PROGRESS IN EXERCISE AND WOMEN'S HEALTH RESEARCH

PROGRESS IN EXERCISE AND WOMEN'S HEALTH RESEARCH

JANET P. COULTER

EDITOR

Nova Science Publishers, Inc.
New York

Copyright © 2008 by Nova Science Publishers, Inc.

NOTICE TO THE READER

The Publisher has taken reasonable care in the preparation of this book, but makes no expressed or implied warranty of any kind and assumes no responsibility for any errors or omissions. No liability is assumed for incidental or consequential damages in connection with or arising out of information contained in this book. The Publisher shall not be liable for any special, consequential, or exemplary damages resulting, in whole or in part, from the readers' use of, or reliance upon, this material.

Independent verification should be sought for any data, advice or recommendations contained in this book. In addition, no responsibility is assumed by the publisher for any injury and/or damage to persons or property arising from any methods, products, instructions, ideas or otherwise contained in this publication.

This publication is designed to provide accurate and authoritative information with regard to the subject matter covered herein. It is sold with the clear understanding that the Publisher is not engaged in rendering legal or any other professional services. If legal or any other expert assistance is required, the services of a competent person should be sought. FROM A DECLARATION OF PARTICIPANTS JOINTLY ADOPTED BY A COMMITTEE OF THE AMERICAN BAR ASSOCIATION AND A COMMITTEE OF PUBLISHERS.

LIBRARY OF CONGRESS CATALOGING-IN-PUBLICATION DATA

Progress in exercise and women's health research / Janet P. Coulter (editor).
    p. ; cm.
 Includes bibliographical references and index.
 ISBN 978-1-60456-014-5 (hardcover)
 1. Exercise for women. 2. Physical fitness for women. 3. Women--Health and hygiene. I. Coulter, Janet P.
 [DNLM: 1. Exercise. 2. Health Behavior. 3. Women's Health. QT 255 P9643 2008]
RA781.P716 2007
613.71082--dc22
            2007034877

Published by Nova Science Publishers, Inc. ✦ *New York*

CONTENTS

PREFACE

In the last 50 years significant numbers of men and women take little exercise in the course of their occupation. The computer keyboard, the rise of private transport, the world by television, household "labor saving" devices mean that with the minimal of physical effort people work and play. The benefits of doing regular exercise include a reduced risk of: heart disease, stroke, bowel cancer, breast cancer, osteoporosis, and obesity. In addition, many people feel better in themselves during and after exercise. Regular exercise is also thought to help ease stress, anxiety, and mild depression. This book presents the latest research in this growing field.

Chapter 1 - The purpose of this chapter is to delve more deeply into the place of exercise in women's lives and bring contemporary social science literature to bear on the challenge of promoting exercise in the lives of two unique subgroups of women: aging women and women with spinal cord injury. The chapter is divided into three major sections: the first section highlights the power of appearance norms to shape women's views of their bodies as well as their aging and disability experiences related to exercise; the second section presents the results of two separate studies on exercise practices and barriers to exercise in aging and disabled women; the third and final section considers these findings in relation to future research and next steps in critical social science research focused on barriers to exercise in understudied populations of women.

Chapter 2 - Ability to use different substrate pathways (oxidative glycolysis, β-oxidation) reflects body functionality and its metabolic flexibility i.e. capacity to shift between lipids or carbohydrates utilization, at rest or during exercise. Metabolic function changes between childhood to oldness. Women are a specific population because of their hormonal variations that occurs during their life. In fact from puberty to menopause women's life is build by large hormonal variation periods which will largely influence metabolic function. Moreover sexual hormone can participate to substrate utilization regulation. At rest and during exercise substrate utilization in women could change depending on both hormonal status (puberty, pregnancy, and menopause) and physical activity status. These last years, using invasive or non invasive methods, a large body of studies has given new insight about women substrate utilization in normal and pathological conditions. Metabolic diseases such as type 2 diabetes or obesity are associated with metabolic inflexibility reflecting alteration of substrate utilization. Obesity and type 2 diabetes are becoming a Mundial health priority because of these associated complications like cardiovascular disease. Women are relatively protected of cardiovascular disease (CVD) because of their adult hormonal status. However this benefice is lost after menopause and the risk of cardiovascular complications is more increased than in men if obesity or diabetes is associated. Hormonal substitution has proved it efficiency on CVD after menopause, but currently many research promote exercise and nutritional adaptation for management of postmenopausal status. Exercise and diet are two therapeutics ways which have showed their efficacy on substrate utilization and complications associated to obesity and diabetes. Those two therapeutics approaches should be largely promoted for well-being of women during their life to decrease development or aggravation of chronic pathologies like obesity and type 2 diabetes.

This review proposes a history of substrate utilization modifications that occurs during women's life when associated to obesity and type 2 diabetes and how to optimize utilization of metabolic fuels.

Chapter 3 - The usefulness of exercise/sport for the humans has been acknowledged ever since antiquity. The present paper constitutes a literature review aiming at the determination of the benefits for the women from their participation in physical activities, which can play a decisive role to the shaping of their personality (social and psychological development) as well as to contribute to the exhibition of health behaviors. These health behaviors, as it has been supported, are the result of the development of the physical, psychological/emotional and intellectual/mental health, as well as of the socialization of women. More specifically, in the framework of socialization, it has been supported that health behaviors constitute the outcome of social, cognitive and moral development. Eventually, exercise and sport seem to form an environment which contributes to the development of health behaviors, yet this environment would be even more effective under more appropriate conditions.

Chapter 4 - The purpose of this study was to examine the importance of satisfying basic psychological needs proposed within Self-Determination Theory (SDT; Deci & Ryan, 2002) to domain-specific well-being in women engaged in regular physical exercise. Employing cross-sectional designs, participants in study 1 ($N = 115$) and study 2 ($N = 247$) completed different self-report instruments measuring perceived psychological need satisfaction felt via exercise as well as an index of physical self-worth. Multivariate analyses using structural equation modeling in study 1 supported the tenability of a model based on SDT positing physical self-worth as a function of a latent variable representing overall psychological need satisfaction in exercise settings. Simultaneous multiple regression analyses reported in study 2 indicated satisfaction of each psychological need was associated with a stronger sense of physical self-worth and these relationships were not moderated by gender. Overall, this investigation supports a major premise embedded within SDT postulating a direct relationship between fulfillment of competence, autonomy, and relatedness needs and enhanced well-being that holds implications for structuring programs to foster women's health.

Chapter 5 - Due to the twin epidemic of obesity and physical inactivity, promoting physical activity has been identified as a major public health priority in the United States. Unfortunately, there is a precipitous decline in physical activity levels among adolescents and this decline is more pronounced for females than males. Improving the effectiveness of school-based physical education is one strategy to promote physical activity for this segment of the population, yet it has been demonstrated that females tend to be less engaged than males in physical education. Advocates for gender equity in physical education have recommended using the Personal-Social Responsibility Model (PSRM) to create a gender-sensitive learning environment. The PSRM is a student-centered instructional model that promotes positive social interactions by emphasizing respect, effort, self-direction, and caring. Moreover, the PSRM promotes the transfer of these responsibilities, or life skills, to other settings. The purpose of this study was to extend previous research by investigating possible gender differences related to the life goals and perceived obstacles of participants in a PSRM physical activity program. Specific research questions included: 1) What are the long- and short-term life goals of participants?; 2) What obstacles do participants perceive in pursuing these goals?; and 3) Are there gender differences in participants' life goals and perceived obstacles? Qualitative analysis revealed several broadly relevant categories related to goals and obstacles, however, the salience of certain categories did seem to vary with gender. Implications for practice and research are discussed.

Chapter 6 - The health status of African American women continues to lag behind their white counterparts. Despite the beneficial effects of physical activity on health African American women remain the least physically active subgroups within the United States. The purpose of this article was to review physical activity promotion and weight loss interventions targeted towards African American women who were 18 years or older. In order to collect the materials for the study, a search of Academic Search Premier, CINAHL, ERIC, and MEDLINE databases was carried out for the time period 2000 June 2007. A total of 11 interventions met the search criteria. Only four out of the 11 interventions were rooted in behavioral theories. The theories used were social action theory, social cognitive theory, behavior choice treatment and the social ecological model. Future interventions need to reify behavioral theories. Seven out of the 11 studies made accommodations for cultural sensitivity while four interventions made no mention of the concept. However, out of the seven studies only one study distinguished cultural sensitivity into its superficial and deep dimensions and addressed both those realms. Future interventions need to be culturally sensitive. With regard to process evaluation only one intervention included a formative and a process evaluation component. Future interventions need to utilize process evaluations. In terms of the duration, three of the interventions were brief (up to 12 weeks), four were middle range (five to six months) and four were 12 months long. Interventions that did not employ theoretical frameworks were longer in duration than the ones which did. If more interventions are theory based they can be more efficient and shorter in duration. Most of the interventions focused on short term changes right after the intervention and it is essential to have measures at least at six months after the intervention to see for the retention of behavior change. On the whole, interventions have resulted in modest changes in behaviors and have shown mixed results with indicators of physical inactivity thereby necessitating more effective use of theoretical approaches.

Chapter 7 - Physical exercise contributes to primary and secondary prevention of heart diseases, hypertension, stroke, diabetes, and cancer. In women physical inactivity is additionally associated with specific risks for mortality and morbidity. However, many women do not engage in sufficient physical exercise. Although women know quite well that this unhealthy habit increases the risk of myocardial infarction, they frequently underestimate their personal risk to die from vascular diseases. But basic knowledge rarely meets with corresponding habits. In addition, women-typical motives (i.e., perceived pros and cons) and high barriers (i.e., low self-efficacy beliefs) play the central role in motivation to engage in regular physical activity which can best be explained by gender roles and corresponding norms, expectations, and experiences. This chapter describes how gender roles and corresponding norms, expectations, and experiences influence women's physical activity and its changes as well as how interventions may be better tailored to women needs. The introduction gives a review about health risks of physical inactivity and health benefits of physical activity; and prevalences, knowledge, motives, and barriers in women are described. This evidence, however, is not sufficient to better design women-specific interventions due to the complex nature of the process of health behaviour change. Consequently, the authors introduce the Health Action Process Approach (HAPA) as theoretical framework to integrate this evidence and identify women-typical characteristics. Implications for theory-based research on women's adoption and maintenance of health enhancing physical exercise is outlined. The chapter concludes with strategies how to design exercise promotion interventions theory-based tailored to particularly women needs.

Chapter 8 - Background: Weight reduction in overweight and obese individuals reduces morbidity and mortality from chronic diseases associated with excess adiposity. Weight loss, however, negatively affects bone health by decreasing bone mass and bone mineral density.

Objective: The purpose of the present study was to examine the effects of short-term weight loss with and without non-weight bearing aerobic exercise on bone mineral content (BMC) and density (BMD) in overweight premenopausal females.

Methods: Twenty overweight to class I obese, sedentary, non-smoking women aged 18 to 35 years, participated in this 6-week weight loss intervention study designed to produce a 5% reduction in body weight. Participants were randomly assigned to either the diet only (D) or the diet plus non-weight bearing exercise (D+E) group. The D group achieved weight loss via moderate energy restriction; the D+E group reduced energy intake and increased energy expenditure by 250-400 kcal/day through non-weight bearing aerobic exercise. Exercise training consisted primarily of cycling on a stationary bike 5 days/week at approximately 60% of measured maximum oxygen consumption (75% maximal heart rate) for 45 minutes/day. Anthropometrics, maximal oxygen consumption (VO_2max), BMD and BMC of the total body, hip and lumbar spine were measured at baseline and post-weight loss. Dietary intake was monitored using written food diaries; pre- and post-weight loss diets were analyzed using Food Processor 8.0. Repeated measures two-way ANOVA was used to test for significant time and group effects, as well as for group by time interactions. Post hoc t-tests and Tukey's test were used for significant main effects and interactions, respectively. Data were analyzed using SigmaStat (Version 2.03, SPSS Inc.).

Results: D and D+E groups were not significantly different at baseline in age, body weight, BMI, percent body fat, or VO_2max. Body weight and BMI decreased significantly in both groups from baseline to post-weight loss ($p<0.05$) and there was no group by time interaction; however, the D+E group exhibited a significant reduction in percent body fat (~5%), while the D group did not. As expected, there was a significant group by time interaction for VO_2max; aerobic capacity increased significantly in the D+E group ($p<0.05$), confirming compliance with the exercise training. Average energy intake decreased by 971±158 and 468±98 kcal/d in the D and D+E groups, respectively. There were no significant group differences in BMD or BMC at any site before or after weight loss. Neither group showed any significant changes in BMD or BMC. However, hip BMD showed a tendency to decline with weight loss (time main effect, $p=0.079$).

Conclusion: The present study suggests that a 6-wk moderate weight reduction with or without non-weight bearing aerobic training does not cause any significant changes in BMD or BMC in premenopausal overweight women. Long-term weight loss, however, may result in measurable reductions in BMD, as suggested by the observed decrease in hip BMD ($p=0.079$). Aerobic exercise, regardless of whether it is weight bearing or non-weight bearing, is known to promote health benefits beyond that of bone density, and, therefore, should be an important component of any weight loss program.

Chapter 9 - BACKGROUND: Women are at heightened risk for loss of strength and functional ability due to sarcopenia as they age. Resistance training (RT) is an effective intervention against muscle loss, while ingestion of a post-exercise protein supplement may have an additive effect on muscle growth.

PURPOSE: The purpose of this study was to determine if timing of protein intake following RT would influence gains in lean mass in women.

METHODS: Fifteen women (age 38 ± 10 years, BMI 27.8 ± 5.1 kg/m^2) completed 12 weeks of RT three times a week (36 sessions). Immediately (T0) or two hours (T2) after each training bout they received a high protein supplement (150 kcal, 25g protein, 5g carbohydrate, 3.5g fat). Maximal strength (1RM chest and leg press) and body composition (air displacement plethysmography) were measured at baseline and after completion of week 12.

RESULTS: There were no significant differences between groups for gains in strength and lean mass. Both groups experienced similar increases in strength ($P < 0.01$) and gained an average of 0.43 ± 0.3 kg lean mass ($P = 0.11$). A significant difference between groups was observed for fat mass. Group T2 lost a significant amount of fat mass (-0.8 ± 0.6 kg) ($P = 0.03$) compared to Group T0 (-0.1 ± 0.7 kg).

CONCLUSION: In women engaged in a 12-week RT program, gains in lean mass are not affected by the timing of protein intake post exercise. However, a two-hour delay in intake following RT sessions results in significant decreases in fat mass.

Chapter 10 - Regular moderate-intensity exercise has been shown to decrease all-cause mortality and age-related morbidity. Improved cardiovascular, metabolic, endocrine, and psychologic health has been documented. The 'effective' dose of exercise needed to elicit effects likely to be of clinical importance as well as and the concept of accumulation of activity has been extensively debated. Despite this, the major part of adult population does not currently exercise at the recommended levels. Italian public health surveillance systems do not usually include assessments of this type of physical activity. The authors examined physical activity behaviours of participants in a lifestyle, nutritional, cardiovascular, and immunologic screening survey conducted in Pisa, central Italy. Demographic, socio-economic and lifestyle information was obtained by Lifestyle European Prospective Investigation of Cancer and Nutrition (EPIC) questionnaire (including questions on education, socioeconomic status, occupation, history of previous illness and disorders of surgical operations, lifetime history of consumption of tobacco and alcoholic beverages, and physical activity). Smoking habits, educational level, occupational status, daily number of hours engaged in housework, weekly number of hours engaged in physical activities during leisure (walking, cycling, gardening, exercise) and during job (sitting most of the time; light activity, walking around; handiwork with some effort; heavy work) were assessed.

Among 116 women (age 44 ± 13 years, range 17 to 73 years) 66% worked, mainly in sedentary and light jobs. Their educational level was the following: 46% secondary, 34% high, 20% graduate. They spent 2.7 ± 1.3 hours/day in housework activities, 2.0 ± 1.7 hours/week in exercise, 1.3 ± 0.5 hours/day in physical activities (including walking, cycling, gardening, and exercise). Increasing physical activity was associated with reduced body mass index. On the contrary, housework activities were not significantly associated with body weight. Time spent in housework decreased with increasing educational level, whereas leisure time physical activities correspondingly increased. Increasing age was associated with reduced physical activity and increased housework. Women' behaviours were compared with those of 93 men of similar age.

These preliminary data are discussed to analyse which could be the most effective methods in lifestyle epidemiology among those presently available. Indeed, although it should be advisable a European survey of lifestyle with particular attention to exercise and physical activity, the lack of standardisation of the assessment methods remains the main methodological drawback for carrying out such studies in practice.

Chapter 11 - The lack of sports activity and its impact on public health is a serious concern in modern society, while its benefical effects are indicated by many empirical researches. Besides many somatic health benefits, physical activity is closely related to higher level of psychosocial health, psychological well-being, positive mood and mental health. Sports activity behavior is established during late childhood and early adolescence, similar to other health behaviors. While regular sports activity is a natural part of children's lifestyle, it starts to decrease during adolescence, particularly among girls, and therefore, they are an important target group to get involved in health promotion programs. The main goal of the present study is to analyze early adolescent girls' psychosocial health in the light of their sports activity behavior. The data collection was going on among elementary school girls (N=247) living in Szeged, Hungary, by using a self-administered questionnaire. Data suggest that in this age period most of them regularly take part in sports activity. In their choice of sports type, primarily they prefer individual sports. In terms of individual sports, they prefer dancing and running. The most popular team sports are the following among them: handball and basketball. Among psychosomatic symptoms, headache, low-back pain and chronic fatigue are the most frequent. The authors have pointed out that in their psychosocial health, sports activity plays an important role. Girls who take part in regular sports activity and are engaged in sports activity at a higher level or in an organized sports club indicate their own health and fitness higher, have lower levels of psychosomatic symptoms. More active girls also tended to avoid regular smoking and drinking and watched for their diet more often. In addition, subjective factors of sports activity (e.g., liking sports and evaluating sports as important) may also contribute to develop motivations towards regular sports activity. The findings suggest that the role of sports activity behavior in psychosocial health is an important focus of research. These research results may be useful in health promotion programs targeted adolescent girls.

EXPERT COMMENTARIES

In: Progress in Exercise and Women's Health Research
Editor: Janet P. Coulter, pp. 3-12

ISBN 1-60456-014-5
© 2008 Nova Science Publishers, Inc.

Expert Commentary 1

THE EFFECT OF EXERCISE ON CARDIOVASCULAR FUNCTION IN WOMEN

Vikram Kumar Yeragani[1,2,3], *Narayana Subramaniam*[1] *Rahul Kumar*[1] and *Pratap Chokka*[2]

[1]Department of Cardiology, M.S. Ramaiah Medical College Hospital, Bangalore, India.
[2]Departemnt of Psychiatry, University of Alberta, Edmonton, Canada
[3]Department of Psychiatry and Behavioral Neurosciences, Wayne State University
School of Medicine Detroit, MI, USA.

ABSTRACT

This article examines some of the findings from recent studies on cardiac autonomic function and the effects of exercise in women. Exercise, in general, induces a state of cardiovascular vagal predominance, which is beneficial to health. This area of research is especially important in relation to the neurohormonal influences on cardiovascular function in health and disease in women, due to the complex interactions that occur during puberty, menstrual cycles, pregnancy and menopause. The literature relating menopause to increased cardiovascular mortality underscores the importance of hormonal mechanisms on cardiovascular autonomic function. However, there are only a few systematic studies in this area, especially in relation to the use of noninvasive measures such as beat-to-beat heart rate and QT interval variability, and blood pressure variability. These studies are extremely important especially in relation to pregnancy and menopause. We have highlighted some of the important differences in cardiovascular function between men and women. We also examine some of the theoretical models of using exercise as a preventive tool to increase relative cardiac vagal function and decrease relative cardiac sympathetic function in women. Hormone replacement therapy, once widely used is not popular any more due to serious side effects including uterine cancer and thromboembolic phenomena leading to cardiovascular mortality. We discuss future directions of research which might yield valuable information on autonomic function during various stages of development in women.

Key Words: menstrual cycle, pregnancy, menopause, exercise, cardiovascular health, autonomic dysfunction, QT interval, heart rate, blood pressure

INTRODUCTION

Physical exercise influences many systems in the human body, of which cardiovascular and respiratory systems deserve special attention. In this commentary, we have made an attempt to briefly highlight the periods of vulnerability in females during different stages of development and how they might influence the health of females, and how exercise can have a beneficial effect.

In simple terms, physical exercise improves the oxygen consumption by the lungs, decreases the heart rate, improves vagal function of the heart, which may decrease relative sympathetic activity. The end result is mostly likely a decrease in the incidence cardiovascular mortality and serious ventricular tachy-arrhythmias. Here let's examine the following aspects of development in females.

HORMONAL INFLUENCES

ECG Changes during Puberty

Steroid hormones have multifold effects on the cardiovascular system [1]. The onset of puberty is influenced predominantly by the release of hypothalamic hormone GnRH (Gonadotropin Releasing Hormone), which causes the release of two hormones, Luteinizing Hormone (LH) and Follicle Stimulating Hormone (FSH). These in turn, mediate the release of estrogen and then progesterone in females, which govern the normal menstrual cycles. In males, testosterone is responsible for primary as well as secondary sexual characteristics. These two hormones, are mainly responsible for the changes that ECG undergoes during puberty.

Testosterone is released from the interstitial cells of Leydig of the testis in males and in minute quantities from the suprarenal glands. It is an anabolic steroidal compound that produces substantial changes on the electrocardiogram (ECG) during puberty. Testosterone acts as a vasoconstrictor and sensitizes smooth muscles of the blood vessels to the vasoconstrictive action of other substances that mediate a sympathetic response, such as epinephrine and nor-epinephrine. This explains why men generally have a higher blood pressure and a lower heart rate. Testosterone also promotes the production and release of erythropoietin from the kidney, which increases red blood cell count, thereby increasing blood viscosity which is partly responsible for an increase in systolic blood pressure. With age, testosterone levels decrease (male climacteric) and there is a gradual reversal of the actions it brings about in puberty.

Estrogen, in the non-pregnant female, is released in significant quantities from the ovaries and in minute quantities from the suprarenal glands. The exact mechanism of estrogen on the cardiovascular system is not known. Initially it was thought to act only as a vasodilator that decreases blood pressure in women, but recent studies have shown that this action is catalyzed by the presence of nitric oxide. Absence of nitric oxide in old age acts as a vasoconstrictor, and a potential hypertensive agent in women. This is one of the reasons why pre-menopausal women have a systolic blood pressure of 4-5 mm of Hg lower than males, but in post-menopausal women, systolic blood pressure is 4-5 mm of Hg higher in women compared to men. Estrogen also causes sodium and water retention to a small degree which is of little significance in a non-pregnant female. Estrogen inhibits the secretion of erythropoietin, which may partly explain the lower blood pressure in females compared to males.

As both these hormones are present in both sexes, their interaction is believed to cause a series of significant changes in the female ECG during puberty. Heart rate is slightly higher in females due to lower arterial pressure, which is mediated by estrogen levels. Till puberty both heart rate and blood pressure are almost identical in males and females. Several ECG changes take place during puberty and there are significant differences between boys and girls [2,3,4]. The QT interval, which represents ventricular repolarization, is prolonged in females. This is most likely due to the difference in potassium permeability in the cardiac muscle mediated by estrogen levels. This variation in the QT interval between males and females is attributable largely to the fact that there is a significant shortening of male QT interval during puberty in addition to a slight increase in the length of QT interval in females after puberty. This puts females at more risk for cardiac arrhythmias. An increase in QT interval beyond 530 ms (normal range is 400-440 ms), results in a disorder called Long QT Syndrome (LQTS). This can cause cardiac arrhythmias and sudden cardiac arrest. A study showed that before puberty, males were four times more likely to develop LQTS than females 10-12 years of age. But in the age group 13-20, no such diversity in risk was seen. This could be due to the differential effects of testosterone and estrogen, creating different risk factors at different stages. After puberty in females, there are no significant age-dependent differences in the distribution of QT interval patterns. Studies also showed no significant difference in the QT intervals during different stages of the menstrual cycle and no significant effect of hormonal therapy on the duration of the QT interval.

A 'typical' female ECG is believed to bear the following features: the amplitude of the J-point<1 mV and ST angle<20 degrees. A 'typical male' ECG is believed to bear the following features: the amplitude of the J-point≥1 mV and ST angle>20 degrees. Some studies of ECG during puberty have found low estrogen levels causing prolonged PR interval and larger variation in female QRS complex but the evidence has not been conclusive.

MALE FEMALE DIFFERENCES IN METABOLISM

The Maximal Oxygen Consumption

The "typical" young untrained male will have an absolute VO_2 max of about 3.5 liters/min, while the typical same-age female will have about 2 liters/min. This is a 43% difference! First, much of the difference is due to the fact that males are bigger on average than females. Humans are all geometrically similar, so heart size scales in proportion to lean body size . If we divide VO_2 by bodyweight, the difference is diminished (45 ml/min/kg vs 38 ml/min/kg) to 15 to 20%, but not eliminated. Thus this is an important difference.

If we compare the average body-fat in males and females, young untrained women average about 25% body-fat compared to 15% in young men. So, if we factor out body composition differences by dividing VO_2 by lean body mass (Bodyweight minus estimated fat weight), the difference in maximal O_2 consumption decreases to perhaps 7-10%. The explanation for the remaining 10% difference may be due to the key limitation on VO2 max and oxygen delivery. On average, females have upto 10% lower blood hemoglobin content than males. Finally, there is some evidence, that the female heart is slightly smaller relative to body size than the male heart. Recent ECG and echocardiographic studies also suggest that the young female heart exhibits less enlargement in response to either endurance or resistance training than the male heart [5]. This may be due to differences in androgen receptor density in the female heart. A smaller heart would be expected to be a less effective pump.

Slightly lower oxygen carrying capacity of the blood (lower hemoglobin levels) plus a somewhat smaller or less adaptive heart are sufficient to account for the gender differences in maximal oxygen consumption that are independent of body size and fat percentage. It is worth noting here the results of a 1996 study by Spina et al. [6], which suggested that the adaptive response of left ventricular filling dynamics to endurance exercise training is influenced by gender in older subjects. Older men show improvement in left ventricular filling dynamics, whereas older women do not. To summarize, there is a growing body of data suggesting that females demonstrate a somewhat different pattern of cardiac adaptation to exercise, which may become more dissimilar with age. They also generally have a lower hemoglobin compared to men. The net effect is a small but significant difference in maximal oxygen consumption, even among similarly trained males and females, and after scaling for differences in size and body composition. It is important to make note of the fact that these differences are "average" values. In reality, there are many women with significantly higher VO_2max values than average men.

The Lactate Threshold

The second component of endurance performance is the lactate threshold. This is the exercise intensity at which lactic acid begins to accumulate in the blood stream at levels significantly above "baseline" values. This intensity sets a (slightly fuzzy) boundary between that exercise intensity, which can be sustained for long periods (over one hour) versus those which lead to fatigue in minutes. Changes in lactate threshold are due to adaptations that occur in the exercising muscle. These are peripheral adaptations (Changes in cardiovascular performance are called central adaptations).

The question here is if women demonstrate a different pattern or capacity for peripheral adaptations then men. First, Female skeletal muscle is not distinguishable from male skeletal muscle. Second, within some margin of error, the fiber type distribution (percentage of slow versus fast fibers) is not different in the male and female population. Third, male and female skeletal muscle responds similarly to endurance exercise. Finally, elite female endurance athletes have similar lactate threshold values compared to men when expressed as a percentage of their VO_2 max. Elite women perform at the same high percentage of their maximal oxygen consumption as their male counterparts.

Efficiency

The third component of endurance performance is efficiency which of course has different constraints, depending on the sport. The research information comparing the efficiency of female and male athletes is both sparse and inconclusive. In running, for example females have been found to be more, less, and equally efficient compared to males depending on the specific study. Some of this confusion comes down to how the differences in bodyweight and body-fat were accounted for. In situations like running or cycling, these may actually favor females in general, due to narrower upper bodies for a given total body mass, and potentially less wind or water drag. Differences in VO2 max alone are sufficient to explain the gender performance gap in rowing.

Fat Metabolism Differences

Back in the 70s, a theory suggested the following: "since women have more fat stores, they will be better at utilizing fat during endurance performance when glycogen stores are depleted." One of the supporting pillars of the theory was that it had been noticed by one female runner/author how "fresh" many female runners looked as they crossed the finish line! This theory did not stand the test of time. In 1979, Costill and colleagues compared males and females who were equally trained during a 60 minute treadmill run [7]. There were no differences in any measures of fat metabolism. There is no gender difference in the ability of men and women to burn fat!

Are Men Sweatier than Women?

On an absolute basis, and per kg bodyweight, women have lower sweat rates than men. However, because of their higher body surface area to volume ratio, they dissipate heat equally well. Men have an advantage in evaporative cooling, but women have an advantage in radiant cooling, so they come out even in this regard.

Muscle Strength and Power

Although maximal muscular strength and anaerobic power has little to do with pure endurance performance, there are many events which can be classified as "power-endurance" events. These events ranging from 2 to about 8 minutes require some combination of aerobic and anaerobic capacity. For this reason, it is important to also consider this "anaerobic" component. When we talk about anaerobic capacity, the critical determinant is muscle mass. Females, on average, have less total muscle mass than males. As a result, maximal strength measures as well as maximal power measures (power = force/time) are reduced. Gross measures of upper body strength suggest an average 40-50% difference between the sexes, compared to a 30% difference in lower body strength.

SPECIAL FACTORS THAT AFFECT FEMALES

Depression in Women

In childhood, rates of Major Depressive Disorder are approximately equal in females and males but in adolescence all studies report a female preponderance with rates of depressive disorders being two to three times higher in girls than in boys [8,9,10]. The reasons for this preponderance of depressive symptoms may partly be related to the hormonal levels. This is further supported by the fact that premenstrual dysphoria and depression associated with the so called premenstrual syndrome occur frequently in women.

Pregnancy

Pregnancy is also associated with depressive symptoms in some females and of particular note is that there is probably decreased heart rate variability during pregnancy.

Menopause

Menopause is a natural event that occurs in the life cycle of women that marks the transition from the reproductive phase to the nonreproductive phase. The average age of menopause is about 51 years. There is an increased incidence of anxiety and depression in women after menopause as both biological and psychological factors play a significant role.

After menopause, there is a significant decrease of estrogens, which prduces degenerative changes in the female reproductive tract. Hot flushes occur in 60 to 90% of women after menopause. Other symptoms include anxiety, depression, sleep disturbances, depression and irritability. Menopause is also associated with significant cardiac dysfunction [11].

Hot Flushes

Though the mechanism of hot flushes is not well understood, Freedman et al. [l2] reported that administration of yohimbine was associated with induction of hot flushes and clonidine had the opposite effect. These findings suggest a central alpha-2 adrenergic mechanism and sympathetic hyperactivity in the initiation of hot flushes.

Cardiovascular Mortality

Post-menopausal women have higher rates of coronary heart disease than premenopausal women. The protective effects of estrogens probably are due to their effect on lipid metabolism. Another contributor to the development of coronary heart disease is the increased cardiovascular reactivity to mental stress. Owens et al. [13] found that menopause is associated with enhanced stress-induced cardiovascular responses and elevated ambulatory blood pressure (BP) during the work day, which may contribute to the risk of cardiovascular morbidity after menopause.

Heart Rate Variability

Heart rate (HR) or the inter-beat interval (R-R interval) changes every beat and the time series appear intrinsically chaotic. Spectral analysis of HR variability using Fourier Transform, usually reveals a peak between 0.040-0.14 Hz (low frequency: LF), and 0.15 – 0.5 Hz (high frequency: HF). In normal controls, orthostatic stress is accompanied by a marked increase of the relative spectral energy in the LF band, and a significant decrease in the HF component [14,15]. Available evidence suggests that the HF power in both postures is modulated by the cholinergic (vagal) system and the LF power is influenced both by cholinergic and adrenergic systems. Decreased IIR variability is a strong independent predictor of cardiovascular mortality [13].

Beat-to-Beat Qt Interval Variability

QT interval on the surface electrocardiogram (ECG) reflects time for repolarization. The usual duration of QT interval corrected for HR is about 400 milliseconds and is dependent upon HR to some extent. Thus, it is customary to correct QT interval for HR (QTc) in clinical situations. Prolongation of QTc may be more dangerous in the setting of a higher HR. QT interval can be prolonged in several different conditions including congenital long QT syndrome. This condition can be associated with serious cardiac arrhythmias including torsades de pointes. Several studies have shown a relationship between prolonged QTc and life-threatening arrhythmias [16]. Increased beat-to beat QT interval variability (QTV) is associated with an increase in cardiac mortality [17,18]. This is especially important due to the fact that an increase in cardiac sympathetic activity is associated with an increased QTV [19].

Blood Pressure

Heart rate and blood pressure (BP) variabilities also appear to be closely coupled together and the beat to beat variation in systolic BP appears to be concentrated in the LF and HF regions as described above. Blood pressure waves around 0.1 Hz are referred to as Mayer waves, which occur at a frequency slower than that of respiration and these produce large amplitude fluctuations in arterial BP around O.1 Hz. These waves can be suppressed by the intake of clonidine and may be elicited by yohimbine, thus reflecting sympathetic activity. An increase in BP variability is usually associated with increased sympathetic activity and results in end organ damage [20].

Risk for Cardiovascular Morbidity and Autonomic Function

A decrease in cardiac parasympathetic tone and an increase in sympathetic tone of cardiovascular neural regulatory mechanisms have been reported after acute myocardial infarction, heart failure, cardiac arrhythmias and in patients who are prone to sudden death. Reduced cardiac vagal function in patients with coronary artery disease and after acute myocardial infarction is a significant predictor of cardiac morbidity. Thus, while an increase in HR variability is generally cardio-protective, an increase in QT interval or BP variability is associated with serious arrhythmias or end organ damage.

Hormone Replacement Therapy (HRT)

Hormone replacement therapy has been in use for several years and several reports suggested the beneficial effects on hot flushes, mood swings and protection against cardio-cerebrovascular events. Several studies have examined the effects of HRT in postmenopausal women [21,22,23,24,25]. Recent studies have shown that there is a considerable risk associated with HRT. Though HRT is associated with an increase in cardiac vagal activity and a decrease in peripheral vascular resistance, it may cause prolongation of QT interval and/or QT dispersion and ventricular repolarization.. However, the evidence is controversial. To our knowledge, there are no reports on the effects of HRT on beat-to-beat QT interval variability in post-menopausal women on HRT.

Importance of Exercise

Lack of exercise may lead to obesity. Obesity impairs muscle blood flow in humans [26]. Vasodilatory control mechanisms such as metabolic control and endothelium-derived factors may be impaired in obesity due to insulin resistance, hyperglycemia, dyslipidemia, and oxidative stress. All these factors can contribute to endothelial dysfunction and eventual cardiovascular disease. Exercise produces functional hyperemia resulting in an increase in blood flow. Oxidative stress results in impaired vasodilatory responses. Regular exercise leads to a decrease of blood pressure and increases the effectiveness of the heart as a "pump". this may help decrease blood pressure variability. Exercise and diet can have a positive influence to sustain synaptic plasticity and mental health, and are therefore important for combating the effects of aging [27]. It is well known that there is a decrease in cardiac vagal function with aging.

In light of the special vulnerability of women to cardiovascular risk during different phases of development, regular exercise can play a very important role to alter some of the risk factors for hypertension, proinflammatory conditions that can cause vascular dysfunction, all of which can eventually lead to fatal ventricular arrhythmias. There has been a great deal of work done on cardiovascular system and exercise and it appears that both regular intense aerobic exercise or long walks have a protective effect on the cardiovascular system in regards to beat-to-beat heart rate variability and QT interval variability, and blood pressure variability in addition to the well known effects of exercise on lipid metabolism. This is especially important after menopause to prevent serious cardiovascular problems.

REFERENCES

[1] Stumpf W. Steroid hormones and the cardiovascular system: direct actions of estradiol, progesterone, testosterone, gluco- and mineralocorticoids, and soltriol (vitamin D) on central nervous regulatory and peripheral tissues. *Experientia. 1990*;46:13-23.

[2] Katz AM: Cardiac ion channels. *N Engl J Med 1993*;328:1244-1251.

[3] Snyders DJ, Tamkun MM, Bennett PB: A rapidly activating and slowly inactivating potassium channel cloned from human heart. *J Gen Physiol.* 1993;101:513-543.

[4] Surawicz B, Parikh SR. Differences between ventricular reopalrization in men and women: description, mechanism and implications. *Ann Noninv Electrocardiol 2003*;8:333-240.

[5] George KP, Wolfe LA, Buggraf GW, Norman R. Electrocardiographic and echocardiograhic characteristics of female athletes. *Med Sci Sports Exerc 1995*:27;1362-1370.

[6] Spina RJ, Miller TR, Bogenhagen WH, Schchtman KB, Ehsani AA. Gneder related differences in left ventricular filling dynamics in older subjects after endurance exercise training. *J Gerontol A Biol Sci Med Sci 1996*; 51:B232-237.

[7] Costill DL, Fink WJ, Getchell LH, Ivy JL, Witzman FA. Lipid metabolism in skeletal muscle of endurance trained males and females. *J Appl Physiol 1979*; 47:787-791.

[8] Cohen P, Cohen J, Kasen S, Valez CN, Hartmark C, Johnson J, Rojas M, Brook J, Streuning EL. An epidemiological study of disorders in late childhood and adolescence- I. Age and gender specific prevalence. *J Child Psychol Psychiatry 1993*;34;851-867.

[9] Reinherz HJ, Giakonia RM, Pariz B, Silverman AB, Frost ak, Lefkowitz ES. Psychosocial risks for major depression in late adolescence: a longitudinal community study. *J Am Acad Child Adolesc Psychiatry 1993*;32:1155-1163.

[10] Reinherz HJ, Giakonia RM, Lefkowitz ES, Pariz B, Frost AK. Prevalence of psychiatric disorders in a community population of older adolescents. *J Am Acad Child Adolesc Psychiatry 1993*;32:369-377.

[11] Kannel W, Hjortland MC, McNamara PM et al. Menopause and risk of cardiovascular disease: the *Framingham Study. Ann Intern Med 1976*;85:447-2.

[12] Freedman RR, Woodward S, Sabharwal SC. Alpha-2 adrenergic mechanism in menopausal hot flushes. Obstet Gynecol 1990; 76: 573-8.

[13] Owens JF, Stoney CM, Mathews KA. Menopausal status influences ambulatory blood pressure levels and blood pressure changes during mental stress. Circulation 1993;88:2794-802.

[14] Malliani A, Pagani M, Lombardi F et al. Cardiovascular neural regulation explored in the frequency domain. Circulation 1991;84:482-92.

[15] Yeragani VK. Heart rate and blood pressure variability: Implications for psychiatric research. *Neuropsychobiology 1995*;32:182-91.

[16] Schwartz PJ, Wolf S. QT interval prolongation as predictor of sudden death in patients with myocardial infarction. *Circulation 1978*;57:1074-7.

[17] Berger RD, Casper EK, Baughman KL et al. Beat-to-beat QT interval variability. Novel evidence for repolarization lability in ischemic and nonischemic dilated cardiomyopathy. Circulation 1997;967:1557-65.

[18] Atiga WL, Calkins H, Lawrence JH et al. Beat-to-beat repolarization lability identifies patients at risk for sudden cardiac death. *J Cardiovasc Electrophysiol 1998*;9:899-908.

[19] Yeragani VK, Pohl R, Jampala VC et al. Effect of posture and isoproterenol on beat-to-beat heart rate and QT variability. *Neuropsychobiology 2000*;41:113-23.

[20] Mancia G, Di Rienzo M, Parati G et al. Sympathetic activity, blood pressure variability and end organ damage in hypertension. *J Hum Hypertens 1997*;(suppl): S3-S8.

[21] Gupta G, Aronow WS. Hormone replacement therapy. An analysis of efficacy based on evidence. *Geriatrics 2002*;57: 18-20.

[22] Farag NH, Nelesen RA, Parry BL et al. Autonomic and cardiovascular function in post-menopausal women: the effects of estrogen versus combination therapy. *Am J Obstet Gynecol 2002;186:954-61.*

[23] Altunkeser BB, Ozdemir K, Icli A et al. Effects of long-term hormone replacement therapy on QT and corrected QT dispersion during resting and peak exercise electrocardiography in post-menopausal women. *Jpn Heart J 2002*;43:1-7.

[24] Vrtovec B, Starc V, Meden-Vrtovec H. The effect of estrogen replacement therapy on ventricular repolarization dynamics in healthy post- menopausal women. *J Electrocardiol* 2001;34:277-83.

[25] Sbarouni E, Zarvalis E, Kyriakides ZS et al. Absence of effects of short-term estrogen replacement therapy on resting and exertional QT and QTc dispersion in post-menopausal women with coronary artery disease. *Reclng Clin Electrophysiol 1998;21:2392-5*

[26] Hodnett BL, Hester RL. Regulation of muscle blood flow in obesity. *Microcirculation 2007; 14:273-288.*

[27] Gomez-Pinilla F. The influences of diet and exercise on mental health through hormesis. *Ageing Res Rev 2007 (in press).*

In: Progress in Exercise and Women's Health Research
Editor: Janet P. Coulter, pp. 13-16

ISBN 1-60456-014-5
© 2008 Nova Science Publishers, Inc.

Expert Commentary 2

RESISTANCE EXERCISE FREQUENCY: CAN INCREASING TRAINING FREQUENCY INCREASE GAINS IN LEAN MASS FOR MIDDLE AND OLDER-AGED WOMEN?

Melissa J. Benton[1]

College of Nursing, Valdosta State University
1300 N. Patterson St., Valdosta, GA 31698

Resistance exercise is an underappreciated modality, especially among middle and older-aged women. It not only provides improvements in lean mass, strength and bone density that are not achieved by aerobic exercise [1-5], but a single bout of resistance exercise results in a greater overall caloric deficit than a similar bout of aerobic exercise [6]. Resistance training has also been found to improve cardiorespiratory status [7, 8], an area of fitness often considered to be exclusively related to aerobic training. Although intense aerobic exercises such as jogging and running can approximate some of the benefits of resistance exercise in terms of improved lower extremity bone density [1, 9, 10] and cardiorespiratory status, many middle-aged and older women are unable to endure the high impact involved in these exercises. Even brisk walking as an alternative to jogging can generate a level of impact that is not well-tolerated [11]. Cycling, as an alternative to jogging or running, may be better tolerated due to its lack of impact; and at higher intensities it can improve cardiorespiratory status and strength [12]. However, it does not increase bone density or lean mass. Only resistance exercise provides such a range of benefits that combat the changes commonly associated with aging, including sarcopenia, sarcopenic obesity, osteoporosis and functional decline. For those who cannot comfortably participate in impact-generating activities, resistance training is a viable alternative that can provide the regular physical activity needed to maintain health.

---

[1] Correspondence to: Valdosta State University 1300 N. Patterson St. Valdosta, GA 31698 Phone: 229-245-3775
email: mjbenton@valdosta.edu

Although minimal recommendations for physical activity frequency include at least five days per week [13], recommendations for resistance training frequency remain only two to three days per week [14]. Unfortunately this is often interpreted as a ceiling on training frequency rather than minimal guidelines. Furthermore, these guidelines are based primarily on maintenance of strength rather than the overall capacity for health-related improvements possible with resistance exercise. Two to three days a week of resistance exercises designed to stimulate the major muscle groups of the body [14] may be sufficient to maintain moderate levels of strength but may not maximize lean mass or bone density.

Although evidence supports the efficacy of resistance training for increasing muscle mass in middle and older-aged women [15], research is lacking regarding the most effective training frequency for maximizing such increases. To date, increased resistance training frequency has not been well studied in relation to accretion of lean mass, although data from young males suggest that increasing the frequency of resistance exercise to five days per week results in greater increases in upper body strength than what is achieved with a frequency of two or three days per week [16]. However, because the need for adequate time to recover from neuromuscular fatigue argues against daily resistance training for individual muscles or muscle groups, it is necessary to develop more advanced resistance training strategies suitable for middle and older-aged women that allow for recovery time within a framework of consecutive day training. This will provide not only greater flexibility in scheduling of exercise bouts but also allow greater frequency of training.

Split training programs are a feasible alternative to traditional total body training that allows frequency to be increased through consecutive day exercise bouts while avoiding repetitive training of muscle groups. Typically used for more advanced training [17], split routines have had limited application to untrained and/or older populations. Although studies by Calder et al. [18] and Candow et al. [19] found that split training did not produce significantly greater gains in lean mass than whole body training in young women, their study designs limited training frequency to two to three times per week and provided equal training volumes for both split and whole body training groups. However, the advantage and appeal of split training programs is that they provide a mechanism for increasing training volume solely by increasing frequency while they allow adequate recovery time for individual muscle groups. Hence, split training at a frequency of two or three times a week would not be expected to achieve greater results than traditional whole body training two or three times a week unless training volume were to be significantly greater with the split training program.

The effect of resistance training frequency on lean mass is an area yet to be explored. Both lean and fat mass have been found to influence functional ability in middle and older-aged women [20, 21]. Although resistance training programs alone may not diminish fat mass without the addition of dietary restriction, they can increase lean mass. If fat mass remains stable, increased lean mass results in an overall decrease in percent body fat. This has significant health implications for middle-aged and older women. Designing resistance training programs that maximize lean mass rather than solely strength will provide a feasible and effective exercise modality that may be more attractive to women who have limited tolerance for impact-type activities.

REFERENCES

[1]   Wood RH, Reyes R, Welsch MA, Favaloro-Sabatier J, Sabatier M, Matthew Lee C, et al. Concurrent cardiovascular and resistance training in healthy older adults. *Med Sci Sports Exerc.* 2001 Oct;33(10):1751-8.

[2]   Binder EF, Yarasheski KE, Steger-May K, Sinacore DR, Brown M, Schechtman KB, et al. Effects of progressive resistance training on body composition in frail older adults: results of a randomized, controlled trial. *J Gerontol A Biol Sci Med Sci.* 2005 Nov;60(11):1425-31.

[3]   Park SK, Park JH, Kwon YC, Kim HS, Yoon MS, Park HT. The effect of combined aerobic and resistance exercise training on abdominal fat in obese middle-aged women. *J Physiol Anthropol Appl Human Sci.* 2003 May;22(3):129-35.

[4]   Martyn-St James M, Carroll S. High-intensity resistance training and postmenopausal bone loss: a meta-analysis. *Osteoporos Int.* 2006;17(8):1225-40.

[5]   Hind K, Truscott JG, Evans JA. Low lumbar spine bone mineral density in both male and female endurance runners. *Bone.* 2006 Oct;39(4):880-5.

[6]   Elliot DL, Goldberg L, Kuehl KS. Effect of resistance training on excess post-exercise oxygen consumption. *Journal of Applied Sport Science Research.* 1992;6(2):77 - 81.

[7]   Vincent KR, Braith RW, Feldman RA, Kallas HE, Lowenthal DT. Improved cardiorespiratory endurance following 6 months of resistance exercise in elderly men and women. *Arch Intern Med.* 2002 Mar 25;162(6):673-8.

[8]   Hautala AJ, Kiviniemi AM, Makikallio TH, Kinnunen H, Nissila S, Huikuri HV, et al. Individual differences in the responses to endurance and resistance training. *Eur J Appl Physiol.* 2006 Mar;96(5):535-42.

[9]   Nevill AM, Burrows M, Holder RL, Bird S, Simpson D. Does lower-body BMD develop at the expense of upper-body BMD in female runners? *Med Sci Sports Exerc.* 2003 Oct;35(10):1733-9.

[10]   Tomkinson A, Gibson JH, Lunt M, Harries M, Reeve J. Changes in bone mineral density in the hip and spine before, during, and after the menopause in elite runners. *Osteoporos Int.* 2003 Jul;14(6):462-8.

[11]   Taylor WR, Heller MO, Bergmann G, Duda GN. Tibio-femoral loading during human gait and stair climbing. *J Orthop Res.* 2004 May;22(3):625-32.

[12]   Macaluso A, Young A, Gibb KS, Rowe DA, De Vito G. Cycling as a novel approach to resistance training increases muscle strength, power, and selected functional abilities in healthy older women. *J Appl Physiol.* 2003 Dec;95(6):2544-53.

[13]   Department of Health and Human Services. *Physical Activity and Health: A Report of the Surgeon General.* Atlanta: U.S Department of Health and Human Services, Centers for Disease Control and Prevention, National Center for Chronic Disease Prevention and Health Promotion; 1996.

[14]   American College of Sports Medicine Position Stand. The recommended quantity and quality of exercise for developing and maintaining cardiorespiratory and muscular fitness, and flexibility in healthy adults. *Med Sci Sports Exerc.* 1998 Jun;30(6):975-91.

[15]   Hakkinen K, Kraemer WJ, Newton RU, Alen M. Changes in electromyographic activity, muscle fibre and force production characteristics during heavy

resistance/power strength training in middle-aged and older men and women. *Acta Physiol Scand.* 2001a Jan;171(1):51-62.

[16] McKenzie Gillam G. Effects of frequency of weight training on muscle strength enhancement. *J Sports Med Phys Fitnes*s. 1981 Dec;21(4):432-6.

[17] Kraemer WJ, Adams K, Cafarelli E, Dudley GA, Dooly C, Feigenbaum MS, et al. American College of Sports Medicine position stand. Progression models in resistance training for healthy adults. *Med Sci Sports Exerc*. 2002 Feb;34(2):364-80.

[18] Calder AW, Chilibeck PD, Webber CE, Sale DG. Comparison of whole and split weight training routines in young women. *Can J Appl Physiol.* 1994 Jun;19(2):185-99.

[19] Candow DG, Burke DG. Effect of short-term equal-volume resistance training with different workout frequency on muscle mass and strength in untrained men and women. *J Strength Cond Res*. 2007 Feb;21(1):204-7.

[20] Lebrun CE, van der Schouw YT, de Jong FH, Grobbee DE, Lamberts SW. Fat mass rather than muscle strength is the major determinant of physical function and disability in postmenopausal women younger than 75 years of age. *Menopause*. 2006 May-Jun;13(3):474-81.

[21] Sowers MR, Crutchfield M, Richards K, Wilkin MK, Furniss A, Jannausch M, et al. Sarcopenia is related to physical functioning and leg strength in middle-aged women. *J Gerontol A Biol Sci Med Sci.* 2005 Apr;60(4):486-90.

SHORT COMMENTARY

In: Progress in Exercise and Women's Health Research ISBN 1-60456-014-5
Editor: Janet P. Coulter, pp. 19-28 © 2008 Nova Science Publishers, Inc.

Short Commentary 1

DO WOMEN AND MEN OVER 70 YEARS OLD SIMILARLY BENEFIT FROM A ONE-YEAR TRAINING PROGRAM?

Gaëlle Deley[1,], Gaëlle Kervio[2],*
Bénédicte Verges[1] and Jean-Marie Casillas[1]
[1] INSERM/ERIT-M 0207 Motricité-Plasticité, Université de Bourgogne, Dijon, France.
[2] Groupe de Recherche Cardio-Vasculaire, Université de Rennes 1, Rennes, France.

ABSTRACT

Background and Aims

Exercise capacity declines with age and is improved with exercise training. The aim of this study was to characterize the effects of a one-year combined exercise training in subjects over 70 years old, and to examine the eventual differences obtained between men and women.

Methods

After baseline evaluation, 24 subjects (12 men and 12 women) over 70 years old underwent moderate intensity training with aerobic and resistance exercises, 3 hours a week over one year. Workload, oxygen uptake (VO2) and heart rate were measured during a symptom-limited exercise test. The distance walked in 6 minutes (6-MWT) was also registered, and the maximal strength was measured on knee extensor muscles.

* Correspondence to : Cardiovascular Research Laboratory, Spaulding Rehabilitation Hospital, 125, Nashua Street,Boston, MA 02114 – USA, Phone: 617.573.2783 Fax: 617.573.2589, Mail: gdeley@partners.org

Results

After training, VO2 at ventilatory threshold was increased both in men (+17%, p<0.01) and women (+20%, p<0.01), as well as peak workload (+8% and +12%, respectively, p<0.05) and peak VO2 (+13%, p<0.05, and +19%, p<0.01, respectively). The 6-MWT distance was also improved both in men (+8%, p<0.01) and in women (+12%, p<0.01), whereas the maximal strength of knee extensor muscles was increased only in women (+28%, p<0.05). The amount of increase after training for these last two parameters was higher in women (p<0.05).

Conclusion

This study have shown that one-year of combined exercise training in healthy subjects over 70 years old is well-tolerated and improves aerobic capacity, performance to field test and muscle strength. Moreover, women seem to better benefit of this program.

Key Words: elderly, gender, aerobic and strength training, exercise capacity, maximal strength, walk test.

Exercise tolerance declines with age due to cardiovascular limitations, *i.e.* decreased maximal cardiac output and/or maximal heart rate (Gertensblith et al. 1976), but also due to age-induced modifications at peripheral level and within skeletal muscles (Conley et al. 2000). These impairments, revealed by reductions of maximal oxygen uptake values (VO$_2$max) (Proctor and Joyner 1997, Paterson et al. 1999, Stathokostas et al. 2004), muscular strength and submaximal endurance to fatigue (Aniansson et al. 1986, Hurley 1995, Hunter et al. 2000, Kent-Braun and Ng 2000), are therefore attributable to the normal process of ageing, but also to the sedentary way of living adopted by most of older people (Kent-Braun and Ng 2000, Hunter et al. 2004). Thus, adapted and regular physical activity is recommended in this population (Evans 1999, Mazzeo and Tanaka 2001, ACSM 2004). Most studies that investigated the effects of exercise training in older subjects were of short-term (less than six month) and have mostly considered (i) the range of 60-70 years, (ii) strength or aerobic exercise training, (iii) institutionalised elderly and (iv) men subjects.

According to the American College of Sports Medicine (2004), long-term participation in programs of physical activity is one of the most effective ways for older adults to make physical activity a part of one's lifestyle and therefore to help prevent chronic disease, promote independence, and increase quality of life. This is a key component in the promotion of physical activity in old age regarding the sedentary way of living adopted by most of older people. The aim of the present study was therefore to determine to what extent, and how differently, a long-term training program with strength and moderate-intensity aerobic exercises, may impact on cardiorespiratory and functional parameters in healthy men and women over 70 years.

METHODS

Subjects

Table 1 presents the characteristics of the twenty-four clinically healthy, community-dwelling older volunteers, who were enrolled in this study (12 women and 12 men).

Exclusion criteria were malignant disease, previous stroke, Alzheimer's disease, major lung pathology, motor neurone disease, musculoskeletal disorders, endocrine disorders, severe diabetes mellitus and a history of hypertension, recent myocardial infarction, use of beta-blockers, and subjects who were not in sinus rhythm, or who had had an acute febrile or systemic disease within the previous 2 years.

An activity pattern profile taking into account the type and number of hours of exercise per week have been determined for each participant. Only those individuals considered as "sedentary", since they took part in recreational, non-competitive physical activities at a frequency of no more than twice a week, have been admitted to the study.

The investigation conforms to the principles outlined in the Declaration of Helsinki. All subjects gave their written consent after being clearly advised about the protocol, which was approved by the Institutional Ethics Committee.

Table 1. Baseline anthropometric data. Mean (SD)

	Women (n = 12)	Men (n = 12)	P value
Age (yrs)	76.9 (4.3)	77.1 (3.1)	ns.
Weight (kg)	59.6 (7.3)	75.9 (9.5)	< 0.001
Height (cm)	158.4 (4.4)	167.4 (4.5)	< 0.001
Body Mass Index (kg/m²)	24.7 (2.4)	27.0 (2.7)	< 0.01

P value: Statistical difference Women group vs. Men group (Student's t-test).

Measurements and Data Analysis

At baseline (PRE) and after the one-year period (POST), subjects underwent a clinical exam, a symptom-limited cardiopulmonary exercise test, a 6-min walk test (6-MWT) and an evaluation of knee extensor muscles maximal strength. All subjects first performed the clinical exam and the symptom-limited cardiopulmonary exercise test, in order to exclude those presenting contra-indications from the study.

Cardiopulmonary Exercise Test

The incremental exercise test was performed on an electromagnetically braked cycle ergometer (Lode, Groningen, Netherlands). Briefly, after a 3-minute rest sitting on the cycle ergometer, the test started, with one minute pedalling at 20 watts and the workload was then increased by 10 watts every minute. The exercise test was terminated when the subject was unable to maintain the imposed pedalling rhythm of 60 rpm. Twelve-lead electrocardiogram derivations (Case, General Electrics Medical Systems, United Kingdom) was monitored throughout the test and left arm blood pressure measurements were obtained every 2 minutes using a standard cuff mercury sphygmomanometer. Gas exchanges were measured breath-by-breath using a computerised system (CPX, Medical Graphics, St. Paul, MN). Before each test, the system was calibrated with a 3-liter Rudolph syringe and a standard gas of known concentrations.

Peak VO_2 and peak heart rate were defined as the mean oxygen uptake and heart rate values during the last 30 seconds of exercise. Three well-trained investigators blinded to the trial, determined the ventilatory threshold using the method of Beaver et al. (1986). The VO_2 corresponding to the ventilatory threshold was noted.

6-Min Walk Test

A therapist, blind to the ergocycle exercise test results, administered this test. Subjects were asked to cover as much distance as possible in 6 minutes. The test was performed in a 50-m long unobstructed corridor and the total distance walked was measured in meters (m) at the end of 6 minutes. Slow-down and stops for resting were authorized. To avoid the learning effect (Kervio et al. 2003), subjects were familiarized with this test before entering the study. The heart rate value at the end of the test was noted.

Maximal Strength

Strength of quadriceps muscles was evaluated as a one-repetition maximum (1-RM) on a leg press machine (Leg Press, Multi-Form', La Roque d'Anthéron, France). The 1-RM was defined as the maximum weight that could be lifted for one complete repetition (Phillips et al. 2004).

Exercise Training

The supervised exercise training was held twice a week in the hospital gym. Each session started with a 10-minute warm-up including light rhythmical, flexibility exercises, and supported stretching exercises.

After the warm-up, subjects underwent a 12-min, instructor-led, group aerobic workout, involving low-impact walking and stepping with changes of direction to challenge balance maintenance. This included, for example, forward, backward, sideways and diagonal heel and toe taps; forward, backward, and sideways walks; knee raises and lunges. Upper body movements such as arm raises, crosses, and curls were also incorporated into these movements. This exercise was set to music paced at 118–124 beats per minute with an HR value of no more than 70 % of maximal HR, controlled using a heart monitor (Polar S610i, Kempele, Finland).

Strength training exercises were then carried out with two variable-resistance machines (Leg Press and Sitting calf, Multi-Form'). Subjects performed two sets of 12 repetitions on each machine at an intensity initially set at 40% of the 1-RM value and gradually increased to

80% within one month. The 1-RM was individually updated every two weeks to adjust the training stimulus. Subjects were asked to execute the concentric phase of each exercise for 2 seconds, followed by the eccentric phase for 3 seconds. The range of motion was 50° on the Sitting Calf and 90° on the Leg Press. A two-minute rest was provided between each set of repetitions.

At the end of the session, the subjects performed a 10-minute cool-down with stretching of the trained muscles. Specialized teachers supervised all training sessions.

Once a week, a training session was held at home with elastic bands (Theraband, Hygenic Corporation, Akron, OH) reproducing the movements generated on the Sitting Calf and Leg Press machines. Subjects were initially familiarized with the elastic bands and were given instructions on how to reach the same intensity as with the machines (Capodaglio et al. 2002). Each session consisted of 20 repetitions of horizontal squatting (Leg Press) and heel-rise from seated (Sitting Calf). Subjects were also asked to perform 30 minutes of brisk walking once a week.

Statistical Analysis

Data are expressed as means ± standard deviations (SD). The baseline values of the two groups were compared by a Student's t-test. A two-way ANOVA was used to assess the effects of gender and exercise training. This was followed by a post-hoc LSD test, when the P value was significant. A Student's t-test was also used to compare between men and women the percentage of modification of each studied parameter. Significant differences were accepted at $P<0.05$.

Results

Baseline

Table 2. Baseline data registered in women and men. Mean (SD).

	Women	Men	P value
VO$_2$ at rest	4.3 (1.1)	4.2 (0.8)	ns.
HR at rest	75.7 (8.4)	70.2 (10.1)	ns.
VO$_2$ at VT	11.8 (2.9)	13.4 (2.3)	= 0.05
HR at VT	106.0 (8.8)	96.9 (17.8)	ns.
Peak VO$_2$	16.2 (3.1)	21.5 (2.2)	< 0.01
Peak WL	79.6 (30.4)	116.5 (28.0)	< 0.01
Peak HR	136.5 (10.5)	134.4 (16.4)	ns.
6 – MWT	399.7 (39.9)	445.9 (38.6)	< 0.01
6 – MWT HR	108.6 (19.1)	100.2 (13.6)	ns.
KE 1-RM	48.6 (14.3)	84.0 (27.4)	< 0.001

VO$_2$: oxygen uptake (mL.min^{-1}.kg^{-1}) ; HR : heart rate (beats.min^{-1}) ; WL: workload (Watts) ;VT: ventilatory threshold ; 6-MWT: distance to the 6-minute walk test (meters) ; KE 1-RM: maximum weight lifted with knee extensor muscles (kg).

P value: statistical difference Women vs. men (Student t-test).

At rest, HR and VO_2 values were not different in men and women. At the ventilatory threshold and at the end of the cardiopulmonary exercise test, HR was not different between men and women, whereas VO_2 was respectively 13.6% (P=0.05) and 32.7% (P<0.01) lower in women. Concerning the 6-MWT, HR was not different between the two groups, whereas the distance walked was 11.6% (P<0.01) lower in women. The muscular strength was 42.0% lower in women (P<0.001).

Effects of Exercise Training in Men and Women (Figure 1).

Heart rate and VO_2 measured at rest were unchanged after exercise training.

As shown in Figure 1, most parameters were improved, both in men and women, after exercise training. At the ventilatory threshold and at the end of the cardiopulmonary exercise test, HR was unchanged whereas VO_2 was increased similarly in men (+ 17% and + 13%, respectively, P < 0.05) and in women (+ 20% and + 19%, respectively, P < 0.01).

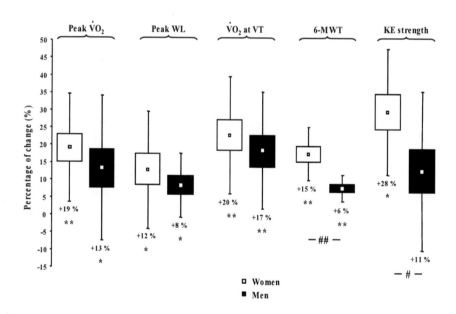

Figure 1. PRE to POST ratio for all parameters. Peak oxygen uptake (peak VO2), peak workload (peak WL), oxygen uptake at ventilatory threshold (VO_2 at VT), distance walked in 6-minute (6-MWT) and knee extensor maximal strength (KE strength). Values are expressed as mean percentage of change ± SD. Statistical differences of the PRE to POST ratio (*, **, ***: p<0.05, p<0.01, p<0.001), and between men and women (#, ##: p<0.05, p<0.01).

After exercise training, the 6-MWT distance was increased both in men and women (+ 8% and 12% respectively, P < 0.01) without any change of HR in both groups. The maximal strength of knee extensor muscles was improved in women only (+28%, P < 0.05). Indeed, the 11% of increase for this parameter measured in men was not significant. The inter-group comparison demonstrated significantly greater improvements in 6-MWT distance and in the knee extensor muscles maximal strength in women (P<0.01 and P<0.05, respectively).

DISCUSSION

Regular physical activity is considered as one of the most effective ways for older adults to help to prevent chronic disease, promote independence and increase quality of life. Numerous studies have already demonstrated the beneficial effects of strength and/or endurance training programs of various durations in elderly subjects (Mazzeo and Tanaka 2001, Ferketich et al. 1998, Cress et al. 1999, Capodaglio et al. 2005, Mian et al. 2006). Our present program is also interesting because it takes into account, on the basis of the recommendations of the American College of Sports Medicine (2004), the three following key components: it is (i) a multidimensional activity program (endurance, strength, balance and flexibility), what is generally considered optimal for older adults, (ii) a long-duration program, what allow making physical activity a part of one's lifestyle and therefore induce greater improvements of exercise tolerance, (iii) composed by exercises of low / moderate intensity, which ensure good adherence, particularly in elderly subjects.

Baseline characteristics of our population are comparable to previous data obtained in age-matched subjects (Capodaglio et al (2005) and Deley et al. (2007)). As expected, women showed lower values in VO_2, both at peak and at ventilatory threshold, distance to the 6-MWT and maximal strength. This gender difference is well described in published data, and is mainly attributed in women to their higher body fat composition, lower haemoglobin content and smaller heart size (Woo et al. 2006, Ogawa et al. 1992). Recently, Musselman and Brouwer (2005) have also suggested that the primary factors relating to gender-specific strength was activity level in men and body weight in women.

Our training program showed beneficial and significant effects on both aerobic capacity and muscular strength. The training-induced improvements in peak VO_2 are of great interest since this parameter is often considered as an important indicator of exercise capacity and aerobic fitness (Stathokostas et al. 2004). However, in our study, peak VO_2 was only increased by 13% in men and 19% in women, what is small in comparison with other studies. For example, Ferketich et al. (1998) have reported, for this parameter, an increase around 30% after a 12-week program. This discrepancy may be explained by the lower intensity used in our program (no more than 70% vs. 70-80%), but also by the lower aerobic exercises duration (12 vs 30 min) and maybe by the lower number of supervised training sessions per week (2 vs 3 days a week).

Maximal strength is also considered as an important determinant of exercise tolerance (Cress et al. 1999), so that we were particularly interested in the effects of training on this parameter. In accordance with previous results (Deley et al. 2007, Cress et al. 1999, Mian et al. 2006), we have shown an improvement of strength by 11% in men and 28% in women. However, the origins of these strength improvements are actually unclear. Further investigation are therefore needed to determine if they are due to increases in motor unit activation, muscle size and muscle quality, i.e. strength per unit of muscle (Evans 1999) and/or due to a reduction in antagonist coactivation (Simoneau et al. 2005).

Submaximal exercise capacity, assessed in our study by VO_2 at ventilatory threshold and 6-MWT distance, was also significantly improved after exercise training. These improvements are very interesting since they suggest an enhancement of the subjects' capacity to perform sustained submaximal activities (Piepoli et al. 2006), that is related to better autonomy, physical independence and increased quality of life for trained elderly subjects (Larsen et al. 2001, Poole-Wilson 2001). Moreover, the distance walked in 6 minutes was increased after training without any modification of the heart rate values. This result confirms also that the patients, probably by adaptations obtained at peripheral level (Paterson et al. 1999, Zhang et al. 2003, Santa-Clara et al. 2002, Piepoli et al. 2006), would be able to extend their daily activities for an equivalent cardiac solicitation.

In our study, improvements were similar in men and women for all parameters measured during the cardiopulmonary exercise test. However, concerning the 6-MWT and the knee extensor muscles strength, it is interesting to notice that these improvements after training are more important in women than in men. This difference could be due to the training intensity, which was insufficient to highly improve strength in men, but enough to improve it in women, and to improve aerobic and functional capacities. Our data confirm and complete those of Capodaglio et al. (2005), who have used a similar training protocol. However, in their study, at baseline, men devoted more time to physical activity than women (8 vs. 3 hours.week^{-1}). Thus, in regard to these studies, it seems that whatever the initial level, women obtained better performances in comparison to men. In practice, these results suggest that the subjects' gender must be so taken into account in the elaboration of individual intensity training.

In conclusion, the main finding of this study is that, even when performed at low intensity, long-term training with both aerobic and strength exercises induces significant improvements in maximal and submaximal indices of functional capacity, and lower limb maximal strength in healthy subjects over 70 years old. Moreover, it appears that women better benefit of this training particularly regarding 6-MWT and strength performances. Thus, these results provide further support for the usefulness of this kind of exercises training in healthy population, and suggest that men probably require higher work intensity to better improve their maximal strength.

ACKNOWLEDGEMENTS

This study was supported by European Commission Framework V grant (QLRT-2001-00323).

REFERENCES

American College of Sports Medicine (2004). Physical activity programs and behavior counseling in older adult populations. *Med Sci Sports Exerc, 36*, 1997-2003.

Aniansson, A; Hedberg, M; Henning, GB; Grimby, G. (1986). Muscle morphology, enzymatic activity, and muscle strength in elderly men: a follow-up study. *Muscle Nerve, 9,* 585-591.

Beaver, WL; Wasserman, K; Whipp, BJ. (1986). A new method for detecting anaerobic threshold by gas exchange. *J Appl Physiol, 60,* 2020-2027.

Capodaglio, P; Capodaglio, EM; Ferri, A; et al. (2005). Muscle function and functional ability improves more in community-dwelling older women with a mixed-strength training programme. *Age Ageing, 34*, 141-147.

Capodaglio, P; Facioli, M; Burroni, E; et al. (2002). Effectiveness of a home-based strengthening program for elderly males in Italy. A preliminary study. *Aging Clin Exp Res, 14*, 28-34.

Cress, ME; Buchner, DM; Questad, KA; et al. (1999). Exercise: effects on physical functional performance in independent older adults. *J Gerontol A Biol Sci Med Sci, 54*, M242-248.

Deley, G; Kervio, G; Van Hoecke, J; Verges, B; Grassi, B; Casillas, JM. (2007). Effects of a one-year training program in adults over 70 years old: a study with a control group. Aging Clin Exp Research. *Aging Clin Exp Res, 19*, 310-315.

Evans, WJ. (1999). Exercise training guidelines for the elderly. *Med Sci Sports Exerc, 31*, 12-17.

Ferketich, AK; Kirby, TE; Always, SE. (1998). Cardiovascular and muscular adaptations to combined endurance and strength training in elderly women. *Acta Physiol Scand, 164*, 259-267.

Gerstenblith, G; Lakatta, EG; Weisfeldt, ML. (1976). Age changes in myocardial function and exercise response. *Prog Cardiovasc Dis, 19*, 1-21.

Hunter, GR; McCarthy, JP; Bamman, MM. (2004) Effects of resistance training on older adults. *Sports Med, 34*, 329-348.

Hunter, GR; Wetzstein, CJ; Fields, DA; Brown, A; Bamman, MM. (2000). Resistance training increases total energy expenditure and free-living physical activity in older adults. *J Appl Physiol, 89*, 977-984.

Hurley, BF. (1995). Age, gender, and muscular strength. *J Gerontol A Biol Sci Med Sci, 50*, 41-44.

Kent-Braun, JA & Ng, AV (2000). Skeletal muscle oxidative capacity in young and older women and men. *J Appl Physiol, 89*, 1072-1078.

Kervio, G ; Carre, F ; Ville, NS. (2003). Reliability and intensity of the six-minute walk test in healthy elderly subjects. *Med Sci Sports Exerc, 35*, 169-174.

Larsen, AI; Aarsland, T; Kristiansen, M; Haugland, A; Dickstein, K. (2001). Assessing the effect of exercise training in men with heart failure; comparison of maximal, submaximal and endurance exercise protocols. *Eur Heart J, 22*, 684-692.

Mazzeo, RS & Tanaka, H. (2001). Exercise prescription for the elderly: current recommendations. *Sports Med, 31*, 809-818.

Mian, OS; Thom, JM; Ardigo, LP; Morse, CI; Narici, MV; Minetti, AE. (2006). Effect of a 12-month physical conditioning programme on the metabolic cost of walking in healthy older adults. *Eur J Appl Physiol, 4*, 1-7.

Musselman K & Brouwer B. (2005). Gender-related differences in physical performance among seniors.. *J Aging Phys Act, 13*, 239-253.

Ogawa, T; Spina, RJ; Martin, WH 3rd; Kohrt, WM; Schechtman, KB; Holloszy, JO; Ehsani, AA (1992). Effects of aging, sex, and physical training on cardiovascular responses to exercise. *Circulation, 86*, 494-503.

Paterson, DH; Cunningham, DA; Koval, JJ.; St. Croix, CM. Aerobic fitness in a population of independently living men and women aged 55–86 years. (1999). *Med. Sci. Sports Exerc, 31*, 1813–1820.

Phillips, WT; Batterham, AM; Valenzuela, JE; Burkett, LN. (2004). Reliability of maximal strength testing in older adults. *Arch Phys Med Rehabil, 85*, 329-334.

Poole-Wilson, PA. (2000). The 6-minute walk. A simple test with clinical application. *Eur Heart J, 21*, 507-508.

Proctor, DN & Joyner, MJ. (1997). Skeletal muscle mass and the reduction of $\dot{V}O_2$ max in trained older subjects. *J Appl Physiol, 82*, 1411-1415.

Santa-Clara, H; Fernhall, B; Mendes, M; Sardinha, LB. (2002). Effect of a 1 year combined aerobic- and weight-training exercise programme on aerobic capacity and ventilatory threshold in patients suffering from coronary artery disease. *Eur J Appl Physiol, 87*, 568-575.

Simoneau, E; Martin, A; Van Hoecke, J. (2005). Muscular performances at the ankle joint in young and elderly men. *J Gerontol A Biol Sci Med Sci, 60*, 439-447.

Stathokostas, L; Jacob-Johnson, S; Petrella, RJ; Paterson DH. (2004). Longitudinal changes in aerobic power in older men and women. *J Appl Physiol, 97*, 781-789.

Task Force of the Italian Working Group on Cardiac Rehabilitation Prevention; Working Group on Cardiac Rehabilitation and Exercise Physiology of the European Society of Cardiology; Piepoli, MF; Corra, U; Agostoni, PG; Belardinelli, R; Cohen-Solal, A; Hambrecht, R; Vanhees, L. (2006). Statement on cardiopulmonary exercise testing in chronic heart failure due to left ventricular dysfunction: recommendations for performance and interpretation. Part I: definition of cardiopulmonary exercise testing parameters for appropriate use in chronic heart failure. *Eur J Cardiovasc Prev Rehabil, 13*, 150-64.

Woo, JS; Derleth, C; Stratton, JR; Levy, WC. (2006). The influence of age, gender and training on exercise efficiency. *J Am Coll Cardiol, 47*, 1049-1057.

Zhang, JG; Ohta, T; Ishikawa-Takata, K; Tabata, I; Miyashita, M. (2003). Effects of daily activity recorded by pedometer on peak oxygen consumption (VO2peak), ventilatory threshold and leg extension power in 30- to 69-year-old Japanese without exercise habit. *Eur J Appl Physiol, 90*, 109-113.

RESEARCH AND REVIEW STUDIES

In: Progress in Exercise and Women's Health Research
Editor: Janet P. Coulter, pp. 31-69

ISBN 1-60456-014-5
© 2008 Nova Science Publishers, Inc.

Chapter 1

THE PLACE OF EXERCISE IN THE EVERYDAY LIVES OF AGING WOMEN AND WOMEN WITH PHYSICAL DISABILITIES

Catherine L. Lysack[1] and Heather E. Dillaway

Associate Professor, Gerontology and Occupational Therapy, Wayne State University, Detroit, Michigan

Assistant Professor, Sociology, Wayne State University, Detroit, Michigan

INTRODUCTION

Physical exercise has been increasingly defined as a critical health-promoting behavior. *The Surgeon General's Report on Physical Activity and Health* in the mid-1990s, *The Surgeon General's Call To Action To Prevent and Decrease Overweight and Obesity* in 2001, and *Healthy People 2010* all state the dire importance of routine physical exercise (U.S. Department of Health and Human Services, 2007). The Center for Disease Control and the American College of Sports Medicine have put out similar calls for increased physical activity (Burns, 1996). These measures have been taken because it is now well established that routine physical exercise reduces the risk of premature death or disability caused by health conditions such as coronary heart disease, some cancers (e.g., colon cancer), non-insulin-dependent diabetes, osteoarthritis, osteoporosis, hypertension, mental health concerns, and obesity (Newson & Kemps, 2007; Janiszewski & Ross, 2007; Eyler et al., 1998; Henderson & Ainsworth, 2000; Brownson et al., 2000). Specific populations get special benefit from routine exercise, due to the risks of disease or disability that they face. Considerable research has documented the benefits of exercise for menopausal and postmenopausal women, for example. They are more at risk than younger women for the conditions cited above (Brownson et al., 2000; Simkin-Silverman et al., 2003), yet these risks are lessened by exercise (Periera et al., 1998). Research also documents the benefits of

[1] Correspondence to: Rm. 231 Knapp Bldg., Institute of Gerontology, 87 E. Ferry St., Wayne State University, Detroit, Michigan, 48202. Email: c.lysack@wayne.edu

exercise for women with physical disabilities. Studies show that the prevalence of obesity, for example, is 2 to 4 times higher in the disabled population than in the general population (Rimmer & Wang, 2005; Weil et al., 2002). Again, research shows meaningful health benefits are realized through exercise, even for those with severe physical disabilities like spinal cord injury (Nash & Gator, 2007).

Despite the widely publicized health benefits of exercise, many American adults remain sedentary (Belza et al., 2004; Janiszewski & Ross, 2007; Newson & Kemps, 2007). Further, studies show that women remain less active than men, older adults are less active than younger adults, and older women are typically the least active of all (CDC, 2006; Newson & Kemps, 2007; Periera et al., 1998). The situation for adults with disabilities is not dissimilar. Finch, Owen, and Price (2001) found that 20% of the individuals in their study identified current injury or disability as one of several barriers to greater physical activity, with half of those respondents citing it as the number-one reason why they do not participate more in physical activities. Studies suggest that in the U.S. alone, more than 112,000 preventable deaths each year are due to obesity and physical inactivity, and that relatively small increases in regular exercise could cut these numbers substantially (Flegel, Graubard, Williamson, Gail, 2005). Quality of life in general would also improve. While some studies have begun to examine the sociocultural contexts and demographic factors surrounding sedentary lifestyles, these contexts have not been explored in full (Manson, Skerrett, Greenland, & VanItallie, 2004). In addition, while a handful of studies have begun to compare gender, age, and racial-ethnic groups for their rates of and reasons for exercise, there have been few efforts to study diversity of perspectives or experiences within one group -- for instance, women – and how different groups of at-risk women (e.g., menopausal women and disabled women) might experience and think about exercise very differently. Specifically, while studies are underway to outline some of the barriers or motivations to exercise in general for women versus men, old versus young, or different racial-ethnic groups (e.g., Newson & Kemps, 2007;), the complexities of exercise for these specific groups needs greater investigation (Rimmer, Rubin & Braddock, 2000; Adams, 1995).

The purpose of this chapter is to delve more deeply into the place of exercise in women's lives and bring contemporary social science literature to bear on the challenge of promoting exercise in the lives of two unique subgroups of women: aging women and women with spinal cord injury. The chapter is divided into three major sections: the first section highlights the power of appearance norms to shape women's views of their bodies as well as their aging and disability experiences related to exercise; the second section presents the results of two separate studies on exercise practices and barriers to exercise in aging and disabled women; the third and final section considers these findings in relation to future research and next steps in critical social science research focused on barriers to exercise in understudied populations of women.

SECTION I

Appearance Norms and Female Beauty

Feminist scholars have extensively documented the importance of external appearances in western cultures (Bartky, 2003; Bordo, 1993; Dinnerstein & Weitz, 1998; Markson, 2003; Markey, Markey, & Birch, 2004; Rogers, 1997; Witt, 1994/1995; Wolf, 1991; Zones, 2000) and described the corporeal physical body as a "text of culture… a symbolic form upon which the norms and practices of society are inscribed" (Lee, 2003, p. 82). Zones (2000) argues that "of all the characteristics that distinguish one human being from the next, physical appearance has the most immediate impact…and… the power of physical appearance pushes people to assimilate in order to avoid unwanted attention or to attract desired attention" (p. 87). Often this means looking "conventionally attractive", and at any given time and place there are fairly "uniform and widely understood models of how groups of individuals (e.g., women) 'should' look" (Zones, 2000, p. 87). In the U.S., the contemporary standard for female beauty dictates slenderness/thinness, youth, Whiteness, upper-class status (in that one must be able to spend considerable amounts to adhere to beauty standards), and "no noticeable physical imperfections or disabilities" (Zones, 2000, p. 91). In addition, social constructions of women's external appearances or public bodies do not accommodate change-- women's appearances should remain the same over time; any visible alterations are ideologically defined as "negative," "abnormal," or "deviant" (Martin, 1992; Wolf, 1991; Zones, 2000). To maintain a feminine/gendered body is to maintain an *unchanging* body. [Even pregnant women are not immune to this, as there is medical and cultural pressure to gain minimal weight and continue to exercise during pregnancy so that one can regain one's pre-pregnancy shape/weight as quickly as possible (Dworkin & Wachs, 2004).] Idealized norms of beauty and physical appearance are everywhere. They influence us all, and alter perceptions and daily practices of women themselves. Nowhere is this more obvious than in the lives of women who are aging and women with visible physical disabilities.

Women and Menopause: Questioning the "Aging" Body

Women entering and experiencing menopause provide a useful context in which explore body image and beauty norms and how aging and health are intertwined. Menopausal bodies have often been conflated with aging bodies, and an assumption is sometimes made that a negative definition of aging is what makes menopause negative for some women. Menopause is a biosocial experience at midlife. It is sometimes called the "change of life." Feminist social science literature suggests that biomedicine and popular culture reduce menopausal women to "the internal secretions of their reproductive organs" (Dickson, 1990, p. 17; Adler et al., 2000; Kuh, Wadsworth & Hardy, 1997; Melby, Lock, & Kaufert, 2005). Popular culture suggests that aging female bodies are ignored and negated specifically because these women's bodies have lost their reproductive (and by implication, sexual) charm. Markson (2003) writes that the aging female body is rarely "an object of the appreciative male gaze" (p. 30). Nor does it fit the contemporary cultural discourse about "ideal" female beauty. Thus, both medical literature and popular culture suggest that women's menopausal bodies might be experienced negatively simply because they are aging bodies and that aging (and not menopause per se) is what brings the negativity. An important contribution of feminist social science is the idea that women experience menopause within particular social contexts, emphasizing its socio-cultural dimensions (Barbre, 1993; Adler et al., 2000; Melby et al., 2005; Gold et al., 2000). Because feminist social scientists contextualize menopause and talk to individual women, they find that menopause is shaped by physiological symptoms *and* life circumstances, along with a complex set of social locations including ethnicity, socio-economic status and sexuality.

Although there can be no doubt that women worry about the bodily effects of aging in general, they may specifically worry about the bodily "changes" they experience during midlife that "blast the image of the fecund sex goddess" (Markson, 2003, p. 81). Rogers (1997) explains that the bodily experiences to which we assign importance are those that "disturb identity, system, order" (p. 226). Menopause takes on significance in our society specifically because it disturbs the ideological distinctions between women (and their bodies) and men (and their bodies). Menopausal women become "different" from an ideologically defined (i.e., reproductive, fertile, sexual, attractive) "woman," and cross over into an "other" (i.e., non-reproductive, infertile, asexual, unattractive) category – a category that must represent something "abnormal" and "unnatural" and that ought to be eradicated if gender distinctions are to remain undisturbed (Epstein, 1995; Garber, 1992). Control and discipline of the body therefore comes into sharp relief – the beauty industry reminds women that as they age they need specialized products and costly services including plastic surgery to prevent or reverse visibly undesirable consequences of aging like flabby arms, wrinkled skin, and sagging breasts; the fitness industry reminds women that by disciplining the body through physical exercise they too can "look and feel young".

But aging is a natural human process. There are many problems in equating beauty with youth. For instance, this equation denies the inevitability of normal human development and life course changes and can distort a healthy self-identity. In the case of menopause, the general message encountered by midlife women is: if your body is changing, it is probably due to menopause, but bodily change is negative, and therefore you should work to prevent or mask any changes that might occur (Barbre, 1993; Gullette, 1997; Lyons & Griffin, 2003; Rogers, 1997).

In addition to concerns about external appearance and bodily change that parallel cultural norms about beauty, midlife women begin to be exposed to a "discourse of prevention: (Murtagh & Hepworth, 2003). Murtagh and Hepworth (2003, p. 188) describe how, beginning in the 1980s, "menopause became identified in the medical literature as a crucial point in a woman's life because of the possible onset of preventable diseases." Since menopause has been defined as the time when women begin to experience a decrease in particular hormones (e.g., estrogen), they are now told that they are at a greater risk for osteoporosis (and subsequent injuries such as hip fractures). Studies in the 1980s also began to make the links between aging women's lack of estrogen and an increased risk of cardiovascular disease (Murtagh & Hepworth, 2003; Bush et al., 1987). Thus, women begin to be told at midlife (or at the onset of menopause) that they are now at considerable risk for long-term health problems, and they need to engage in health-promoting behavior in order to curb this risk (e.g., exercise, diet, vitamin supplementation). In addition, they have been told to seek out traditional medicine in the form of hormone therapies to alleviate some of these risks (Murtagh & Hepworth, 2003). Nonetheless, there is an emphasis placed on self-management of these risks, which means exercise and other individual behaviors have attained heightened importance in recent years. This leaves women to face two dictates that point them towards exercise and related health-promoting activities: (1) the importance of maintaining a particular physical appearance in the face of beauty norms, and (2) the importance of minimizing long-term health risks because of a midlife/menopausal life stage that means a decrease of estrogen.

Women with Physical Disabilities: A Challenge to Stereotypes

"Disabled bodies" or bodies that are no longer "able" or "normal" may challenge the myths of beauty and bodily perfection to an even greater extent than aging bodies do. Stone (1995) argues that a myth of bodily perfection plays an integral role in creating a category of people labeled disabled and of relegating them to the status of "other". Women's traditional roles as nurturers, mothers, wives, homemakers, and lovers are usually not seen as appropriate for women with disabilities. Thus, women with disabilities are no longer seen as women; disability has trumped their womanhood, leaving them with a single negative "master status" – disabled. Research has shown in compelling terms how women with disabilities are rendered "deficient" and "devalued" by virtue of these distorted cultural norms about physical appearance and female beauty (Cash & Pruzinsky, 2002; Fine & Asch, 1988). Even simple demographics bear this out. The U.S. Census (2005) shows that compared to both men with disabilities and non-disabled women, women with disabilities are more likely to never marry, marry later, and be divorced if they do get married. Furthermore, while 60 percent of non-disabled women and men with disabilities are married, only 49 percent of women with disabilities are married. Women with disabilities are viewed as a second class of woman who does not fit the idealized norms for women's bodies or place in society (Fine & Asch, 1988; Wendell, 1996). Scholars have variously described women with disabilities as "doubly disadvantaged" or as experiencing "double jeopardy" – a multiplicative burden of oppression due to gender and disability that can only be "made worse" by race ("triple jeopardy").

While feminist scholars and disability scholars have made small strides in exploring the experience of disability and the impact of appearance norms in groups of women with various types of disabilities, the literature is small. However, studies of these topics and the valuable insights they provide are virtually non-existent in the mainstream medical literature. This leaves unacknowledged profound social pressures on women who do not have full use of their bodies. Feminist scholars and disability scholars (Calasanti, 2004; Gill, 1997; Wendell, 1996) rightfully argue that such pressures push women with disability into trying to hide their disability or pass for "normal". Of course, in the case of severe visible physical disabilities that require a wheelchair for example, hiding disability is impossible. But hiding parts of the body and shielding them from the glare of public scrutiny and stigma *are* possible. In the realm of disability, just as in aging, there are social pressures to control and discipline the body in order to reduce the public's discomfort with reminders that human bodies can fail.

Beyond appearances, there are professions charged with "reforming" the body. Rehabilitation professionals, for example, provide treatments and therapies meant to repair and retrain disabled bodies. Exercise is one means of doing this. So the question must be asked: Is exercise merely a set of mechanical movements mean to bring health and vitality to all who dedicate themselves properly to the task? This may be the view of rehabilitation professionals and others who prescribe exercise, but what of the view of aging women and women with disabilities themselves? How do they perceive the need to exercise, the goals of exercise, the experience of exercise? Do they ever perceive exercise as an unwelcome "fix" for bodies others view as "deficit"? More provocatively, and from a critical social science perspective, could exercise be conceptualized as yet another extension of biomedicine's "clinical gaze" (Foucault, 1975). But much more simply, since exercise is known to bring many health benefits and if we wish to extent those most beneficial elements of exercise to all women, how can we learn more about the experience of exercise in the daily lives of aging women and women with physical disabilities – two groups where so little is currently known?

Exercise: Disciplining Aging and Disabled Bodies

Exercise and physical fitness in the context of women's health is a topic enjoying renewed interest in medical research. There are a variety of reasons why this is so. The quickly growing aging population may be one reason but it must be acknowledged that the contemporary concern with America's "obesity epidemic" is another (Flegel, Graubard, Williamson, & Gail, 2005). Yet, most models of health behavior change which provide the theoretical footing for exercise are grounded in the assumptions that effort and self-awareness are all that are needed to achieve exercise success. These assumptions require critical scrutiny, since at the very least, they have not been adequate to solve the current "obesity crises". Decades of research has proven that adherence to exercise programs is a tremendous barrier to achieving the potential public health benefits associated with it (Janiszewski & Ross, 2007). In addition to well-known problem of sticking to exercise regimes, one must ask how realistic is it to rely on self-awareness and effort alone in the face of powerful of gender norms about physical attractiveness and female beauty and a variety of other serious barriers to exercise?

In the case of women living with more pronounced chronic health conditions and severe physical disabilities, the range of issues is much wider. Degenerative orthopedic conditions like arthritis and hip fractures, for example, are more common as women age. So is cardiovascular disease and stroke. All leave visible "marks" on the body   diminished strength, pain, a change in gait and mobility. But relatively speaking these assaults to the body are mild. There are more severe physical disabilities which cause much more significant consequences. Such is the situation with traumatic spinal cord injury (SCI).

Traumatic SCI is one of the most severe, lifelong and publicly visible disabilities there are (Dijkers, 2005). From a physiological perspective, women with SCI must learn to live their lives in bodies that are partially or completely paralyzed and accept that some parts of their bodies will feel little or no physical sensation. The cause may have been a car accident or a fall or something else, but it is immediately evident that this disability makes any form of exercise more difficult. Most obviously, SCI means impaired motor function, but other systems like the autonomic nervous system and endocrine systems which lead to abnormal perspiration, erratic blood pressure fluctuations, and fainting for example, are affected as well. The very nature of this injury makes exercise potentially more risky. From a psychosocial or emotional point of view, women with SCI must also contend with the radically altered appearance of their bodies and learn to deal with their personal feelings about their altered appearance and their identities as disabled women (McColl, 2002;

Pentland, Walker, Minnes, Tremblay, Brouwer, & Gould, 2002). Specific aspects of one's physical appearance as a women with SCI will also change dramatically over time. Without electrical impulses to move muscles in one's limbs, there is "muscle wasting" and the limbs grow progressively thin. For some, limbs can also appear very rigid and contracted at the joints. Some experience "invisible symptoms" like pain and fatigue, while other women must content with uncontrolled spasticity and tremors in their limbs, and even their bladder and bowel (Nosek et al., 2006; Sipski, Jackson, Gómez-Marín, Estores, & Stein, 2004). The physiological aspects of this physical disability takes time to adjust to. It is not surprisingly that the disability may alter women's perceptions of themselves as women, wives, mothers, workers and lovers. Pertinent to this chapter on exercise is the question of whether the major bodily changes associated with SCI negatively impacts women's participation in exercise, and the reasons why/why not. Given the depth of idealized beauty norms in society, how willing are women who do not fit these norms to have their bodies "exhibited" during exercise? Does having one's body viewed (and thereby judged) negatively impact one's desire and ability to attain the benefits associated with regular physical exercisee? Discomfort with one's physical appearance is known to be a significant barrier to exercise for "normal" women (Cash & Pruzinsky, 2002). For women with visibly altered bodies due to aging and disability, are those challenges even greater?

Aging and Disability Research: A Critical Approach

Social scientists and feminist researchers have critically engaged a wide array of topics in aging and disability, and done so in ways that privilege the perspectives of women themselves. Their embrace of critical but also empowering methodological research approaches are invaluable in illustrating how most women do not have an illness or disease orientation toward aging (Calasanti, 2004; Lock 1993; Kaufert & Gilbert, 1986); nor do they have a view of disability as "deficit, disorder and deviance" (Conrad & Schneider, 1992). Research in this tradition recognizes the inherently social experience of aging and disability. Shifts in the forms of acceptable data collection methods has meant greater acceptance of qualitative interviews and observational methods. This has been very useful since personal experiences, beliefs, and values are not easily captured using standardized formats and quantitative approaches like surveys and opinion questionnaires. So-called qualitative (or "naturalistic" or "interpretive") methods are ideal when the purpose of the research is to elicit personal ideas, perceptions, and meanings (Lysack, Luborsky & Dillaway, 2006). Bipartisan research organizations like the National Institutes of Health have also recognized the value of these methodologies and social science research in general and underscored the fundamental role played by social and cultural factors in health:

The social sciences are important in efforts to prevent and treat illness and to promote health. Research in the social sciences can pinpoint environmental contexts, social relationships, interpersonal processes, and cultural factors that lead people to engage in healthy behaviors, seek health services before disease symptoms worsen, and participate with medical professionals in treating illness. The incorporation of social science research and theory into prevention, treatment, service, and health-promotion programs is likely to result in more effective interventions (NIH, PA 07-045, online).

It is useful to ask what research findings there are to guide our understanding of the complex relationships that likely exist between exercise and women's aging and disabled bodies. The answer is very little. Exercise research itself is a relatively new enterprise and studies that document even basic prevalence of exercise and physical activity levels in people with various types of disabilities are rare. In one of the first studies of this type, Rimmer and Wang (2005) found that minority women with disabilities had the greatest risk of being overweight and obese and were nearly 8 times more likely to be in the category of extreme obesity compared with non-disabled white women. An important explanation for this is found in the important report published by the *Center for Research on Women with Disabilities*: "We now have evidence that women with disabilities practice about the same health maintenance behaviors as women without disabilities, with one important exception, exercise" (cited in Rimmer, Rubin & Braddock, 2000). The explanations for why, however, are much harder to find. Rimmer and colleagues (2000) used telephone interviews to discover the major types of barriers confronted by a sample of 50 African American women with disabilities. The four major barriers were cost of the exercise program (84.2%), lack of energy (65.8%), transportation (60.5%), and not knowing where to exercise (57.9%). Remarkably, this is the first study ever published on barriers to exercise in this population. The literature on barriers to exercise for aging women is not a great deal more advanced. In one of the few studies there are that examine barriers and motivators to exercise in the same study, Crombie et al. (2004) found aging women were less likely to exercise than aging men, and health concerns (e.g., painful joints, having a limiting health condition, lack of energy) were the major barriers to exercise. Women were also more likely than aging men to cite a lack of exercise facilities and exercise-specific knowledge as factors that prevent them from exercising. Although research is accelerating quickly on many aspects of exercise in the context of older women and women with disabilities, it is very early days for identifying the key factors that facilitate and restrict participation in exercise for all of these women.

Why Study Exercise in Aging Women and Disabled Women?

Aging and disability offer two highly compelling contexts for studying the complex relationships that exist between body image, personal identity and womanhood. The two studies that follow were conducted by the authors of this chapter in diverse samples of women living in metropolitan Detroit. Many of the women were African American women; some were "low-income" women living in the inner city. The studies illustrate how powerful women's social locations (e.g., race and class) are in shaping exercise experience and exercise behaviors. The studies highlight the unique perceptions about exercise not often studied in the mainstream exercise literature, and they draw to our attention the way invisible socio-cultural norms infuse women's daily lives, particularly the lives of low-income minority women as they work to find ways to maintain and better their lives. The studies also highlight practical barriers to exercise.

Common perceived barriers to exercise in minority women include lack of time, family priorities, lack of motivation, lack of energy, lack of accessibility of fitness facilities, and lack of social support (Eyler, Wilcox, Matson-Koffman, Evenson, & Sanderson, (2002). The most commonly cited barrier is lack of time (Wilcox, Richter, Henderson, Greaney, & Ainsworth, 2002). For low-income women, limited finances may be a problem. For older women, barriers to exercise also include perceptions that exercise is "hard work" and tiring, that places to exercise are too far away, and that walking in their neighborhoods may not be safe (Jones & Nies, 1996; Williams, Bezner, Chesbro & Leavitt, 2006). For women with physical disabilities, barriers to exercise are only just beginning to be explored. While women with disabilities confront many of the same barriers as other women, there are likely a variety of unique barriers to exercise that to date remain undiscovered.

SECTION II: EXERCISE PRACTICES AND EXERCISE BARRIERS: TWO STUDIES OF WOMEN IN METROPOLITAN DETROIT

Study 1: Health, Bodies, and Exercise in a Sample of Menopausal Women (Dillaway)

Method

Between January and September 2001, the second author (Dillaway) interviewed 61 women in the Detroit metropolitan area about their menopausal experiences. Participants ranged in age from 38 to 60 years, and considered themselves to be "perimenopausal" (i.e., experiencing symptoms of the stages leading up to menopause) or "menopausal" (i.e., having had no menstrual period for 12 consecutive months). Eight women participated in focus groups first, and then another 53 were interviewed separately.

The sample was developed through snowball and purposive sampling procedures. Participants were recruited via women's organizations, targeted businesses (a real estate office and a school), doctor's offices and women's health clinics, churches, advertisements in women's newsletters/listserves/magazines, sports leagues, fitness clubs, community centers, word of mouth, and flyers. Institutional Review Board approval was secured for focus groups and individual interviews for the 2001 year, and all procedures undertaken followed the ethical standards of the university. Participation in the study was voluntary, and, therefore, interviewees were self-selected. In addition to an interview, participation included a questionnaire that elicited demographic as well as reproductive history information.

Table 1 depicts the demographic profile of the sample. Three-quarters of the sample identified as European American and "White". Most women were financially stable at the time of the interview. The majority (53 or 87%) worked outside the home and had some sort of autonomy and authority in paid work (based on their job titles). Almost two-thirds had graduated with an undergraduate degree and many held a graduate or professional degree. Given the income and education distributions in Table 1, 54 women (88.5%) were designated as "middle class" and 7 women (11.5%) as "working-class." The sample was also overwhelmingly heterosexual, with only 4 women identifying as lesbian (n=3) or bisexual (n=1)

Table 1. Characteristics of Participants in the Menopause Study

Women's Age (N = 61)		*Individual Income* (N = 52)	
35-39	1 (1.6%)	$0-9,999	7 (13.5%)
40-44	4 (6.6%)	$10,000-19,999	5 (9.6%)
45-49	16 (26.2%)	$20,000-29,999	6 (11.5%)
50-54	23 (37.7%)	$30,000-39,999	10 (19.2%)
55-59	14 (23.0%)	$40,000-49,999	8 (15.4%)
60 and over	3 (4.9%)	$50,000-59,999	7 (13.5%)
		$60,000-69,999	3 (5.8%)
		$70,000 and over	6 (11.5%)
Race (N=61)		*Marital Status (N=61)*	
A. American	11 (18.0%)	Never Married	2 (3.3%)
Chicana	3 (4.9%)	Married[2]	34 (55.7%)
Asian American[3]	2 (3.3%)	Divorced	19 (31.1%)
White	43 (70.5%)	Widowed[4]	2 (1.6%)
Other[5]	2 (3.3%)	Domestic Partner[6]	3 (4.8%)
		Separated	1 (1.6%)
Education (N=53)		*Parental Status (N=61)*	
Some H.S.	1 (1.9%)	Biological Parent	52 (85.2%)
H.S. Diploma	5 (9.4%)	Adoptive Parent	4 (6.6%)
Some College	15 (28.3%)	Foster Parent	1 (1.6%)
College Diploma	11 (20.8%)	Step Parent	4 (6.6%)
Some Graduate Work	7 (13.2%)		
Graduate Degree	14 (26.4%)		
Family Income (N=48)		*Sexuality (N=61)*	
$0-9,999	1 (2.1%)	Heterosexual	57 (93.6%)
$10,000-19,999	2 (4.2%)	Lesbian	3 (4.8%)
$20,000-29,999	4 (8.3%)	Bisexual	1 (1.6%)
$30,000-39,999	5 (10.4%)		
$40,000-49,999	1 (2.1%)		
$50,000-59,999	5 (10.4%)		
$60,000-69,999	5 (10.4%)		
$70,000 and over	25 (52.1%)		

Despite its ethnic bias, this sample includes women with varied family and reproductive experiences. Slightly more than one-half of the women interviewed (34 or 56%) were married at the time of the interview, and approximately one-third (19 or 31%) were divorced from at least one partner. Twenty-three (38%) described themselves as "single," and often were

---

[1] I do not include dichotomous demographic variables in this table and, rather, only talk about them in the text.

[2] Includes two women who reported they were in their 2nd marriages. I suspect a few other women were also in their 2nd and 3rd marriages (based on the prevalence of divorce and remarriage in the U. S. population at large), but I did not explore this. I also did not ask how many times women had been divorced.

[3] Both were South Asian in descent.

[4] Includes one woman who was also formerly divorced.

[5] Includes one multiracial women and one West Indian woman. Both women were careful to distinguish themselves from "African American" individuals, since usually they are characterized based on the color of their skin. The multiracial women reported Native American as well as African American descent. The West Indian woman was from Jamaica.

[6] Includes one woman formerly divorced and one woman formerly widowed.

actively looking for a romantic partner. The majority (52 or 85%) had biological children. Of those who were parents, almost one-half (28 or 46%) had children under age 18 living in their homes.

The investigator conducted 2 focus groups on a university campus and scheduled them on weekends for women's convenience. The first focus group included 3 women and the second included 5 women. Each focus group lasted approximately 3 hours. Individual interviews took place in private settings (e.g., a woman's home, workplace, a university conference room, a bookstore). Individual interviews varied in length but, on average, lasted 90 minutes. The interview schedule followed a focused interview format (Rubin & Rubin, 1995). Focus groups and interviews were audio-taped and transcribed.

The purpose of this study was to explore the social meanings and experiences of menopause, broadly defined. Although the investigator included specific categories of questions on the interview schedule, questions were designed to be general enough to elicit a variety of responses. Women were asked to (1) describe their menopause experience (e.g., symptoms, length of experience, and general feelings about the experience); (2) outside influences (i.e., experiences with medical institutions and what they had heard from doctors, lay people, family members, and the media); (3) how menopause shapes/is shaped by other facets of their lives (e.g., families, workplace, peer relationships); (4) whether social locations (e.g., gender, race, social class, sexuality) impacted menopause; (5) aging issues and whether they related menopause to aging; (6) bodily changes they experienced and how they viewed and reacted to their bodies; and (7) current concerns about menopause. Questions about bodily change included a direct question about whether women exercised or changed their diet in response to menopause or aging concerns, but women also brought up exercise in response to other questions.

This project was exploratory. Therefore the investigator tried to maintain an inductive, rather than a deductive, approach throughout data collection, coding, and analysis. During coding and analysis she specifically looked for patterns within women's answers to particular questions, concentrating on the similarities and differences across women's discussions of various topics. The analysis presented here is based on just one of the major themes that emerged from women's discussions of their views and responses to bodily change at midlife. The investigator reports on other themes in the women's interviews, including other themes about bodies, elsewhere (e.g., Dillaway, 2005; Dillaway, 2008).

Findings

Overall, twenty-nine women (48%) discussed some sort of current exercise program or routine. Thus, approximately half of the sample of menopausal women attempted some sort of fairly regular physical activity. Participants reported different reasons for exercising however. Four women currently exercised because they had always been physically active; for them, then, exercise was a lifestyle. Of these four, two were long-term soccer players and still played on a local women's team (both White, middle class). Another White middle class woman was a personal trainer at a fitness club. The fourth was a very driven, professional, African American woman in her mid-forties who explained that exercising (i.e., aerobics, gym workouts) was just a part of her life. Other reasons for exercising were to improve current or long-term health, or to lose weight.

Health Reasons: General and Specific

Four more women exercised simply to improve their general health. Two of these latter women (both White, middle class) worked out alongside their husbands; as couples, they had decided to improve their physical wellbeing yet exercising also became a pleasurable activity because they could do it together. One African American professor and mother of three described how her efforts to exercise were a part of a general effort to utilize more natural, holistic methods to ensure her own and her family's health over time. A second African American woman (a middle-level manager in a small company and a mother of one) had just started exercising for general health reasons.

Three women reported exercising because of some prior health condition. For instance, one White, middle class woman relayed that her multiple sclerosis necessitated her daily exercise. Another White, middle class woman exercised only because of a recent hip replacement surgery. A third White, middle class woman reported that her obesity was directly related to a recent diagnosis of sleep apnea. Thus, she was exercising mostly to prevent additional weight gain due to this condition. All three of these women felt as if they had no choice but to exercise because of these conditions. Pre-existing health problems did not always encourage exercise, however. One White middle class woman reported that her arthritis often did not allow her to engage in physical activity; thus, she did not exercise regularly. Similarly, an African American, working class woman explained that her type-two diabetes and high blood pressure prevented her from currently being active. Thus, depending on the previous health condition, women made different decisions about regular exercise.

Nine women (15%) immediately stated that they exercised in order to prevent osteoporosis. As might be expected the majority (8 or 89%) of these women were White; the only African American woman who was worried about osteoporosis was very small and slight in stature and had already been warned by a doctor that she might be a greater risk for bone health problems in her later years. Several of the other women who reported exercising for this reason had also received a warning from their doctors or female relatives about osteoporosis. One woman relayed how the doctor originally diagnosed her with arthritis but then found out "I'm on borderline for osteopenia, and it's really unusual at my age. . . . I don't know why I'm like that, but following that they monitored me with this Miacalcitonin and an increase in exercise, and I did great. I really am making an improvement."

Several other women in this category also felt that their exercise was paying off, with another White middle class woman even reporting that she had recently cancelled a follow-up bone density test because her "bones even felt stronger" since she had been exercising (a secondary reason for the cancellation, however, was that she lacked health insurance at the time of the interview). Often encouraged by their doctors or by media attention to bone health in recent years, these participants were physically active because they did not want to end up like their mothers, grandmothers, and the women they saw depicted on the posters in doctors' offices. Often these women specifically took on weight-bearing exercise (e.g., water aerobics with weights) or weight-lifting, in response to their long-term health concerns. One woman proposed that the Baby Boom "generation is very lucky because we do, did, get this information [about bone health] and we've been able to do a lot of things that other generations haven't been able to do. And I'm stressing this to my daughter. I do believe that how you take care of your body really is important and you can't start young enough." Thus, women were often very glad to receive information from doctors so that they could feel like they were warding off long-term health problems.

On the other hand, some women received mixed signals from doctors about the benefits of certain types of exercise for osteoporosis. One middle class White woman described how her doctor was encouraging her to discontinue jogging.

It was the concern for osteoporosis which got me into starting to walk about three years ago and that built into jogging. My doctor tells me [to] stop jogging. "It's not good on your knees. She said [to] swim instead. Well, you just don't tell that to a jogger to swim. . . . And then she said -- you know, [a] reason I stopped, too -- she said, 'You know, it's bad for your insides. Women jogging breaks things up inside and it makes you old and makes you [i.e., your breasts] hang.' That's what she told me. And I mean, I did read that in one of those books. So I don't know. I mean, that sounds almost like an old wives' tale-ish kind of thing."

While trying to prevent osteoporosis via an activity she enjoyed, this participant bumped up against the power of beauty norms and an "expert" who made sure that appearance norms came to the forefront in her exercise decisions. The next section details other women's concerns about beauty norms and their consequent efforts to lose weight through exercise.

Exercise as a Response to Gendered Beauty Norms

Some women in this study talked about beauty and exercise routines as attempts to maintain a gendered body. Specifically, ten (17%) reported exercising to lose weight. Of those who were not exercising, eight additional women (13%) knew that they should exercise because they were concerned about weight and/or appearance issues. Thus, a total of 18 women (30%) at least contemplated exercise because of weight issues.

According to the women in this sample, the most problematic change in physical bodies upon menopause or midlife was weight gain (the "worst" "side effect" of menopause, according to many women). Specifically, 36 women (59%) highlighted weight gain as current bodily problem. The majority directly attributed these particular physical changes to a decrease in estrogen and/or, more broadly, to a perimenopausal/menopausal life stage. That is, interviewees considered these changes to be some of the bodily "side effects" of passing through this developmental transition. However, a few decided that these bodily changes were simply due to aging or laziness/lack of effort. Previous research indicates that physical changes in women's bodies may not be directly caused to menopause, but rather due to other related processes of chronological aging or environmental exposure; in fact, whether or not menopause causes any visible changes or symptoms is still uncertain (Fausto-Sterling, 1992; Martin, 1992). Bertero (2003), however highlighted weight gain as a physical symptom related to the onset of menopause. The fact that interviewees thought that weight changes are related to menopause illustrates how menopause is characterized by them as bringing on negative change in physical appearance. The following interview excerpts illustrate women's constructions of their changing shape and weight.

The only thing that's bothered me [about menopause] is the weight. And . . .my doctor said, 'Just ride it out.' It's probably a hormone thing and . . . it's not that bad. It's just I don't like it 'cause I've been pretty slender my whole life so...and, like I said, my mom had gone through the same thing. I can remember her kind of pudging up a little. . . I mean, oh my God, I'm going to have the shape like my great-grandmother. You know, she was just robust. . . .I'm being positive about it [i.e., menopause] overall. That's the only thing I have not particularly been happy about. I look at all the women's magazines... [European American, middle class]. Other women's comments were similar:

I gained 20 pounds. [*HD: And you would attribute this to menopause?*] Yes. Yes, because my eating habits haven't changed, I don't think. I gained 22 pounds, like, in maybe 3 or 4 months, which is significant. [*HD: When you started experiencing menopause?*] Yeah. Right at the onset. The first 6 months, I would say, and I haven't been able to get it off. [European American, middle class]

[M]enopause started, and it was like, oh! I was never this size. I'm big now. . . .You can see me in that picture. That's when [my daughter] was young: 135 [pounds], you know? That was my weight for many years. Even after I had her [a daughter], I went back down to that size 10, you know? It's 14, now, you know? [West Indian American, middle class]

Lamenting her increased weight and other bodily changes upon menopause, one European American middle class woman said that physical appearance is "what our value is. It is our womanliness." Previous literature on women's bodies suggests that women's weight, skin, and breasts visually define who a "woman" is and are the focal points for public gaze (Bordo, 1993; Bartky, 2003; Lee, 2003; Young, 2003). Despite the fact that some women in the sample realized that the beauty ideal is unattainable, many – regardless of their race/ethnicity or class -- upheld cultural norms when thinking about their own bodies. For example, a few women discussed wanting to be able to wear certain types of clothing (e.g., tighter clothing, bathing suits) in public or knowing that they would get more respect for their actual accomplishments from others (e.g., bosses, coworkers) if they looked "younger," thinner, "prettier," or "tighter." As one African American middle class woman announced, "I want to be able to wear a thong." Many other women referred to movie stars (e.g., Raquel Welch), musicians (e.g., Tina Turner), and supermodels (e.g., Farah Fawcett) as they discussed what they wanted their bodies to look like.

Possible Race/Class Differences?

Scholars have noted that the quest to lose weight and therefore meet gendered beauty ideals is not limited to European American middle class women (Witt, 1994/1995; Zones, 2000). Disadvantaged women in my sample were engaged in conscious weight-altering activities. Nonetheless the ways in which women controlled (or thought about controlling) their weight (e.g., exercise, diet foods, pills, surgeries) differed somewhat based on how much disposable income they had, the adherence to ideals of thinness/slenderness seemed relatively uniform among the group of women I interviewed. Working-class women often discussed trying to eat less sugar or less food. If they exercised, walking was often the activity of choice. Many middle class women talked about being enrolled in Weight Watchers or other diet programs, as well as attempts at regular exercise routines (e.g., daily walking, regular weightlifting, joining fitness clubs, aerobic swimming, horseback riding, and team sports). Women of all racial/ethnic and class locations also debated about whether taking hormone therapies (HT) would increase or decrease their weight, and they discussed making HT decisions with this concern in mind. Nonetheless, when we look at the numbers of White and non-White exercisers, White women in the sample (22 or 51%) were more likely than women of color (7 or 39%) to report current exercise. (Of these women of color, three exercised for weight loss, two exercised for general health concerns, one exercised because she always had exercised, and one exercised because of other bodily changes.) Further, only one working class woman (14%) reported a current exercise routine, compared to 28 middle class women

(52%). (Further, this working class woman was someone who had been heavily involved in exercise over her lifetime, so reasons for exercise were not health-related.) While the numbers in this sample are small, these discrepancies in reporting hint at race/class differences in women's commitment to formal exercise. While the discrepant concerns for osteoporosis explain some of this difference (in that White women are told to be more concerned about bone health problems (Moynihan, Heath & Henry, 2002; Murtaugh & Hepworth, 2003), two women commented specifically on why these race/class differences in exercise rates might exist:

> [W]e don't tend to exercise, you know. . . African-American women are coming out, they just always feel because they've always been movers and shakers and, you know, and going and doing that they don't need an exercise plan, you know. . . .But we already doing it, you know. We don't get on an exercise plan, you know, as quick and as easy you know as you know, ah Caucasian women because they know that this is part. . . of what you got to do. This is part of the program. . . . [T]he majority that African-American women is like, "Hey, I don't need to diet, I've always ate this way, you know, I'll keep on, I'm healthy this is just what is supposed to be." . . . [H]ey, I'm always on the go, you know, and I'm 50 years old and I still look good. So, what in the heck I got to do all of this for? So I think that, ah, I think, you know, we pushing [exercise] underneath the rug. And another thing [we] say, this is just this white woman telling us what we have to do. . . . Now we trying to be white, you know. . . . So we look at our bodies and everything differently, you know and we try to find other ways, you know, to curb it to be honest about it, you know. . . .[W]e will psych ourselves out, you know in the mind, you know, with well that's not for us. [African American, middle class]

> The reason why I can't exercise too much now is because of my foot, but I plan on doing a lot of walking, doing aerobics in the water, that's what helps me. . . . Exercising, along with what I have, will make me feel a hundred percent better. . . . If I were a woman who had lots of money, I'd have money to go exercise, I'd have money to be able to do different things I want to do. . . . [I]t would be different because right now, today, if I had the money, I'd go join an exercise club, or I'd go pay the money to get into water aerobics, and that would make a big difference, but I don't have the money. [African American, working class]

These quotes illustrate the potential reasons for race and class differences in regular exercise, at least within this sample of menopausal women. First, as the first woman notes, perhaps cultural differences step in to make African American women less likely to think they should exercise, especially if they might think that menopause and exercise separately are both "white women's" issues. Second, as suggested by the second interviewee, access to economic resources eases one's entry into regular exercise as there are many more options for physical activity (and perhaps more options for those who actually have health conditions that necessitate machine workouts or water workouts). On the other hand, a few women of color referred to themselves as "still active," but did not consider themselves to be exercisers. That is, they were still actively involved in paid work, caregiving, and social activities that kept them on the move (as the first woman quoted above also notes). This latter group has also been described in previous research (e.g., Eyler, et al., 1998; Henderson & Ainsworth, 2003; Tudor-Locke et al., 2003), but other potential differences in the meanings and experiences of exercise among race and class groupings of women must be explored further.

Common Barriers to Exercise

The 32 women in the sample who were not exercising at the time of interview often suggested that they knew that they should exercise. Many discussed how their doctors, family members or friends discussed the benefits of exercise with them, or how they read about the benefits of exercise in books or on websites. Thus, a lack of exercise did not correspond to a lack of knowledge about the importance of physical activity. They reported easy access to many different sources of information about the benefits of formal exercise at midlife.

Lack of Effort. Many women (12 or 20%) admitted that a lack of formal regular exercise was simply due to a lack of effort or "laziness," in one participant's words. Nonetheless, their lack of effort was often associated with particular feelings about their life stage, their health, or with exercise itself. Two women suggested that their lack of effort was induced by feelings that they were not at risk for any major health problems. So, in their minds, there was no urgent need to remain active.

> There are things I know I should do like exercise and watch my diet and every...you know I...and since I don't really feel yet like I'm at risk for any of that stuff I don't do it but I think about it a lot more than used to. Um...um...I think I should take care...better care of myself. [White, middle class]

A third woman suggested that her lack of exercise was due to the fact that she felt better now than she did when she was 30:

> I turned 50 two years ago and I go, 50? I mean, I'm supposed to be you know with a bun in my hair and hunched over. I don't know! You know our society is so strange about aging and yet I like myself better than I did when I'm 30. You know? I...I feel more interesting. I feel more solid. I feel more vital than I ever have so...Gee! They don't tell you that part. So, I don't know what...and I read all the...you know, gloomy [information about menopause and aging]... I don't know. I don't feel like I have to please anybody. . . . And it's not that I've gotten ornery or anything in my old age I just feel I know who I am. I feel like I'm confident. I know the things that interest me. I don't bother with the things that don't. I don't feel like I really have to please anybody. . . . I, I think the only discouraging thing I'd have to say about [menopause] if there's one thing is I've put on weight. And I've always been very thin my whole life so I'm kind of fighting with that. . . . I don't like this grandmotherly shadow of myself anymore but . . . I don't do anything. . . .I don't exercise as much as I should. [White, middle class]

This woman continued by suggesting that menopause, overall, was a positive experience for her and that, really, being in a midlife stage just meant "going from pumps to loafers... It's like not a really big deal for me." Her comments signify her acquiescence to a midlife stage (that may be accompanied by inevitable bodily and lifestyle changes, in her mind) alongside a renewed sense of self. Both her acceptance of midlife and the fact that she feels "better than she did when she was 30" result in a lack of exercise but she admits later in the interview that, really, it came down to a lack of effort.

Even when women characterized aging or menopause negatively, however, they still did not always invest time in physical exercise. For instance, a White, middle class participant proposed, "I guess I see aging more as a physical assault. (laugh) You know? It's slowly our deteriorating physically. . . .[O]f course I don't take care of myself very well with eating and exercise. You know, so I could physically feel younger, I'm sure, than I do but. . . I keep saying to myself I could do something about the physical stuff." A second woman defined her weight gain in very negative terms but still did not exercise.

> In the last two years I've put on twenty-five pounds. . . . I think my metabolism is slower, but I don't know if that's because of menopause, or if it's just being lazier. It could just be part of the big picture [of aging], because I don't have the desire to do the things I used to do. I used to be a real exercise freak. Now, I'm just as happy to sit back and read a book, or do a crossword puzzle. . . . I think back, and I know my mother was always relatively thin, but then when she went through her change, then, that's when she gained all her weight, and I always thought, what a cop-out. But maybe now I'm doing the exact same thing. So I've really been trying to get back in the routine of riding a bike and stuff like that, but I just don't have the enthusiasm for it that I had in the years gone by. But, again, it could just be me copping out.

Another woman suggested, however, that she simply did not care enough to change her lifestyle, even if it meant an increased chance for health problems.

> I still smoke and I will not quit. I know it's shortening my life but oh well. I don't diet. I don't exercise. I don't wear make-up. I haven't had any cosmetic surgery. . . .You know, I am what I am. What you see is what you get. You know, if you think I'm 65 that's fine, too. I don't care. . . . I always tell people how old I am. I have no problems. And I don't do anything really. I mean I will get as old as I will get and then I will die and that's, that's life. [White, middle class]

As can be seen from the above quotes, the reasons for a lack of effort invested in exercise varied, since participants in this category often had very different opinions about menopause, aging, and bodily change. Collectively, however, they admitted to a lack of effort and/or lack of interest in formal exercise.

Three additional women in the sample, however, had exercised previously and had not seen or felt any short-term benefits; therefore, they discontinued physical activity because of a lack of visible result. As one White, middle class woman explained, formal exercise was a "pain in the butt," and if one didn't see results (e.g., weight loss, increased energy, improved sleeping patterns) in the short-term, they might stop exercising. A second White, middle class woman who participated in a focus group exemplified this feeling:

> [At the onset of perimenopause] I was really making an effort to exercise more and stuff. But then, really, you know, as I got more into [menopause], . . . I went back to my physicians assistant, and told her that the herbal stuff and my [exercise] routine wasn't working anymore, and I did a lot of praying and that wasn't working either (everyone's laughing), so whatever! (At this point everybody laughing.) She said, "You know, you've given it a good year with the stuff, how do you feel about trying this hormone replacement stuff?" And I was like, "I don't think we have any other choice!" I was a wreck, I was just a wreck. So I respond pretty quickly to medication, and so that was, that was fine.

While attempting to find a more natural route to symptom relief at the beginning of perimenopause – one that included exercise – this woman eventually resorted to traditional medicine to eradicate her symptoms. For her, this meant a discontinuation of herbal remedies, exercise and other, non-invasive activities (e.g. praying). A third White, middle class woman suggested that she had tried to exercise to reduce her insomnia, discussing how she "should have been dead by the time I hit the pillow" because of exercise but she was not. She also discussed exercising in the anticipation of a trip to Hawaii but "you can't keep the weight off. You just can't." Frustration over a lack of results while exercising was loud and clear.

Full and Busy Lives. Many women also suggested that they did not exercise due to the business of their lives. Delaying childbearing, delaying marriage, getting divorced and remarried, raising children through menopause, helping other family members with health problems, and having elderly parents that need constant care are all reasons why women live busy lives at midlife. In contrast to generations before them, 53 of the 61 menopausal women interviewed (87%) also are typically still working for pay – often full-time -- and plan to continue working for many years to come (barring disability, layoff, or family calamities). (At the time of the interview, 39 White women (90.7%) and 14 women of color (77.8%) were working for pay. Of the eight women who were not working, four were White and four were women of color. Five of the seven working-class women (71.4%) were currently out of work.) Thus, menopause and aging (and the accompanying bodily changes and health concerns) become a small blip in an otherwise still busy and full life. Participants recognized that they still have at least half their lives to lead and that their lives will continue to be full. Many women discussed how, despite a lack of formal exercise or recreational physical activity, they "stayed active" because of their multiple responsibilities and roles; women therefore inferred that they did not need to add formal exercise to their lives. An interview question about whether participants exercised often led to comments about how they could not fit anything else into their schedules or exactly how tired they were at the end of the day and, therefore, could not fathom formal exercise.

> I'm 51 and, you know, I have a teenager and I'm working. [My friend] described it as bone tiredness, where I've had it that in the middle of the day at work I could just climb up on the table and fall asleep. I don't know if you've seen the episode of [Seinfeld] where George has that futon under his desk (laughs), and nobody knows you're there. . . . It's . . . the kind of tired that you'd never believe, and then, um, the irony of it is that you go to bed at night and you can't sleep. . . . [White, middle class]

> I have a lot of lower back pain and I get extremely tired by the end of the day. . . and I have not yet really dealt with this other than [doing] exercises for my lower back. Um, so that has affected my sex drive [too]. Sometimes by the end of the day I'm, I'm just whipped. You know, it's very hard. So I guess that's my major issue [preventing me from exercise], you know, being very, very tired at the end of the day. [White, middle class]

> My life is busy with other things. [White, middle class]

Another middle class, African American woman discussed how she was "carrying a heavy load." Two other women formally cited recent personal tragedies (the realization of infertility and a recent miscarriage) as reasons for a lack of formal exercise. These personal situations simply added to the complex nature of their midlife stage. Menopause and aging are fully lodged within family and life stage contexts, and the business of their lives affects how much importance they attach to exercise.

There were a few other reasons for participants' lack of formal exercise. For instance, a few women called on race, class, or gender to help explain why they didn't exercise. As explained earlier in this section, one woman suggested that concerns about menopause and exercise are only for "White women." Another suggested that a lack of economic resources necessitated her lack of exercise. A third explained how her doctor discouraged her from jogging because of what it did to her feminine figure. Finally, and also as covered earlier, two women felt that they were prevented from exercising by pre-existing health conditions (one with arthritis and one with diabetes and high blood pressure).

Overall, barriers to exercise were not based on knowledge or access to information about the benefits of exercise. By far, the most frequent reason for the lack of exercise was an individual lack of effort but many different perspectives bolstered this reason. In addition, midlife women's busy lives prohibited some from following through on an exercise routine. Others did not give reasons for their lack of exercise, just stating that they did not exercise. While only about half of the participants were currently engaged in regular exercise, though, the vast majority were involved in other health-promoting activities, such as diet alteration, supplementation of vitamins or herbal remedies, etc. Exercise, then, was less of a priority than some of these other behaviors or options.

Summary/Conclusion

Overall, the major reasons for exercising in this sample seemed to be what the literature already assumes: (1) concerns about physical appearance, and (2) concerns about new long-term health risks at midlife, such as women's worries about osteoporosis. Murtagh and Hepworth (2003) suggest that perhaps long-term health concerns take precedence over cultural norms (such as concerns about feminine appearances), but the data in our study contradict this proposal and suggest that gendered beauty norms still remain important for aging women. In addition to these reasons, familial support for exercise seemed to encourage women to keep a regular routine of physical activity, as two women reported how exercise became a fun, less burdensome activity since they did it jointly with their husbands. Other women (n=4) exercised because they had always exercised; thus the strength of well-established habits exerted an influence on current lifestyles. Additional women exercised to alleviate specific health problems (e.g., conditions related to multiple sclerosis, a previous hip replacement surgery, sleep apnea). Thus, overall, motivations for exercise included concerns for appearance, general and specific health concerns, the presence of familial support, and continuation of past lifestyles.

Barriers to exercise reported in our study differ somewhat from what is usually reported in the literature on women's lack of exercise. Specifically, the major barriers to exercise for our women seemed to be a lack of effort and busy lives at midlife. Other specific barriers mentioned were women's inability to see visible results of their exercise (and therefore, if they had exercised previously, they had stopped) and issues surrounding their specific social locations (that is, either race, gender, or socioeconomic issues prevented them from exercising the way they preferred). A few women also mentioned their current physical health conditions (e.g., diabetes, high blood pressure, arthritis) prevented them from exercising. The fact that women's busy lives and a lack of effort were the major barriers, though, means that much more research is needed on the sociocultural contexts for exercise.

Study 2: Exercise Barriers for Women with Spinal Cord Injury (Lysack)

Method

Data presented here are drawn from a larger mixed-methods study of adults living with traumatic spinal cord injury (SCI) (n=72). The study, entitled 'Community Participation after Spinal Cord Injury: Idioms of Beliefs and Behaviors' was cross-sectional in design and used standardized instruments and in-depth qualitative interviews to explore life in the community after SCI [NIDRR: #H133G020151; PI: Lysack].

Study participants met the following inclusion criteria: (1) between the ages of 18 and 70 years, (2) African American or White, (3) medical diagnosis of traumatic SCI, and (4) current wheelchair use, all self-reported. Recruitment centered on the city of Detroit and the surrounding metropolitan area. Recruitment strategies included word-of-mouth, i.e., the snowball technique, as well as advertisements in local disability newsletters, internet postings, flyers posted in community centers, grocery stores and pharmacies, brochures distributed to SCI support groups, and information sheets posted in local physician waiting rooms. Interested individuals called the project office for more information were administered a brief screening tool over the telephone to assess study eligibility. Volunteers were excluded if they revealed any signs of cognitive impairment or English speaking difficulties during the telephone screener. Participation consisted of one 2-3 hour, face-to-face interview at a time and place of the participant's convenience, most often in the participant's home, but also at the research office and in a few instances, at a workplace or local coffee shop. Interviews were audiotaped and professionally transcribed to increase the quality of the data. Ethics approval was obtained in advance of data collection and each participant in the study received $30 at the conclusion of the interview.

The purpose of the exploratory study was to identify and describe the perceived social and material barriers to participation in daily life. This analysis focuses exclusively of the women in the sample (n=35) and the barriers they confronted in relation to exercise.

Variables and Measurement Instruments

Craig Hospital Inventory of Environmental Factors (CHIEF). The CHIEF is a 25-item instrument designed to quantify the frequency, magnitude and overall impact of *perceived* environmental barriers. The CHIEF total score has high test-retest reliability (intraclass correlation coefficients [ICC] = .93) and high internal consistency (Cronbach α = 0.93 (Whiteneck, Harrison-Felix, Mellick, Brooks, Charlifue, & Gerhart, 2004). This instrument is widely recognized to be the 'gold standard' for the measurment of environmental barriers in the context of SCI. The CHIEF-Short Form, used in this study, utilized the 12 items of the longer version that the original developers report have "the greatest conceptual clarity and discriminant validity" (Whiteneck et al., 2004a). Internal consistency of the CHIEF-SF in our sample was acceptable (Cronbach α = 0.75). The CHIEF-SF items reference the past year. For example, CHIEF-SF item 2 reads: "In the past 12 months, how often has the natural environment – temperature, terrain, climate – made it difficult to do what you want or need to do?" CHIEF-SF item 5 reads: "In the past 12 months, how often has the availability of health care services and medical care been a problem for you?" Three scores are obtained for each item: (1) a score indicating the frequency of each type of barrier (daily=4, weekly=3, monthly=2, less than monthly=1, never=0); (2) a magnitude score indicating the extent of the problem (little problem=1 or big problem=2); and (3) a product score indicating the overall impact of the barriers. Product scores are derived from the first two scores, by multiplying the frequency score by the magnitude score to yield a product score on a scale of 0-8. The maximum and minimum values on this scale have conceptual meaning. For example, a value of 0 means there are no environmental barriers on the domain in question. The CHIEF-SF is reported to take 5 to 10 minutes to administer (although in our experience it took closer to 20 minutes). The measure is published in Whiteneck et al. (2004b).

Qualitative Interview Data. The qualitative dimension of this study was designed to explore the life-altering impact of SCI. The women were asked to describe the environmental barriers they encountered in daily life, and each time a barrier was identified, the interviewers were trained to probe the circumstances surrounding that particular barrier, including how the barrier impacted the women's daily responsibilities, personal mobility, and community participation overall. Questions were also asked about physical activity and recreation and leisure pursuits. For those who were physically active, follow-up questions were asked about body image to better understand how the women felt about the appearance of their bodies and their identities as physically disabled women. Interviewers were trained to use probes and prompts whenever possible to obtain responses that were as complete and descriptive as possible.

Findings

Table 2 presents the sociodemographic and injury variables for the women with SCI. Fifty-seven percent of the women (n=20) were African American and 43% (n=15) were White. Their mean age at the time of interview was 38.8 years (range: age 22-61 years), and their average length of time since injury was 11.4 years (range: 2 months-37 years). There were slightly more women with tetraplegia (n=19, 54%) than paraplegia (n=16, 46%). Nearly three-quarters of the women (n=25, 71%) had some college education while the remainder (29%) were either highschool graduates (n=7) or had less than highschool (n=3) education. A small number were married or cohabitating (n=9, 26%); the remainder were unmarried and living alone (26, 74%). The majority (n=30, 86%) were unemployed; only five women (14%) worked for pay. The causes of SCI in this sample of women with SCI were threefold: motor vehicle accidents (n=17, 49%), followed by violent causes (n=13, 37%) and falls (n=5, . More details can be found in Table 2.

Environmental Barriers for Women with Spinal Cord Injury

Figure 1 depicts the mean CHIEF-SF product scores (environmental barriers) for the 12 items in this instrument. The top five barriers reported by our sample of women with SCI were, in descending order: the natural environment, transportation, help at home, attitudes at home, and the policies of government. Recalling that a mean CHIEF-SF item score between 2 and 3 means that on average, a barrier causes a "little problem" on a "weekly" basis (or alternatively, a "big problem" on a "monthly" basis), it is evident that the top two barriers, the natural environment and transportation were most problemmatic. And even though the remaining barriers were reported with less frequency and magnitude, the barriers reported by the women in our study far exceed those reported in the SCI literature. In one of the largest studies of environmental barriers after SCI to date Whiteneck, Harrison-Felix, et al., (2004) found that 20% of their sample (n=2760) had no barriers whatsoever (mean total product score of zero) and 75% had a mean score less than one. In contrast, not a single woman in our sample reported "no barriers whatsoever" and only 40% scored less than one. This left 60%

of the women in our study with significant environmental barriers (versus 5% in Whiteneck, Harrison-Felix, et al., (2004)).

Table 2: Characteristics of the Participants in the SCI Study (n=35)

DEMOGRAPHICS	
Age (in years): Mean, Range	38.8 (22-61 years)
Ethnicity	
African American	20, 57%
White	15, 43%
Marital Status:	
Married/cohabitating	9, 26%
Living alone	26, 74%
Education:	
Less than highschool	3, 9%
Highschool grad/GED	7, 20%
Some college	25, 71%
Work status:	
Paid employment	5, 14%
Unemployed	30, 86%
Financial situation:	
Paycheck only	5, 14%
SSI/SSD only	15, 43%
SSD & other	9, 26%
Other	6, 17%
Transportation:	
Owns a vehicle	22, 63%
Currently driving	17, 49%
INJURY-RELATED FACTORS	
Duration of SCI (in years):	
Mean, Range	11.4 (1-37 years)
Level of injury:	
Paraplegia	16, 46%
Tetraplegia	19, 54%
Cause of injury:	
Motor vehicle crash	17, 49%
Violence	13, 37%
Falls	5, 14%
Self-rated health:	
Poor	2, 6%
Fair	6, 17%
Good	15, 43%
Excellent	5, 14%
Missing	7, 20%

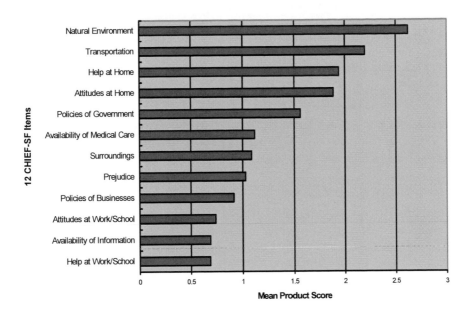

Figure 1: CHIEF-SF Item Scores for Women with Spinal Cord Injury (n=35), in Descending Order of Mean Total Product Score

Barriers to Exercise for Women with SCI

The top environmental barriers identified on the standardized CHIEF-SF scale provided important clues to barriers to physical exercise for women with SCI. The natural environment and transportation, the top two general barriers reported, posed the most obvious barriers to exercise. The natural environment of Michigan (mid-western U.S.) meant that many outdoor activities become that much more difficult in the winter months due to snow, windy conditions and cold weather. One woman with SCI in this study said: "I just hate it that I can't get out more during the winter months, you know, cause of the slush and snow!" This was very common. Another said: "I go out quite a bit in summer...but now [during winter] I can't do that because I've done that before, and then got my chair all wet... And just the mess it makes! Plus cleaning it up is way too hard." For individuals with SCI, life in a wheelchair is a 24-7 enterprise. It is easy to understand that managing life from a wheelchair can be a barrier to many aspects of life, slowing women down and causing them to do less, simply to reduce the difficulties involved. Thus, it was not surprising to learn that most women in this study were not regular exercisers, and those who considered themselves "regular exercisers" prior to their injuries were the same women who considered themselves regular exercisers after their injuries. Unfortunately, that group of regular exercisers consisted of only 5 of the 35 women in the study.

Regular Exercisers after SCI (n=5/35 women)

Despite the challenges posed by inclement weather and reliance on a wheelchair for mobility, a small group of women with SCI (n=5) gave exercise a prominent place in their daily lives. These women said they were "regular exercisers" before their injuries and they continued to exercise regularly afterwards. Their rationales seemed to support the idea of exercise as a life-long lifestyle or identity; something that was an essential part of who they were throughout their lives. One middle class woman explained the benefits of exercise she perceived this way: "Working out makes me stronger and better able to do more during the day. Also, by making sure that I take care of my body, feeding it well, then um, working out, exercising... That all makes my, my spirits higher. That gives me more stamina to do so many different tasks beyond my obligations, those things I have to do." Another woman who had been a regular jogger before a car accident disabled her thought of exercise in similar terms. She had always been active in sports earlier in her life and now more than a decade after injury, she was active, and still interested in trying new sports. In fact, she had recently taken up a completely new activity, hand-cycling. She was enthusiastic about the sport and believed strongly that participation in it would keep her healthy, just as other sports had done earlier in her life. At one point in her interview she said: "I'm looking forward to doing the marathon. I want to do the marathon, because I'm thinking that will help with my health and strength. You know, the hand cycling, it helps with cardiovascular fitness, and it will help with socializing, and it'll be fun, so I want to get into that right now." A third woman explained that once you enjoy fitness and exercise it does not take that much effort and creativity to adapt to exercise again after injury or illness. Describing her youth as a period of "fun and sports" this woman explained how it only took some minor changes to equipment or the way of doing the exercise (or sport) to be able to do it with her disability. She summed up her efforts matter-of-factly: "You know the different mode or the different apparatus or whether I need to wrap my hand when I play table tennis or whether I need to strap my legs when I play wheelchair basketball... it's all just little accommodations. But basically, all those things that I was doing before, I still like to do them, and I do them."

Adjusting One's Expections. Beyond the physical adaptations necessary to exercise and engage in physical activities, some women in our study described how they also needed to adjust their personal expectations and their competitiveness. One woman who was an avid tennis player before her injury said "A tennis racket is really kind of heavy. I can strap a table tennis racket onto my hand, but a tennis racquet? I'm somewhat apprehensive about it because I used to be a pretty good tennis player. I liked being number 1 and I don't want to be number 2!" She freely admitted that she had to deal with her expectations about her new level of ability; she had to accept that some things, including the level of success she was going to enjoy in future would be comprised due to reduced grip strength, reduced joint range of motion, reduced speed, and other physical limitations. She recognized that she would have to adjust mentally to "not being the player I was". Living as a woman with disability and becoming a recreational athlete with a disability meant, for her, dealing with the reality that she could not play as well or in the same way as she did before. She admitted this was difficult. She said "You know, your self-esteem is challenged all the time. You are challenged physically by way of just getting around, getting in and out of places. So, that's a transition, you know. It affects everything. But, coming in contact with people, peers, people who share your disability, people who have disabilities, and getting to know them and talking about how they cope... those are important too. That's what transitioning is all about, you know, you have to come to know yourself all over again." This idea, that adjustments must be made and self-acceptance is part of the adjustment process, was a view that was generally shared by the women who identified as "exercisers". It appeared that the adjustments that this group of five women made were worthwhile, since at the point of interview these five women had lived with their mobility impairments for more than a decade and still considered themselves "exercisers".

"Exercisers" Had Financial Means. Who were these five "regular exercisers"? Further analysis showed that they were White women: four worked for pay, either full-time or part-time, and all owned and drove their own cars. Because their employment left them better off financially than many of the other women in this study, they had the means to afford gym memberships, for example, and participate in fitness programs that interested them. They had choices. Of course, even women with disabilities who are regular exercisers confront barriers. When the exercisers were asked what barriers they confronted in their efforts to be physically active, the most frequent response was finding an accessible and welcoming place to exercise. Since the women in this study were, on average, 11 years post-injury, they had years to find satisfactory exercise environments. These women reported numerous barriers to exercise encountered post-injury, both in the past, barriers they had overcome, and barriers to exercise they continued to encounter at present. A common problem was identifying an exercise location which included an accessible bathroom. It was surprising to learn the extent to which women had to work, even before leaving their homes, to determine if there would be an accessible bathroom at the exercise location. Because bladder and bowel function are often impaired as a result of SCI, women with SCI need to use a catheter or other equipment to manage their toileting needs. It is very important that women with SCI are able to find a bathroom when needed. This should have been easier, but it was not. One woman related a story of being trapped inside a bathroom and being unable to exit due to the small turning radius inside the bathroom and the position of the door. She said:

> I have yet to find a bathroom door that's easy to open. Oh it's crazy. They're very heavy. They're so awkward sometimes, and to try to open the door and get yourself around it... Yeah, that's one of the little things that really become one of the biggest things... Handicap bathrooms, so often they're not in working order, I swear! Either the seats are broken or they're out of order. Of course it's unpredictable too. You can call and they say 'Its OK' but then you get there, and it's not.

Inaccessible Exercise Environments. Beyond accessible bathrooms is the accessibility of other aspects of the physical environment where exercise takes place. For women who use wheelchairs, the absence of ramps into the building where exercise takes place, and a lack of accessible parking, are two significant additional barriers to exercise. Two women in the study swam regularly before their injuries but reported that afterwards, they had difficulty finding a swimming pool that was accessible to persons using a wheelchair. In one case, the woman couldn't attend the neighborhood pool she had been going to for years because there was no ramp to the facility. In the other case, the woman could get inside the facility, but the locker rooms were inaccessible and there was no reasonable place for her to change her clothes or to shower. Undeterred, this woman sought out and found an accessible facility 14 miles from her home. This woman, who had swam competitively for years talked about her old pool and then the new facility she finally found: "I wish I could've got in the [old] pool or the sauna, but I couldn't. You'd think in this day and age... So, I drove across town where I heard there was an accessible pool... and then I couldn't park because there was only one accessible spot and someone was always in it! [with no handicapped sticker] I tried going a few times, but I gave up. I guess I should have gone back and told them, look, don't take my parking spot cause I can't roll across the grass, you know, so leave my parking spot. Do not park there, you know, 'cause I need the sidewalk right there so I can get out." The combination of driving distance and unpredictable parking took its toll and this woman stopped swimming completely for nearly five years. Fortunately, motivated by a friend, she sought another facility with a swimming pool that also included more accessible parking. She resumed her swimming routine and was swimming twice a week at the time of the study.

Transportation is a Barrier to Exercise. The final major barrier to women with SCI who exercised regularly was transportation. Fears about being stranded were not uncommon, although the fears did not prevent them from going out and doing what they wanted and needed to do, including exercise: "I think about my vehicle breaking down" one woman said, "What are you gonna do, who's gonna pick you up? That's probably the biggest thing I worry about when I take off on my own. But I still go." An older woman with SCI expressed her feelings of vulnerability in terms of personal safety: "When you're in a chair … people see you as easy prey. You're simply more vulnerable." This woman lived alone in Detroit and drove her car alone nearly every time she went out. She talkied about "just trying to be careful and sensible" about the places she went, and when during the day she would go there. She reported how she tried to do all her driving in the daytime. She also carried a cell phone. Overall, however, the five women who exercised regularly found ways to overcome their fears related to physical vulnerability. They continued to "get out there and do things". All knew they were taking some small risk being out on their own as women in wheelchairs, but none considered this so significant a barrier that it limited their community participation. One of the women with SCI in the study put it this way:

> At any time my wheelchair can fail... something can happen where it makes me stop in the middle of the sidewalk or something. Then I'd have to rely on other people. The same thing with my vehicle... It can malfunction at any time. So I'm never truly independent. I'm always relying on the grace of God to get me anywhere. But so is everybody else! It's just a little more obvious with me.

All five of the "regular exercisers" acknowledged that added physical vulnerability was a part of being physically disabled and relied upon a wheelchair. Still, they were not prepared to let life pass them by. They enjoyed exercising and they valued the health benefits they saw accruing from exercise. For all five women, "going for a roll" in the neighborhood in their wheelchairs was their most frequent form of exercise. On average, these women went "out for a roll in the fresh air" two to three times a week during the summer, and once winter arrived, they turned to swimming and work-out routines in indoor community centers and gyms. Exercise was part of their life-long identity.

Exercise 'Makes me Tired' and Other Exercise Barriers (n=30/35 women)

The majority of women with SCI in our study did not engage in any regular exercise. Although most considered themselves "busy" and "pretty active", none participated in intentional physical activity that had as its goal, increased fitness or weight reduction. Interview data revealed that most of the women were not interested in sports as a recreational or leisure pursuit and none had done any regular exercise since their school days. Since the mean age of our sample at interview was nearly 39 years of age and the mean time since injury was 11 years, this meant that most women had been sedentary for 20 years – 10 years before their disability, and 10 years afterwards. In part, this was because "being fit" was not viewed as being a critical dimension of their self-identity as women. This finding was central in the interview data, particularly for the African American women. The African American women with SCI in our study, in general, did not want to "get skinny" because they did not view thinness as beautiful or attractive to African American men. For the most part, they "liked their curves" and many felt that carrying a small amount of extra weight was actually a buffer against further health problems. Coupled with being busy mothers and

'Exercise is Bad for Me'. Another important barrier to exercise was the belief that if they exercised too much they might actually compromise their health. Although nearly all felt exercise was "probably a good idea" and "good for you", many women with SCI in our study suggested the physical effort required of living in a wheelchair and carrying out all of their daily activities tired them out enough. One African American woman with young children asked "Now why would I go lookin' to get more tired than I already am!" During her interview, one woman [a part-time advocate at a disability organization] expressed some surprise and even some frustration at the question: "Girl, there is simply no reason for me to do more to wear myself out! I don't have that much left, you know, and I need it all!" The idea that physical disability left women with with less physical strength and stamina was prevalent in our data, although it was expressed most frequently by African American women. Most felt the physical exertion related to childcare and carrying out activities of daily living like grocery shopping, cooking, laundry and taking care of their homes was about all they could handle. Efforts to probe the reasons for this view more deeply were not that fruitful. Still, it was clear that the general sentiment was that they had endured one major trauma to their bodies in the form of SCI, and they were not prepared to stress their bodies unnecessarily. They felt their bodies were not as robust as they were pre-injury (which in some results is true). Thus, exercise was generally seen by this group as something to be avoided since it would just "wear you down" further and this was not something they would welcome.

Cost is a Barrier to Exercise. Given that the thirty "non-exercisers" in the study were unemployed, and relied mostly on social security and disability pensions for their income, it was not surprising that cost was an anticipated barrier for the few women who expressed any interest in exercise. Lack of financial resources poses barriers to exercise in a variety of different ways. First and foremost, one's finances radically restricted transportation options. Eighteen of the 30 women who did not exercise did not drive a car. This fact made getting to an exercise location (even if they wanted to exercise) much more difficult and time-consuming. These women were dependent on public transportation or "handicapped transit" or else taxis, or family and friends. This group of women was very dissatisfied with their transportation situation. One African American woman living in the inner-city was highly critical of the public transit system and very frustrated with the buses in her neighborhood. She said, "You can sit out there and get sunstroke waiting on the bus in a wheelchair because they don't have all accessible buses in certain areas. I hate to say it, but... they don't ever have many buses with lifters [wheelchair lifts] on them... so I spend hours waiting to get transportation sometimes." A White woman who also lived in the inner-city of Detroit relied exclusively on taxis, when she could afford them, or "Dial-A-Ride" a local private company that provided transportation to older adults and people with disabilities. She related several situations where she felt unsafe as a direct result of the driver's behaviors. For her, the environmental barrier she faced was not the lack of transportation per se, but rather the quality of the service:

> When I'm riding in the transportation vans, you know, I'm not in control of where I'm going. You've got this guy driving and I mean 90% of the time they drive like maniacs and you're in back, you're bouncing around in the back of the van. One time, someone did forget to tie down my [wheel]chair and I wasn't even thinking, and we're pulling off and I forget what had happened but I started to tip over. I didn't tip all the way, thank god! But think what *could* have happened?

Other women stressed the advance planning involved in finding bus routes to new destinations. They emphasized how all this effort took so much of the fun and spontaneity out of doing things that they would decide not to go out as much. One woman said "I hate not being able to just get in a car and go when I get ready. I got to call transportation, and wait and wait until they come get me. I can't go when I want." Due to the time spend searching for accessible buses on the desired schedule and to the desired destination, public transportation was "far too much trouble" unless the trip was a very high priority trip like a doctor's visit or overdue trip to the grocery store or pharmacy. Thus, the idea of taking a bus to go exercise somewhere was a very low priority. In fact, it was not even something most women ever thought contemplated. And if they thought about it, it was quickly dismissed. The advance planning, the time and effort, plus the range of potential risks and inconveniences involved all operated as barriers to going out to exercise.

Interviewers asked follow-up questions at many points in the study to try to learn whether removal of these barriers (e.g., financial, transportation, physical accessibility) might make a difference to these women who did not exercise now. Would removal of barriers help facilitate future participation in exercise? Two discoveries were made in this realm. The first speaks to the issue of social support, and the second returns us to one of the first topics discussed in this chapter on exercise and aging and disabled bodies – the complicated issue of body image and appearance and its relationship to perceptions of health.

Exercise Requires a Friend. Study investigators were surprised to learn that many non-exercising women with SCI would exercise if they had a friend or family-member to exercise with. Some of the women who had been more physically active several years earlier talked about retreating from physical activities because they sensed their friends no longer wanted to participate with them. Most did not blame their friends for this, but they sense their friends' social discomfort being with them, and would eventually stop asking their friends to accompany them. One woman said: "I'd like to do more exercising but I feel like people don't want to go out with me, and I don't really know why, but I hear people say after the fact they've gone out and done things or they've been places... I feel like I don't have uh, many friends to go out with at all." For these women, the diminishment of physical activity came over time and the decision to curtail exercise was made by the women themselves. This issue was more pronounced in White women. They, more often than African American women, stated how they did not want to impose any sort of burden on their friends or family. Some related stories about going shopping or out to restaurants with their friends and then noticing how their friends did subtle things to minimize attention drawn in their direction. One young newly injured African American woman admitted she had a similar feeling about some members of her family. She related how she always had a lifelong enjoyment of dancing and going out to social clubs on weekends. Dancing was also her most frequent form of exercise. Before her SCI dancing was a regular occurrence, but afterwards, much less so. She said: "I used to go out dancing a lot. My sister and my niece and I used to hang out at the same club. But they don't even bother to ask anymore." And then, somewhat less convincingly: "It doesn't bother me... I don't have the desire to really go, *I guess*..." Other African American woman echoed this sentiment about friends making her feel "unwanted": "My friends were going somewhere, to the park or something, and they were making like it was gonna be-- they were making excuses, you know—to say anything but to say I can go. Well, I was like, well, I just wanna go, just to be there with y'all. That really made me feel not wanted." In short, the vast majority of women with SCI in this study were seeking more social interaction with their female friends and family members and friends. This included a desire to having friends go with them to exercise. However, if they sensed their disability imposed undue demands on their friends and familiy, then the women with SCI in this study acted to curtail their activities. When confronted with the choice of imposing on others and achieving their goal of exercise, friends feelings won out. This finding highlights directions for further research.

Exercise and 'Displaying' Disability. The final barrier to exercise for women with SCI in this study takes us right back to the issue of physical appearance discussed at the outset of this chapter. For all of the women with SCI in the study, African American and White, getting used to the way their bodies looked immediately after injury was very difficult. Even many years after SCI, some women found self-acceptance difficult. One White woman revealed that in the first two years after her injury she didn't have any mirrors in her house "because I didn't want to see myself." Another described how she "even stopped dressing like a woman" because she felt so poorly at the time. Describing the impact of her injury on her self-care routine and alluding to the complicated relationship that exists between a woman's own opinions of her appearance and her sense of self-worth, she says:

> I wouldn't take the time to really do that primping, all that lady stuff...I don't have time, I'm not going to places I used to go, you know, I'm not really going to work, I'm just going out to the market. Because I was in that chair, and I couldn't get up and walk, and you know, uh, I didn't want to take the time to tell the people who were helping me to get dressed that this is- you know, I thought it was too difficult. I wanted to make it easy for them. I wasn't happy, and then I had a couple of people say, you don't look like yourself. You know. Where is- where is your makeup at? And I knew... This is not me. I know it's not. Let me get back to doing, you know, putting my makeup on, getting my hair done, getting my nails done, you know, and things like that, and uh, I felt better. You know, I felt better. I started back then with an attitude, and that brought on an even better attitude".

Analysis of the study data showed that in time however, most of the women with SCI gained greater confidence about who they were as women. For some, physical appearance more and for others it mattered less, but the most important factor in their confidence was having a sense of control over what mattered most to them. If appearance mattered they worked hard to appear how they wished to be seen to others. And if physical appearance was not as central to their identity then time and effort spent on appearance was less, and the views of others were deemed less important. Some women also spoke about how time and experience as women living life from a wheelchair had enabled them to become more vocal and assertive about their needs overall. This included speaking up for oneself and becoming more confident and empowered self-advocates. One woman said "The first thing they [the public] see is the chair, so you have to break that barrier. *You have to overcompensate.* You have to be *more* than charming, *more* than personable, *more* than approachable, you know? It takes time, but you have to learn to do it." This same woman also felt she had to accept her "disabled self" before she assume greater control and assertiveness in other aspects of her life, and suspects this might be true of other women. In reference to the impact of SCI on her physical body she remarked that "Your self-esteem is challenged all the time ... you have to come to know yourself all over again." An important step in this process is accepting there are some aspects of the disability that you can do almost nothing about, but that you have control over how you deal with it. When asked what she would like other women with SCI to know about how she had become so self-accepting, she described how women with physical disabilities "must think for themselves" and "don't let other people's perceptions become your reality." This was not easy for many women in the study, and was especially true in the earlier months and years post-injury. Women repeatedly spoke of the emotional energy that was required, day after day, as they confronted people who did not see the person, but rather only the " disabled body":

> People see you as different in a wheelchair. They don't know that you're basically the same. So they see you as different. They see the disability, but they don't see you. And sometimes I don't know if they see it as both a mental and a physical disability. I remember the first time I went somewhere out to lunch. And it was difficult because it was something different and I was new at it all. And it was so embarrassing, feeling like all those people were watching me and knowing they were like appalled at how I was trying to eat. That type of feeling. That is not comfortable at all. But eventually, and now I am nearly 10 years after my injury, I have changed my entire lifestyle, you know, how I go about my daily living now... You just can't say, well, I'm just gonna get up and do it. You can't. You just have to re-plan it... and just do it a different way. And wait, and try again. It does take time.

Study Summary and Conclusions

One of the main findings of our study of women and SCI was that our study participants, as a group, perceived environmental barriers at rate that is roughly double that reported in previous studies (Whiteneck et al, 2004a&b, & 2001; Forcheimer, Kalpakjian & Tate, 2004). We suggest our finding of relatively high environmental barriers is due to the comparatively worse objective barriers in urban environments (a significant number of women in our sample resided in "inner-city Detroit") and the fact that more than half of our sample were African American. This is relevant since women and African Americans with SCI have been shown to have higher rates of environmental barriers than men and Whites (Forchheimer, Kalpaljian & Tate, 2004; Krause & Broderick, 2004; Whiteneck, 2004a&b, 2001).

The second major finding was how few women actually participated in any form of regular physical exercise. Only five of the 35 women with SCI in this study engaged in regular exercise post-SCI. The exercise consisted mostly of "going for roll" in the neighborhood, but also working out with weights, taking exercise classes, hand-cycling and swimming. This finding too is partially related to the proportion of African American women in our sample and research that shows that African American women have the lowest rates of exercise participation of all (Williams et al., 2006).

The third set of findings are most important. These findings relate to the identification and description of key barriers to exercise and how they operate in the individual lives of women with SCI. These barriers include a lack of accessible, efficient and save transportation, a lack of accessible fitness facilities, and limited financial resources to dedicate to exercise and improved health. Importantly, this study also highlights unique barriers to exercise on the basis of race/ethnicity. Study findings point to perceptions about additional health risks assumed when exercise is added to the physical burden of disability, for example. The idea that doing too much physically can stress a disabled body leaving it less robust, not more, is an idea that future research must pursue. Another new finding centered on the place of female friendships and the delicate balance of reciprocity that exists between women with physical disabilities and their close female friends. Women in this study were aware that being seen with a disabled person could embarrass a friend. This awareness was sufficient to stop some women from asking their friends to accompany them out in the community, including to exercise. The subtleness of these forces is noteworthy. Friendship is a clearly valued resource that the women with SCI hesitated to draw upon too often and this was a real barrier to participation in exercise. Finally, there are important dimensions to exercise participation that appear different for African American women with SCI. For example, this group did not strongly identify with the weight-reducing benefits of exercise since they did not equate thinness with beauty. The physically demanding nature of their daily lives as mothers who conducted their lives from a wheelchair, coupled with beliefs that exercise would deplete their energy levels, created additional barriers to exercise. Many of these barriers are not immediately appreciated by rehabilitation professionals and others charged with dispensing advice about exerciseand health living. For too many "experts", exercise is an obvious, straightforward "good thing" that everyone should do if they care about their health. This exploratory study of women with SCI shows how much more complicated exercise is and how more attention must be paid to women's personal experiences and the reasons they do, or do not, exercise.

CONCLUDING REMARKS

Aging women and menopause and women with spinal cord injury present unique contexts. Historically, in the medical literature, these groups have received relatively little attention. The social experience of natural transitions such as menopause and the realities of unexpected injury and disability are very unique situations where critical social methods are helpful. These methods can explicate these processes and the reactions that women, and others, have toward them. Menopause and physical disability are also important contexts for further research since the population is aging and women with disabilities are living longer.

The Future for Menopause Research

Over 52 million women were estimated to be older than 45 years and in menopausal or post-menopausal life stages in the year 2000 (Ferguson et al., 1989; Hampson & Hibbard, 1996; Lemaire & Lenz, 1995). Conservative estimates project another 40 million women will experience menopause within the next two decades (Hampson & Hibbard, 1996; Meyer, 2001). With the highly publicized "aging" of the "Baby Boomer" generation, menopause, a normal part of women's aging and reproductive processes, has finally become a legitimate topic of interest in clinical research circles (Hampson and Hibbard, 1996; Lemaire and Lenz, 1995; Lock, 1993; Rostosky & Travis, 1996; Coney, 1993). The recent recognition of menopause parallels the "graying of America" (Baca Zinn and Eitzen, 1999; Browne, 1998; Pearsall, 1997; Arendell & Estes, 1994).[7] Barbre (1998) refers to this demographic trend as a "Meno-boom." The fact that so many women – *more than ever before* -- are experiencing menopause simultaneously will have widespread social, political and medical consequences (Barbre, 1998; Fisher, 1999).

Testimonies to women's desire for knowledge and understanding of menopause, as well as documented gaps between women's and physicians' perceptions of menopause, are providing an impetus for the contemporary expansion of social science literature on menopause (Lock, 1993; Lemaire and Lenz, 1995; McElmurry and Huddleston, 1991; Dickson, 1990; Hampson & Hibbard, 1996; Ferguson et al., 1989; Rothert et al., 1990; Preves, 1995; Kaufert & Gilbert, 1986). Yet, sociological literature on menopause is fairly sparse (Rostosky & Travis, 1996). Many feminist scholars attribute this dearth first, to the fact that the understanding of meanings and experiences of aging and gender in United States has not been considered important or high-priority until recently (Dickson, 1990; Greer, 1993; Ruzek et al., 1997; Grambs, 1989). Because of the intersection of aging and gender ideology, Melamed (1983, p. 9) suggests there has been an "information blackout" on the conditions, experiences and thoughts of women as they reach their 40s, 50s, and beyond. This is particularly the case when we turn to how women think about and promote their own health at menopause, for instance, whether, how or when they exercise. That is, while epidemiologists and social science scholars have begun to document how women feel about menopausal symptoms and treatments, or how particular family contexts affect women's experiences of aging or menopause, there is little known about the health-related actions women initiate (or don't initiate, as the case may be) at midlife. Especially in the face of literature that suggests that individuals are responsible for creating their own "success" in aging and/or their own "good" health (e.g., Rowe & Kahn, 1998), social scientists should be more concerned than we currently are with the meanings and experiences of exercise at midlife.

The Future of Disability Research

An estimated 253,000 people in the United States are currently living with a spinal cord injury (SCI) (National Spinal Cord Injury Statistical Center, 2006), and 75% are men (NSCISC, 2006). As a result, less is known about physical recovery processes and the social consequences of SCI from a woman's perspective. Sexuality (Estores & Sipski, 2004), reproduction (Jackson & Wadley, 1999), psychosocial adaptation (Nosek & Walter, 1998), physical fitness, body image, and aging issues have only become a focus of rigorous study within the last decade (Nosek, Hughes, Petersen, Taylor, Robinson-Whelen, Byrne, & Morgan, 2006). An additional challenge for those interested in understanding the personal meaning and impact of SCI in women's lives is the relatively longstanding focus on biomedical models of disability and deficit models of coping and adjustment that have limited our understanding of how women reconstruct their lives post-injury and re-establish

---

[7] Specifically, the two largest 5-year age groups in the 2000 Census were 35-to-39 and 40-to-44 year olds, and the 50-to-54-year age group experienced the largest percentage growth (Meyer, 2001, p. 2).

personally satisfying and productive lives (Lutz & Bowers, 2005; Pentland, Walker, Minnes, Tremblay, & Gould, 2003). In one of only a handful of studies to examine women with SCI at mid-life, Pentland and colleagues (2003) found that their sample (n=29) had little in common with their same-aged able-bodied peers, locating their day-to-day difficulties predominantly in the physical and social environment and not with their bodies. They characterized their difficulties as including a "lack of information and understanding of women and disability" in general, and more specifically, "isolation from peers for support and information sharing, and physical and attitudinal barriers that limit participation and recognition of their needs and issues" (p. 28). Pentland and colleagues (2003) concluded that the women with SCI in their study were fearful about the future since they understood their overall adjustment to SCI and to aging with SCI as "an accumulation of losses and multiple jeopardizes" (p.29). Yet, it is difficult to imagine there would not be greater heterogeneity in the experiences of women living with SCI. Socioeconomic factors, individual personal circumstances, family and community support are all known to exert a powerful force on community integration, quality of life and participation in the community after SCI for both men and women (Boschen, Tonack, & Gargaro, 2003; Duggan & Dijkers, 2001; Estores & Sipski, 2004; Forchheimer, Kalpakjian, & Tate, 2004; Hammel, 2004 & 2007; Krause & Broderick, 2004). Research with more diverse samples of women with SCI is needed. Also, if Pentland's (2003) more general finding is true, that is that women with SCI locate their difficulties in the environment and not with their bodies, then further research is necessary to discover *how* and *why* the environment limits women with SCI's opportunities to live full and satisfying lives. Further, these early data propel us to ask new questions about how women living with SCI reconstruct their lives post-injury, including questions about how women re-claim their identities as women after a severe injury like SCI that permanently alters their physical appearance and perhaps even threatens their sense of femininity and womanhood.

The Future for Exercise Research for Aging Women and Women with SCI

Upon reflection, it is evident that the two studies presented highlight key similarities between able-bodied women in mid-life experiencing menopause and the experiences of women living with spinal cord injury. As it pertains to exercise, their beliefs and behaviors are notably similar. Familial support (i.e., having someone to exercise with) and the importance of body image/physical appearance was a motivator for exercise in both studies, just as a lack of economic resources was a barrier in both. The inability to find and get to exercise facilities was also an issue for both aging women and disabled women, although the reasons were different for each: for disabled women, the barriers to exercise were more about transportation and physical design of bathrooms and buildings and equipment; for menopausal women, the challenges were more deeply tied to finding time in busy lives or in some cases, a lack of effort and interest. This fundamental inability to get oneself to the point of exercise – i.e., the work and amount of effort/negotiation with self and others – needs further study.

Another clear commonality is that when women do exercise, they are either doing it because they have always done it or they are exercising for health or appearance reasons. All of the women in the studies described above knew that exercise was beneficial. Thus, the inability to or lack of exercise in each sample has more to do with practical/logistical reasons than knowledge.

All of the findings reported here need to be replicated in other contexts because the studies relied on small samples in specific geographic as well as socio-cultural locations. Furthermore, as originally designed, the studies were not focused exclusively on exercise. Thus, the findings we report are tempered by those limitations. Much still needs to be known. More research on exercise beliefs, experiences and barriers is urgently needed with different groups of women and with different health conditions, and we need to learn more about and have a deeper understanding of how people conceptualize and experience exercise overall. However, listening to and documenting how disabled and able-bodied older women voice their opinions and experiences regarding exercise are perhaps fruitful and useful first steps.

REFERENCES

Arendell, T. & Estes, C. (1994). Older women in the post-Reagan era. In Fee, Elizabeth and Nancy Kreiger (eds.). *Women's health, politics, and power: Essays on sex/gender, medicine, and public health* (pp. 333-49). Amityville, NY: Baywood Publishing Company, Inc.

Baca Zinn, M. & Eitzen, D. (1999). *Diversity in families (fifth edition).* NY: HarperCollins College Publishers.

Barbre, J. W. (1993). Meno-boomers and moral guardians: An exploration of the cultural construction of menopause. In J. Callahan (Ed.), *Menopause: A midlife passage* (pp. 23-35). Bloomington, IN: Indiana University Press.

Bartky, S. L. (2003). Foucault, femininity, and the modernization of patriarchal power. In R. Weitz (Ed.), *The politics of women's bodies: Sexuality, appearance, and behavior* (pp. 25-45). New York: Oxford University Press.

Belza, B., Walwick, J., Shiu-Thornton, S., Schwartz, S., Taylor, M., & LoGerfo, L. (2004). Older adult perspectives on physical activity and exercise: Voices from multiple cultures. *Prevention of Chronic Disease*, 1(4), A09.

Bertero, C. (2003). What do women think about menopause? A qualitative study of women's expectations, apprehensions, and knowledge about the climacteric period. *International Nursing Review*, 50, 109-118.

Bordo, S. (1993). *Unbearable weight: Feminism, western culture, and the body.* Berkeley, CA: University of California Press.

Boschen, K., Tonack, M., & Gargaro, J. (2003). Long-term adjustment and community reintegration following spinal cord injury. *International Journal of Rehabilitation Research*, 26, 157–164.

Browne, C. (1998). *Women, feminism, and aging.* New York: Springer Publishing Company.

Brownson, R., Eyler, A., King, A., Brown, D., Shyu, Y., & Sallis, J. (2000). Patterns and correlates of physical activity among US women 40 years and older. *American Journal of Public Health*, 90, 264-270.

Burns, K. J. (1996). A new recommendation for physical activity as a means of health promotion. *Nurse Practitioner*, 21(9), 26-28.

Bush, T., Barrett-Connor, E., Cowan, L. et al. (1987). Cardiovascular mortality and non-contraceptive estrogen use in women: Results from the lipid research clinics' program follow-up study. *Circulation*, 75, 1102-9.

Calasanti, T. (2004). New directions in feminist gerontology: An introduction. *Journal of Aging Studies*, 18, 1-8.

Cash, T., & Pruzinsky, T. (2002). *Body image: A handbook of theory, research, and clinical practice*. New York: Guilford Press.

CDC 2006. *http://www.cdc.gov/mmwr/preview/mmwrhtml/mm5528a7.htm*

Christakis, N. & Fowler, J. (2007). The spread of obesity in a large social network over 32 years. *New England Journal of Medicine*, 357, 370-379.

Coney, S. (1993). *The menopause industry: A guide to medicine's discovery of the mid-life woman*. North Melbourne, Victoria: Pinifex.

Conrad, P. & Schneider, J. (1992). *Deviance and medicalization: From badness to sickness*. Philadelphia, PA: Temple University Press.

Crombie, I., Irvine, L.,Williams, B., McGinnis, A., Slane, P., Alder, E. et al. (2004). Why older people do not participate in leisure time physical activity: A survey of activity levels, beliefs and deterrents. *Age and Ageing*, 33, 287-292.

Dickson, G. (1990). A feminist poststructuralist analysis of the knowledge of menopause. *Advanced Nursing Science*, 12(3), 15-31.

Dijkers, M. (2005). Quality of life of individuals with spinal cord injury: A review of conceptualization, measurement, and research findings. *The Journal of Rehabilitation Research and Development*, 42, 87-110.

Dillaway, H. (2008). Why can't you control this?: Women's characterizations of intimate partner interactions about menopause. *Journal of Women & Aging*, in press.

Dillaway, H. (2005). (Un)changing menopausal bodies: How women think and act in the face of a reproductive transition and gendered beauty ideals. *Sex Roles*, 53(1-2), 1-17.

Dinnerstein, M. & Weitz, R. (1998). Jane Fonda, Barbara Bush, and other aging bodies: Femininity and the limits of resistance. In R. Weitz (Ed.), *The politics of women's bodies: Sexuality, appearance, and behavior* (pp. 189-204). New York: Oxford University Press.

Duggan, C. & Dijkers, M. (2001). Quality of life after spinal cord injury: a qualitative study. *Rehabilitation Psychology*, 46: 3–27.

Dworkin, S. & Wachs, F. (2004). Getting your body back: Postindustrial fit motherhood in Shape Fit Pregnancy Magazine. *Gender & Society*, 18, 610-625.

Epstein, J. (1995). *Altered conditions*. New York: Routledge.

Estores, I., & Sipski, M. (2004). Women's issues after SCI. *Topics in Spinal Cord Injury Rehabilitation*, 10, 107-125.

Eyler, A., Baker, E., Cromer, L., King, A., Brownson, R.C., & Donatelle, R.J. (1998). Physical activity and minority women: A case study. *Health Education & Behavior*, 25(5), 640-652.

Eyler, A., Brownson, R., Donatelle, R., King, A., Brown, D., & Sallis, J. (1999). Physical activity social support and middle- and older-aged minority women. *Social Science & Medicine*, 49(6), 781-9.

Eyler A., Wilcox, S., Matson-Koffman, D., Evenson, K., Sanderson, B. (2002). Correlates of physical activity among women from diverse racial/ethnic groups. *Journal of Women's Health and Gender Based Medicine*, 11, 239-253.

Fausto-Sterling, A. (1992). *Myths of gender (revised edition)*. New York: Basic Books.

Ferguson, K., Hoegh, C., & Johnson, S. (1989). Estrogen replacement therapy: A survey of women's knowledge and activism. *Archives of Internal Medicine*, 149, 133-136.

Finch, C., Owen, N., & Price, R. (2001). Current injury or disability as a barrier to being more physically active. *Medicine & Science in Sports & Exercise*, 33(5), 778-782.

Fine, M. & Asch, A., (1988). Introduction: Beyond pedestals. In Michelle Fine and Adrienne Asch (Eds.)'s *Women with disabilities: Essays in psychology, culture, and politics*, pp. 1-37. Philadelphia: Temple University Press.

Fisher, H. (1999). *The first sex: The natural talents of women and how they are changing the world.* New York: Ballantine Books.

Flegel, K., Graubard, B., Williamson, D. & Gail, M. (2005). Excess deaths associated with underweight, overweight and obesity. *Journal of the American Medical Association*, 293(15), 1861-1867.

Forchheimer, M., Kalpakjian, C., & Tate, D. (2004). Gender differences in community integration after spinal cord injury. *Topics in Spinal Cord Injury Rehabilitation*, 10, 163-174.

Foucault, M. (1975). *Birth of the clinic: An archaeology of medical perception* (Vintage). (A. M. Sheridan Smith, trans.) New York: Vintage Books.

Garber, M. (1992). *Vested interests: Cross-dressing & cultural anxiety*. New York: Routledge.

Gill, C. (1997). The last sisters: Disabled women's health. In S.B. Ruzek, V. Olesen, & A. Clarke (Eds.) *Women's Health: Complexities and Differences*. Columbus, OH: Ohio State University Press.

Grambs, J. (1989). *Women over forty: Visions and realities* (revised edition). New York: Springer Publishing Company.

Greer, G. (1993). *The change: Women, aging, and menopause.* New York: Alfred Knopf.

Gullette, M. (1997). Menopause as magic marker: Discursive consolidation in the United States, and strategies for cultural combat. In P. Komesaroff, P. Rothfield, & J. Daly (Eds.), *Reinterpreting menopause: Cultural and philosophical issues* (pp. 176-199). New York: Routledge.

Hammell, K. (2004). Quality of life among people with high spinal cord injury living in the community. *Spinal Cord,* 42, 607-620.

Hammell, K. (2007). Quality of life after spinal cord injury: A metasynthesis of qualitative findings. *Spinal Cord*, 45, 124-139.

Hampson, S, & Hibbard, J. (1996). Cross-talk about the menopause: Enhancing provider-patient interactions about the menopause and hormone therapy. *Patient Education and Counseling*, 27, 177-184.

Henderson, K. & Ainsworth, B. (2000). Sociocultural perspectives on physical activity in the lives of older African American and American Indian women: A cross cultural activity participation study. *Women & Health*, 31(1), 1-20.

Henderson, K. & Ainsworth, B. (2003). A synthesis of perceptions about physical activity among older African American and American Indian women. *American Journal of Public Health*, 93(2), 313-317.

Janiszewski, P. & Ross, R. (2007). Physical activity in the treatment of obesity: Beyond body weight reduction. *Applied Physiology and Nutritional Metabolism*, 32, 512-522.

Jones, M. & Nies, M. (1996). The relationship of perceived benefits of and barriers to reported exercise in older African-American women. *Public Health Nursing*, 13, 151-158.

Kaufert, P. & Gilbert, P. (1986). Women, menopause, and medicalization. *Culture, Medicine and Psychiatry*, 10, 7-21.

Krause, J., & Broderick, L. (2004). Outcomes after spinal cord injury: comparisons as a function of gender and race and ethnicity. *Archives of Physical and Medical Rehabilitation*, 85, 355-362.

Lee, J. (2003). Menarche and the (hetero)sexualization of the female body. In R. Weitz (Ed.), *The politics of women's bodies: Sexuality, appearance, and behavior* (pp. 82-99). New York: Oxford University Press.

Lemaire, G., & Lenz, E. (1995). Perceived uncertainty about menopause in women attending an educational program. *International Journal of Nursing Studies* 32(1): 39-48.

Lock, M. (1993). *Encounters with aging: Mythologies of menopause in Japan and North America.* Berkeley: University of California Press.

Lysack, C., Luborsky, M. & Dillaway, H. (2006). Gathering qualitative data (Ch.20). In G. Kielhofner (Ed.)'s *Research in occupational therapy*. Philadelphia: F.A. Davis.

Lyons, A. C., & Griffin, C. (2003). Managing menopause: A qualitative analysis of self-help literature for women at midlife. Social Science & Medicine, 56, 1629-1642.

Manson, J., Skerrett, P., Greenland, P., & VanItallie, T. (2004). The escalating pandemics of obesity and sedentary lifestyle. *Archives of Internal Medicine*, 164:249-258.

Markey, C., Markey, P., & Birch, L. (2004). Understanding women's body satisfaction: The role of husbands. *Sex Roles,* 51, 209-216.

Markson, E. W. (2003). The female aging body through film. In C. Faircloth (Ed.), *Aging bodies: Images and everyday experiences* (pp. 77-102). Walnut Creek, CA: AltaMira Press.

Martin, E. (1992). *The woman in the body: A cultural analysis of reproduction* (2nd edition). Boston: Beacon Press.

McColl, M. (2002). A house of cards: Women, aging and spinal cord injury. *Spinal Cord*, 40, 371-373.

McElmurry, B., & Huddleston, D. (1991). Self-care and menopause: Critical review of research. *Health Care for Women International*, 12, 15-26.

Melamed, E. (1983). *Mirror, mirror: The terror of not being young.* Linden Press: New York.

Meyer, J. (2001). Age: 2000. Census 2000 Brief, C2KBR/01-12. U. S. Census Bureau, Washington, D. C. Downloaded on 5/22/02: *www.census.gov/prod/2001pubs/c2kbr01-12.pdf.*

Moynihan, R., Heath, I., & Henry, D. (2002). Selling sickness: The pharmaceutical industry and disease mongering. *British Medical Journal*, 324 (April 13), 886-891.

Murtagh, M. J., & Hepworth, J. (2003). Menopause as a long-term risk to health: Implications of general practitioner accounts of prevention for women's choice and decision-making. *Sociology of Health & Illness*, 25, 185-207.

Newson, R, & Kemps, E. (2007). Factors that promote and prevent exercise engagement in older adults. *Journal of Aging & Health*, 19(3), 470-481.

Nosek, M., Hughes, R., Petersen, N., Taylor, H., Robinson-Whelen, S., Byrne, M., & Morgan, R. (2006). Secondary conditions in a community-based sample of women with physical disabilities over a 1-year period. *Archives of Physical Medicine and Rehabilitation*, 87, 320-7.

Pearsall, M. (1997). *The other within us: Feminist explorations of women and aging*. Boulder, CO: Westview Press.

Pentland, W., Walker, J., Minnes, P., Tremblay, M., Brouwer, M., & Gould, . (2002).Women with spinal cord injury and the impact of aging. *Spinal Cord,* 40, 374-387.

Pereira, M., Kriska, A., Day, R., Cauley, J., LaPorte, R., & Kuller, L. (1998). A randomized walking trial in postmenopausal women: Effects on physical activity and health 10 years later. *Archives of Internal Medicine*, 158, 1695-1701.

Powell, K., & Blair, S. (1994). The public health burdens of sedentary living habits: Theoretical but realistic estimates. *Medical Science and Sports Exercise*, 26(7), 851-6.

Preves, S. (1995). *Transforming the hot flash into the power surge: Observation and interviews of women in midlife*. Unpublished paper presented at the 1995 Pacific Sociological Meetings. April 7, 1995.

Rimmer, J., & Wang, E. Obesity prevalence among a group of Chicago residents with disabilities. *Archives of Physical Medicine and Rehabilitation*, 86(7), 1461-1464.

Rogers, W. (1997). Sources of abjection in western responses to menopause. In P. Komesaroff, P. Rothfield, & J. Daly (Eds.), *Reinterpreting menopause: Cultural and philosophical issues* (pp. 225-238). New York: Routledge.

Rostosky, S, & Travis, C. (1996). Menopause research and the dominance of the biomedical model 1984-1994. *Psychology of Women Quarterly*, 20, 285-312.

Rothert, M., Rovner, M., Holmes, N., Schmitt, G., Talarczyk, J., Kroll, & Gogate, J. (1990). Women's use of information regarding hormone replacement therapy. *Research in Nursing and Health*, 13, 355-366.

Rowe, J. W., & R. L. Kahn. (1998). *Successful aging*. New York: Random House.

Ruzek, S., Olesen, V., & Clarke, A. (1997). What are the dynamics of difference? In Ruzek, S, Olesen, V, & Clarke, A (Eds.), *Women's health: Complexities and differences* (pp. 51-95). Columbus, OH: The Ohio State University Press.

Rubin, H., & Rubin, I. (1995). *Qualitative interviewing: The art of hearing data*. London: Sage.

Schulz, A., Parker, E., Israel, B., & Fisher, T. (2001). Social context, stressors, and disparities in women's health. *Journal of the American Medical Women's Association*, 56, 143-149.

Simkin-Silverman, L., Wing, R., Boraz, M., & Kuller, L. (2003). Lifestyle intervention can prevent weight gain during menopause: Results from a 5-year randomized clinical trial. *Annals of Behavioral Medicine*, 26(3), 212-220.

Sipski, M., Jackson, A., Gómez-Marín, O., Estores, I., & Stein, A. (2004). Effects of gender on neurologic and functional recovery after spinal cord injury. *Archives of Physical Medicine and Rehabilitation*, 85, 1826-1836.

Stone, S. D. (1995). The myth of bodily perfection. *Disability & Society*, 10(4), 413-424.

Tudor-Locke, C., Henderson, K., Wilcox, S., Cooper, R., Durstine, J., Ainsworth, B. (2003). In their own voices: Definitions and interpretations of physical activity. *Women's Health Issues,* 13(5), 194-199.

Waxman, B. & Finger, A. (1989). The politics of sexuality and disability. *Disability Studies Quarterly*, 9(3), 2-5.

Weil, E., Wachterman, M., McCarthy, E., Davis, R., O'Day, B., Iezzoni, L., Wee, C. (2002). Obesity Among Adults With Disabling Conditions. *Journal of the American Medical Association*, 288, 1265-1268.

Wendell, S. (1996). *The rejected body: Feminist philosophical reflections on disability.* London: Routledge.

Whiteneck, G., Harrison-Felix, C., Mellick, D., Brooks, C., Charlifue, S., & Gerhart, K. (2004). Quantifying environmental factors: A measure of physical, attitudinal, service, productivity, and policy barriers. *Archives of Physical Medicine and Rehabilitation*, 85, 1324-1335.

Whiteneck, G., Meade, M., Dijkers, M., Tate, D., Bushnik, T., & Forchheimer, M. (2004). Environmental factors and their role in participation and life satisfaction after spinal cord injury. *Archives of Physical Medicine and Rehabilitation*, 85, 1793-1803.

Wilcox, S., Richter, D., Henderson, K., Greaney, M., & Ainsworth, B. (2002). Perceptions of physical activity and personal barriers and enablers in African-American women. *Ethnicity and Disease*, 12, 353-362.

Williams, B., Bezner, J., Chesbro, S., & Leavitt, R., (2006). Effects of a walking program on perceived benefits and barriers to exercise in postmenopausal African American women. *Journal of Geriatric Physical Therapy*, 29(2), 43-49.

Witt, D. (1994/1995). What (n)ever happened to Aunt Jemima: Eating disorders, fetal rights, and Black female appetite in contemporary American culture. *Discourse*, 17, 98-122.

Wolf, N. (1991). The beauty myth: How images of beauty are used against women. New York: Morrow.

Young, I. M. (1990). *Justice and the politics of difference.* Princeton, NJ: Princeton University Press.

Young, I. M. (2003). Breasted experience: The look and feeling. In R. Weitz (Ed.), *The politics of women's bodies: Sexuality, appearance, and behavior* (pp. 152-163). New York: Oxford University Press.

Zones, J. S. (2000). Beauty myths and realities and their impacts on women's health. In M. B. Zinn, P. Hondagneu-Sotelo, & M. Messner (Eds.), *Gender through the prism of difference* (2nd ed.) (pp. 87-103). Boston: Allyn and Bacon.

In: Progress in Exercise and Women's Health Research
Editor: Janet P. Coulter, pp. 71-106

ISBN 1-60456-014-5
© 2008 Nova Science Publishers, Inc.

Chapter 2

SUBSTRATE UTILIZATION IN WOMEN WITH OBESITY AND TYPE 2 DIABETES: EFFECTS OF EXERCISE AND NUTRITIONAL ADAPTATION

Lore Metz and Karen Lambert *

Laboratory of Biology and Physical activity and Sports, EA 3533, Biologie Bat B,
Université Blaise Pascal, Les Cézeaux, BP 104, 63172 Aubière, France
*INSERM, ERI25 Muscles and pathologies, F-34295 Montpellier, France
Université Montpellier I, EA4202, F-34295 Montpellier, France

ABSTRACT

Ability to use different substrate pathways (oxidative glycolysis, β-oxidation) reflects body functionality and its metabolic flexibility i.e. capacity to shift between lipids or carbohydrates utilization, at rest or during exercise. Metabolic function changes between childhood to oldness. Women are a specific population because of their hormonal variations that occurs during their life. In fact from puberty to menopause women's life is build by large hormonal variation periods which will largely influence metabolic function. Moreover sexual hormone can participate to substrate utilization regulation. At rest and during exercise substrate utilization in women could change depending on both hormonal status (puberty, pregnancy, and menopause) and physical activity status. These last years, using invasive or non invasive methods, a large body of studies has given new insight about women substrate utilization in normal and pathological conditions. Metabolic diseases such as type 2 diabetes or obesity are associated with metabolic inflexibility reflecting alteration of substrate utilization. Obesity and type 2 diabetes are becoming a Mundial health priority because of these associated complications like cardiovascular disease. Women are relatively protected of cardiovascular disease (CVD) because of their adult hormonal status. However this benefice is lost after menopause and the risk of cardiovascular complications is more increased than in men if obesity or diabetes is associated. Hormonal substitution has proved it efficiency on CVD after menopause, but currently many research promote exercise and nutritional adaptation for management of postmenopausal status. Exercise and diet are two therapeutics ways which have showed their efficacy on substrate utilization and complications associated to obesity and diabetes. Those two therapeutics approaches should be largely promoted for well-being of women during their life to decrease development or aggravation of chronic pathologies like obesity and type 2 diabetes.

This review proposes a history of substrate utilization modifications that occurs during women's life when associated to obesity and type 2 diabetes and how to optimize utilization of metabolic fuels.

INTRODUCTION

Women life is organized in function of large hormonal cyclic period *i.e* puberty, pregnancy, and menopause. These main periods represent the acquisition and loss of reproductive function respectively. Hormonal variation during those different periods is accompanied of weight modification and especially of adipose mass. These morphological changes represent an open way to possible pathological alterations increasing risk of obesity or metabolic disease as diabetes. Substrate utilization represents an important metabolic activity which is governed by hormonal status including sexual female hormones. Ability to use different substrate pathways (oxidative glycolysis, β-oxidation) reflects body functionality and its metabolic flexibility *i.e.* capacity to shift between lipids or carbohydrates utilization, at rest or during exercise. Here we try to summarize how every hormonal phase in women life can influence substrate utilization. Moreover as incidence of insulin resistant states increase and because women are at particularly high risk to develop it, we also focus here on substrate utilization in those pathological states. Thus in regard of the public health impact of obesity and type 2 diabetes there is a need to promote life style intervention as regular physical activity and nutritional adaptation. In this chapter we will first present hormonal variation during women's life and regulation of substrate utilization in non pathological states. Then interaction between substrate utilization and hormonal status of women will be presented before approaching insulin resistant states. Finally this chapter will focused on the two main life style interventions which should be largely promoted as physical exercise and nutritional adaptation.

1. WOMEN HORMONAL VARIATION

Sexual female hormones, estrogens and progesterone are both derived from cholesterol. Progesterone is a steroid hormone released from the corpus luteum, placenta, and adrenal glands. It is a precursor to the male and female hormones testosterone and estrogen. Estrogen is a collective term for a group of 18-carbon steroid hormones. The most biologically active estrogen is 17β-estradiol. Estrogens are secreted mainly by ovaries and to a lesser extend by adrenal glands. In adipose and muscle tissues, estrogens are synthesized from androgens such as testosterone.

From puberty to menopause women are submitted to cyclic variation in estrogen and progesterone concentration occurs over the course of on average a 28-32 day menstrual cycle. The level of estrogen and progesterone are mediated by luteinising hormone (LH) and follicle-stimulating hormone (FSH) which are in turn regulated by gonadotropin releasing hormone (GnRH) released by the hypothalamus (Figure 1). We present in this first part how those sexual hormones appear and disappear in women's life.

From Childhood to Puberty and Menarche

Growth can be classified into two phases: pre and postnatal periods. Prenatal growth is not dependant on GH or estrogen whereas postnatal growth and early adult life largely relies on. During this first part of life the major fact is the growth of different tissues and organs of the body. Even if all humans follow the basic S-shaped curve, environment can alter the progression of the growth and particularly nutritional environment.

Normal physical growth and sexual maturation require time-evolving coordination among growth hormone and Insulin Growth factor 1 (IGF-1), thyroid hormone, androgens, estrogens, glucocorticoides and insulin. Growth hormone (GH) secreted by pituitary gland acts via mechanisms dependant and independent of IGF-1. GH increases during growth for the development of tissues and organs and regulates growth. Thyroid hormones secreted by thyroid gland, work synergistically to enhance the action of growth hormone and have a permissive effect on sexual maturation. Estrogens are responsible for the development of secondary sexual characteristics and play a major role in reproductive function in women

In newborn GH levels are elevated. Then, concentration decreased and GH secretion rates are stable in the decade before puberty. During puberty, a 1.5 to 3-fold increase in the pulsatile secretion of GH occurs associated with an increase in serum IGF-1 concentration which peaks at 14.5 year in girls and 1 year later in boys. There is a close interplay between estrogens and GH in the regulation of growth and development as exemplified in puberty [1]. The increase in GH and estrogen trigger a growth spurt, which is accompanied by dramatic changes in physical development resulting in the attainment of gender-specific body composition.

Puberty

Puberty results from the awakening of complex neuroendocrine machinery submit to various environments. From a simplified viewpoint, the timely onset and effectual progress of puberty would require, at a minimum, interaxis coordination of GH/IGF-1 and GnRH/LH/sex-steroid production. In children, gonads can be stimulated by gonadotropin although they are not secreted by hypophyse as GnRH by hypothalamus. Then it seems that there is a mechanism before puberty leading for the absence of pulsative secretion of GnRH. The mechanism leading to activation of GnRH secretion is actually not known.

To date, one question is rising: is the timing of normal puberty have changed and is it in relation with body size? In fact, one hypothesis is that body needs a critical weight and possibly a body fat percentage for beginning puberty process. In fact, during puberty a gradual increase in fat mass occurs in girls. Although leptin levels are similar between prepubertal boys and girls, they increase significantly in girl at late puberty [2]. In fact, children who develop puberty earlier are more likely to be overweight children during childhood. Moreover, the age at menarche has fallen rapidly since the 19th century by up to 12 months per decade [3]. There is also growing evidence to suggest that early postnatal weight gain may represent a long-term programming of various outcomes in humans [4].

Pregnancy

Pregnancy is accompanied by important changes in hormonal status, energy needs and body weight leading a suitable environment for the fetus and the mother. There is an increase in energy need due to an increase in resting metabolic rate, increased deposition of fat but no major changes in energy intake [5]. Changes in fat mass occurring mainly during the two primary trimesters of pregnancy are associated with a concomitant loss in fat-free mass favoring an accumulation of body fat. Serum estrogen levels correlated negatively with fat oxidation, suggesting that endogenous estrogen status may regulate total body fat using varying physiological states [2]. During pregnancy there is a dramatic increase in circulating estrogen levels such that by term, the production rate of estradiol is approximately 200 times that of nonpregnant state. In the same time, secretion of pituitary GH is progressively suppressed and replaced by secretion of placenta GH into circulation. Placenta GH is the major regulator of maternal serum IGF-1 levels and has similar metabolic and somatogenic effects as pituitary GH.

Menopause

With age, human ovary is less sensitive to gonadotropin and thus its activity decrease with a concomitant loss of menstrual cycle. With menopause, ovary secretes insufficient amount of progesterone and 17β-estradiol thus increasing secretion and serum levels of LH and FSH. Some of the menopause inconvenient can be corrected by hormonal therapy with exogenous estrogen.

During adult life, GH continues to stimulate the same metabolic processes and is a major regulator of substrate utilization and thus body composition. The main effect is on protein and fat metabolism. GH stimulates lipolysis in order to increase fat utilization thereby keeping protein for nutrient deprivation. GH regulates positively body protein and negatively body fat. Moreover, all the components of fat-free mass are all positively regulated by GH. Regardless of regional difference in the fat and muscle mass, the difference in body composition that exist between genders are contrary to what may be predicted from a greater level of GH secretion in women. This observation suggests again a significant effect of gonadal steroids on body composition and possibly an action of estrogen opposite to that of GH [2]. Nevertheless, several studies seems suggest that menopause is associated with an altered distribution of body fat toward the abdomen thus increasing risk for the development of insulin resistance.

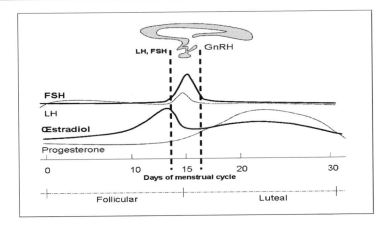

Figure 1. Cyclic variation of oestrogen during menstrual state

If estrogen allows development of specific female characteristic it is also largely implied in substrate partitioning in women. Substrate utilization represents a vast research field which permits to better understand normal and pathological mechanisms.

2. SUBSTRATE UTILIZATION

The main goal of human body for surviving is the production of energy *i.e* ATP. The storage of this highly rich phosphate molecule is very poor and requires contribution of food which brings different nutriments to the body: carbohydrates and lipids. Those nutriments are stored under two forms: triglyceride in adipose tissue and glycogen in liver and muscle. This storage capacity allows the human body autonomy between two feeding period. Invasive and non invasive methods allow measurements of substrate utilization at rest and during exercise.

How to Measure Substrate Utilization?

Several methods can be used to evaluate substrate utilization. The main non invasive method is the indirect calorimetry based on variations of respiratory volumes (VO_2 and VCO_2) and the interpretation of Respiratory Quotient ($RQ=VCO_2/VO_2$). From these measures, different indexes of substrate utilization can be measured. This method is based on the assumption that the physical activity is performed in a steady state and protein make up only a small portion of the energy and can therefore be ignored [6]. The exclusive use of carbohydrate results in a RQ of 1.0, the exclusive use of fat results in a RQ of 0.7. Since it is unlikely that either substrate would be the sole source of energy during submaximal exercise, the typical use of glucose and fat for energy results in a RQ between 0.7 and 1.0.

In the recent years, several research groups have work on different indexes for substrate utilization based on indirect calorimetry. Brooks and Mercier [7] have proposed the crossover concept which allows the determination of the crossover point. There is equilibrium between lipids and carbohydrates utilization during exercise. At the beginning of exercise lipids oxidation provide the major part of energy fuel but with increasing intensity glucose become progressively the major substrate used. For each subjects when exercise intensity increases there is a crossover point between the utilization of lipid and carbohydrate. According Brooks and Mercier concept, the crossover point is defined as the power output at which the increase in energy derived from carbohydrate predominates over the energy derived from lipids (Figure 2). This crossover point can be moved to higher intensities by training, an adaptation that reflects an increase in lipids utilization. This point can also be moved to lower intensities by activity of sympathetic nervous system which increases carbohydrate dependence.

Another index of substrate utilization determined by indirect calorimetry has been established by different research team. This index is known as the $Lipox_{max}$ [8] or Fat_{max} [9] depending on the research group. This index reflects the maximal lipid oxidation point during exercise and can be compared between different populations (Figure 3).

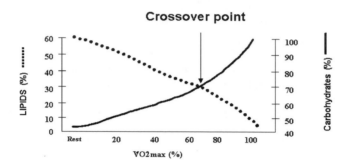

Figure 2. Crossover concept proposed by Brooks and Mercier (1994).

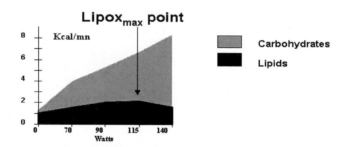

Figure 3. Determination of Lipoxmax point during exercise

Nuclear magnetic resonance has been also used those last years in numerous studies to measure modification of phosphates molecules like ATP stores or production (oxidative phosphorylation) or glycogen stores [10]. More invasive technique can be used to measure physiological evolving of glucose or lipids intermediates. Thus, the use of labelled isotope gives information on the rate of appearance (Ra) or disappearance (Rd) and the clearance of different substrate (glucose, glycerol, palmitate) at rest or during exercise [10].

Muscular biopsy appeared those last years as a new fundamental technique to study cellular substrate utilization. In fact, enzymatic activities can be measured but also mitochondrial functionality. The later can be measured using isolated mitochondria which are obtained by centrifugation or skinned muscle sample which leave the mitochondria in its environment. Functionality of mitochondrial metabolic pathways and activity of respiratory chain complexes can be measured using mitochondrial respiration technique.

At Rest

The main tissues involved in partitioning of substrate utilization are adipose tissue, skeletal muscle and the principal regulator is the liver. In fact the later maintains glycemia by glycogenolysis and neoglucogenesis until the next meal. Moreover glucose from liver is mainly used by glucose dependent organ like brain, kidneys or red blood cells. Adipose tissue produces free fatty acids (FFA) which contribute largely to energy production at rest. Skeletal muscle uses mainly circulating FFA, glucose and lactate provided by the circulation. Actually, lactate is recognized as substrate which could be oxidized by skeletal muscle and heart [11-13].

In postprandial state, there is an increased concentration of carbohydrate triglycerides and amino acids in blood obtained from meal and from the digestive system. The increased availability of different substrate decrease glucose hepatic production and increase different metabolic processes of substrate storage as neoglycogenesis, production of triglycerides in adipose tissue and muscle, synthesis of protein and elimination of amino acids in excess.

In starvation state, glycogen stores and FFA oxidation are the main source of energy production. A decrease in glycemia will induce an increase in glucose hepatic production by glycogenolysis. If starvation lasts for a long time, glycogen storage will end and body will survive using triglycerides from adipose tissue for ketones body production by liver, which could be used as energetic substrate by different tissues like muscle or brain.

Gender difference of substrate utilization have been sometimes [14, 15] but not always [16, 17] identified. Basal fatty acid oxidation have been found to be lower in women than in men, even after adjusting for confounding variable (peak VO_2 and FFM) [14]. This data suggest that a lower basal fat oxidation may contribute to the increased fat storage in women compared with men.

During Exercise

The relative contribution of fat and carbohydrate utilization to total energy expenditure is under hormonal control (se below) and is designed to promote an optimal balance of glucose supply between brain and muscle. Moreover, the balance between carbohydrate and lipids oxidation during exercise depends on exercise characteristics *i.e.* duration and intensity.

Mobilization of Carbohydrate during Exercise

Moderate Intensity Exercise

Between rest and moderate exercise, glycogen stores contribute to energy supply. After few minutes of exercise glycogen stores will participate for half of the energy demand and lipids oxidation for the other half. With increased duration of exercise, lipids will contribute to a larger extend to energy supply. During moderate intensity of exercise women use less glucose and glycogen stores than men [18].

High Intensity Exercise

During high intensity exercise the source of energy supply is the degradation of hepatic and muscular glycogen. When duration of exercise increases, there is an important contribution of hepatic glucose production for energy supply. One hour of high intensity exercise decrease about 55% of hepatic glycogen store and two hours of high intensity work decrease completely glycogen store in liver and active muscles. In fact, due to limited glycogen stores high intensity exercise can not be maintained for very long time.

Effect of Training on Carbohydrate Utilization

Endurance training leads to multiples adaptation of muscle metabolism but essentially to:

- Increase of glycogen stores
- Increase of mitochondrial content and functionality

Those two main adaptation process leads to an increase of glycogen availability and of oxidative pathways capacity in trained subjects. However in those subjects, blood glucose and glycogen store became less used for same exercise intensity, due to lipids utilization. Freidlander and *al* [18] have shown that women respond differently to training than man. The major difference in training response between men and women was that, at the same relative intensity after training women have a significant reduction in RQ whereas the men did not. The possible explanation proposed was that in women, training had a greater glycogen-sparing effect than in men.

Mobilisation of Lipids during Exercise

During light and moderate exercise, lipids mobilization results from peripheral adipose tissue for one part and from the intramuscular lipids droplets for the other part.

Adipocytes from abdominal sub-cutaneous adipose tissue are more active for lipolysis than adipocyte from glutei adipose tissue because of different adrenoreceptor stimulation. At 25% of VO_{2max}, lipids oxidation represents almost the totality of energy supply. When exercise intensity increases to a moderate level, carbohydrate and lipids provide the same energy proportion. The maximal level of lipid oxidation ($Lipox_{max}$ or Fat_{max}) has been determined by indirect calorimetry to range between 55-70% VO_{2max} [9]. Moreover, when exercise last more than one hour, lipids oxidation increase progressively as carbohydrate store become exhausted. During very long duration exercise lipids oxidation can represents 80% of energy supply.

Different studies using indirect calorimetry, muscle biopsy or isotope tracer have largely demonstrated that premenopausal women oxidize proportionately more lipid and less carbohydrate during submaximal exercise than men [16, 19]. In fact women have in general a higher percentage of body fat which could potentially promote this higher lipid utilization. Some studies have speculated that the relative abundance of oestrogen or progesterone or both may alter the regulation of metabolic pathways to favour fat oxidation and conserve carbohydrate [16, 19, 20]. Sex differences in substrate utilization seems likely to be mediated in part by the higher 17-β estradiol concentration in women [21]. It should be mentioned that some studies have not found this difference in substrate utilization between sexes [22, 23]. Potential mechanisms have been proposed to explain sex differences of substrate utilization. First explanation could be the lower sympathetic activity in women for submaximal intensity [24]. Second explanation is the difference in muscular typology between genders. It appears that most of the studies have found a relatively greater amount of type 1 fiber and type 2a in women than in men [25, 26]. This difference may be due to the higher testosterone concentration in men. Finally the last explanation is the possibility of a gender difference in capacity of GLUT 4 translocation in response to physiological stimuli [27-29].

Effects of Training on Lipids Mobilisation

Training increases adipocytes sensibility to lipolytic activity and FFA availability in blood for energy production in peripheral tissue. Regular exercise training in women can increase skeletal muscle capacity to oxidize FFA [30]. In fact, endurance training increases muscular oxidative capacity and then the utilization of FFA as substrate. Healthy women have higher intramuscular lipid droplet compared to men [31, 32] but training induce in both an increase in the number of this lipid pool [32].

Metabolic Flexibility

In healthy subjects, skeletal muscle present a metabolic flexibility to switch from predominant utilization of lipids during starvation to carbohydrate utilization in insulin-stimulated conditions like post-absoptive state. This concept was proposed by Kelley and *al* to characterize the change of muscle capacity to use different substrate in insulin resistant state [33]. Interest of this concept is that metabolic flexibility is a health metabolic indicator. In pathological states as insulin resistance there is a metabolic inflexibility.

3. HORMONAL INFLUENCE OF SUBSTRATE UTILIZATION

As mentioned previously substrate utilization is under hormonal control. Pancreatic and suprarenal hormones are the main actors which act to increase or decrease glycemia. Those hormones are equally helped by other hormones, as thyroid (T3, T4), pituitary or sexual hormones.

Pancreatic Hormones

Insulin and glucagon derived from pancreatic islet are the main hormones which regulate glycemia. Insulin is the hypoglycaemic hormone mainly secreted during postprandial state in view of glucose storage in peripheral tissues. By its action, 10% of glucose providing by the intestine bed is stored as glycogen in liver and skeletal muscle. An excess of glucose will be stored as triglycerides in adipose tissue.

Glucagon is the main hyperglycaemic hormone which acts when a decrease in glycemia occurs. Thus, glucagon is secreted during exercise to maintain glucose available for skeletal muscle activity. After it activation there is a mobilisation of hepatic glycogen and if glycogen store are completely depleted glucagon will increase FFA influx in the liver to increase production of ketone bodies which can be used by brain, cardiac and skeletal muscle as substrate.

Suprarenal and Hypothalamic - Pituitary Hormones

Catecholamines are considered as stress hormones. They are secreted in response to a physiological stress such as exercise or fear situation to increase substrate availability. Catecholamine, act through α-adrenoreceptor (inhibition) or β-adrenoreceptor (stimulation). Lipolytic effect of catecholamine depends on their plasma level and on local density of α- or β- adrenoreceptor. Norepineprine has essentially a β-adrenergic effect whereas epinephrine acts thought α- or β- adrenoreceptor. During exercise there is an increase in catecholamine action which promotes lipid oxidation at submaximal intensity. Epinephrine secretion is lower in women for a given exercise intensity. Thus there is a lower α-adrenergic inhibition comparatively to men. This can contribute to explain the increased lipid oxidation found in women during submaximal exercise. Action of catecholamine is reinforced by cortisol and growth hormone (GH) which stimulate neoglucogenesis by liver.

Thyroid Hormones

T3 and T4 act on metabolism essentially increasing resting energy expenditure. In fact it appears that T3 may act on mitochondria function increasing ATP consumption. Thyroid hormone can increase activity as biogenesis of mitochondria [34].

Sexual Hormones

The variation of estrogen and progesterone concentrations across the normal menstrual cycle, do not allow the analysis of separate effect of female sex hormones on substrate utilization. Thus, animal studies have permitted to highlight specific effect of each of these hormones on substrate utilization. In ovariectomized rat (model of menopause) after administration of 17-β estradiol or progesterone or both, there was no effect of treatment on glucose or lipid utilization at rest. However during exercise there was a decrease in muscular glucose uptake with progesterone alone and progesterone+17-β-estradiol [35]. Glycogen stores are also affected by progesterone during exercise as GLUT4 expression, providing an explanation for the decrease muscular glucose utilization mediated by progesterone [29]. Estrogen appears to have positive effects only in the absence of progesterone or when supraphysiological dose are coupled with normal dose of progesterone [35]. The effect of ovarian hormone on lipid metabolism has also been investigated in particular estrogen action. Estrogen administration decrease adipocyte lipoprotein lipase (LPL) activity but increase its activity in muscle. These actions promote FFA utilization in skeletal muscle by increasing activity of lipid mitochondrial transporters carnitne palmitoyl transferase 1 (CPT1) and lipolytic enzyme hydroxyl-acylcoA dehydrogenase (HADH) [36]. Recently D'Eon et *al* [37] have shown that estrogen act on adiposity and fuel partitioning by genomic and non genomic regulation. In ovariectomized rats, estrogen treatment reduce adipose mass and adipocytes size. Those modification were explained by down-regulation of lipogenic genes in adipose tissues, liver and skeletal muscle. Moreover estrogen treatment promotes oxidation of FFA in skeletal muscle via an up regulation of Adenosine Mono Phosphate Kinase (AMPK) pathways activity and Peroxisomal Proliferator Activator Receptor (PPAR) genes expression. In fact, based on those results, it appear that estrogen increase lipids oxidation while the effect on carbohydrate oxidation remains unclear.

Human studies focused on the effect of estrogen and progesterone on substrate utilization are not easy to conduct. In fact, it is difficult to differentiate estrogen and progesterone effect in women from cyclic variation. However evidences seem to comfort results from animals studies that report an increase lipid oxidation effect of estrogen [16, 21, 38].

The literature strongly suggests that estrogen promote lipid oxidation without alteration of carbohydrate oxidation or with a sparing effect on glycogen stores. Interrestingly, it has been suggested that estrogen can increase metabolic flexibility of skeletal muscle. Conversely, progesterone which seems to decrease lipid and carbohydrate oxidation could therefore increase the development of a state of relative inflexibility as it is observed in insulin resistance states [39].

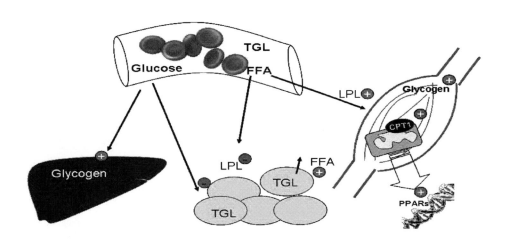

Figure 4. Effects of estrogen on peripheral tissues. Data are collected from animal models and human investigations. TGL, triglycerides; FFA, free fatty acids; LPL, llpoprotein lipase; CPT1, carnitine palmito transferase 1. Estrogen increase LPL activity of skeletal muscle as glycogen storage, CPT-1 activity and Peroxisomal Proliferator Activator Receptor (PPAR) genes expression. Estrogen decrease LPL activity in adipose tissue which limit TGL storage.

Regarding the role of gender difference in hormonal regulation of substrate utilization (catecholamine) and the potential implication of estrogen on lipid mobilization, there is probably a specific female life variation in substrate utilization.

4. Variation of Substrate Utilization during Women's Life

From Puberty to Oral Contraception

This period is characterized by the instauration of menstrual cycle. Hormonal changes lead to morphological and metabolic modification. During this stage there is an increase in fat mass and fat free mass. In girls there can be a 20-25% increase in fat mass as opposed to only a 15-20% increase in boys. This could promote development of obesity in girls during puberty. Skeletal muscle is also affected by this stage [40]. Puberty is characterized at cellular level, by acquisition of glycolytic capacity in skeletal muscle. Thus children have a greater proportion of type 1 fibers than sedentary adult [41]. The proportion of type 2 fibers increases between the age of 5 and 20. Because of this muscular typology, children have a low glycolytic potential which increase during and after puberty [42]. In fact during submaximal exercise children have a low lactate increase compared to adult. This low lactate level can also be explained by the absence of lactate deshydrogenase enzyme system during prebubertary stage. Moreover there is a low activity of PFK, which is a key glycolytic enzyme, and a slower glycogen concentration in children compared to adult. However, after puberty there is an increase in glycolytic enzyme activity and glycogen utilisation. Those cellular adaptations during puberty are reflected by a lower RQ in pubertal girls compared to women (20-32 years old) [43, 44].

When sexual maturity occurs, most of young women start an oral contraception. Synthetic steroids used as oral contraceptives can influence carbohydrate and lipids partitioning during exercise. Literature seems to provide evidence that oral contraception reduces glucose flux [45] during exercise and increase lipids mobilisation [46] without change in RQ during submaximal exercise (45-65%). In fact, with oral contraception there is no change in total carbohydrate or lipid utilization. However, it seems that oral contraception increase use of alternative carbohydrate energy sources (like glycogen) in skeletal muscle, to compensate reduced glucose availability. Concerning lipids, the elevated fatty acids mobilization is accompanied by increased reesterification of mobilized FA [10]. Thus oral contraceptives do not modify whole body substrate utilization but modify the dynamic of energy sources used.

Pregnancy

In general the resting metabolic rate increases as pregnancy progresses [47, 48]. The increase is related to the increased work of respiration, cardiovascular functioning, uterine, placental demands and the fetal demands for growth [47]. The increased metabolism causes an increased demand on the maternal glucose such that blood level may decline. There is an increase level of epinephrine during the first and the second trimester but not in the third trimester. This could explain the rapid glycogen depletion observed during pregnancy probably in order to maintain glucose level. Circulating cortisol levels increase during pregnancy which allows the reduction of glucose cellular uptake. Since maternal glucose conservation prevails, the maternal use of fats appears to increase as pregnancy progress.

The majority of evidence for substrate utilization obtained by indirect calorimetry suggests that there is no difference in substrate utilization during exercise in pregnant women compared with non pregnant ones [48, 49]. However some studies have shown opposite results therefore, other markers of metabolic activity should be examined. In fact, glucose level during or after exercise have shown a decrease in pregnant women compared to non pregnant women. However, those results should be interpreted in light of the RQ which was not different between groups. In fact, despite a decrease in blood glucose level, there is not necessarily a change in RQ. It suggests that there is no difference in substrate utilization, but there could be an impairment of glucose production rather than an actual increase of glucose utilization. Concerning fat utilization during exercise and pregnancy, it appears that moderate exercise increase triglycerides and FFA levels without changing RQ. This suggests that even if fat availability increases, their utilization for energy production do not.

Before and after Menopause

To assess the effect of ovarian hormone on substrate utilization some authors have compared women metabolism in follicular or in luteal phase. Influence of ovarian hormone on insulin mediated glucose uptake has been largely discussed in the literature. There are reports [50] on reduced insulin action in luteal phase as well as data showing that cycle phase has no impact on insulin action [51, 52]. However, no studies have shown a reduced insulin action during the follicular phase, suggesting that if the ovarian hormones impair insulin action, progesterone is more likely a candidate than estrogen. This possible effect on insulin mediated glucose uptake should be blunted during exercise due to the effect of muscle contraction on glucose uptake. Several authors have shown that carbohydrate oxidation was significantly lower in the luteal phase during sub maximal exercise. This effect was abolished for higher exercise intensity [35, 36, 53]. Regarding the whole literature on this subject, there is not a strong support for a physiologically relevant cycle phase difference in substrate utilization during exercise. However, it should be kept in mind that the range of hormone concentrations observed across cycle phases is trivial compared to the differences observed between men and women.

With the progressive decrease of the ovarian function, there is a decrease in estrogen secretion which is associated with a degradation of physiological aspects like increased adipose tissue. In fact, there is little information on the comparison of substrate utilization before and after menopause. However, it has been suggested that reduced fat oxidation in older women both at rest and during exercise is related to fat free mass loss, but may also result of estrogen deficiencies and/or a reduction in the intrinsic capacity of muscle for fat oxidation.

5. OBESITY AND TYPE 2 DIABETES

Obesity and type 2 diabetes represent world wide diseases. Estimated prevalence is above 100 million and projections are that the prevalence will double to 200 million by 2020 [54]. The prevalence of type 2 diabetes is associated to aging, increasing calorie intake and decreasing calorie expenditure and obesity. Obesity is defined as an excess of adipose tissue and can be associated with insulin resistance. Obesity represents a risk factor for development of cardiac complication and type 2 diabetes.

Type 2 diabetes is characterized by resistance to the normal action of insulin. It is presumed that insulin can bind normally to its receptor on the surface of cells but polygenic abnormalities underlying the disease attenuate the transmission of the insulin signal within the cells resulting in insulin resistance. This, lead to increased glucose production from the liver (owing to inadequate suppression by insulin), and inadequate uptake of glucose by skeletal muscle and peripheral tissues.

Complications

Cardiovascular diseases is the most common cause of death in type 2 diabetes, with risk among diabetic being increased by up to five times compared to the non diabetic population [55]. This increased risk is particularly apparent in women with diabetes [56], where the relative protection due to gender is lost [57]. Insulin resistance may contribute to the pathogenesis of these diseases by altering carbohydrate and lipid metabolism. The association between diabetes and coronary heart disease has been suggested to be stronger in women than in men prompting the idea that diabetes eliminates or attenuates the advantages of being female.

The concept that clustering of cardiovascular risk factors can occur in individuals more often than would be expected by chance, led to the identification of a constellation or syndrome called syndrome X, Reaven's syndrome or the metabolic syndrome [58]. The risk factors are linked in such a way that the prevalence of each factor is increased in individuals with other factors. Approximately 10-20% of type 2 diabetics people have this syndrome depending on how it is defined. The components of the metabolic syndrome are: hypertension, dyslipidemia, obesity, microalbuminaemia.

In fact, alterations in lipids and carbohydrate metabolism are implicated in development of cardiovascular complications in obesity and type 2 diabetes. Potentially with their increased cardiovascular risk, women with diabetes have more to gain from any managing strategy like hormones therapy but also life style adaptation by physical activity or nutritional adaptation.

To limit complications associated to obesity and type 2 diabetes, it is important to underscore the pathological aspects of tissue and organ implicated in substrate utilization and how they are affected by insulin resistance.

Pathological Aspects of Tissue Involved in Substrate Utilization

Substrate utilisation is under hormonal regulation which has been described in preceding section. In fact, pancreatic hormone are implicate in maintain of glycemia and substrate storage in insulin sensitive tissue. Liver is a central organ in the organisation of substrate flux and adipose tissue is the principal implicated in development of obesity. Substrate utilization is mainly influenced by skeletal muscle because of the mass of insulin sensitive tissue that it represents. All those tissue are profoundly altered in insulin resistant states. However we will focus especially on adipose and muscular tissue. Adipose tissue is particularly altered in women life and muscular tissue represents quantitatively the principal insulin sensitive tissue and is mainly implied in substrate utilization.

Pancreas

In healthy subject, insulin secretion during basal state is for the great part regulated by glucose level. During post-prandial state glucose load induce a biphasic response of insulin secretion. The pattern of insulin secretion involves an initial peak which corresponds to the early or cephalic phase fallowed by a more sustained release driven by rising blood glucose. In insulin resistant states there is an absence of the first phase response. In human characterized by insulin resistance a clear characteristic is the absence of this initial peak of insulin secretion. Thus there is a increased glucose levels after a meal and failure to inhibit plasma FFA levels. This phenomenon is the first sign of a lack of flexibility of physiological function to achieve optimal fuel handling.

Liver

Insulin inhibits production and release of glucose by blockage of neoglucogenesis. Moreover insulin inhibits glycogen degradation [59]. In fact, in insulin resistant states there is a decrease in action of insulin which is reflected by an increase in hepatic glucose production (HGP) by liver contributing to hyperglycemia. Increased level of circulating FFA can participate to this increased HGP and to steatosis.

Adipose Tissue

It is well-known that women have a higher amount of body fat than men. Additionally women have a higher proportion of body fat in the gluteal-femoral region, whereas men have more body fat in the abdominal region [60]. Men also have a higher incidence of cardiovascular disease than women, and menopause in women increase the incidence of cardiovascular disease and the central distribution of adipose tissue [61]. Thus upper body obesity is referred as android and lower body obesity as gynoid.

In Insulin resistant states, anti-lipolytic action of insulin is decreased, consequently there is an increase in circulating FFA. It seems that FFA excess can decrease glucose utilization and glycogen synthesis [62]. Moreover FFA can also accumulate in different tissue as skeletal muscle or liver.

Adipose tissue is not only an energy storage location but is also an endocrine tissue. Many adipokine are secreted by adipose tissue and play a role in development or aggravation of insulin resistant states. Numerous hormones secreted by adipose tissue have been recently discovered and some of them play a role in energy regulation such as adiponectine or leptin.

Leptin play a key role in food intake energy expenditure and body weight. In insulin resistant states circulating level of leptin is increased suggesting a resistance to it action [63]. There is a gender difference in circulating leptin level which is much higher in women than in men. Because women have more body fat and different distribution of fat than men, it has been difficult to relate sex steroids hormones to blood leptin concentration. Some studies have investigated the effect of estrogen in regulation of leptin production, but there is still controversy. However, it appears that leptin can act on estrogen synthesis and inversely, that estrogen supplementation during hormone therapy can act on leptin profile [64, 65]. More studies are needed to investigate how leptin and estrogen can interact in normal and insulin resistant states.

Adiponectin is the most abundant gene product in adipose tissue. Much remain to be learnt about its physiological functions, but evidence is accumulating for a role in the inhibition of inflammatory processes and protection against the consequence of the insulin resistance syndrome [66]. In contrary of leptin, it appears that adiponectin have no clear relation with female sex hormones.

Lipolysis and lipogenesis are regulated by catecholamine and insulin respectively. As previously mentioned, catecholamines act through α-adrenoreceptor (inhibition) or β-adrenoreceptor (stimulation). In insulin resistant states, most of time subjects are overweighed or obese. Increases adipose tissue, and size of adipocyte affect lipid mobilisation. In fact, in large adipocyte there is a majority of α2-adrenoreceptor which have an anti-lipolytic effect [67]. Thus, in overweight or obese subjects there is a shift toward reduced β-adrenergic stimulation and an increase of α-adrenergic inhibition. Recent data have found that atrial natriuretic peptide have greater lipolysis activity than catecholamine [68]. This new insight on endocrine mobilisation of adipose tissue can be promising in terms of managing of insulin resistant states.

Muscular Tissue

This tissue represent as far as 70% of insulin sensible peripheral tissue of human body. As in liver, there is a pathological accumulation of muscular triglycerides during insulin resistant states [69]. Numerous studies have shown that muscular triglycerides are inversely related to insulin sensibility [70]. Furthermore it well admitted that obese and type 2 diabetic subjects have an increase in muscular triglycerides. This relation is independent of total adiposity which suggest that repartition of adipose tissue in specific location can be more deleterious than consideration of total adiposity. Excess of muscular triglycerides lead to accumulation of acyl-CoA intermediary known for their bad effects on insulin sensibility [71]. However this relation between intramuscular lipids and insulin sensitivity must be used carefully because in endurance trained subjects there in a non pathological increase in muscular triglycerides [72]. Accumulation of intramyocellular lipids found in insulin resistant states is pathological because of many other alterations of oxidative metabolism. Actually, it is well admitted that there is a decrease in type 1 fibers (the more sensible to insulin action) and concomitantly an increase in type 2b fibers in insulin resistant states. Moreover the proportion of glucose transporters 4 (GLUT4) in type 1 fibers is also decrease in insulin resistant state explaining therefore a part of the mechanism of peripheral insulin resistance [73]. Concomitantly, with this typology modification, there is a decrease in oxidative enzyme capacity in obese subject and this alteration is even more important in type 2 diabetic subjects [74]. Mitochondrial activity have been largely studied, however there is a controversy about possible alteration in insulin resistant states [75, 76]. At genetic level, it appears clearly that expression of genes implied in mitochondrial biogenesis or oxidative phosphorylation (OXPHOS) are down-regulated in insulin resistant states [77, 78]. In fact, modification genetic expression during obesity and type 2 diabetes can have important impact on whole muscular metabolism. Gender difference in mitochondrial energetic pathways (cellular and genetic level) have been studied in animal and have shown higher mitochondrial mass and oxidative capacity in female [79]. However there is not data on gender differences in human pathological states as insulin resistance.

Insulin Resistance and Substrate Utilization

Genetic factors associated to insulin resistance could influence physical capacity of subjects as capacity to adapt to training stimulation [80, 81]. Reduced physical capacity is know recognize as a risk factor for development of insulin resistance [82]. It is also well established that type 2 diabetic women present a lower VO_{2max} compared to healthy ones [83]. Alteration of muscular tissue as presented previously, could largely contribute to this phenomenon. Although physical capacity is linked with the capacity of body to use different substrate and it has been largely investigated these last years.

At Rest

Two mechanisms are implicated in glucose utilization: an insulin dependant way which take place solely in insulin sensitive tissue and an insulin independent way which can take place in insulin or non insulin sensitive tissue. Insulin sensitive tissues are well known: adipose tissue, liver, and skeletal muscle. Organs who use glucose by insulin independent way is principally brain, nerves and the splanchnic bed. Baron and al have shown that non insulin dependant utilization of glucose during euglycemic situation does not imply skeletal muscle [84]. However during hyperglycaemic situation as encountered in type 2 diabetes non insulin dependant utilization of glucose is increased in muscle resulting of mass effect. In general, glucose utilization at rest is the same or higher in type 2 diabetic than in healthy women [85, 86]. This could be illustrated by the increased RQ found in insulin resistant subjects at rest.

There is an elevated circulating FFA level (blunted anti-lipolytic effect of insulin) at rest and during postprandial situation. However, circulating FFA utilization is diminished at rest and in post absorptive states in obese subjects and contribute to this increased FFA level found in insulin resistant states. Weight loss do not change FFA utilization, this suggest that this defect is more linked to insulin resistance than to obesity [86]. Gender differences of substrate utilization in insulin resistant states have not been studied a lot. It seems that there are no gender difference in resting metabolic rate when adjusted for FFM [87].

Those substrate utilization modifications during insulin resistant states measured at whole body level have also cardiovascular implication. Abnormality of substrate utilization in obese women can have repercussion on myocardial substrate metabolism and efficiency [88]. Peterson et al showed that in obese women, BMI and insulin resistance was associated with shift in myocardial substrate metabolism toward greater fatty acid use. This shift in substrate utilization in obesity was associated with decrease in the efficiency of myocardial energy transduction to contractile work.

During Exercise

For intensity varying from 40 to 60% of peak VO_2 insulin resistant subjects present an increased glucose utilisation [86, 89]. Thus, a single bout of exercise can decrease glycaemia in type 2 diabetic subject even without a clear normalisation. Glycogen utilization is decreased in insulin resistant subjects during moderate exercise and even more if they are diabetic [90, 91]. Our study group has shown that crossover and $Lipox_{max}$ points are decreased in insulin resistant subject without gender differences [8]. Those results suggest that insulin resistant subject present decrease lipid utilization during exercise and a glucodependance pronounced. Some recent data have given new insight about explanation of this glucodependance. Obese and type 2 diabetic subjects present an increase in blood and muscular lactate level. We have shown that this increase blood lactate level is correlated to crossover and $Lipox_{max}$ point in insulin resistant women, suggesting that this increased in lactate level can promote carbohydrate pathway utilization thus early glucodependance during exercise [92].

Lipids utilization investigated by different technique has given controversy results. Obese or post-obese women present a decrease in lipids oxidation [8, 93]. This can be explained by adrenergic status in obesity. With increased adipose mass, there is an increase of anti-lipolytic effect of α2-adrenoreceptor and a decrease in β-adrenegic lipolytic effect. Moreover, using invasive technique it has been shown that there is an pathological increase in intramuscular lipids pool in insulin resistant women [94][95]. But it has also been shown that lipid oxidation in diabetic subject is not different from healthy subjects [96]. An overview of the literature shows that we have to be careful considering the status of substrate utilization in insulin resistant states and particularly in type 2 diabetes. This last is a heterogeneous disease, and adaptation at the substrate level differs between obese and non obese patients and may contribute to differences in the final appearance of the various phenotypes.

Metabolic Inflexibility

As previously mentioned, in patient with type 2 diabetes [97] there is no peak of insulin secretion after a normal glucose load, only a small progressive increase which reflect the incapacity of pancreas to respond to a glucose load [98]. In parallel after a meal there is a blunted anti-lipolytic effect of insulin as mentioned before. The idea of a metabolic inflexibility comes from all these observations which reflect the incapacity of the body to respond normally to a glucose load.

Kelley and *al* have studied the energetic balance of leg muscle during starvation or insulin stimulated condition using indirect calorimetry and arterio-venous difference in obese and type 2 diabetic subjects [33]. This experience gave an appreciation of metabolic flexibility. Kelley and *al* found a decrease of lipid oxidation at rest in obese and diabetic subjects. As previously mentioned insulin resistant subject present higher RQ at rest than healthy subject. However, during insulin-stimulated condition lipids oxidation was higher in obese and diabetic subjects than in controls. Those results reflect the incapacity to use lipids during fasting, and carbohydrate during insulin stimulation.

Recently, it have been suggested a racial difference in metabolic flexibility in healthy premenopausal women. Thus, African-American women have a metabolic inflexibility compared to matched Caucasian women, which could contribute to the higher prevalence of obesity and insulin resistance found in this population [99]. In fact, Berk et *al* submitted two groups of women (African-American *vs* Caucasian) to high-fat diet and low fat diet and measured substrate utilization before and after those nutritional intervention. They found that Caucasian women adapt to high fat diet by increasing they capacity to oxidize fat. African–American women did not change their pattern of substrate utilization during different diet intervention. Moreover, it appears that African-American women failed to increase their fat oxidation and decrease their carbohydrate oxidation after stimulation by epinephrine. This last study underlies maybe, the necessity to promote life style intervention in subpopulation at high risk to develop insulin resistant state.

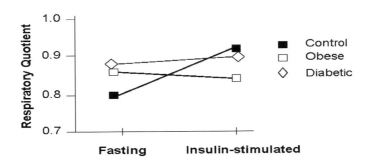

Figure 5. Concept of metabolic inflexibility adapt from Kelley et al (2000)

In fact, decrease capacity to switch between different substrate does not only represent a local phenomenon (*i.e* skeletal muscle) but have an impact on whole body, and certainly contribute to complications seen in insulin resistant states. This, with reduced physical capacity contributes to insulin resistant state. It underlies the absolute necessity to develop and promote life style intervention which will improve metabolic disturbances found in insulin resistant states.

6. MANAGEMENT OF INSULIN RESISTANCE BY PHYSICAL ACTIVITY

In the literature, there is a paucity of data about the utility of exercise without association with caloric restriction as a strategy for obesity reduction in women. However, exercise-induced weight loss is associated with a reduction in fat (total and abdominal), an improvement in both cardiorespiratory parameters and skeletal muscle oxidative capacity [100].

Because exercise is known to increase insulin sensitivity it represents one of the first therapeutic approaches for obese and type 2 diabetic subjects. Physical activity can also improve metabolic profile and cardiovascular complication. However, there is still poor information on this last point concerning effect of exercise in women before and after menopause.

Prescription of physical activity to insulin resistant subject is very heterogeneous in terms of protocol proposed.

What Kind of Exercise?

Endurance training: the goal of this kind of training is the improvement of cardiorespiratory fitness as muscle oxidative capacity. Those protocols are on long time (10-16 weeks), intensity vary between 40 and 60% of VO_{2max} and on a frequency of 3-4 time per week [101, 102].

Circuit-training: this concept is based on alternation between endurance and resistance exercises. The interest of that protocol is improvement cardiorespiratory fitness and muscular weight promoting by this way an increase in insulin sensitive tissue [103, 104].

Strength training: there are few studies on this kind of protocol. Here the goal is to increase muscle mass by hypertrophy mechanism [105].

Training at the Crossover or the $Lipox_{max}$ point: our study group has proposed training protocols based on utilization of crossover or $lipox_{max}$ point as the intensity of training. Subjects are trained at de cardiac frequency corresponding to crossover point or $lipox_{max}$ previously determined by indirect calorimetry. The interest of this protocol is that training is individualized for each subject who is trained at a specific cardiac intensity. Crossover point intensity is of interest for type 2 diabetic subjects because this intensity favour use of a great majority of carbohydrate (60%) but still imply use of an interesting proportion of lipids (40%) for energy demand. The use of $lipox_{max}$ allows a training program at the intensity of maximal lipids oxidation, this is particularly interesting for obese subjects who need to decrease adipose tissue mass.

Effects of Training on Substrate Utilization

At Physiological Level

Health benefits of regular exercise are well established in the prevention and the treatments of diseases. In addition to its effects on insulin sensibility and on body weight composition, regular exercise increase cardiorespiratory and muscle fitness and decrease risks of cardiovascular diseases [106, 107]. Blood pressure is strongly improved by moderate intensity training in type 2 diabetes and in obesity. Exercise provides also less atherogenic lipid profile. Surprisingly effect of exercise on glycaemic control appears controversy but literature suggests strongly improvements in glycogen utilization and cellular pathways promoting glucose uptake. However the positive metabolic effects of training are rapidly reversible and 5 day of detraining can significantly induced improvement in insulin action and in muscular glucose uptake [108].

Lipid metabolism also appears to be improved after training leading to increased oxidative capacity and fatty acid utilization. In addition, exercise improves tissues sensitivity to catecholamine, thereby enhancing lipolysis and providing more FFA to working muscle.

However, after training, the main source of FFA utilization during exercise appears to be increased intramuscular TG breakdown in healthy subjects and it appears that this triglyceride pool is also mobilised in insulin resistant subjects [109].

Using a training program at Lipox$_{max}$ point, Brandou et *al* have shown increased lipid oxidation in obese adolescent whereas diet alone did not improve substrate utilization [110]. Higher intensity training seems to increase carbohydrate utilization with no change in lipid oxidation [111]. In fact low intensity training provides a greater improvement in metabolic profil than high intensity training because of it action on lipid oxidation [112]. Dietary intervention in obese adult is relatively ineffective without concomitant exercise training. Prevention of obesity in childhood and adolescence should emphasise increased physical activity rather than diet because of fears relating to the adverse effects of inappropriate eating patterns.

Pregnancy is a stage in women life which presents a risk for development of future diabetes. In fact exercise can reduce risk to develop gestational diabetes by increasing glucose utilization. The same advice should be given to obese or type 2 diabetic women during pregnancy to limit complications or pre-eclampsia risk [113].

Concerning effect of exercise on substrate utilization and cardiovascular risk before and after menopause, there are very few data. In postmenopausal women regular exercise training as 1h of walking 3 days a week can improve metabolic profile and despite decrease cardiovascular risk [114]. More intense exercise training is needed to decrease fat mass in postmenopausal women [115]. We should point out the difficulty to work on substrate utilization in postmenopausal women because of effect of hormone replacement therapy on lipid oxidation [116].

At Cellular Level

The main effect of exercise on glucose metabolism in working muscle is insulin independent and in a large part explained by the exercise induced translocation of the GLUT 4 transporters. Training have also a large beneficial effect on oxidation pathways, promoting lipid mobilisation and utilization. Moreover, strength training can improve muscle quality modifying muscular typology in insulin resistant subjects [117].

Mitochondria ...A Gold Mine

Effect of training on mitochondrial activity in skeletal muscle of insulin resistant subjects is at this time a goal research for many groups. Because of the heterogeneity of anthropometric characteristic of insulin resistant subjects (BMI, % fat mass, age, and physical aptitude), recent results on mitochondrial activity should be interpreted carefully. In fact there have been suggested that obese and type 2 diabetic subjects present [75, 118] or not [76] decrease in mitochondrial activity. This first point is under debate actually and need more investigation to determine mitochondrial alteration in subjects with specific anthropometric characteristics. The effect of training on mitochondrial activity in insulin resistant subjects has been investigated these two last years. Endurance training, at relatively moderate intensity increases, both in men and women muscular lipid oxidation and mitochondrial electron chain transport activity in insulin resistant subjects [119-121]. Those modifications could be accompanied or not [121] by an increase in mitochondrial content. Most of the studies works on sample including men and women or only men, there is no study on comparison of men and women substrate utilization at cellular level in insulin resistant states. However studies which have worked on a population including men and women did not report differences between sexes on cellular parameters.

Because mitochondria is the central organelle of oxidative metabolism the transcription factors as Peroxisomal proliferator activator receptor γ Coactivator (*PGC1*), Peroxisomal Proliferator Activator Receptor (PPARs) and Nuclear Repiratory Factor 1 (NRF1) have been studied in healthy and insulin resistant states. Those transcription factors are involved in mitochondrial biogenesis. Patti et *al* [78] have shown that prediabetic and type 2 diabetic muscle is characterized by decreased expression of OXPHOS genes, many of which are regulated by NRF-dependent transcription. Furthermore, expression of PGC1α and -β, coactivators, PPAR γ and NRF-dependent transcription, is significantly reduced in both prediabetic and diabetic subjects. Both men and women where studied and no gender differences have been noted. Actually there is no information about effect of training on insulin resistant women on the expression of these transcription factors. This way of research should be emphasized to better understand genetic adaptation of skeletal muscle of insulin resistant subjects. Moreover, it would equally be of great interest to study effect of gender difference on this adaptation.

At Molecular Level

There is a related direct effect of muscular contraction on signalisation pathways implicated in intracellular glucose transport. Two pathways are principally concerned: Adenosin Mono Phosphate Kinase (AMPK) and Mitogen Activated Protein Kinase (MAPK) pathways.

AMPK is a stress activated protein which act to promote the repletion of muscular ATP stores. In fact, AMPK increase activation of metabolic pathways which produce energy (glycolysis…oxidation) and increase GLUT4 membrane translocation cellular glucose uptake. This way is not modified by insulin resistance, thus there are no differences in AMPK activation between lean and obese women [122]. However, recent finding on animal model suggest that at the onset of menopause an increase in androgen to estrogen ratio can promote visceral fat accumulation by inhibiting AMPK activation and stimulating lipogenesis [123]. Exercise training can increase AMPK activation both in healthy or insulin resistant subjects (both men and women) this provide a interesting management of increase fat storage during menopause [124].

The MAPK pathways play a role in genetic regulation of muscular adaptation at exercise. There are poor information on insulin resistance and MAPK pathways. It have been shown in obese animal that the pathways was decreased but that training could reverse this situation [125].

AMPK and MAPK pathways are interesting in insulin resistance context in regards of their effect on increase glucose tolerance after exercise. Those ways is activated during high or moderate intensity of exercise. In fact, those findings suggest that it could be of interest in a training program for obese and/or type 2 diabetic subjects, to diversify exercise type (low, moderate or high intensity training).

Effects of Training on Metabolic Flexibility

Low or moderate intensity training which have an effect on lipid oxidation as previously mentioned, should influence the metabolic inflexibility towards a better flexibility. Thus it should be recommended that insulin resistant subject exercise at intensity and frequency which allow improvement of lipid oxidation at rest and during submaximal exercise. Moreover exercise training can improve insulin sensibility and then a more correct response to a glucose load (insulin stimulating situation).

7. Management of Insulin Resistance by Nutritional Adaptation

The study of McCay et al. [126] in 1935 at Cornell University which report for the first time that calorie restriction in rats extend maximal life span and prevent the severity of chronic disease due to aging have been the first on a long list now.

Subsequently, data have shown that calorie restriction i.e. reduction in calorie intake below usual ad libitum intake without malnutrition, slows aging and associated-diseases in a wind variety of species from animal regna.

The mechanisms responsible for calorie restriction-mediated beneficial effects on aging observed in rodents involved metabolic adaptations including: decrease in body weight and fat mass, in glycemia and insulinemia, oxidative stress, circulating triiodothyronine (T3) levels and sympathetic nervous system activity leading to a decrease in body temperature and whole-body resting energy expenditure, reduction in systematic inflammation and protection against aging-associated alteration in immune function [127]. In human is it difficult to evaluate the impact of calorie restriction on aging and longevity. However, there is some data on lean subject submitted voluntary to calorie restriction. Interestingly, the data available indicated that human on calorie restriction have many of the metabolic alteration seen in rodents. Then, what happening in overweight / obese human patient on calorie restriction? Because, many type 2 diabetic patients presented also an obesity state and it is well admitted that a weight reduction could normalized or improved glucose metabolism and many of the metabolic alterations. Therefore, calorie restriction is the cornerstone of overweight, obesity therapy in insulin resistant or not patients.

8. Caloric Restriction

Effects on Metabolic Alteration

The effects of moderate caloric restriction on substrate utilization are well known in animal models. Classically in rodent a reduction of 40% of total caloric intake has been used in order to prevent all age-associated diseases and increase maximal life time [128]. In such model, an increase in insulin sensitivity is often seen. On muscles, caloric restriction plays an important role mainly by facilitated insulin-stimulated glucose uptake participating in glucose regulation. This response is mediated by an increase in sarcolemmal GLUT4 after insulin stimulation. Is it to note that the basal GLUT4 content is not changed suggesting a better GLUT4 translocation after calorie restriction [129]. Associated with such data is the increase in insulin-stimulated glucose uptake glucose after calorie restriction. In human, depending of the weight loss desired caloric restriction in obese patient could be moderate to severe. Thus, in human and particularly in women there is a greater variability in the response to diet.

The metabolic response to calorie restriction in obese and type 2 diabetic patients seems to induce the same adaptation concerning glucose metabolism: improvement of insulin resistance and insulin secretion [130] as well as a decrease in hepatic glucose production [131, 132]. Furthermore, caloric restriction and weight reduction are beneficial in enhancing insulin action on peripheral tissues [133, 134] and preventing the development of type 2 diabetes. Even if is it widely accepted that such dietary intervention permit a better management of metabolic alteration the underling mechanism are not known.

Recent data obtain from CALERIE team (The Comprehensive Assessment of the Long Term Effects of Reducing Intake of Energy) illustrate that in healthy overweight men and women patient a 6-month calorie restriction induces a ~10% weight reduction with a fasting insulin concentration significantly reduced whereas surprisingly glucose and dehydroepiandrosterone sulphate (DHEAS) levels were not. The 24-hour energy expenditure was decreased in a greater order than expected by loss of fat-free mass [135]. In the same cohort of patients these authors have reported the effect of ~25% energy restriction due to caloric restriction alone or in combination with exercise on body composition and fat distribution. Their data suggest both experimental groups which induce a negative energy balance to 25% of baseline change body composition and abdominal fat distribution in same magnitude. This result was unexpected because previous studies have found a greater reduction in fat mass and particularly visceral adipose tissue after exercise training [100]. In the subgroup of overweight women, the 25% calorie restriction induce a significant decrease in fat-free mass and surprisingly the reduction of visceral adipose tissue was smaller than in men as well as the average reduction in fat from any depot was ~30% for men but only ~25% for women. Then, this result underline the precise calculation of energy cost of exercise because when exercise and the combination of calorie restriction + exercise are compared, the energy deficit achieved by the exercise groups exceed those of the calorie restriction groups. However, previous data obtained in obese type 2 diabetic patient found that calorie restriction *per se* had an important regulatory effect on metabolism of such patient that is independent of weight loss [132, 136].

Effects on Cellular Alteration

In insulin resistant skeletal muscle, numerous metabolic alteration are present. Since calorie restriction improves insulin resistance the mechanisms involved have been investigated. Several conflicting data are available on the effect of energy-deficit on enzyme activities. Because of the metabolic alteration in oxidative pathway during insulin resistance [74, 118] it was expected that weight loss by calorie restriction could alter enzyme activities and mitochondria functioning. In rat female the effect of weight loss is associated with a decrease in glycolytic key-enzyme: phosphofructokinase in a tissue-specific manner [137]. In human the effect of calorie restriction on enzyme activities seems to indicate that oxidative enzyme activity does not improve after weight loss in obese humans [138-140]. In fact the main effect of calorie restriction is not on enzyme activities but rather on mitochondria function in relation to the decrease in oxidative stress. In rodent, as in human, calorie restriction seems to induce mitochondria proliferation [141] and efficiency [142] associated or not with exercise [143]. In overweight and obese patients, calorie restriction also improves mitochondria function. Civitarese et al.,[140] have give new insight about how calorie restriction acts on mitochondria biogenesis. The implication of transcription factor A mitochondrial (TFAM) and the peroxisome proliferators-activated receptor gamma coactivator 1α (PGC1 α) as well as sirtuin 1 (SIRT1) as been implicated in the mitochondria biogenesis after 6 months of calorie restriction in overweight healthy patients [140]. The induction of mitochondria biogenesis was associated with a lower energy-expenditure and a decreased level DNA damage thus suggesting that calorie restriction induces biogenesis of efficient mitochondria.

Moreover, in this latter study only restricted subject presented an increased in AMP-activated protein kinase alpha2 (AMPKα2) mRNA in contrast to calorie restriction associated with exercise group who did not. This latter enzyme seems to act as a metabolic sensor inside cell and it is interesting to note that only the metabolic stress induce by calorie restriction without exercise which can activated it. Nevertheless, a great part of metabolic adaptation observed with calorie restriction could come from hormonal alteration. One candidate is leptin which is an anorexigenic hormone secreted by adipose tissue able to reduce spontaneous food intake. The comparison, in rodent, of calorie restriction *per se* and calorie restriction due to a physiological hyperleptinemia, illustrates that hyperleptinemia was not sufficient to induce after one week hepatic mitochondrial-lipooxidative gene expression and oxidative capacity. Thus, based on this result it seems that in calorie restriction the decrease in leptin did not plays a central role in metabolic adaptations. Consistent with this latter explanation is the study of Torgerson JS et al. [144] where reduced levels of leptin in response to severe calorie restriction in men and women obese patients do not appear to regulate the hormonal starvation response. Leptin levels seem do not predict weight relapse but rather a maintained weight reduction. Moreover, leptin stimulates thyroid stimulating hormone (TSH) production and thus thyroid hormones which participated in resting energy expenditure and metabolic regulation [145]. Then in obese premenopausal women, diurnal TSH secretion is significantly enhanced and appears to be positively correlated with circulating leptin levels and body mass index (BMI). A very low calorie calorie diet (VLCD) for ~4 months in these patients induces a reduction in T3 and 24-h TSH secretion which correlates with the decline of mean 24-h leptin concentration. It has been previously reported that estrogens from oral contraceptive raise TSH concentrations. Even if in the latter study there was a significant decrease in estrogen concentration after the VLCD, there was not any significant relation between estradiol concentrations and TSH secretion suggesting a minor role of estrogen in hypothalamic-pituitary-thyroid axis after calorie restriction.

One substrate often forgotten during metabolic alteration is lactate. This monocarboxylate is a preferential substrate for oxidative tissues as muscle or heart and an important precursor of gluconeogenesis in liver. Since subcutaneous adipose tissue could produce lactate, lactate metabolism could be altered during caloric restriction [146]. To date even if lactatemia has been recognized as an independent risk factor for the development of insulin resistance there is no data available on the effect of calorie restriction on lactate metabolism in human. In rodent, both 6-week of calorie restriction or anorexia due to hypoxia induce an increase in sarcolemmal lactate transport capacity without changes in skeletal muscle isoforme protein expression [147, 148]. Then calorie restriction is able to alter lactate transport capacity and since lactate compete with glucose for ATP synthesis in oxidative tissue is it reasonable to take into account this substrate in metabolic alteration.

9. NUTRITIONAL SUPPLEMENTATION

Conjugated Linoleic Acid

Nutritional supplementation is another strategy to prevent insulin resistance or to counterbalance the metabolic alterations. However, this latter therapeutic help is much related to up to date data concerning molecules or metabolic alteration theories then depending of the current opinion. Nevertheless, a well executed nutritional supplementation associated with weight loss/management or exercise could facilitate the result to obtain. Inside the entire available supplement one is currently extensively studied: the conjugated linoleic acid (CLA). CLA is a polyunsaturated fatty acid naturally occurring in foods from ruminant sources. CLA refers to all the positional and geometric isomers of linoleic acid which contains two double bonds in positions 9 and 12. The cis-9,trans-11 CLA is the most abundant isomer representing 90% of CLA isomer in natural food products and its counterpart the trans-10,cis-12 CLA represent the remainder. The interest for this molecule comes from its effects against a variety of modern diseases: cancer, atherogenese, obesity, adiposity and inflammation [149]. Based on the excellent review of Toomey S et al. it appears that the promising effects of CLA on rodent are not efficient on obese human. In obese and type 2 diabetic patients, CLA induce discrete improvement in fat accumulation but depending on insulin resistance background could be detrimental. However, recent data obtain from obese patient with a greater proportion of women found some positive effect of CLA. These studies have found that CLA increases lean body mass [150] and reduces body fat associated with a prevention of weight gain during holiday season [151]. Thus, if food supplemented with such molecule could induce beneficial effect on metabolic alteration without exercise or calorie restriction we can speculate that in the future such intervention will be preferred to "classical "management of metabolic alterations. However, to date the longest human trial was only on 22 years of supplementation of mixed isomer [152]. Thus, the potential benefice of CLA need further studies in order to determine the precise dose and isomer, depending on the background of the subject (age, insulin sensitivity, pathologies-associated) and duration of the supplementation…

Resveratrol

Like calorie restriction, resveratrol has long been known to have interesting properties. Resveratrol is a natural polyphenolic flavonoid component found in the skin of red grapes and thus in small proportion in red wine. The properties of resveratrol include antioxidant effects accounted for in part in its beneficial effects on cardioprotective and anticancer activities. Interestingly it as been shown that resveratrol in vitro can enhances sirtuin/Sir2 activity through an allosteric interaction, resulting in the increase of SIRT1 affinity for both NAD+

and acetylated substrate [153]. This family of NAD+- dependent deacetylases have been previously implicated in the life span increase by calorie restriction. In mammals, seven sirtuin genes have been identified (SIRT1-7) with SIRT1 which senses nutritional status via NAD+ levels (as AMPK) and induces modulation of cellular metabolism. The metabolic effect of SIRT1 implicate glucose and insulin production, fat metabolism and cell survival [154] highlighting a role in mediating calorie restriction effects. Moreover, SIRT1 physically interacts with and deacetylates PGC1α at multiple lysine sites and thus activated it leading to induction of downstream gene transcription implicated in mitochondria biogenesis. Several studies have illustrated the beneficial effect of high and low doses of resveratrol against high-calorie diet-induced obesity in mice. In mice submitted to high-calorie diet mainly, resveratrol improves mitochondrial function and increases mitochondrial number, insulin sensitivity, AMPK and PGC1 α. These results are closed to those with calorie restriction and mice on high-calorie diet associated with resveratrol seem to get longer lifespan [154]. Moreover, the effects of resveratrol on muscle are very interesting. Mice show an increase motor function with an increased running time and consumption of oxygen in muscle fibers [155]. Thus these results are promising for pathologies-associated with high-calorie diet. However, is it to note that resveratrol failed to decrease weight gain associated with such diet. Then even if resveratrol improves most of the pathologies-associated with high-calorie diet the impact of increase fat mass in the long term need to be assess both in mice and human. In human, there is a crucial need of data on the effect of resveratrol in healthy, diabetic, insulin resistant patients. To date, the promising result in mice can not be extrapolated to human due to the lack of data on safety of long term exposure [156].

10. Conclusion and Perspectives

Substrate utilization in women is influenced by hormonal variation and especially by estrogen. This latter, with concomitant specific adrenostimulation of adipose tissue, regulate fat storage and mobilization. Those two last parameters are of importance in development of chronic disease as obesity. Despite some comprehensive works on animal, more studies on women pre and post menopause are needed, to validate results obtained on animals.

Mitochondria represent a central point of investigation which is of particular importance in obesity and type 2 diabetes. In fact, mitochondrion is the central location of oxidative energetic pathways. In light of the new data on gender differences on mitochondria functionality, there are still numerous questions to answer: does estrogen play a role in this different mitochondrial activity? is there a gender difference in metabolic flexibility in normal and pathological states? how exercise training and nutritional adaptation can influence it?.

Exercise training has been largely promoted to limit or reverse metabolic and cardiovascular complication associated with type 2 diabetes. Even if exercise training have proved it effects on physiological and cellular alterations found in insulin resistant states, precaution should be taken when exercise training is prescribe to obese or type 2 diabetic subjects. In fact, it is not easy to assess an important strength or endurance training in daily life of obese or type 2 diabetic subjects. We should keep in mind the feasibility of a life style intervention because compliance of subjects is hard to keep if training program is too heavy. Moreover, there is still question about effect of training on muscular genetic adaptation in men and women. Because women with insulin resistance are more exposed to cardiovascular complication, exercise training should be promoted in this subpopulation. Training programs based on substrate utilisation allow a good compliance because of moderate intensity proposed. It also increases fat oxidation which the major substrate alteration encountered in insulin resistant state.

The management of insulin resistance in human by dietary intervention alone is effective as therapeutic tools. It implies a very low calorie diet in the first part for inducing a weight lost then low calorie and weight stabilization program are needed for a long time. Then we can understand the interest in pills counteracting the deleterious effects of high-calorie diet often rich in fat. However, yet these pills as calorie restriction mimics are not available. There is some indication about molecules or pathway implicated in insulin resistance alteration and thus therapeutic target. Future work is necessary to extrapolated results from mice to human and to found a combination between diet recommendation and pill use. The fight against insulin resistance needs the combination of all tools available as calorie restriction for weight loss with exercise for increasing substrate utilization as why not one or two selected pills for accelerating the result. By now, instead of pill patient are recommend to eat an equilibrated food with …..one or two glasses of red wine…..

11. REFERENCES

[1]   Veldhuis, J.D., et al., Endocrine control of body composition in infancy, childhood, and puberty. *Endocr Rev*, 2005. 26(1): p. 114-46.

[2]   Leung, K.C., et al., Estrogen regulation of growth hormone action. *Endocr Rev*, 2004. 25(5): p. 693-721.

[3]   Ong, K.K., M.L. Ahmed, and D.B. Dunger, Lessons from large population studies on timing and tempo of puberty (secular trends and relation to body size): the European trend. *Mol Cell Endocrinol*, 2006. 254-255: p. 8-12.

[4]   Dunger, D.B., M.L. Ahmed, and K.K. Ong, Early and late weight gain and the timing of puberty. M*ol Cell Endocrinol*, 2006. 254-255: p. 140-5.

[5]   Kopp-Hoolihan, L.E., et al., Longitudinal assessment of energy balance in well-nourished, pregnant women. *Am J Clin Nutr*, 1999. 69(4): p. 697-704.

[6]   Peronnet, F. and D. Massicotte, Table of nonprotein respiratory quotient: an update. *Can J Sport Sci*, 1991. 16(1): p. 23-9.

[7]   Brooks, G.A. and J. Mercier, Balance of carbohydrate and lipid utilization during exercise: the "crossover" concept. *J Appl Physiol*, 1994. 76(6): p. 2253-61.

[8]   Perez-Martin, A., et al., Balance of substrate oxidation during submaximal exercise in lean and obese people. *Diabetes Metab*, 2001. 27(4 Pt 1): p. 466-74.

[9]   Achten, J., M. Gleeson, and A.E. Jeukendrup, Determination of the exercise intensity that elicits maximal fat oxidation. *Med Sci Sports Exerc*, 2002. 34(1): p. 92-7.

[10]   Jacobs, K.A., et al., Fatty acid reesterification but not oxidation is increased by oral contraceptive use in women. *J Appl Physiol*, 2005. 98(5): p. 1720-31.

[11]   Ahlborg, G., Mechanism for glycogenolysis in nonexercising human muscle during and after exercise. *Am J Physio*l, 1985. 248(5 Pt 1): p. E540-5.

[12] Gertz, E.W., et al., Myocardial substrate utilization during exercise in humans. Dual carbon-labeled carbohydrate isotope experiments. *J Clin Invest*, 1988. 82(6): p. 2017-25.

[13] Jorfeldt, L., Metabolism of L(plus)-lactate in human skeletal muscle during exercise. *Acta Physiol Scand* Suppl, 1970. 338: p. 1-67.

[14] Nagy, T.R., et al., Determinants of basal fat oxidation in healthy Caucasians. *J Appl Physiol*, 1996. 80(5): p. 1743-8.

[15] Toth, M.J., et al., Gender differences in fat oxidation and sympathetic nervous system activity at rest and during submaximal exercise in older individuals. *Clin Sci (Lond)*, 1998. 95(1): p. 59-66.

[16] Horton, T.J., et al., Fuel metabolism in men and women during and after long-duration exercise. *J Appl Physiol*, 1998. 85(5): p. 1823-32.

[17] Levadoux, E., et al., Reduced whole-body fat oxidation in women and in the elderly. *Int J Obes Relat Metab Disord*, 2001. 25(1): p. 39-44.

[18] Friedlander A.L., et al., Training-induced alterations of carbohydrate metabolism in women: women respond differently from men. *J Appl Physiol*, 1998. 85(3): p. 1175-86.

[19] Tarnopolsky, L.J., et al., Gender differences in substrate for endurance exercise. *J Appl Physiol*, 1990. 68(1): p. 302-8.

[20] Ruby B.C. and R.A. Robergs, Gender differences in substrate utilisation during exercise. *Sports Med*, 1994. 17(6): p. 393-410.

[21] Carter, S., et al., Short-term 17beta-estradiol decreases glucose R(a) but not whole body metabolism during endurance exercise. *J Appl Physiol*, 2001. 90(1): p. 139-46.

[22] Romijn, J.A., et al., Substrate metabolism during different exercise intensities in endurance-trained women. *J Appl Physiol*, 2000. 88(5): p. 1707-14.

[23] Goedecke, J.H., et al., Determinants of the variability in respiratory exchange ratio at rest and during exercise in trained athletes. *Am J Physiol Endocrinol Metab*, 2000. 279(6): p. E1325-34.

[24] Davis, S.N., et al., Effects of gender on neuroendocrine and metabolic counterregulatory responses to exercise in normal man. *J Clin Endocrinol Metab*, 2000. 85(1): p. 224-30.

[25] Carter, S.L., et al., Changes in skeletal muscle in males and females following endurance training. *Can J Physiol Pharmacol*, 2001. 79(5): p. 386-92.

[26] Staron, R.S., et al., Fiber type composition of the vastus lateralis muscle of young men and women. *J Histochem Cytochem*, 2000. 48(5): p. 623-9.

[27] Hansen, P.A., et al., Effects of ovariectomy and exercise training on muscle GLUT-4 content and glucose metabolism in rats. *J Appl Physiol*, 1996. 80(5): p. 1605-11.

[28] Barros, R.P., et al., Muscle GLUT4 regulation by estrogen receptors ERbeta and ERalpha. *Proc Natl Acad Sci U S A*, 2006. 103(5): p. 1605-8.

[29] Campbell, S.E. and M.A. Febbraio, Effect of the ovarian hormones on GLUT4 expression and contraction-stimulated glucose uptake. *Am J Physiol Endocrinol Metab*, 2002. 282(5): p. E1139-46.

[30] Stisen, A.B., et al., Maximal fat oxidation rates in endurance trained and untrained women. *Eur J Appl Physiol*, 2006. 98(5): p. 497-506.

[31] Roepstorff, C., et al., Gender differences in substrate utilization during submaximal exercise in endurance-trained subjects. *Am J Physiol Endocrinol Metab*, 2002. 282(2): p. E435-47.

[32] Tarnopolsky, M.A., et al., Influence of endurance exercise training and sex on intramyocellular lipid and mitochondrial ultrastructure, substrate use, and mitochondrial enzyme activity. *Am J Physiol Regul Integr Comp Physiol*, 2007. 292(3): p. R1271-8.

[33] Kelley, D.E. and L.J. Mandarino, Hyperglycemia normalizes insulin-stimulated skeletal muscle glucose oxidation and storage in noninsulin-dependent diabetes mellitus. *J Clin Invest*, 1990. 86(6): p. 1999-2007.

[34] Weitzel, J.M., K.A. Iwen, and H.J. Seitz, Regulation of mitochondrial biogenesis by thyroid hormone. *Exp Physiol*, 2003. 88(1): p. 121-8.

[35] Campbell, S.E. and Febbraio, M.A, Effect of the ovarian hormones on GLUT4 expression and contraction-stimulated glucose uptake. *Am J Physiol Endocrinol Metab*, 2002. 282(5):E1139-46.

[36] Campbell, S.E. and M.A. Febbraio, Effect of ovarian hormones on mitochondrial enzyme activity in the fat oxidation pathway of skeletal muscle. *Am J Physiol Endocrinol Metab*, 2001. 281(4): p. E803-8.

[37] D'Eon, T.M., et al., Estrogen regulation of adiposity and fuel partitioning. Evidence of genomic and non-genomic regulation of lipogenic and oxidative pathways. *J Biol Chem*, 2005. 280(43): p. 35983-91.

[38] Hamadeh, M.J., M.C. Devries, and M.A. Tarnopolsky, Estrogen supplementation reduces whole body leucine and carbohydrate oxidation and increases lipid oxidation in men during endurance exercise. *J Clin Endocrinol Metab*, 2005. 90(6): p. 3592-9.

[39] Campbell, S.E. and M.A. Febbraio, Effects of ovarian hormones on exercise metabolism. *Curr Opin Clin Nutr Metab Care*, 2001. 4(6): p. 515-20.

[40] Dietz, W.H., et al., Effect of sedentary activities on resting metabolic rate. *Am J Clin Nutr*, 1994. 59(3): p. 556-9.

[41] Bell, R.D., et al., Muscle fiber types and morphometric analysis of skeletal msucle in six-year-old children. *Med Sci Sports Exerc*, 1980. 12(1): p. 28-31.

[42] Boisseau, N. and P. Delamarche, Metabolic and hormonal responses to exercise in children and adolescents. *Sports Med*, 2000. 30(6): p. 405-22.

[43] Eriksson, O. and B. Saltin, Muscle metabolism during exercise in boys aged 11 to 16 years compared to adults. *Acta Paediatr Belg*, 1974. 28 suppl: p. 257-65.

[44] Mahon, A.D., et al., Blood lactate and perceived exertion relative to ventilatory threshold: boys versus men. *Med Sci Sports Exerc*, 1997. 29(10): p. 1332-7.

[45] Suh, S.H., et al., Effects of oral contraceptives on glucose flux and substrate oxidation rates during rest and exercise. *J Appl Physiol*, 2003. 94(1): p. 285-94.

[46] Casazza, G.A., et al., Menstrual cycle phase and oral contraceptive effects on triglyceride mobilization during exercise. *J Appl Physiol*, 2004. 97(1): p. 302-9.

[47] McMurray, R.G., et al., The effect of pregnancy on metabolic responses during rest, immersion, and aerobic exercise in the water. *Am J Obstet Gynecol*, 1988. 158(3 Pt 1): p. 481-6.

[48] Bessinger, R.C., R.G. McMurray, and A.C. Hackney, Substrate utilization and hormonal responses to moderate intensity exercise during pregnancy and after delivery. *Am J Obstet Gynecol*, 2002. 186(4): p. 757-64.

[49] Lotgering, F.K., et al., Respiratory and metabolic responses to endurance cycle exercise in pregnant and postpartum women. *Int J Sports Med*, 1998. 19(3): p. 193-8.

[50] Braun, B., et al., Women at altitude: changes in carbohydrate metabolism at 4,300-m elevation and across the menstrual cycle. *J Appl Physiol*, 1998. 85(5): p. 1966-73.

[51] Diamond, M.P., et al., Glucose metabolism during the menstrual cycle. Assessment with the euglycemic, hyperinsulinemic clamp. *J Reprod Med,* 1993. 38(6): p. 417-21.

[52] Toth, E.L., et al., Insulin action does not change during the menstrual cycle in normal women. *J Clin Endocrinol Metab,* 1987. 64(1): p. 74-80.

[53] Hackney, A.C., M.A. McCracken-Compton, and B. Ainsworth, Substrate responses to submaximal exercise in the midfollicular and midluteal phases of the menstrual cycle. *Int J Sport Nutr,* 1994. 4(3): p. 299-308.

[54] Pereira, M.A., et al., Fast-food habits, weight gain, and insulin resistance (the CARDIA study): 15-year prospective analysis. *Lancet,* 2005. 365(9453): p. 36-42.

[55] Panzram, G., Mortality and survival in type 2 (non-insulin-dependent) diabetes mellitus. *Diabetologia,* 1987. 30(3): p. 123-31.

[56] Kannel, W.B. and D.L. McGee, Diabetes and cardiovascular disease. The Framingham study. Jama, 1979. 241(19): p. 2035-8.

[57] Barrett-Connor, E. and D.L. Wingard, Sex differential in ischemic heart disease mortality in diabetics: a prospective population-based study. *Am J Epidemiol,* 1983. 118(4): p. 489-96.

[58] Reaven, G.M., Why Syndrome X? From Harold Himsworth to the insulin resistance syndrome. *Cell Metab,* 2005. 1(1): p. 9-14.

[59] Michael, M.D., et al., Loss of insulin signaling in hepatocytes leads to severe insulin resistance and progressive hepatic dysfunction. *Mol Cell,* 2000. 6(1): p. 87-97.

[60] Kissebah, A.H., et al., Relation of body fat distribution to metabolic complications of obesity. *J Clin Endocrinol Metab,* 1982. 54(2): p. 254-60.

[61] Tchernof, A., E.T. Poehlman, and J.P. Despres, Body fat distribution, the menopause transition, and hormone replacement therapy. *Diabetes Metab,* 2000. 26(1): p. 12-20.

[62] Bergman, R.N. and M. Ader, Free fatty acids and pathogenesis of type 2 diabetes mellitus. *Trends Endocrinol Metab,* 2000. 11(9): p. 351-6.

[63] Ahima, R.S. and J.S. Flier, Adipose tissue as an endocrine organ. *Trends Endocrinol Metab,* 2000. 11(8): p. 327-32.

[64] Catalano, S., et al., Leptin enhances, via AP-1, expression of aromatase in the MCF-7 cell line. *J Biol Chem,* 2003. 278(31): p. 28668-76.

[65] Chu, M.C., et al., A comparison of oral and transdermal short-term estrogen therapy in postmenopausal women with metabolic syndrome. *Fertil Steril,* 2006. 86(6): p. 1669-75.

[66] Kubota, N., et al., Disruption of adiponectin causes insulin resistance and neointimal formation. *J Biol Chem,* 2002. 277(29): p. 25863-6.

[67] Stich, V., et al., Activation of alpha(2)-adrenergic receptors impairs exercise-induced lipolysis in SCAT of obese subjects. *Am J Physiol Regul Integr Comp Physiol,* 2000. 279(2): p. R499-504.

[68] Sengenes, C., et al., Natriuretic peptides: a new lipolytic pathway in human adipocytes. *Faseb J,* 2000. 14(10): p. 1345-51.

[69] Malenfant, P., et al., Fat content in individual muscle fibers of lean and obese subjects. *Int J Obes Relat Metab Disord,* 2001. 25(9): p. 1316-21.

[70] Pan, D.A., et al., Skeletal muscle triglyceride levels are inversely related to insulin action. *Diabetes,* 1997. 46(6): p. 983-8.

[71] Ruderman, N.B. and D. Dean, Malonyl CoA, long chain fatty acyl CoA and insulin resistance in skeletal muscle. J Basic Clin Physiol Pharmacol, 1998. 9(2-4): p. 295-308.

[72] Hoppeler, H., et al., Endurance training in humans: aerobic capacity and structure of skeletal muscle. *J Appl Physiol*, 1985. 59(2): p. 320-7.

[73] Gaster, M., et al., GLUT4 is reduced in slow muscle fibers of type 2 diabetic patients: is insulin resistance in type 2 diabetes a slow, type 1 fiber disease? *Diabetes*, 2001. 50(6): p. 1324-9.

[74] Simoneau, J.A. and D.E. Kelley, Altered glycolytic and oxidative capacities of skeletal muscle contribute to insulin resistance in NIDDM. *J Appl Physiol*, 1997. 83(1): p. 166-71.

[75] Petersen, K.F., S. Dufour, and G.I. Shulman, Decreased insulin-stimulated ATP synthesis and phosphate transport in muscle of insulin-resistant offspring of type 2 diabetic parents. *PLoS Med*, 2005. 2(9): p. e233.

[76] Boushel, R., et al., Patients with type 2 diabetes have normal mitochondrial function in skeletal muscle. *Diabetologia*, 2007. 50(4): p. 790-6.

[77] Mootha, V.K., et al., PGC-1alpha-responsive genes involved in oxidative phosphorylation are coordinately downregulated in human diabetes. *Nat Genet*, 2003. 34(3): p. 267-73.

[78] Patti, M.E., et al., Coordinated reduction of genes of oxidative metabolism in humans with insulin resistance and diabetes: Potential role of PGC1 and NRF1. *Proc Natl Acad Sci* U S A, 2003. 100(14): p. 8466-71.

[79] Colom, B., et al., Skeletal muscle of female rats exhibit higher mitochondrial mass and oxidative-phosphorylative capacities compared to males. *Cell Physiol Biochem*, 2007. 19(1-4): p. 205-12.

[80] Berntorp, K., K.F. Eriksson, and F. Lindgarde, The importance of diabetes heredity in lean subjects on insulin secretion, blood lipids and oxygen uptake in the pathogenesis of glucose intolerance. *Diabetes Res*, 1986. 3(5): p. 231-6.

[81] Colman, E., et al., The role of obesity and cardiovascular fitness in the impaired glucose tolerance of aging. *Exp Gerontol*, 1995. 30(6): p. 571-80.

[82] Nyholm, B., et al., Insulin resistance in relatives of NIDDM patients: the role of physical fitness and muscle metabolism. *Diabetologia*, 1996. 39(7): p. 813-22.

[83] Regensteiner, J.G., et al., Abnormal oxygen uptake kinetic responses in women with type II diabetes mellitus. *J Appl Physiol*, 1998. 85(1): p. 310-7.

[84] Baron, A.D., et al., Rates and tissue sites of non-insulin- and insulin-mediated glucose uptake in humans. *Am J Physiol*, 1988. 255(6 Pt 1): p. E769-74.

[85] Colberg, S.R., et al., Skeletal muscle utilization of free fatty acids in women with visceral obesity. *J Clin Invest*, 1995. 95(4): p. 1846-53.

[86] Kang, J., et al., Substrate utilization and glucose turnover during exercise of varying intensities in individuals with NIDDM. *Med Sci Sports Exerc*, 1999. 31(1): p. 82-9.

[87] De Luis, D.A., R. Aller, and O. Izaola, Resting energy expenditure and insulin resitance in obese patients, differences in women and men. *Eur Rev Med Pharmacol Sci*, 2006. 10(6): p. 285-9.

[88] Peterson, L.R., et al., Effect of obesity and insulin resistance on myocardial substrate metabolism and efficiency in young women. *Circulation*, 2004. 109(18): p. 2191-6.

[89] Martin, I.K., A. Katz, and J. Wahren, Splanchnic and muscle metabolism during exercise in NIDDM patients. *Am J Physiol*, 1995. 269(3 Pt 1): p. E583-90.

[90] Braun, B., et al., Effects of insulin resistance on substrate utilization during exercise in overweight women. *J Appl Physiol*, 2004. 97(3): p. 991-7.

[91] Colberg, S.R., et al., Utilization of glycogen but not plasma glucose is reduced in individuals with NIDDM during mild-intensity exercise. *J Appl Physiol,* 1996. 81(5): p. 2027-33.

[92] Metz, L., et al., Relationship between blood lactate concentration and substrate utilization during exercise in type 2 diabetic postmenopausal women. *Metabolism,* 2005. 54(8): p. 1102-7.

[93] Guesbeck, N.R., et al., Substrate utilization during exercise in formerly morbidly obese women. *J Appl Physiol,* 2001. 90(3): p. 1007-12.

[94] Goodpaster, B.H., et al., Skeletal muscle lipid content and insulin resistance: evidence for a paradox in endurance-trained athletes. *J Clin Endocrinol Metab,* 2001. 86(12): p. 5755-61.

[95] Blaak, E.E., et al., Impaired oxidation of plasma-derived fatty acids in type 2 diabetic subjects during moderate-intensity exercise. *Diabetes,* 2000. 49(12): p. 2102-7.

[96] Borghouts, L.B., et al., Substrate utilization in non-obese Type II diabetic patients at rest and during exercise. *Clin Sci (Lond),* 2002. 103(6): p. 559-66.

[97] Bergman, R.N., L.S. Phillips, and C. Cobelli, Physiologic evaluation of factors controlling glucose tolerance in man: measurement of insulin sensitivity and beta-cell glucose sensitivity from the response to intravenous glucose. *J Clin Invest,* 1981. 68(6): p. 1456-67.

[98] Bruce, D.G., et al., Physiological importance of deficiency in early prandial insulin secretion in non-insulin-dependent diabetes. *Diabetes,* 1988. 37(6): p. 736-44.

[99] Berk, E.S., et al., Metabolic inflexibility in substrate use is present in African-American but not Caucasian healthy, premenopausal, nondiabetic women. *J Clin Endocrinol Metab,* 2006. 91(10): p. 4099-106.

[100] .Ross, R., et al., Exercise-induced reduction in obesity and insulin resistance in women: a randomized controlled trial. *Obes Res,* 2004. 12(5): p. 789-98.

[101] .Brandenburg, S.L., et al., Effects of exercise training on oxygen uptake kinetic responses in women with type 2 diabetes. *Diabetes Care,* 1999. 22(10): p. 1640-6.

[102] .Poirier, P., et al., Impact of moderate aerobic exercise training on insulin sensitivity in type 2 diabetic men treated with oral hypoglycemic agents: is insulin sensitivity enhanced only in nonobese subjects? *Med Sci Monit,* 2002. 8(2): p. CR59-65.

[103] .Eriksson, J., et al., Aerobic endurance exercise or circuit-type resistance training for individuals with impaired glucose tolerance? *Horm Metab Res,* 1998. 30(1): p. 37-41.

[104] .Maiorana, A., et al., Combined aerobic and resistance exercise improves glycemic control and fitness in type 2 diabetes. Diabetes Res Clin Pract, 2002. 56(2): p. 115-23.

[105] .Holten, M.K., et al., Strength training increases insulin-mediated glucose uptake, GLUT4 content, and insulin signaling in skeletal muscle in patients with type 2 diabetes. *Diabetes,* 2004. 53(2): p. 294-305.

[106] .Vanninen, E., et al., Habitual physical activity, aerobic capacity and metabolic control in patients with newly-diagnosed type 2 (non-insulin-dependent) diabetes mellitus: effect of 1-year diet and exercise intervention. *Diabetologia,* 1992. 35(4): p. 340-6.

[107] .Lehmann, R., et al., Loss of abdominal fat and improvement of the cardiovascular risk profile by regular moderate exercise training in patients with NIDDM. *Diabetologia,* 1995. 38(11): p. 1313-9.

[108] .Vukovich, M.D., et al., Changes in insulin action and GLUT-4 with 6 days of inactivity in endurance runners. *J Appl Physiol,* 1996. 80(1): p. 240-4.

[109] .Kim, H.J., J.S. Lee, and C.K. Kim, Effect of exercise training on muscle glucose transporter 4 protein and intramuscular lipid content in elderly men with impaired glucose tolerance. *Eur J Appl Physiol*, 2004. 93(3): p. 353-8.

[110] Brandou, F., et al., Effects of a two-month rehabilitation program on substrate utilization during exercise in obese adolescents. *Diabetes Metab*, 2003. 29(1): p. 20-7.

[111] Brandou, F., et al., Impact of high- and low-intensity targeted exercise training on the type of substrate utilization in obese boys submitted to a hypocaloric diet. *Diabetes Metab*, 2005. 31(4 Pt 1): p. 327-35.

[112] Sartorio, A., et al., Effects of different training protocols on exercise performance during a short-term body weight reduction programme in severely obese patients. *Eat Weight Disord*, 2003. 8(1): p. 36-43.

[113] Damm, P., B. Breitowicz, and H. Hegaard, Exercise, pregnancy, and insulin sensitivity – what is new? *Appl Physiol Nutr Metab*, 2007. 32(3): p. 537-540.

[114] Fritz, T., et al., Walking for exercise--does three times per week influence risk factors in type 2 diabetes? *Diabetes Res Clin Pract*, 2006. 71(1): p. 21-7.

[115] Giannopoulou, I., et al., Exercise is required for visceral fat loss in postmenopausal women with type 2 diabetes. *J Clin Endocrinol Metab*, 2005. 90(3): p. 1511-8.

[116] Chmouliovsky, L., et al., Beneficial effect of hormone replacement therapy on weight loss in obese menopausal women. *Maturitas*, 1999. 32(3): p. 147-53.

[117] Brooks, N., et al., Strength training improves muscle quality and insulin sensitivity in Hispanic older adults with type 2 diabetes. *Int J Med Sci*, 2007. 4(1): p. 19-27.

[118] Kelley, D.E., et al., Dysfunction of mitochondria in human skeletal muscle in type 2 diabetes. *Diabetes*, 2002. 51(10): p. 2944-50.

[119] Cortright, R.N., et al., Skeletal muscle fat oxidation is increased in African-American and white women after 10 days of endurance exercise training. *Obesity (Silver Spring)*, 2006. 14(7): p. 1201-10.

[120] Bruce, C.R., et al., Endurance training in obese humans improves glucose tolerance and mitochondrial fatty acid oxidation and alters muscle lipid content. *Am J Physiol Endocrinol Metab*, 2006. 291(1): p. E99-E107.

[121] Menshikova, E.V., et al., Effects of exercise on mitochondrial content and function in aging human skeletal muscle. *J Gerontol A Biol Sci Med Sci*, 2006. 61(6): p. 534-40.

[122] Steinberg, G.R., et al., AMP-activated protein kinase is not down-regulated in human skeletal muscle of obese females. *J Clin Endocrinol Metab*, 2004. 89(9): p. 4575-80.

[123] McInnes, K.J., et al., Regulation of adenosine 5',monophosphate-activated protein kinase and lipogenesis by androgens contributes to visceral obesity in an estrogen-deficient state. *Endocrinology*, 2006. 147(12): p. 5907-13.

[124] Bluher, M., et al., Circulating adiponectin and expression of adiponectin receptors in human skeletal muscle: associations with metabolic parameters and insulin resistance and regulation by physical training. *J Clin Endocrinol Metab*, 2006. 91(6): p. 2310-6.

[125] Osman, A.A., et al., Exercise training increases ERK2 activity in skeletal muscle of obese Zucker rats. *J Appl Physiol*, 2001. 90(2): p. 454-60.

[126] McCay, C.M., M.F. Crowell, and L.A. Maynard, The effect of retarded growth upon the length of life span and upon the ultimate body size. 1935. *Nutrition*, 1989. 5(3): p. 155-71; discussion 172.

[127] Fontana, L. and S. Klein, Aging, adiposity, and calorie restriction. *Jama*, 2007. 297(9): p. 986-94.

[128] Weindruch, R. and R.L. Walford, Dietary restriction in mice beginning at 1 year of age: effect on life-span and spontaneous cancer incidence. *Science*, 1982. 215(4538): p. 1415-8.

[129] Dean, D.J., et al., Calorie restriction increases cell surface GLUT-4 in insulin-stimulated skeletal muscle. *Am J Physiol*, 1998. 275(6 Pt 1): p. E957-64.

[130] DeFronzo, R.A., Lilly lecture 1987. The triumvirate: beta-cell, muscle, liver. A collusion responsible for NIDDM. *Diabetes*, 1988. 37(6): p. 667-87.

[131] Henry, R.R., P. Wallace, and J.M. Olefsky, Effects of weight loss on mechanisms of hyperglycemia in obese non-insulin-dependent diabetes mellitus. *Diabetes*, 1986. 35(9): p. 990-8.

[132] Kelley, D.E., et al., Relative effects of calorie restriction and weight loss in noninsulin-dependent diabetes mellitus. J Clin Endocrinol Metab, 1993. 77(5): p. 1287-93.

[133] Goodpaster, B.H., et al., Effects of weight loss on regional fat distribution and insulin sensitivity in obesity. *Diabetes*, 1999. 48(4): p. 839-47.

[134] Kelley, D.E., et al., Skeletal muscle fatty acid metabolism in association with insulin resistance, obesity, and weight loss. *Am J Physiol*, 1999. 277(6 Pt 1): p. E1130-41.

[135] Heilbronn, L.K., et al., Effect of 6-month calorie restriction on biomarkers of longevity, metabolic adaptation, and oxidative stress in overweight individuals: a randomized controlled trial. *Jama*, 2006. 295(13): p. 1539-48.

[136] Harrison, D.E., J.R. Archer, and C.M. Astle, Effects of food restriction on aging: separation of food intake and adiposity. *Proc Natl Acad Sci* U S A, 1984. 81(6): p. 1835-8.

[137] Ballor, D.L., et al., PFK activity in muscle and heart tissue is differentially affected by dietary restriction. *Int J Obes Relat Metab Disord*, 1995. 19(2): p. 138-42.

[138] Kempen, K.P., et al., Skeletal muscle metabolic characteristics before and after energy restriction in human obesity: fibre type, enzymatic beta-oxidative capacity and fatty acid-binding protein content. *Eur J Clin Invest*, 1998. 28(12): p. 1030-7.

[139] Simoneau, J.A., et al., Markers of capacity to utilize fatty acids in human skeletal muscle: relation to insulin resistance and obesity and effects of weight loss. *Faseb J*, 1999. 13(14): p. 2051-60.

[140] Civitarese, A.E., et al., Calorie Restriction Increases Muscle Mitochondrial Biogenesis in Healthy Humans. *PLoS Med*, 2007. 4(3): p. e76.

[141] Nisoli, E., et al., Calorie restriction promotes mitochondrial biogenesis by inducing the expression of eNOS. *Science*, 2005. 310(5746): p. 314-7.

[142] Lopez-Lluch, G., et al., Calorie restriction induces mitochondrial biogenesis and bioenergetic efficiency. *Proc Natl Acad Sci* U S A, 2006. 103(6): p. 1768-73.

[143] Menshikova, E.V., et al., Effects of weight loss and physical activity on skeletal muscle mitochondrial function in obesity. *Am J Physiol Endocrinol Metab*, 2005. 288(4): p. E818-25.

[144] Torgerson, J.S., et al., A low serum leptin level at baseline and a large early decline in leptin predict a large 1-year weight reduction in energy-restricted obese humans. *J Clin Endocrinol Metab*, 1999. 84(11): p. 4197-203.

[145] Chan, J.L., et al., The role of falling leptin levels in the neuroendocrine and metabolic adaptation to short-term starvation in healthy men. *J Clin Invest*, 2003. 111(9): p. 1409-21.

[146] Hagstrom, E., et al., Subcutaneous adipose tissue: a source of lactate production after glucose ingestion in humans. *Am J Physiol*, 1990. 258(5 Pt 1): p. E888-93.

[147] Lambert, K., et al., Effect of food restriction on lactate sarcolemmal transport. *Metabolism*, 2003. 52(3): p. 322-7.

[148] Py, G., et al., Role of hypoxia-induced anorexia and right ventricular hypertrophy on lactate transport and MCT expression in rat muscle. *Metabolism*, 2005. 54(5): p. 634-44.

[149] Toomey, S., J. McMonagle, and H.M. Roche, Conjugated linoleic acid: a functional nutrient in the different pathophysiological components of the metabolic syndrome? *Curr Opin Clin Nutr Metab Care*, 2006. 9(6): p. 740-7.

[150] Steck, S.E., et al., Conjugated linoleic acid supplementation for twelve weeks increases lean body mass in obese humans. *J Nutr*, 2007. 137(5): p. 1188-93.

[151] Watras, A.C., et al., The role of conjugated linoleic acid in reducing body fat and preventing holiday weight gain. *Int J Obes (Lond)*, 2007. 31(3): p. 481-7.

[152] Gaullier, J.M., et al., Supplementation with conjugated linoleic acid for 24 months is well tolerated by and reduces body fat mass in healthy, overweight humans. *J Nutr*, 2005. 135(4): p. 778-84.

[153] Howitz, K.T., et al., Small molecule activators of sirtuins extend Saccharomyces cerevisiae lifespan. *Nature*, 2003. 425(6954): p. 191-6.

[154] Baur, J.A., et al., Resveratrol improves health and survival of mice on a high-calorie diet. *Nature*, 2006. 444(7117): p. 337-42.

[155] Lagouge, M., et al., Resveratrol improves mitochondrial function and protects against metabolic disease by activating SIRT1 and PGC-1alpha. *Cell*, 2006. 127(6): p. 1109-22.

[156] Check, E., A votre sante: now in pill form? *Nature*, 2006. 444(7115): p. 11.

Reviewed by Professor Denis Joanisse, Centre de recherche de l'université de Laval, Division Kinesiologie, Université Laval, 0223 PEPS, St- Foy Québec.

In: Progress in Exercise and Women's Health Research   ISBN 1-60456-014-5
Editor: Janet P. Coulter, pp. 107-137   © 2008 Nova Science Publishers, Inc.

Chapter 3

THE BENEFITS OF EXERCISE AND SPORT ON THE PSYCHOLOGICAL AND PERSONAL HEALTH OF WOMEN

Miltiadis Proios

Department of Physical Education & Sport Science,
Aristotle University of Thessaloniki, Hellas

ABSTRACT

The usefulness of exercise/sport for the humans has been acknowledged ever since antiquity. The present paper constitutes a literature review aiming at the determination of the benefits for the women from their participation in physical activities, which can play a decisive role to the shaping of their personality (social and psychological development) as well as to contribute to the exhibition of health behaviors. These health behaviors, as it has been supported, are the result of the development of the physical, psychological/emotional and intellectual/mental health, as well as of the socialization of women. More specifically, in the framework of socialization, it has been supported that health behaviors constitute the outcome of social, cognitive and moral development. Eventually, exercise and sport seem to form an environment which contributes to the development of health behaviors, yet this environment would be even more effective under more appropriate conditions.

INTRODUCTION

Exercise and sport constitute human activities which a great number of people perform on a daily basis; the reason being the fact that participation in physical activities contributes to the improvement of the participants' health (Blair & Connelly, 1996). The merit from the participation of women in these activities is undeniable (Giuliano, Popp, & Knight, 2000), with the opportunities for sport participation having significantly increased in the last two decades for both young girls and women (Weiss & Barber, 1995).

The perception that physical exercise contributes to the maintenance of health in humans is something that has been formulated ever since antiquity, while the scientific confirmation of this view has been established throughout the previous century. However, the ancient Greek dictum "a healthy mind in a healthy body" reveals that as early as that period it was clear that exercise, apart from the maintenance of physical health, contributes to the mental euphoria as well. This proclaims that the mental condition of the humans is far from unrelated to their physical condition, while a healthy mind finds its shelter in a healthy body.

The participation of women in games and sport is reported to exist ever since antiquity, for instance in the Ancient Greek and Egyptian society. In the latter, the women held a rather admirable position; Nile River was a place where the Egyptian women could swim and fish. On the frescos gracing the Egyptian palaces, there are scenes representing females dancing and performing acrobatic exercises. Similar activities performed the women in ancient Greece as well (e.g. in Mycenae and Crete). In Sparta, women participated also in games, contrary to Athens where this form of education was not provided for women, something that urged some ancient philosophers, such as Xenophon and Plato, to write about the need of the females to exercise.

By a diachronic study of the prevailing views concerning women in sport it is evident that the latter were differentiated depending on how each society wanted women to be. Lutter (1994) stated that the prevailing view concerning woman in sport is the one that represents a popular person but at the same time an inappropriate mother. Miller and Levy (1996) concluded that "Sports participation by females routinely carries a negative stigma" (p. 112). Even traditional perceptions concerning sport seem to be incompatible with the women's traditional roles (e.g., Bunker, 1996; Miller & Levy, 1996). All these probably have been reasons for the limited participation of females in sport, compared to men, at least until mid 20th century.

Today, however, the social changes that took place as well as the current more liberal notions concerning the role of women in society have contributed to the increase of the females' and women's participation in sport (Acosta & Carpenter, 2004; Finkenberg & Moode, 1996; Marsh, 1993; Suitor & Reavis, 1995; Weiss & Barber, 1995). This increase seems to be even more intense during the last four decades (Baum, 1998). Nevertheless, Daniels, Sincharoen and Leaper (2005) claim that, despite the ever increasing participation of women in sport, this has not led to any substantial differentiation of the social attitudes, such as sport being equally applicable to both men and women. The stance supporting that the increased interest and participation in sport represent only surface social changes, as no deep ideological change has actually occurred also moves to this direction (Kane & Greendorfer, 1994). The claim that social attitudes concerning the participation of women in sport have not dramatically changed is further supported by the fact that, although the rates of participation in sport and exercise of girls, at least today, during their childhood seem to be similar to those of boys, however in adolescence they decrease and continue doing so throughout their life time (Hovell et al., 1999; United States Department of Health and Human Services, 2000).

MOTIVES FOR PARTICIPATION

In exercise and sport several activities (e.g., motor, mental) are developed. Participation in such activities imposes some form of motivation in order an individual to accept to perform them. In sport social psychology, motivation has been examined in context of achievement such as sport and several other physical activities (e.g., physical education, recreation). The first theories have interpreted motivation as the expression of human instincts and needs. More contemporary theories adopt the cognitive approach, which interprets motivation on the basis of cognitive procedures of humans, such as their thoughts, perceptions or goals. Motivation can be considered as a set of motives that lead the individual to participate in exercise and sport.

The efforts made in order to satisfy the motives play a significant role in humans' life. Humans based on motives set goals, make plans, envision the future, struggle, fight for their personal progress and improvement. At the same time, motives also dictate the individuals' social behavior, meaning that humans along with their personal prosperity aim at the general advancement of society as well. Birch and Veroff (1966) have supported that motives are factors that contribute to the exhibition of such behaviors by people that are necessary for the achievement goal.

The motives that make youths participate in sport have been classified in three categories (Weiss & Williams, 2004, p. 224): "(a) to develop or demonstrate physical competence or adequacy (e.g., learn and improve skills, be physically fit, get stronger, achieve goals), (b) to attain social acceptance and approval (e.g., make friends, feel part of a group, receive coach/parent approval), and (c) to enjoy experiences related to sport involvement (i.e., have fun, feel excited)". However, because of the different social messages sent by sport, girls contrary to boys are considered to participate in sport under different motives/ goals (Daniels, Sincharoen, & Leaper, 2005). For instance, studies have maintained that females consider stronger motives for sport participation the body-related (appearance) and social factors (social acceptance and approval), while the competition and competence (physical competence/adequacy) motives are more valued by males (e.g., Flood & Hellstedt, 1991; Gill et al., 1996; Koivula, 1999).

BENEFITS FROM THE PARTICIPATION

It has previously been stated that specific motives actually motivate the individuals to participate in exercise and sport. Of course, these activities are expected to provide certain benefits to the participants, since this is their ultimate goal. Indeed, studies have revealed that exercise and sport have a positive effect on the individuals' physical, psychological/emotional, social and mental health (e.g., Daniels et al., 2005; Danish & Nellen, 1997; Kellinske, Mayer, & Chen, 2001; NRCIM, 2002; Siegenthaler & Gonzalez, 1997).

Many sport psychologists consider the above mentioned results of exercise able to play a decisive role in the shaping of the individuals' personality (social and psychological development) (see Rees, 2001; Shields & Bredemeier, 1995, 2001; Weiss & Smith, 2002). The term "personality" is used with many meanings in the different scientific fields (e.g., in psychology), however the meaning that could be best apprehended is the one that refers to the dynamic organization of physical, mental, moral and social qualities of the individual, demonstrated in his/her social life (Papadopoulos, 1994). The word "personality" was considered as having a similar meaning to the word "character" and thus they are used interchangeably (Shields & Bredemeier, 1995). According to Fromm (1947) and Allport (1961), the world character reflects those traits or qualities which are culturally valued and, more specifically, which reflect ethical or morally appropriate orientations and behavior.

Personality is considered to consist of two structures that "(a) are products of social development; and (b) they regulate social (and moral) conduct. These structures promote responsiveness or sensitivity to the social expectations of peers and the greater social community, and foster the ability to interpret one's social experiences in terms of a religious, philosophical, or political theory." (Hogan & Emler, 1995, p. 224). In the present study, my intention is to examine the two above mentioned structures of females' and women's personalities in comparison to the performance of activities (physical and competitive). More specifically, the aim of the present paper is to examine the contribution of the benefits from exercise and sport in the psychological and personal health (i.e., the development of an appropriate personality exhibiting health behaviors) in both females and women. Additionally, I would like to clarify that the term "health" in the present study is not attributed only with the narrow meaning of this word (namely, referring to some physical or psychological disease), but it has a rather broad meaning. According to the World Health Organization (1946) "Health is a state of complete physical, mental, and social well-being and is not merely the absence of disease and infirmity."

PHYSICAL HEALTH

Exercise and sport are activities in which every individual has the opportunity to participate. This is the reason why the traditional stigmas and limitations to the female sport participation have changed, since sport is now considered as a context where both boys and girls can equally participate (Le Unes & Nation, 1993). Thus, participation in the respective activities enables the woman to discover her natural abilities providing her this way with the potential to claim and realize her ambitions. Sport participation has been found to promote positive self-concepts in female athletes such as physical appearance, athletic competence etc. (e.g., Marsh & Peart, 1988; Sage & Loudermilk, 1979). Desertain and Weiss (1988) and Jackson and Marsh (1986) suggest that female athletes are more masculine than female non-athletes, something that reveals that such self-concepts lead females to aspire and assert the performance of masculine activities (professions). Whitley (1983) suggested that female athletes may use positive self-concepts related to athletic participation to discount gender role conflict.

Indeed, sport – as it has been supported – is a context which promotes physical development (NFHS, 2002), and seems to offer the girls even more benefits than the boys in the context of health/ fitness (Kelinske, Mayer, & Chen, 2001). More specifically, researchers have shown that women acquire physical benefits from a strength training program (Ebben & Jensen, 1998; Fleck, 1998; Freedson, 2000). Harne and Bixby (2005) reported that the physiological benefits for women from a strength program include increase of muscular strength, lean of body mass and decrease of body fat rate. This result further supports the women's perception concerning their ability to perform traditional male jobs (i.e., jobs that demand much muscular strength). This perception of self-efficacy on part of females increases their convictions that they are able to behave towards the achievement of the goals they have set. Perceived self-efficacy has been found to be a major instigating force in forming intentions to exercise and in maintaining the practice for an extended period of time (e.g., Feltz & Riessinger, 1990; McAley, 1992, 1993; Weinberg, Grove, & Jackson, 1992).

Significant are also the benefits from the exercise in health issues concerning the exhibition of health behaviors. Individuals who exhibit high levels of physical activity have less chance to develop diseases, while they are more likely to show decrease of the negative implications of chronic diseases (e.g., Blair et al., 1984; Blair et al., 1989; Lee, 1994; Manson et al., 1991; Salonen et al., 1982). These results of exercise may well be due to the positive effect of physical activities on cardio-pulmonary and circulatory systems, and suppression of several pathogenic risks (Health Kanada, 2003; Viru & Smirnova, 1995). Thus, the effects of the physical activities can be considered as positively contributing to the general well-being of women. The women who participate in physical activities exhibit a more positive attitude towards life, a better perception of their role, they are characterized by an intense empathy towards family and friends, they feel more healthy and better, while they anticipate more effectively any difficult situation that may occur (Kull, 2002).

PSYCHOLOGICAL/ EMOTIONAL HEALTH

The psychological and emotional health helps the better composition of an individual's personality, having as a result the exhibition of health behaviors by the latter. Many researchers have supported the contribution of sport and physical activities in the development of psychological (e.g., Health Kanada, 2003; NFHS, 2002; Paffenberger, Hyde, Wing, & Hsieh, 1986) and emotional health (e.g., Danish & Nellen, 1997; Health Kanada, 2003; NFHS, 2002; Svoboda, 1995). The main characteristic of the individuals experiencing a healthy psychological and emotional condition is the high levels of satisfaction they feel for life (Gilman, 2001), something that helps the creation of a good life (Park, 2004). When a person feels satisfied from his/ her life then it can also be useful for society by creating a good family, by good performance to his/ her work, and by having good relations with others.

More specifically, as far as women are concerned, research has indicated that the benefit from exercise on part of their psychological state is rater significant (Ebben & Jensen, 1998; Fleck, 1998; Freedson, 2000). For instance, a psychological trait of the women which improves greatly with exercise in general is self-esteem (e.g., Hayes, Crocker, & Kowalski, 1999; Taylor, 1995; Young & Bursik, 2000). This means that the women who participate in exercise/ sport acquire self-perception, they respect their own self for what they are and in addition they have the feeling that they are rather good (Rosenberg, 1965, 1986). Carron, Hausenblas and Estabrooks (2003) reported that self-esteem is a global, self-evaluative personality disposition that reflects the degree to which an individual feels positive about the self. Papanas (2004) reported that individuals with high self-esteem are productive, creative, imaginative, receptive to challenges, optimistic, have a leading personality, consider themselves worthy to be loved, good listeners, acknowledge the other people's worth, are interested in others, know their limits and anticipate future with optimism and enthusiasm.

Apart from the development of self-esteem, the experiences from the participation in exercise and sport contribute to the development of another psychological trait as well, which in its turn contributes to the development of personal competence, self-confidence (Feltz, Landers, & Raider, 1979). The individual in general, and the females in particular, characterized by high self-confidence confides in herself concerning the successful outcome of her actions in several situations. Bandura (1977, 1986) has reported that an individual's self-confidence that he/ she can organize and implement an action plan for the achievement of certain goals is related to a specific intrapersonal skill, self-efficacy. The term "self-efficacy" has been alternatively used by many researchers (Byrne, 1996; Novick, Cauce, & Grove, 1996) to replace the term "self", and it stresses the mutual relationship among environmental, behavioral and personal factors (Bandura, 1977).

The individuals participating in physical activities come in contact and converse with other individuals from their environment. This has as a result the shaping of the individual's self, i.e. the organization of notions that are accepted by each individual's conscience (Rogers, 1951). The organization of these perceptions results in the individual's adoption, mainly, of ways of behavior harmonized with the image of his/her self (Rogers, 1951). Many researchers have maintained that self-concept is directly related to the performance at school, the professional choices and ambitions, as well as with aspects of behavior that are considered significant for the creation of satisfactory interpersonal relations and the individuals' heartsease (e.g., Markus & Nurius, 1987; Wigfield & Karpathian, 1991). Thus, it can be considered that the love and acceptance of the self developed in the females who participate in exercise and sport can contribute to their psychological balance and their ability to accept others and create satisfactory interpersonal relations.

According to Kalliopuska (1992), empathy is another psychological trait which seems to develop with physical activity in both girls and boys, despite the opposite views on the function of competition (Bredemeier & Shields, 2006). However, studies have found females to be more emotionally expressive and more empathetic to the emotional states of others than males (e.g., Eagly & Wood, 1991; Kalliopuska, 1987; Riggio, Tucker, & Coffaro, 1989). However, despite the reports concerning the competition tendencies to repel experiences and expressions of empathy, Bredemeier and Shields (2006) have maintained that sport produces emotional experiences and provides opportunities for developing empathic skills. Individuals exhibiting a developed feeling of empathy try to compete the statements, behaviors or feelings of others and actually from the point of view – for instance under the conditions – experience these "others". Eisenberg and Strayer (1987) supported that empathy is currently perceived as the sharing of feelings with the others. While, Hoffman (1987) claimed that empathy suggests the perception of other's problems as an injustice, the taking of all responsibility towards the others and the obligation to restore dignity.

INTELLECTUAL/ MENTAL HEALTH

Exercise and sport activate different cognitive procedures (e.g., teaching, learning) when performed. For this reason, physical activities and sport can play a significant role in the encouragement of cognitive development in youths (both males and females) (Mize, 1991; Stevens, 1994). Marcia and Fridman (1970) and Prager (1983) found that women in the various identity statuses resemble their male counterparts in cognitive and personality characteristics. Indeed, research has shown a positive relationship between physical activity and academic performance (California Department of Education, 2002; Dwyer et al., 2001). More specifically as far as women are concerned, research indicated that female student athletes had the highest graduation rates, exceeding those of the general student body and of the female student body (Eitzen & Sage, 1997). The participation in high school sport was found to be positively related to the school grades, the educational aspirations during and after high school courses, and college attendance (e.g., Eccles & Barber, 1999; Whitley, 1999).

Contrary to the above mentioned is the finding that the men's basketball players gradually detached from academic goals and ideals (Adler & Adler, 1985). In the same, above mentioned research, conducted by Eitzen and Sage (1997), it was found that the lowest graduation rates occurred for men in highly commercialized sport, such as football and basketball. The professionalization of sport in the school framework seems actually to turn the participants away from health behaviors such as the improvement of their cognitive level and consequently their performance at school. A recent study confirms the view that the commercialization of college sport disorientates the participants from their academic commitment (Reimer, Beal, & Schroeder, 2000). As far as the women's college sports is concerned, it is supported that it is being more and more commercialized and that the participants anticipate similar issues to those anticipated by men (Eitzen & Sage, 1997).

Apart from the effect of exercise and sport on the intellectual health of youths, it seems that it has also a significant impact on their mental health as well. Research has shown that physical activity can be beneficial to mental health (Camacho et al., 1991; Paluska & Schwenk, 2000; Ross & Hayes, 1988; Stephens, 1988). According to Fox (1999), physical activity activates and produces a more positive mood. Boutchr (2000) and Etnier et al. (1997) suggested that physical activity affects cognitive functions (reaction time, memory, and fluid intelligence) in older people. The improvement of mental health can be attributed to the development of self-esteem in the contexts of physical activity and sport, as it has been previously supported. Sonstroem and Potts (1996) showed that physical self-worth is related to the emotional adjustment and socially desirable responding, to have mental well-being properties in its own right.

As concerning the affect of physical activity on the women's mental health, research has confirmed this result in this group. Stephens (1988) showed that physical activity is positively related with good mental health (positive mood, general well-being) in women. Another study has shown that the limited participation in physical activities can constitute a factor that leads to depressive symptoms (Farmer et al., 1988). A recent study confirms the above mentioned claim. More specifically, Kull (2002) having sampled women aged 18-45 years found that the low levels of physical activity are associated to poor mental health and depressiveness.

SOCIALIZATION

Humans as beings of developed intellect interrelate with others, lives in groups (social groups) seeking this way a healthy life. Human beings are relational by nature. No individual can achieve completion as a human being (e.g., the Aristotelian $ευδαιμονία$ = bliss) on its own and without the contribution of the other humans. In sport, the presence of others – teammates, opponents, officials (e.g., agents, referees, and coaches) – is compulsory in order sport to exist. Competition cannot exist in absence of opponents. The need for humans to coexist can also be attributed to the fact that they by nature have feelings that motivate them to coexist with other humans. Indeed, feelings can constitute the source of compassion relations with others (Proios, 2007). All these maintain that human beings have in some way to learn to live together (Nucci & Young-Shim, 2005).

Learning to live together for humans is an issue, mainly, of developing certain psychological skills. Such skills are those of social learning and social and cognitive development (Greendorfer, 2002). These skills form the term "socialization". More specifically, the term "socialization" refers to the lifelong social experiences by which individuals develop their human potential and learn culture. According to the socialization theory, the individual is considered as a passive subject (Vanreusel et al., 1997). On the contrary, McPherson (1986) suggested that socialization should be viewed as an interactive rather than a passive process.

Greendorfer (2002) reports that "the broad process of socialization has been examined systematically by three disciplines: psychology, sociology and anthropology." (p. 379). In the present study, main interest focuses on the procedure of socialization which has psychological traits. The most popular psychological approaches of socialization have been supported to be those of the psychoanalytic approach, namely by means of learning based on life experiences and the cognitive approach which focuses on the development of cognitive structures (Greendorfer, 2002).

The participation of humans in physical activities and sport is considered an effective means for the former to learn to live together, namely their socialization, (Bloom & Smith, 1996). Sport has been suggested to be an effective means for the development of the positive values of life (socialization) in youths, since it constitutes an environment extremely sentimental and interactive, providing opportunities for the demonstration of the individuals' personal and social traits (Hellison, 1995; Gough, 1997). The applicability of sport to the socialization of youths is also supported, as many of the social and moral requirements for participation in sports are parallels to how individuals must function in a law-abiding society (Seefeldt & Ewing, 1996). However, Coakley (1986) supported that the situations experienced by children in the context of sport can not be fully exploited by them, since they are not yet able to apprehend their roles in relation to the others. This is achieved from eight to ten years of age, when children develop the skills necessary for role-taking which allows them to perceive another person's point of view (Selman, 1971, 1976).

As far as gender differences in sport socialization are concerned, the researchers' views are contradictory (Greendorfer, 2002). Thus, it is considered that the benefits for socialization through participation in physical activities are to be almost similar for both females-girls and men-boys. More specifically, it has been supported that participation in physical activities affects the social, cognitive and moral development, as well as the acquisition of cultural values by children (Greendorfer, 2002). So, the impact of exercise/sport contributes to the acquisition of the psychosocial benefits that affect the social and cognitive components of the behavior exhibited by both women and men (e.g., Brustad, 1992; Trew, Kremer, Gallagher, Scully, & Ogle, 1997). Below, an effort is made to present these psychosocial benefits associated with children's behavior.

Social Development

Exercise and sport is a context where social skills such as cooperation, assertion, responsibility and commitment can be developed (Cote, 2002; Kleiber & Roberts, 1981; Scanlan et al., 1993; Shogan, 1999; Telama, 1999; Weiss & Smith, 2002). Wankel and Berger (1990) claimed that the crucial point of sport is that the youths have the opportunities to create positive relations within groups, achieve completion in the community they live, social status and social mobility.

Cooperation for Rawls (2001) includes the meaning of fair terms of cooperation's, which shape the perception of mutuality or reciprocity. Rawls, in addition, assumed that cooperation includes the "idea of the rational advantage or each participant's advantage", referring particularly to what the cooperators seek to obtain from their own point of view. Finally, Rawls claimed that every individual complies with the rules of cooperation accepted in public; the specific allocation that derives from this is accepted as fair, no matter what this allocation actually is.

The ability of children to cooperate with each other enables them to develop and perform their own moral power (Rawls, 2001). This is possible because the individuals – during their course of development – form, review and follow in a rational way their own notions on what is the right thing to do under each situation. The developmental process of children, according to the cognitive-developmental theory, is an interactive process and it is manifested in a different way in each context (rules, lies and justice) (Piaget, 1932/1965).

Responsibility, as it has been mentioned above, constitutes another social skill. The term "responsibility" reveals that someone has a developed sense of personal prosperity and of the others' prosperity as well. Individuals with a developed sense of responsibility feel the obligation to keep a promise or behave squarely in their transactions with others (Lickona, 1991).

An aforementioned social skill that improves with exercise/sport participation and contributes to the social development of children is the skill of commitment. The ability to be committed is one of the characteristic traits a leader (Murray & Mann, 2001). Additionally, one's ability to be committed can reveal his/her moral identity. Hart, Atkins and Ford (1998) determined this moral identity as "one's commitment to one's idea of oneself in association with the action they promote or their protection of the prosperity of others" (p. 515). In sport, for instance, the commitment to sport participation reveals one of the dimensions of sportspersonship (Shields & Bredemeier, 1995; Vallerand et al., 1996).

Sport is a context whose function is based on rules. Thus, commitments resulting from full sport participation, such as compliance with the rules, significantly contribute to the socialization of the participants in sport through the development of social skill commitment. For instance, the commitment for compliance with the rules of the game helps to avoid deceptive behaviors. The violation of this kind of commitment or promise by the athletes is a form of lie. This form of lie can not be justified in the greater social context (Bok, 1978). Bok, also supported that reliance and integrity constitute a wealth that should not be thriftlessly wasted as it is hard to obtain; the reason being that through lying no one can structure the traits of reliance and integrity, which are necessary for the individual's prosperity in society.

Commitment to full sport participation, however, does not include only the silent promise for compliance with the rules. Sport is a context where a great number of people participate; consequently, there is interaction among them. Thus, commitments deriving from the interaction among individuals contribute to the assimilation of information, accommodation to new ideas and building conceptual networks' and schemas' (general knowledge schemas). Schema theorists (e.g., Derry, 1996; Rumelhart, 1980; Taylor & Crocker, 1981) support that general knowledge contributes to the better memorization of new information (e.g. stories). Schemas are formed as people notice similarities and recurrences among experiences (Narvaez, 2002).

Research also indicated that exercise and sport participation foster citizenship, social success, positive peer relationship, and leadership skills (e.g., Manjone, 1998; Elley & Kirk, 2002; Wright & Cote, 2003). These results can be considered as contributing to a health behavior on part of the participants. Indeed, it has been supported that the development of positive peer relationships influences health behavior (Brown, Dolcini, & Leventhal, 1977). This is due to the fact that relationships with peers can have a significant impact on their psychosocial development (Brustad, Babkes, & Smith, 2001). The relationships among peers are relationships among equals, while the relations among adult athletes exhibit a disproportion of potency.

A significant result of peer relationship has been supported to be the development of friendship among them (Brustad, Babkes, & Smith, 2001; Bukowski & Hoza, 1989; Weinberg & Gould, 2003). According to Aristotle, friendship can be characterized as the wish to please others, something that has to do with what is right and desirable (Proios, 2007). For Aristotle, friendship is also a moral phenomenon in every aspect of personal or social life of the humans. Friendship (sport friendship) is reported to allow youths perceive themselves in relation to the others, while at the same time it enables them to develop intimacy and validation (Sullivan, 1953). A study has examined the content of the constituents of friendship developed in the context of sport, comprising 38 sport participants aged from 8 to 16 years (Weiss, Smith, & Theeboom, 1996). Thus, on the basis of the results of this study, the contribution of friendship to the health behavior of the youths can be attributed to the development of companionship by spending time with each other, the pleasure from playing a game with people who know and accept each other, the increase of self-esteem which is the consequence of the support offered to each other, as well as helping and guiding each other. In addition, health behavior can be also explained since friendship contributes to the exhibition of positive prosocial behaviors (for example compliance with the social conventions), it develops an intimacy among individuals by developing mutual feelings and personal affiliations, it develops the virtue of faith, a commitment to one another and, moreover, since conflicts – i.e. renitence – among friends are avoided.

Another peer relationship suggested is that of peer acceptance (Greendorfer, 2002). Peer acceptance pertains to one's experience of status within or liking by the peer group (Bukowski & Hoza, 1989). The peer acceptance shapes perceptions of authority and views toward competition and compromise, also believed that it could affect views toward competition and cooperation, personal attitudes, and other psychological, social, and emotional outcomes (Sullivan, 1953). Weinberg and Gould (2003) suggested that girls are more efficient than boys in determining emotional support as a positive feature of friendship in sport. Moreover, peer acceptance as well as social status might have an effect on perceptions of competence or enjoyment of sport (Coie, Dodge, & Kupersmidt, 1991; Evans & Roberts, 1987; Weiss & Duncan, 1992).

Eventually, it can be considered that indeed peer relationships contribute to the exhibition of health behaviors on part of children. This is believed to be the result of the development of the cognitive skill (e.g., self-perceptions), and learning of social factors that affect social functions (e.g., through positive peer relationships, friendship formation).

As far as the social skill of citizenship is concerned, the term is considered as anything but a simple or unproblematic one (Coalter, 1998). The term "citizenship" includes the social obligations and duties (Roche, 1992) as well as social control (Coalter, 1998). Thus, sport by developing the citizenship skill contributes to the development of individuals who will fulfill their social obligations and duties that they have undertaken within the society they live, while at the same time they will accept the social control of their actions. Yet, it should be stressed that social commitments often are contrary to the moral ones (Harrison, 1973). This is because while society usually demands decreased limitations of personal liberties, the moral function of society demands the constitution of such limitations.

As concerning citizenship, studies have investigated the issue of volunteerism. More specifically, they have examined the differences between genders. The results of these studies, however, have not showed clearly whether volunteerism is more or less developed in girls of boys (e.g., Davis Smith, 1998; Keith et al., 1990; Pancer & Sundeen, 1994; Rasskoff & Sundeen, 1994).

Cognitive Development

The development of the cognitive skill by participating to motor activities is an issue that has occupied many researchers. Etnier et al. (1997) claimed that exercising the body is beneficial to the function of the mind. Etnier et al. (1997) and Thomas et al (1994) showed that exercise had a modest positive relationship with the improved cognitive skill. More specifically, it was supported that chronic exercise, in comparison with acute exercise, showed greater effects on cognitive performance (Etnier et al., 1997).

Exercise and sport are activities in which several types of games are applied. This plurality of games provides different learning opportunities and teaches different kinds of cognitive skills to both girls and boys (e.g., Etaugh & Liss, 1992; Piaget, 1965). More specifically, participation in physical activities contributes to the development of several types of values and attitudes (Berlage, 1982; Coakley, 1998; O'Hanlon, 1980; Sage, 1988, 1998). Webb (1969) indicated that value orientations change with the increase of sport experience. More specifically, in "play orientation" there is an hierarchy of the values of fairness, skill, and success/winning, which change through professional orientation and the success/winning value becomes more significant that fairness. However, this orientation seems to be more intense in boys than in girls, with the latter being socialized into expressive roles (Johnson, 1963; Sage, 1980; Webb, 1969; Zoble, 1972).

According to Kane (1982) females are encouraged to be less competitive and less motivated to win in sports and to be more concerned with the personal, self-expressive rewards of performance. However, the same author in one of his studies indicated that gender-role orientation has a significant influence on professionalization of attitude toward play (Kane, 1982). In addition, Kane (1982) reported that "Women who perceived themselves as having a masculine orientation were more likely to endorse a 'male' or professional attitude toward play. In contrast, only a small number of the women with a feminine orientation were 'professionalized in their attitudes toward play (p. 293). While, Lever (1976) argued that girls learn values which did not prepare them for adult participation in occupational, political, and social life.

It has been supported above that in the context of exercise/sport health behaviors can be developed. Prosocial behaviors can be considered as health behaviors as well. Prosocial behavior – as it is supported – is the behavior which aims to the benefit of others (Papadopoulou & Markoulis, 1999). Cooper (1982) maintained that sport contributes to the development of prosocial behavior because the affinities developed within a team can discourage the exhibition of egoistic (selfish) behaviors while it provides opportunities to exhibit altruistic (unselfish) behaviors. An individual characterized by altruism is interested in the advantage of the others without taking into consideration his/her own advantage. Kleiber and Roberts (1981) showed that the sport experience had a negative effect on prosocial behavior. More specifically, they indicated that boys, contrary to the girls, demonstrated significantly less altruistic behavior. This result confirms the claim that participation in sport can not guarantee the learning of altruistic behaviors (McKenney & Dattilo, 2001).

Other behaviors considered as pro-social is cooperation, empathy, helping behavior and benevolence. As far as cooperation is concerned, research has showed that sport provides the appropriate context for teaching cooperation (Cote, 2002; Kleiber & Roberts, 1981; Orlick, 1981). While the results of other studies indicated that sport provides opportunities for the creation of positive relations among individuals within teams (Wankel & Berger, 1990), it also helps an individual to cooperate with another aiming at the achievement of similar goals (Mannell & Kleiber, 1997), it enables an individual cooperate with another to anticipate issues of justice that arise in the framework of their participation in a team (Kohlberg, 1981), while it also contributes to the decrease of conflict behaviors (Sharpe, Brown, & Crider, 1995). These results support the above mentioned claim that sport is a context which contributes to the development of health behaviors. The benefit from the development of cooperation is that the individuals become obliging and at the same time they acquire the skill to cooperate with others for the achievement of a goal that will benefit all the cooperating parties.

An aforementioned prosocial behavior was empathy, i.e. the interest and participation in the pain or sorrow of the others. Cote (2002), based on the results of the same study mentioned above, supported that sport indeed constitutes a context for the development of social skills such as empathy. Individuals with a developed sense of empathy are considered to share their feelings with others (Eisenberg & Strayer, 1987), acknowledge the others' problems as an injustice, and undertake responsibility towards others (empathy as a moral feeling) as well as the obligation to restore dignity (Hoffman, 1987). According to Eagly and Crowley (1986) many psychologists have argued that females (and girls) are generally more empathic or sympathetic than men (and boys).

In addition, two virtues considered as prosocial behaviors are helping behavior, i.e. the sympathy or help provided to a specific object or goal, and benevolence. However, both these behaviors have not been researched in the context of physical activities, despite the fact that there are many empirical data. As far as helping behavior is concerned, a meta-analytic review on gender and helping behaviors, found that overall, males were more likely than females to help others (Eagly & Crowley, 1986). According to the social-role theory, the female gender role promotes the norm of nurturant and caring helping. While, as far as benevolence is concerned, it is considered as someone's reaction accompanied by some personal cost for the individual itself (Proios, 2007). Benevolence has mainly to do with the others and not with one's self. In addition, the term "benevolence" assumes that someone does not harm another individual, but rather inhibits harm, restores a harm made and makes what is good. For instance, benevolence can be considered the lending of sport equipment from one athlete to another or from one team to another. The study of benevolence in the framework of competitive sport by Lumpkin, Stoll and Beller (2003) was considered as a huge moral stride.

The development of the character is also considered as an additional result of the cognitive development of children, in the context of exercise and sport. The impact of sport on youths has puzzled the researchers enough because eventually conventional knowledge claims that "sport builds up character" (Fejging, 1994; Miracle & Rees, 1994). Shields and Bredemeier (2001) supported that competitive sport, indeed, is a context where the development of the virtues can be achieved. Lipsyte (1999) and Rees (2000) claimed that sport can contribute to the prevention of violence observed in everyday activities. However, the results of the research appear to be mixed. While some studies (Beller, Stoll, & Rudd, 1997; Rudd & Stoll, 2004) have found that participation in sport builds social character (e.g., teamwork, loyalty, self-sacrifice), there is little evidence that sport builds moral character (e.g., honesty, fairness, and responsibility) in athletes (Bredemeier & Shields, 1985; Hodge, 1989; Rudd, Stoll, & Beller, 1997).

In addition, as concerning whether sport affect character, Kniker (1974) claimed that sport does not build but actually reveals a character. Here, the argument is that sport activity reveals the athlete's character without contributing to it (Edwards, 1973; Ogilvie & Tutko, 1971; Sheehan & Alsop, 1972). However, according to Shields and Bredemeier (1995), this assumption is inadequate since it fails to acknowledge that every demonstration of character contributes to it. However, is has been supported that although sport does not build character, the latter can be taught and learned in a sports setting (Bredemeier & Shields, 2006). Physical activity has been supported to have similar results to those of sport (Hellison, 2003). When more specific measures are taken, the consequences of an action provide feedback to the performer and observers of the action. The feedback then updates any future action. Eventually, it is apprehended that the positive character building is not automatically achieved by participating in sport (Gerdy, 2000; Hellison, 2003).

Finally, the participation of youths in sport – as it has been reported – does not guarantee by itself the expected positive psychological results for the children (Shields & Bredemeier, 1995). In addition, Weinberg and Gould (2003) claimed that "Character is not caught but taught in sport, exercise and physical activity settings" (p. 533). However, these views have not been experimentally confirmed. This is because although a limited number of studies have been conducted in the context of physical education, their results can not be generalized in sport (Shields & Bredemeier, 2001).

Moral Development

In the framework of the socialization of both girls and boys, by participating in physical activities, it has been supported that their moral development is affected. Moral development is considered significant as it provides information on what is right and what is wrong. Moral development is the change of reasoning associated with the cognitive structure of an individual. According to the cognitive-developmental theory the changes of reasoning (moral development) take place through a series of six qualitatively different stages (Kohlberg, 1969).

The six stages of moral development cover all ages from preschool to maturity (Kohlberg, 1969). The theory of this model mainly focused on the changes of moral reasoning in relation to age. Although a great number of researches support Kohlberg's viewpoints on the development process of moral reasoning, yet they have been strongly doubted. Some critics have argued that Kohlberg's approach does not adequately represent the moral reasoning of females (Baumrind, 1986; Gilligan, 1982). Gilligan supported that the moral reasoning of the females tends to reflect a care orientation, while males usually adopt justice in order to approach moral dilemmas. The above mentioned differentiation concerning moral orientation in relation to gender (care orientation, justice orientation), has been supported to be clear (Gilligan, 1979) and that care and justice suggest different ways of judgment, the motives of which have different consequences (Power et al., 1989; Power & Makogon, 1995). In addition, as far as gender differences are concerned, Gilligan (1982) suggested that these can be traced to specific childhood experiences, the development of the self-identity and the socialization in different types of play in childhood.

Walker (1989), based on Gilligan's arguments and Kohlberg's descriptions, suggests that it seems reasonable to be gender differences in moral reasoning. He, more specifically, reports that "males should have a normative or fairness orientation because of their presumed focus on right, duties, and justice, whereas females should have a utilitarianism or perfectionism orientation because of their focus on relationship, welfare, and caring" (p. 158). However, the same author has reservations concerning the fact that the care/ response mode of moral reasoning is reflected in the utilitarianism and perfectionism orientations, because Kohlberg's orientations are not synonymous to Gilligan's.

Although, research in social context has suggested that there are gender-linked differences in moral maturity in boys-men and girls-females (see Walker, 1984; Cohn, 1991 for a review of the literature), however apart form their opinion on the gender-related differentiation in moral reasoning, researchers have supported that gender differences in moral reasoning are quite controversial (e.g., Walker, 1995). Overall, it seems that both genders have both justice and care orientations available, and use them differently, depending on a variety of contextual and background factors (see Jaffe & Hyde, 2000 for further details).

Sport constitutes part of the greater social environment where the development process of moral reasoning takes place in a way similar to both contexts (Proios, 2006; Proios & Doganis, 2006). As in the social context, in sport context as well the views that prevail concerning the gender-related differences are controversial, too. A number of researches showed significant differences in moral reasoning gender-related (Abrahamsen & Roberts, 2003; Bredemeier & Shields, 1984; Guivernau & Duda, 2002; Kavussanu & Roberts, 2001; Miller, Roberts, & Ommundsen, 2005). More specifically, the above mentioned studies revealed that females have a higher level of moral reasoning than males. This revelation of the female athletes' higher level of moral reasoning, in comparison to that of the male athletes, might as well be due to the fact that the value of cooperation and teamwork, developed by sport, is acquired more quickly by females than by males. According to Gill (2002), this type of results can be expected, as boys and girls are differently socialized into competitive sport. In the opinion of Bredemeier and Shields (1984), however, the influence of sport on girls' moral reasoning development can be attributed to the different influence of sport commercialization on females than on males, to different career opportunities, as well as to the way the females' participation in sport is perceived in every culture. On the contrary, results of other researches maintained that the differences between males and females in moral reasoning are not significant (Bredemeier, 1994, 1995; Bredemeier & Shields, 1984). All the above reveal that gender constitutes a controversial factor affecing moral development.

Thus, the claim that there are two different moral 'voices' – 'justice' and 'care' (Gilligan, 1982; Gilligan & Attancucci, 1998) – "voices" that lead individuals to perceive moral problems in a different way, as well as to different strategies for their resolution, can not be strongly supported. This viewpoint is further supported by the results of another study which indicated that with regard to what is perceived from sport participation, both caring and fairness traits were equally acceptable for the respective gender (Kelinske, Mayer, & Chen, 2001). In addition, Jaffee and Hydy (2000) suggested that care and justice orientations are not strongly gender differentiated. At the same time, this was verified by Kohlberg's (1984) claim that there are no significant gender-based differences in moral reasoning, as well as that the issue remains quite controversial (Baumrind, 1986; Gilligan, 1986; Haan, 1985; Walker, 1984, 1991). Thus, it is concluded that sport is an environment that offers unique opportunities for a wide range of moral decisions which reflect both concepts related to justice or fairness and considerations of care (Fisher & Bredemeier, 2000).

In addition, Gilligan and Attanucci (1988) supported that individuals can employ both justice and care orientations, but asserted that only one of them (either justice or care) prevails in people's way of thinking. However, the results of a research indicated that female bodybuilders used both justice and care reasoning in their considerations of moral dilemmas encountered in the bodybuilding context (Fisher & Bredemeier, 2000).

As it has already been mentioned in this chapter, sport constitutes an environment in which virtues can be developed. This is further supported by the fact that exercise and sport are activities that contribute to the development of the cognitive and emotional maturity. These skills are considered as crucial for moral development (Telama, 1999). Thus, it is apprehended that since participation in the above mentioned activities support the participants' cognitive and emotional skill, the improvement of their moral development is also expected.

On the contrary, results of researches have found that the participation of sport does not lead to the expected outcome, i.e. the improvement of moral maturity of youth. Other researches have showed that participation in sport is negatively related to the development of moral reasoning (e.g., Bredemeier & Shields, 1986b; Stevenson, 1998), while some others that sport does not affect moral reasoning at all (e.g., Bredemeier & Shields, 1986b; Proios, Doganis, & Athanailidis, 2004). Thus, these results support the claim that sport, by itself, does not bring the expected positive psychological results to children (Shields & Bredemeier, 1995).

However, because sport and play are separate from real life (Coakley, 2001), the moral reasoning of participants should be examined through some specific variables. More specifically, through the tendency to aggression, the attitude towards sportspersonship and the belief in the fair play of participants. According to Bredemeier and Shields (2006), research has shown that the moral reasoning level is significantly related to moral variables such as aggression, sportspersonship, and belief in fair play.

AGGRESSION

Aggression is an action exhibited by the participants in sport. It is a behavior characterizing a negative personality trait. According to Bredemeier and her colleagues, moral reasoning maturity is inversely correlated with aggressive tendencies among diverse samples of sport participants (Bredemeier, 1985, 1994, 1995; Bredemeier et al., 1987; Stephens & Bredemeier, 1996). Gender-related differences in aggressive tendencies have been reported to be equivocal (Guivernau & Duda, 2002). This is because not all studies have confirmed differences in aggressive tendencies that are gender-related (e.g., Keeler, 2007). More specifically, in a study conducted by Guivernau and Duda (2002), the results of other studies, that had showed that boys were characterized by more intense aggressive tendencies, were not confirmed (e.g., Bredemeier, 1994; Bredemeir et al., 1986). However, this disagreement among researchers was attributed to the different traits of the participants used in those investigations and their own research.

Silva (1983) suggested that females are less likely to accept or participate in overly aggressive or violent than males. More specifically, it has been supported that such a behavior can start being exhibited after the age of 15 (Conroy et al., 2001). In addition, Silva (1983) supported that "some forms of sport participation may actually serve to decrease the legitimacy of rule violating behavior for female participants." (p. 446). These findings may suggest that sport experience provides more beneficial moral stimulation for females. This claim is further supported by the results of another study which showed that girls (10-13 years old) who participated in low contact sports did not exhibit physical aggression tendencies in daily life (Bredemcicr ct al., 1986).

SPORTSPERSONSHIP

Sportspersonship is a meaning rather difficult to be determined (Malloy, Ross, & Zakus, 2000). This is due to the fact that not all the types of behaviors have been illustrated by research concerning their relation to this notion. Despite the already mentioned difficulty, efforts have been made in the past for the determination of sportspersonship. For instance, Shields and Bredemeier (1995) determined sportspersonship as a virtue that contributes to the promotion of competition on the basis of moral goals. Sportspersonship is an attitude through which the value of morality in sport is examined. This attitude is expressed through a set of five dimensions: (1) full commitment toward sport participation, (2) respect and concern for the rules and officials (e.g., coaches), (3) respect for social conventions (such as the good behavior of the defeated), (4) respect and concern for one's opponent, and (5) a negative approach to the participation in sport and manifests itself by a "win at all costs" (Vallerand et al., 1996; Vallerand, Deshaies, & Cuerrier, 1997).

The participation of youths in sport has been associated to poor sportspersonship (Bredemeier & Shields, 1987; Bredemeier, 1995; Lemyre, Roberts, & Ommundsen, 2002). However, gender-related differences in sportspersonship have also been reported (Allison, 1982; Duda et al., 1991). More specifically, results of studies shown that women exhibit a higher sportspersonship orientation than men (Chantal & Bernache-Assollant, 2003; Tsai & Fung, 2005). As concerning the finding that females scored higher than males in principled reasoning, as for instance sportspersonship, this can be attributed to the fact that commitment to sport may provide a more growth-producing experience for females than for males (Bredemeier & Shields, 1984).

Although women were found to exhibit a more intense sportspersonship orientation that men, yet this orientation seems to be even more intense in the case of younger female players than older female players (Tsai & Fung, 2005). Thus, the detrimental function of sports is evident also in the female domain as well. Finally, the results of a study have shown that female athletes perceive the virtue of "respect" in many dimensions, despite the fact that it is a clear aspect of sportspersonship (Gano-Overway et al., 2005). This result found by the same researchers was attributed to the possibility that this group of adolescent female athletes has no clear viewpoint concerning the aspects of moral functioning (ethic of justice, ethic of care, and fairness).

FAIR PLAY

Fair play is one of the terms used for the evaluation of behaviors in sport. Although the definition of this term is rather difficult, as in the case of sportspersonship, however, what it could at least mean is that the game should be played in compliance with the rules and more generally to observe what the Olympic ideal proclaims: "respect to one another", "mutual understanding", "friendship", "a better and peaceful world", "friendly efforts and fair play" and "equal treatment". Gabler (1998) perceived fair play as adherence to compliance with the rules, equal opportunities and respect to the opponent individually as well as to his/ her cooperators. Tuxill and Wigmore (1998) claim that the idea of fair play can be based on the fundamental moral ideas having to do with "respect to the individual".

In sport, winning is what matters (Heeren & Requa, 2000; Rees, 2003); yet this commitment to victory can cause problems to the observance of fair play (May, 2001). The results of a study have shown that female players approve behaviors aiming at the acquisition of an unfair advantage with a view to win (Stephens, 1993). All these lead to the reflection that the fair play spirit is not something that can be expected to be applied by females in the framework of sport.

CONCLUSION

The effect of exercise and sport on humans is an issue that has occupied the scholars for centuries now. Participation in exercise and sport is motivated by several motives. More specifically, as far as girls are concerned, the most significant motives are claimed to be appearance, social acceptance and approval. The benefits for the females from their participation in physical activities have to do with physical health, which among others includes the ability to discover their physical potential, to improve their health/fitness, as well as their general well-being.

The improvement of both psychological and emotional health is a set of other benefits obtained by women through their participation in physical activities. It is supported that this condition is the result of the development of psychological traits such as self-esteem, self-confidence, self-efficacy, self-concept as well as empathy. Among the benefits from the participation of the women in physical activities it has been claimed to be the intellectual and mental health. The improvement of the intellectual health is the result of the activation of several cognitive procedures caused by participation in exercise/sport; while, the beneficial results in mental health are actually those of improvement of the mood and cognitive functions such as reaction time, memory, and fluid intelligence.

Another benefit from participation in exercise/sport is said to be the provision of opportunities for the socialization of youths. It has been supported that differences in the socialization process between females and males are not clear. More specifically, participation in physical activities has been claimed to affect the social, cognitive and moral development of youths and especially that of females. The ability to develop social skills such as cooperation, responsibility and commitment, as well as to become a good citizen and develop positive peer relationships are constituents contributing to the social development of females. As far as the women's cognitive development is concerned, it has been supported that it is the result of the opportunities provided by sport for the development of several values, attitudes, pro-social behaviors as well as the development of the women's character. Up to now, the findings of the researches have confirmed that the increase of sport experiences changes, partly, the females' value orientation with success/wining becoming more significant that fairness. They are led to professional attitudes towards play. The increase of sport experiences contributes to the development of prosocial behaviors such as altruistic, cooperative, helping, and empathic and benevolence behaviors. As concerning the development of the women's character, it has been supported that this is not automatically achieved by participating in sport, but rather through the creation of the appropriate conditions.

The development of moral reasoning is an additional benefit from the women's participation in sport. This, however, does not seem to be significantly different than that of men. The improvement of the women's moral reasoning can be evident in their reduced disposition to violate the rules and in the absence of physical aggression tendencies in daily life. However, the increase of sport experiences seems to decrease the women's sportspersonship orientation, as well as their disposition to exhibit fair play behaviors.

To conclude with, it could be stated that the experiences from the participation in activities (physical, competitive and recreational) can have a positive contribution to the psychological and personal health of the women, resulting in the exhibition of health behaviors. This contribution is even more intense when exercise is performed under the appropriate conditions that lead to the improvement, mainly, of moral development. Thus, it is suggested that the individual exercise programs, and especially those aiming at women, should be appropriately prepared for the maximization of the benefits from the participation in them.

REFERENCES

Abrahamsen, F. E., & Roberts, G. C. (2003). Moral functioning in youth soccer. In R. Stelter (Ed.), *Proceeding of the XIth European Congress of Sport Psychology*. Copenhagen.

Acosta, R., & Carpenter, L. (2004). *Women in intercollegiate sport: A longitudinal, national study twenty seven year update 1977-2004*. Retrieved October 11, 2004, from http://webpages.character.net/womeninsport/AcostaCarp_2004.pdf.

Adler, P., & Adler, P. A. (1985). From idealism to pragmatic detachment: The academic performance of college athletes. *Sociology of Education, 58*, 241-250.

Allison, M. T. (1982). Sportsmanship: variation based on sex and degree of competitive experience. In A. Dunleavy, A. Miracle, & C. Ress (Eds.), *Studies in the sociology of sport* (pp. 143-165). Fort Worth, TX: Texas Christian Press.

Allport, G. W. (1961). *Pattern and growth in personality*. New York: Holt, Rinehart & Winston.

Bandura, A. (1977). *Social learning theory*. Englewood Cliffs, NJ: Prentice-Hall.

Bandura, A. (1986). *Social foundations of thought and action: A social cognitive theory*. Englewood Cliffs, NJ: Prentice-Hall.

Baum, A. (1998). Young females in the athletic area. *Sport Psychiatry, 7*, 745-755.

Baumrind, D. (1986). Sex differences in moral reasoning: Response to Walker's (1984) conclusion that there are none. *Child Development, 57*, 511-521.

Beller, J. M., Stoll, S. K, & Rudd, A. (1997). The "great character experience." Assessing the effectiveness of a great books approach to teaching moral character with competitive populations. *Research Quarterly, 68*, 72.

Berlage, G. I. (1982). Are children's competitive team sports teaching corporate values? *Arena Review, 6*, 15-21.

Birch, D., & Veroff, J. (1966). *Motivation: A study of action*. Belmont, CA: Brooks/Cole.

Blair, S. N., & Connelly, J. C. (1996). How much exercise should we do? The case for moderate amounts and intensities of exercise. *Research Quarterly for Exercise & Sport, 67*, 193-205.

Blair, S. N., Goodyear, N. N., Gibbons, L. W., & Cooper, K. N. (1984). Physical fitness and incidence of hypertension in healthy normotensive men and women. *Journal of the American Medical Association, 252*, 487-490.

Blair, S. N., Kohl, H. W., Paffenbarger R. S.Jr., Clark, D. G., Cooper, K. H., & Gibbons, L. W. (1989). Physical fitness and all-cause mortality. A prospective study of healthy men and women. *Journal of the American Medical Association, 262*, 2395-2401.

Bloom, G. A., & Smith, M. D. (1996). Hockey violence: A test of cultural spill-over theory. *Sociology of Sport Journal, 13*, 65-77.

Bok, S. (1978). *Lying: Moral choice in public and private*. London: Quarter Books Limited.

Boutcher, S. H. (2000). Cognitive performance, fitness and ageing. In S. J. H. Biddle, K. R. Fox, & S. H. Boutcher (Eds.), Physical activity and psychological well-being (pp. 118-129). London: Routledge.

Bredemeier, B. (1985). Moral reasoning and the perceived legitimacy of intentionally injurious sport acts. *Journal of Sport Psychology, 7,* 110-124.

Bredemeier, B. (1994). Children's moral reasoning and their assertive, aggressive, and submissive tendencies in sport and daily life. *Journal of Sport & Exercise Psychology, 16,* 1-14.

Bredemeier, B. (1995). Divergence in children's moral reasoning about issues in daily life and sport specific contexts. *International Journal of Sport Psychology, 26,* 453-463.

Bredemeier, B. J., & Shields, D. L. (1984). The utility of moral stage analysis in the investigation of athletic aggression. *Sociology of Sport Journal, 1,* 138-149.

Bredemeier, B. J., & Shields, D. L. (1985). Moral growth among athletes and nonathletes: A comparative analysis. *The Journal of Genetic Psychology, 147,* 7-18.

Bredemeier, B., & Shields, D. (1986a). Moral growth among athletes and nonathletes: A comparative analysis. *The Journal of Genetic Psychology, 147*(1), 7-18.

Bredemeier, B., & Shields, D. (1986b). Game reasoning and interactional morality. *The Journal of Genetic Psychology, 142,* 257-275.

Bredemeier, B., & Shields, D. (1987). Moral growth through physical activity: A structural developmental approach. In D .R. Gould & M. R. Weiss (Eds.), *Advances in pediatric sport sciences* (Vol. 2) (pp. 143-165). Champaign, IL: Human Kinetics.

Bredemeier, B., & Shields, D. (2006 March). Sports and character development. *President's Council on Physical Fitness and Sport. Research Digest, 7*(1).

Bredemeier, B., Weiss, M. R., Shields, D., & Cooper, B. (1986). The relationship of sport envelopment with children's moral reasoning and aggression tendencies. *Journal of Sport Psychology, 8,* 304-318.

Bredemeier, B., Weiss, M. R., Shields, D., & Cooper, B. (1987). The relationship between children's legitimacy judgments and their moral reasoning, aggression tendencies and sport involvement. *Sociology of Sport Journal, 4,* 48-60.

Brown, B. B., Dolcini, M. M., & Leventhal, A. (1997). Transformations in peer relationships at adolescence: Implications for health-related behaviour. In J. Schulenberg, J. L. Maggs, & K. Hurrelmann (Eds.), *Health risks and developmental transitions during adolescence* (pp. 161-189). New York: Cambridge University Press.

Brustad, R. J., (1992). Integrating socialization influences into the study of children's motivation in sport. *Journal of Sport & Exercise Psychology, 14,* 59-77.

Brustad, R. J., Babkes, M. L., & Smith, A. L. (2001). Youth in sport: Psychological considerations. In R. N. Singer, H. A. Hausenblas, & C. M. Janelle (Eds.), *Handbook of sport psychology* (2nd ed.) (pp. 604-635). New York: John Wiley & Sons.

Bunker, L. K. (1996). Psychological barriers to girls' participation in sports. In Women's Sports Foundation (Ed.), *Sports Psychology Resource Packed*. East Meadow, NY: Author.

Bukowski, W. M., & Hoza, B. (1989). Popularity and friendship: Issues in theory, measurement, and outcome. In T. J. Berndt & G. W. Ladd (Eds.), *Peer relationships in child development* (pp. 15-45). New York: Wiley.

Byrne, B. M. (1996). *Measuring self-concept along the life span.* Washington, DC: American Psychological Association.

California Department of Education (2002). State study proves physically fit kids perform better academically. News Release. Retrieved 23 November 2003, from http://www.cde.ca.gov/news/releases2002/rel37.asp

Camacho, T. C., Roberts, R. E., Lazarus, N. B., Kaplan, G. A., & Cohen, R. D. (1991). Physical activity and depression: Evidence from the Alameda County Study. *American Journal of Epidemiology, 134,* 220-231.

Carron, A. V., Hausenblas, H. A., & Estabrooks, P. A. (2003). *The psychology of physical activity.* New York: McGraw-Hill.

Chantal, Y., & Bernache-Assollant, I. (2003). A prospective analysis of self-dermined sport motivation and sportspersonship orientations. *Athletic Insight, 51*(4). Retrieved 25 march 2004, from the web: http://www.athleticinsight.com/vol5Iss4/sportspersonship.htm.

Coakley, J. J. (1986). When should children begin competing? A sociological perspective. In M. R. Weiss & D. R. Gould (Eds.), *Sport for children and youths* (pp. 59-63). Champaign, IL: Human Kinetics.

Coakley, J. J. (1998). *Sport in society: Issues and controversies* (6th ed.). Boston: McGraw-Hill.

Coakley, J. J. (2001). *Sport in society: Issues and controversies* (7th ed.). Boston: McGraw-Hill.

Coalter, F. (1998). Leisure studies, leisure policy and social citizenship: the failure of welfare or the limits of welfare? *Leisure Studies, 17,* 21-36.

Cohn, L. D. (1991). Sex differences in the course of personality development: A meta-analysis. *Psychological Bulletin, 109,* 252-266.

Coie, J. D., Dodge, K. A., & Kupersmidt, J. (1991). Peer group behaviour and social status. In S. R. Asher & J. D. Coie (Eds.), *Peer rejection in childhood* (pp. 17-59). New York: Cambridge University Press.

Conroy, D. E., Silva, J., Newcomer, R. R., Walker, B. W., & Johnson, M. S. (2001). Personal and participatory socializers of perceived legitimacy of aggressive behavior in sport. *Aggressive Behavior, 27,* 405-418.

Cooper, W. E. (1982). Association: An answer to egoism. *Journal of the Philosophy of Sport, 9,* 66-68.

Cote, J. (2002). Coach and peer influence on children's development through sport. In J. M. Silva & D. E. Stevens (Eds.), *Psychological foundations of sport* (pp. 520-540). Boston, MA: Allyn & Bacon.

Daniels, E., Sincharoen, S., Leaper, C. (2005). The relation between sport orientations and athletic identity among adolescent girl and boy athletes. *Journal of Sport Behavior, 28,* 315-332.

Danish, S. J., & Nellen, V. C. (1997). New roles for sport psychologists: Teaching life skills through sport to at-risk youth. *Quest, 49,* 100-113.

Davis Smith, J. (1998). *The 1997 national survey of volunteering.* London: Institute of Volunteering Research, National Centre for Volunteering Research.

Derry, S. J. (1996). Cognitive schema theory in the constructivist debate. *Educational Psychology, 31*(3/4), 163-174.

Desertain, G. S., & Weiss, M. R. (1988). Being female and athletic: A cause for conflict? *Sex Roles, 18*, 567-582.

Duda, L. J., Olson, L, K., & Templin, T. J. (1991). The relationship of task and ego orientation to sportsmanship attitudes and the perceived legitimacy of injurious acts. *Research Quarterly for Exercise and Sport, 62*, 79-87.

Dwyer, T., Sallis, J. F., Blizzard, L., Lazarus, R., & Dean, K. (2001). Relation of academic performance to physical activity and fitness in children. *Pediatric Exercise Science, 13*, 225-238.

Eagly, A. H., & Crowley, M. (1986). Gender and helping behavior: A meta-analytic review of the social psychological literature. *Psychological Bulletin, 100*(3), 283-308.

Eagly, A. H., Wood, W. (1991). Explaining sex differences in social behavior: A meta-analytic perspective. *Personality and Social Psychology Bulletin, 17*, 306-315.

Ebben, W. P., & Jensen, R. L. (1998). Strength training for women: Debunking myths that block opportunity. *The Physician and Sportsmedicine, 26*, 86-97.

Eccles, J. S., & Barber, B. L. (1999). Student council, volunteering, basketball, or marching band: What kind of extracurricular involvement matters? *Journal of Adolescent Research, 14*, 10-43.

Edwards, H. (1973). *Sociology of sport*. Homewood, IL: Dorsey.

Eisenberg, N., & Strayer, J. (1987). Critical issues in the study of empathy. In N. Eisenberg & J. Strayer (Eds.), *Empathy and its development* (pp.3-16). New York: Cambridge, University Press.

Eitzen, D. S., & Sage, G. (1997). *Sociology of North American sport*. Dubugue, IA: Brown & Benchmark publishers.

Eitzen, D. S., & Sage, G. (2003). *Sociology of North American sport*. Boston, MA: McGraw Hill.

Elley, D., & Kirk, D. (2002). Developing citizenship through sport: The impact of a sport-based volunteer programme on young sport leaders. *Sport, Education and Society, 7*(2), 151-166.

Etaugh, C., & Liss, M. B. (1992). Home, school, and playroom: Training grounds for adult gender roles. *Sex Roles, 26*, 129-147.

Etnier, J. I., Salazar, W., Landers, D. M., Petruzello, S. J., Han, M., & Nowell, P. (1997). The influence of physical fitness and exercise upon cognitive functioning: A meta-analysis. *Journal of Sport & Exercise Psychology, 19*, 249-274.

Evans, J., & Roberts, G. G. (1987). Physical competence and the development of peer relations. *Quest, 39*, 23-35.

Farmer, M. E., Locke, B. Z., Mosciki, E. K., Dannenberg, A. L., Larson, D. B., & Radloff, L. S. (1988). Physical activity and depressive symptoms: The NHANES I epidemiologic follow-up study. *American Journal of Epidemiology, 6*, 1340-1351.

Fejgin, N. (1994). Participation in high school competitive sports: A subversion of school mission or contribution to academic goals. *Sociology of Sport Journal, 11*(3), 211-230.

Feltz, D. L., & Riessinger, C. A. (1990). Effects of in vivo emotive imagery and performance feedback on self-efficacy and muscular endurance. *Journal of Sport and Exercise Psychology, 12*, 132-143.

Feltz, D. L., Landers, D. M., & Raider, V. (1979). Enhancing self-efficacy in a high-avoidance motor task: A comparison of modeling techniques. *Journal of Sport Psychology, 1*, 112-122.

Finkenberg, M. E., & Moode, F. M. (1996). College students' perceptions of the purposes of sports. *Perceptual and Motor Skills, 82,* 19-22.

Fisher, L. A., & Bredemeier, B. (2000). Caring about injustice: The moral self-perceptions of professional female bodybuilders. *Journal of Sport & Exercise Psychology, 22,* 327-344.

Fleck, S. J. (1998). Strong evidence. *Athletic Business, 22,* 51-57.

Flood, S. E., & Hellstedt, J. C. (1991). Gender differences in motivation for intercollegiate athletic participation. *Journal of Sport Behavior, 14,* 159-167.

Fox, K. R. (1999). The influence of physical activity on mental well-being. *Public Health Nutrition, 2,* 411-418.

Freedson, P. S. (2000). Strength training for women. *Idea Personal Trainer, 11,* 36-44.

Fromm, E. (1947). *Man for himself.* New York: Rinehart.

Gabler, H. (1998). Fairness/fair play in *Lexikon der Ethik im Sport.* Schorndorf: Karl Hoffmann.

Gano-Overway, L. A., Guivernau, M., Mayar, T. M., Waldron, J. J., & Ewing, M. (2005). Achievement goal perspectives, perceptions of the motivational climate and sportspersonship: Individual and team effects. *Psychology of Sport and Exercise, 6,* 215-232.

Gerdy, J. (2000). *Sport in school: The future of an institute.* New York: Teachers College Colubmia.

Gill, D. L. (2002). Gender and sport behavior. In T. Horn (Ed.), *Advances in sport psychology* (2nd ed.) (pp. 355-376). Champaign, IL: Human Kinetics.

Gill, D. L., Williams, L., Dowd, D. A., Beaudoin, C. M., & Martin, J. J. (1996). Competitive orientations and motives of adult sport and exercise participants. *Journal of Sport Behavior, 19,* 307-318.

Gilligan, C. (1979). Woman's place in man's life cycle. *Harvard Educational Review, 49*(4), 431-466.

Gilligan, C. (1982). *In a difference voice.* Cambridge, Mass: Harvard University Press.

Gilligan, C. (1986). Remapping the moral domain: New images of self in relationship. In T. C. Heller, M. Sosna, & D. E. Wellbery (Eds.), *Reconstructing individualism* (pp. 327-252). Stanford, CA: Stanford University Press.

Gilligan, C., & Attanucci, J. (1988). Two moral orientations: Gender differences and similarities. *Merrill-Palmer Quarterly, 34,* 223-237.

Gilman, R. (2001). The relationship between life satisfaction, social interest, and frequency of extracurricular activities among adolescent students. *Journal of Youth and Adolescence, 20,* 749-767.

Giuliano, T. A., Popp, K. E., Knight, J. L. (2000). Footballs versus barbies: Childhood play activities as predictors of sport participation by women. *Sex Roles, 42,* 159-181.

Gough, R. W. (1997). *Character is everything: Promoting ethical excellence in sports.* Fort Worth, TX: Harcourt Brace.

Greendorfer, S. L. (2002). Socialization processes and sport behavior. In T. Horn (Ed.), *Advances in sport psychology* (2nd ed.) (pp. 377-401). Champaign, IL: Human Kinetics.

Guivernau, M., & Duda, J. (2002). Moral atmosphere and athletic aggressive tendencies in young soccer players. *Journal of Moral Education, 31*(1), 67-85.

Haan, N. (1985). Processes of moral development: Cognitive or social disequilibrium? *Developmental Psychology, 21,* 996-1006.

Harne, A. J., & Bixby, W. R. (2005). The benefits of and barriers to strength training among college-age women. *Journal of Sport Behavior, 28*, 151-166.

Harrison, B. (1973). State intervention and moral reform in 19th century England. In P. Hollis (Ed.), *Pressure from without in Victorian*. London: Edward Arnold

Hart, D., Atkins, R., & Ford, D. (1998). Urban America as a context for the development of moral identity in adolescence. *Journal of Social Issues, 54*, 513-530.

Hayes, S. D., Crocker, P. R. E., & Kowalski, K. C. (1999). Gender differences in physical self-perceptions, global self-esteem and physical activity: Evaluation of the physical self-perception profile model. *Journal of Sport Behavior, 22*, 1-14.

Health Canada (2003). *Canada's physical activity guide to healthy active living*. Retrieved 10 May 2007, from http://www.hc-sc.ca/hppb/paguide/pdf/guideEng.pdf

Heeren, J., & Requa, M. (2001). Constructing values on a girls high school field hockey team. *Journal of Sport and Social Issues, 25*(4), 417-429.

Hellison, D. (1995). *Teaching responsibility through physical activity*. Champaign, IL: Human Kinetics.

Hellison, D. (2003). *Teaching responsibility through physical activity* (2nd ed.). Champaign, IL: Human Kinetics.

Hodge, K. P. (1989). Character-building in sport: Fact or fiction? New Zealand. *Journal of Sports Medicine, 17*(2), 23-25.

Hoffman, M. L. (1987). The contribution of empathy to justice and moral judgment. In N. Eisenberg & J. Strayer (Eds.), *Empathy and its development* (pp. 59-94). New York: Cambridge, University Press.

Hogan, R., & Emler, N. (1995). Personality and moral development. In W. M. Kurtines & J. L. Gewirtz (Eds.) *Moral development: An introduction* (pp. 209-227). Boston: Allyn and Bacon.

Hovell, M., Sallis, J., Kolody, B., & Mckenzie, T. (1999). Children's physical activity choices: A developmental analysis of gender, intensity levels, and time. *Pediatric Exercise Science, 11*, 158-168.

Jackson, S. A., & Marsh, H. W. (1986). Athletic or antisocial? The female sport experience. *Journal of Sport Psychology, 8*, 198-211.

Jaffee, S., & Hyde, J. S. (2000). Gender differences in moral orientation: A meta-analysis. *Psychological Bulletin, 126*, 703-726.

Johnson, M. (1963). Sex role learning in the nuclear family. *Child Development, 34*, 319-333.

Kalliopuska, M. (1987). Relation of empathy and self-esteem to active participation in Finnish baseball. *Perceptual and Motor Skills, 65*, 107-113.

Kalliopuska, M. (1992).Self-esteem and narcissism among the most and least empathetic Finnish baseball players. *Perceptual and Motor Skills, 75*, 945-946.

Kane, M. (1982). The influence of level of sport participation and sex-role orientation on female professionalization of attitudes towards play. *Journal of Sport Psychology, 4*, 290-294.

Kane, M., & Greendorfer, S. (1994). The media's role in accommodating and resisting stereotyped images of women in sport. In P. Creedon (Ed.), *Women, media and sport* (pp. 2-44). Thousand Oaks, CA: Sage.

Kavussanu, M., & Roberts, G. C. (2001). Moral functioning in sport: An achievement goal perspective. *Journal of Sport & Exercise Psychology, 23,* 37-54.

Keeler, L. A. (2007). The differences in sport aggression, life aggression, and life assertion among adult male and female collision, contact, and non-contact sport athletes. *Journal of Sport Behavior, 30*(1), 57-76.

Keith, A., Nelson, B., Schlabach, C., & Thompson, D. (1990). The relationship between parental employment and early adolescent responsibility: family-related, personal, and social. *Journal of Early Adolescent, 10*, 399-415.

Kelinske, B., Mayer, B. W., & Chen, K. L. (2001). Perceived benefits from participation in sports: A gender study. *Women in Management Review, 16*, 75-84.

Kleiber, D. A., & Roberts, G. C. (1981). The effect of sport experience in the development of social character: An exploratory investigation. *Journal of Sport Psychology, 3,* 114-122.

Kniker, C. R. (1974). The values of athletes in schools: A continuing debate. *Phi Delta Kappan, 56,* 116-120.

Koivula, N. (1999). Sport participation: Differences in motivation and actual participation due to gender typing. *Journal of Sport Behavior, 22*(3), 360-380.

Kohlberg, L. (1969). Stage and sequence: The cognitive-developmental approach to socialization, In D. A. Goslin (Ed.), *Handbook of socialization theory and research* (pp. 347-480). Chicago: Rand McNally.

Kohlberg, L. (1981). *Essays on moral development (Vol. I): The philosophy of moral development.* San Francisco: Harper & Row.

Kohlberg, L. (1984). *Essays on moral development: Vol. 2. The psychology of moral development.* New York: Harper & Row.

Kull, M. (2002). The relationship between physical activity, health status and psychological well-being of fertility-aged women. *Scandinavian Journal Medicine Science Sports, 12,* 241-247.

Lee, I. M. (1994). Physical activity, fitness and cancer. In C. Bouchard, R. J. Shepard, & T. Stephens (Eds.), *Physical activity, fitness and health: International. Proceedings and Consensus Statement* (pp. 814-831). Champaign, IL: Human Kinetics.

Lemyre, P., Roberts, G. C., & Ommundsen, Y. (2002). Achievement goal orientations, perceived ability, and sportspersonship in youth soccer. *Journal of Applied Sport Psychology, 14,* 120-136.

LeUnes, A., & Nation, L. (1996). *Sport psychology* (2nd ed.). Chicago: Nelson-Hall.

Lever, J. (1976). Sex differences in the games children play. *Social Problems, 23*(4), 478-487.

Lickona, T. (1991). *Educating for character: How our schools can teach respect and responsibility.* New York: Bantam Books.

Lipsyte, R. (1999, May, 9). The jock culture: Time to debate the questions. *The New York Times,* Section 8, p. 11.

Lumpkin, A., Stoll, S. K., & Beller, J. M. (2003). *Sport ethics: Applications for fair play* (3rd ed.). New York: McGraw-Hill.

Lutter, J. M. (1994). History of women in sports. *The Athletic Woman, 13*(2), 263-279.

Malloy, D. C., Ross, S., & Zakus, D. H. (2000). *Sport ethics: Concepts and cases in sport and recreation.* Toronto: Thompson Educational Publishing, Inc.

Manjone, J. (1998). International youth tour benefits. *The Sport Journal, 1*(1). Retrieved 15 September 1999, from www.thesportjournal.org/vol1no1/travel.htm.

Mannell, R. C., & Kleiber, D. A. (1997). *A social psychology of leisure.* State College, PA: Venture.

Manson, J. E., Rimm, E. B., & Stampfer, M. J., Colditz, G. A., Willett, W. C., Krolewski, A. S., et al. (1991). Physical activity and incidence of non-insulin dependent diabetes mellitus in women. *Lancet, 338*, 774-778.

Marcia, J., & Friedman, M. (1970). Ego identity status in college women. *Journal of Personality, 38*, 248-263.

Markus, H., & Nurius, P. (1987). Possible selves: The interface between motivation and self-concept. In K. Yardley & T. Honess (Eds.), Self and identity: Psychological perspectives (pp.157-172). Suffolk: John Willey & Sons.

Marsh, H. (1993). The effects of participation in sport during the last two years of high school. *Sociology of Sport Journal, 10*, 18-43.

Marsh, H., & Peart, N. D. (1988). Competitive and cooperative physical fitness training programs for girls: Effects on physical fitness and multi-dimensional self-concepts. *Journal of Sport and Exercise Psychology, 10*, 390-407.

May, R. A. B. (2001). The sticky situation of sportsmanship. *Journal of Sport and Social Issues, 25*(4), 372-389.

McAuley, E. (1992). The role of efficacy cognitions in the prediction of exercise behaviour in middle-aged adults. *Journal of Behavioral Medicine, 15*, 65-88.

McAuley, E. (1993). Self-efficacy and the maintenance of exercise participation in older adults. *Journal of Behavioral Medicine, 16*, 103-113.

McKenney, A., & Dattilo, J. (2001). Effects of an intervention within a sport context on the pro-social and antisocial behavior of adolescents with disruptive behavior disorders. *Therapeutic Recreation Journal, 35*, 123-140.

McPherson, B. D. (1986). Socialization theory and research: Towards a "New Wave" of scholarly inquiry in a sport context. In C. R. Rees & A. W. Miracle (Eds.), *Sport and social theory* (pp. 111-134). Champaign, IL: Human Kinetics.

Melnick, M. J., & Mookerjee, S. (1991). Effects of advanced weight training on body-cathexis and self-esteem. *Perceptual and Motor Skills, 72*, 1335-1345.

Miller, B. W., Robers, G. C., & Ommundsen, Y. (2005). Effect of perceived motivational climate on moral functioning, team moral atmosphere perceptions, and the legitimacy of intentionally injurious acts among competitive youth football players. *Psychology of Sport and Exercise, 6*, 461-477.

Miller, J. L., & Levy, G. D. (1996). Gender role conflict, gender-typed characteristics, self-concepts, and sport socialization in female athletes and non athletes. *Sex Roles, 35*, 111-122.

Miracle, A., & Rees, C. R. (1994). *Lessons of the locker room: The myth of school sports*: Amherst, NY: Prometheus Books.

Mize, M. (1991). Cognitive development: The physical education connection. *Teaching Elementary Physical Education, 2*(1), 14-15.

Murray, M. C., & Mann, B. L. (2001). Leadership effectiveness. In J. M. Williams (Ed.), *Applied sport psychology* (4th ed.) (pp. 82-106). Mountain View: Mayfield Publishing Company.

Narvaez, D. (2002). Does reading moral stories build character? *Educational Psychology Review, 14*(2), 155-171.

National Federation of State High School Association (2002). *The case for high school activities.* Retrieved 5 February 2004, from http://www.nfhs.org/case.htm.

National Research Council and Institute of Medicine (2002). *Community programs to promote youth development*. Washington: National Academy Press.

Novick, N., Cauce, A. M., & Grove, K. (1996). Competence self-concept. In B. A. Bracken (Ed.), *Handbook of self-concept: Developmental, social and clinical considerations* (pp. 210-258). New York: Wiley.

Nucci, C., & Young-Shim, K. (2005). Improving socialization through sport: An analytic review of literature on aggression and sportsmanship. *Physical Educator, 62*(3), 123-129.

Ogilvie, B., & Tutko, T. (1971). Sport: If you want to build character, try something else. *Psychology Today, 5*, 60-63.

O'Hanlon, T. (1980). Interscholastic athletics, 1900-1940: Shaping citizens for unequal roles in the modern industrial state. *Educational Theory, 30*(2), 89-103.

Orlick, T. (1981). Cooperative play socialization among preschool children. *Journal of Individual Psychology, 37*, 54-63.

Paffenberger, R. S., Hyde, R. T., Wing, A. L., & Hsieh, C. (1986). Physical activity, all cause mortality and longevity of college alumni. *New England Journal of Medicine, 3/4*, 605-613.

Paluska, S. A., & Schwenk, T. L. (2000). Physical activity and mental health: Current concepts. *American Journal of Epidemiology, 29*, 167-180.

Pancher, S. M., & Pratt, M. W. (1999). Social and family determinants of community service involvement in Canadian youth, In M. Yates & J. Youniss (Eds.), *Roots of civil identity* (pp. 32-55). Cambridge: Cambridge University Press.

Papadopoulou, D., & Markoulis, D. (1999). *Positive and negative types of prosocial behaviors*. Thessaloniki: Kiriakidis

Papadopoulos, N. J. (1994). *Dictionnaire of psychology*. Athens: Author. (In Greek language).

Papanas, E. (2004). *Self-esteem and their measure*. Athens: Atrapos. (In Greek language).

Park, N. (2004). The role of subjective well-being in positive youth development. *The Annals of the American Academy of Political and Social Science, 59*(1), 25-39.

Piaget, J. (1965). *The moral judgment of the child. M. Gabain, trans*. New York: Free Press (work original published 1932).

Power, F. C., Higgins, A., & Kohlberg, L. (1989). *Lawrence Kohlberg approach to moral education*. New York: Columbia University Press.

Power, F. C., & Makogon, T. (1995). The just community approach to care. *Journal for a Just and Caring Education, 2*, 9-24.

Prager, K. (1983). Identity status, sex-role orientation, and self-esteem in late adolescent females. *Journal of Genetic Psychology, 143*, 159-167.

Proios, M. (2006). Validation of the questionnaire Defining Issues Test in the sport contexts. *Sport Psychology, 17*, 41-54 (In Greek language).

Proios, M. (2007). *Moral education: A psycho-social approach of moral education in contexts of physical education and sport*. Thessaloniki: University Studio Press *(In Greek language)*.

Proios, M., & Doganis, G. (2006). Influence of developmental characteristics age and education on moral judgment in team sport. *Perceptual and Motor Skills, 102*, 247-253.

Proios, M., Doganis, G., & Athanailidis, I. (2004). Moral development and form of participation, type of sport, and sport experience. *Perceptual and Motor Skills, 99*, 633-642.

U. S. Department of Health and Human Services (2000). *Healthy People 2010* (Conference Edition, in Two Volumes). Washington, D. C.

Raskoff, S., & Sundeen, R. (1994). *The ties that bond: Teenage volunteers in the United States*. Paper presented at the International Sociological Association meetings. Bielefeld, Germany.

Rawls, J. (2001). *Justice as fairness: A restatement*. Cambridge, MA: Harvard University Press.

Rees, C. R. (2000). School sports in America: The production of 'winners' and 'losers'. Perspectives: *Interdisciplinary Series of Physical Education and Sport Science, 1*, 115-129.

Rees, C. R. (2001). Character development, moral development, and social responsibility in physical education and sport: Towards a synthesis of subdisciplinary perspectives. *International Journal of Physical Education, 38*, 52-58.

Rees, C. R. (2003). Fair play in sport: Game reasoning and the moral orientation of Adelphi University Physical Education Majors. *International Journal of Physical Education, 40*(2), 54-64.

Riemer, B. A., Beal, B., & Schroeder, P. (2000). The influences of peer and university culture on female student athletes' perceptions of career termination, professionalization, and social isolation. *Journal of Sport Behavior, 23*, 364-378.

Riggio, R. E., Tucker, J., & Coffaro, D. (1989). Social skills and empathy. *Personality and Individual Differences, 10*, 93-99.

Roche, M. (1992). *Rethinking citizenship: Welfare, ideology and change in modern society*. Cambridge: Polity Press.

Rogers, C. R. (1951). *Client centered therapy*. Boston: Houghton Mifflin.

Rosenberg, M. (1965). *Society and the adolescent self-image*. Princeton, NJ: Princeton University Press.

Rosenberg, M. (1986). *Conceiving the self*. New York: Basic.

Ross, C. E., & Hayes, D. (1988). Exercise and psychology well-being in the community. *American Journal of Epidemiology, 127*, 762-771.

Rudd, A., & Stoll, S. K. (2004). What type of character do athletes possess? An empirical examination of college athletes versus college non-athletes with the RSBH Value Judgment hventory. *The Sport Journal* (On-line), *7*. Retrieved 7 march 2005, from http://www.thespoi'tiournal.or~/2004Journal/Vo17-No2/RuddSto1l.asp

Rudd, A., Stoll, S. K., & Beller, J. M. (1997). Expressed coaching behavior and its effect on athlete moral development. *Research Quarterly, 68, 1* 14-1 1 5.

Rumelhart, D. E. (1980). Shematica: The building blocks of cognition. In R. J. Spiro, B. C. Bruce, & W. F. Brewer (Eds.), *Theoretical issues in reading comprehension*. Hillsdale, NJ: Erlbaum.

Sage, G. (1980). Orientations towards sport of male and female intercollegiate athletes. *Journal of Sport Psychology, 2*, 355-362.

Sage, G. (1988). Sport participation as a builder of character? *The World and I, 3*(10), 629-641.

Sage, G. (1998). Does sport affect character development in athletes? *Journal of Physical Education, Recreation & Dance, 69*(1), 15-18.

Sage, G., & Loudermilk, S. (1979). The female athlete and role conflict. *Research Quartrly, 50*, 88-96.

Salonen, J. T., Pusk, P., & Toumilehto, J. (1982). Physical activity and risk of myocardial infarction, celebral stroke and death: A longitudinal study in Eastern Finland. *American Journal of Epidemiology, 115*, 526-537.

Scanlan, T. K., Carpenter, P., Schmidt, G., Simons, J., & Keeler, B. (1993). An introduction to the sport commitment model. *Journal of Sport & Exercise Psychology, 15*, 1-15.

Seefeldt, V. D., Ewing, M. E. (1996). Youth sports in America: An overview. *Research Digest of the PCPFS, 2(11)*.

Selman, R. L. (1971). The relation of role-taking to the development of moral judgment in children. *Child Development, 42*, 79-92.

Selman, R. L. (1976). Social-cognitive understanding: A guide to educational and clinical practice. In T. Lickona (Ed.), *Moral development and behaviour: Theory, research, and social issues* (pp. 299-316). New York: Holt, Rinehart & Winston.

Sharpe, T., Brown, M., & Crider, K. (1995). The effects of sportsmanship curriculum intervention on generalized positive social behaviour of urban elementary school students. *Journal of Applied Behavior Analysis, 28*, 401-416.

Sheehan, T. J., & Assop, W. L. (1972). Educational sport. *Journal of Health, Physical Education and Recreation, 43*, 41-45.

Shields, D., & Bredemeier, B. (1995). *Character development and physical activity.* Champaign IL: Human Kinetics.

Shields, D., & Bredemeier, B. (2001). Moral development and behavior in sport. In R. N. Singer, H. A Hausenblas, & C. M. Janelle (Eds.), *Handbook of sport psychology* (2nd ed.) (pp. 585-603). New York: Wiley & Sons.

Shogan, D. (1999). The making of high-performance athletes: Discipline, diversity, and ethics. Toronto: University of Toronto Press.

Siegenthaler, K. I., & Gonzalez, G. I. (1997). Youth sports as serious leisure. *Journal of Sport and Social Issues, 21*, 298-314.

Silva, J. M. (1983). The perceived legitimacy of rule violating behaviour in sport. *Journal of Sport Psychology, 5*, 438-448.

Smith, M. D. (1979). Towards an explanation of hockey violence: A reference other approach. *Canadian Journal of Sociology, 4*, 105-124.

Soenstroem, R., & Potts, S. A. (1996). Life adjustment correlates of physical self-concepts. *Medicine Science Sports Exercise, 28*, 619-625.

Stephens, T. (1988). Physical activity and mental health in the United States and Canada: Evidence from four population surveys. *Preventive Medicine, 17*, 35-47.

Stephens, D. E. (1993). *Goal orientation and moral atmosphere in youth sport: An examination of lying, hurting, and cheating behaviours in girls' soccer.* Unpublished Doctoral Dissertation, University of California at Berkeley.

Stephens, D. E., & Bredemeier, B. (1996). Moral atmosphere and judgment about aggression in girl's soccer: relationships among moral and motivational variables. *Journal of Sport & Exercise Psychology, 18*, 158-173.

Stevens, D. A. (1994). Movement concepts: Stimulating cognitive development in elementary students. *Journal of Physical Education, Recreation & Dance, 65*(8), 16-23.

Stevenson, M. J. (1998). *Measuring in the cognitive moral reasoning of collegiate student-athletes: The development of the Stevenson-Staff Social Responsibility Questionnaire.* Unpublished doctoral dissertation, University of Idaho.

Suitor, J. J., & Reavis, R. (1995). Football, fast cars, and cheerleading: Adolescent gender norms. *Adolescence, 30,* 265-272.

Sullivan, H. S. (1953). *The interpersonal theory of psychiatry.* New York: Norton.

Svoboda, B. (1995). Scientific review part 1. In I. Vuori, P. Fentem, B. Svoboda, G. Partiksson, W. Andreff, & W. Weber (Eds.), *The significance of sport for society: Health, socialization, economy.* Strasbourg: Council of Europe Press.

Taylor, D. (1995). A comparison of college athletic participants and nonparticipants on self-esteem. *Journal of College Student Development, 36,* 444-450.

Taylor, S. E., & Crocker, J. (1981). Schematic bases of social information processing. In E. T. Higgins, C. P. Herman, & M. P. Zanna (Eds.), *Social cognition: The Ontario Symposium* (Vol. I) (pp. 89-134). Hillsdale, NJ: Erlbaum.

Telama, R. (1999). Moral development. In Y. V. Auweele, F. Bakker, S. Biddle, M. Durand & R. Seiler (Eds.), *Psychology for physical educators* (pp. 321- 342). Champaign, IL: Human Kinetics.

Thomas, J. R., Landers, D. M., Salazar, W. J., & Etnier, J. (1994). Exercise and cognitive functioning. In C. Bouchard, R. J. Shepard, & T. Stephens (Eds.), *Physical activity, fitness, and health* (pp. 521-529). Champaign, IL: Human Kinetics.

Trew, K., Kremer, J., Gallagher, A., Cully, D., & Ogle, S. (1997). Young people's participation in sport in Northern Ireland. *International Review for the Sociology of Sport, 32,* 419-431.

Tsai, E., & Fung, L. (2005). Sportspersonship in youth basketball and volleyball players. *Athletic Insight* [The Online Journal of Sport Psychology], *51*(4). Retrieved from the web http://www.athleticinsight.com/vol7Iss2/sportspersonship.htm, 18/10/2005.

Tuxill, C., & Wigmore, S. (1998). Merely Meat? Respect for persons in sport and games. In M. J. McNamee & S. J. Parry (Eds.), *Ethics and sport* (pp. 104-116). London: E & FN Spon.

Vallerand, R. J., Deshaies, P., & Cuerrier, J. P. (1997). On the effects of the social context on behavioral intententions of sportsmanship. *International Journal of Sport Psychology, 28,* 126-140.

Vallerand, R. J., Deshaies, P., Cuerrier, J. P., Briere, N., & Pelletier, L. G. (1996). Toward a multidimensional definition of sportspersonship. *Journal of Applied Sport Psychology, 8,* 123-135.

Vanreusel, B., Renson, R., Beunen, G., Claessens, A. L., Lefevre, J., Lysens, R., & Vanden Eynde, B. (1997). A longitudinal study of youth sport participation and adherence to sport in adulthood. *International Review for the Sociology of Sport, 32*(4), 373-387.

Viru, A., & Smirnova, T. (1995). Health promotion exercise training. *Sport Medicine, 19*(2), 123-136.

Walker, L. J. (1984). Sex differences in the development of moral reasoning: A critical review. *Child Developmental, 55,* 677-691.

Walker, L. J. (1989). A longitudinal study of moral reasoning. *Child development, 60,* 157-166.

Walker, L. J. (1991). Sex differences in moral reasoning. In W. M. Kurtines, & J. L. Gewirtz (Eds.), *Handbook of moral behavior and development: Vol. 2, Research* (pp. 333-364). Hillsdale, NJ: Erlbaum.

Walker, L. J. (1995). Sexism in Kohlberg's moral psychology? In W. M. Kurtines, & J. L. Gewirtz (Eds.), *Moral development: An introduction* (pp. 83-107). Boston: Allyn & Bacon.

Wankel, L. M., & Berger, B. G. (1990). The psychological and social benefits of sport and physical activity. *Journal of Leisure Research, 22*(2), 176-182.

Webb, H. (1969). Professionalization of attitudes toward play among adolescents. In G. S. Kenyon (Ed.), *Sociology of sport.* Chicago: The Athletic Institute.

Weinberg, R., & Gould, D. (2003). *Foundations of sport & exercise psychology* (3rd ed.). Champaign, IL: Human Kinetics.

Weinberg, R., Grove, R., & Jackson, A. (1992). Strategies for building self-efficacy in tennis players: A comparative analysis of Australian and American coaches. *Sport Psychologist, 6*, 3-13.

Weiss, M. R., & Barber, H. (1995). Socialization influences of collegiate female athletes: A tale of two decades. *Sex Roles, 33*, 129-140.

Weiss, M. R., & Duncan, S. C. (1992). The relationship between physical competence and peer acceptance in the context of children's sport participation. *Journal of sport & Exercise Psychology, 14*, 177-191.

Weiss, M. R., & Smith, A. L. (2002). Moral development in sport and physical activity: Theory, research, and intervention. In T. S. Horn (Ed.), *Advances in sport psychology* (2nd ed.) (pp. 243-280). Champaign, IL: Human Kinetics.

Weiss, M. R., Smith, A. L., & Theeboom, M. (1996). "That's what friends are for": Children's and teenagers' perceptions of peer relationships in the sport domain. *Journal of Sport & Exercise Psychology, 18*, 347-379.

Weiss, M. R., & Williams, L. (2004). The why of youth sport involvement: A developmental perspective on motivational processes. In M. R. Weiss (Ed.), *Developmental sport and exercise psychology: A lifespan perspective* (pp. 223-268). Morgantown, WV: Fitness Information Technology, Inc.

Whitley, B. E. (1983). Sex-role orientation and self esteem: A critical meta-analytic review. *Journal of Personality and Social Psychology, 44*, 765-778.

Whitley, R. L. (1999). Those "dumb jocks" are at it again: A comparison of the educational performances of athletes and nonathletes in North Carolina high school from 1993 through 1996. *High School Journal, 82*, 223-233.

Wigfield, A., & Karpathian, M. (1991). Who am I and What can I do? Children's self-concepts and motivation in achievement situations. *Educational Psychologist, 26*, 233-261.

World Health Organization. (1946). *Constitution.* Geneva: Author.

Wright, A. D., & Cote, J. (2003). A retrospective analysis of leadership development through sport. *The Sport Psychologist, 17,* 268-291.

Young, J., & Bursik, K. (2000). Identity development and life plan maturity: A comparison of women athletes and nonathletes. *Sex Roles, 43*, 241-254.

Zoble, J. (1972). Femininity and achievement in sports. In D. Harris (Ed.), *Women and Sport.* University Park, PA: Penn State HPER Series Number 2.

In: Progress in Exercise and Women's Health Research
Editor: Janet P. Coulter, pp. 139-158

ISBN 1-60456-014-5
© 2008 Nova Science Publishers, Inc.

Chapter 4

HOW IMPORTANT ARE BASIC PSYCHOLOGICAL NEEDS TO WOMEN'S WELL-BEING?

Philip M. Wilson[1], Diane E. Mack and Virginia L. Lightheart

Department of Physical Education & Kinesiology, Faculty of Applied Health Sciences
Brock University, St Catharines, Ontario, L2S 3A1, Canada

ABSTRACT

The purpose of this study was to examine the importance of satisfying basic psychological needs proposed within Self-Determination Theory (SDT; Deci & Ryan, 2002) to domain-specific well-being in women engaged in regular physical exercise. Employing cross-sectional designs, participants in study 1 ($N = 115$) and study 2 ($N = 247$) completed different self-report instruments measuring perceived psychological need satisfaction felt via exercise as well as an index of physical self-worth. Multivariate analyses using structural equation modeling in study 1 supported the tenability of a model based on SDT positing physical self-worth as a function of a latent variable representing overall psychological need satisfaction in exercise settings. Simultaneous multiple regression analyses reported in study 2 indicated satisfaction of each psychological need was associated with a stronger sense of physical self-worth and these relationships were not moderated by gender. Overall, this investigation supports a major premise embedded within SDT postulating a direct relationship between fulfillment of competence, autonomy, and relatedness needs and enhanced well-being that holds implications for structuring programs to foster women's health.

Key Words: Self-Determination Theory, well-being, construct validity

[1] Corresponding author: Tel: (905) 688-5550 Ext. 4997, Fax: (905) 688-8364, Email: phwilson@brocku.ca

Understanding the factors contributing to women's health and well-being has become a central research priority for policymakers and public health professionals (Landry & Solomon, 2002). This is hardly surprising given that substantive evidence indicates that women who engage in regular physical exercise report lower all-cause mortality risk, enhanced physical functioning, and improved management of both acute and chronic diseases (Bouchard, Blair, & Haskell, 2007). Corroborating evidence suggests that elevated quality of life (Fox, 2000) and reductions in markers of ill-being such as the prevalence of depression (Lindwall, Rennemark, Halling, Berglund, & Hassmén, 2007) are commonly reported in women who exercise regularly. Considering the implications of this evidence-base for the promotion of women's health, an important public health question concerns identifying the mechanisms that promote (or forestall) well-being for women within physical activity contexts such as exercise.

One theory accounting for socio-contextual factors influencing variation in well-being is Self-Determination Theory (SDT; Deci & Ryan, 2002; Ryan & Deci, 2006). SDT represents a constellation of sub-theories that delineate the processes involved in human motivation and development (Deci & Ryan, 2002; Ryan & Deci, 2006). An integral sub-theory within the SDT framework concerns the concept of basic psychological needs (Deci & Ryan, 2002). The satisfaction of the psychological needs for competence, autonomy, and relatedness are considered innate and essential conditions fostering growth, development, integration, and adjustment (Deci & Ryan, 2002; Ryan, 1995; Ryan & Deci, 2006). Competence involves effectively interacting with challenging tasks in one's environment (White, 1959). Autonomy concerns feeling a sense of volition and self-determination over one's behaviour rather than feeling like a pawn to external contingencies (deCharms, 1968). Finally, relatedness refers to feeling a sense of meaningful connection to others within one's social milieu (Baumeister & Leary, 1995). In addition to identifying viable avenues for intervention to foster and maintain well-being (Sheldon Elliot, Kim, & Kasser, 2001), the concept of basic psychological needs postulated within SDT holds pragmatic currency given the breadth of human functioning that can be explained using this approach (Ryan & Deci, 2006; Sheldon, Williams, & Joiner, 2003).

Considering the broad appeal of SDT's basic psychological needs sub-theory, it seems surprising that relatively few studies have examined the possibility that fulfilling competence, autonomy, and relatedness needs through exercise participation can influence well-being (Vallerand, 2001; Wilson & Rodgers, 2007). Early work using SDT as a guiding framework conceptualised well-being as a consequence of motivational processes articulated largely within Vallerand's (1997) hierarchical model of motivation and to a lesser extent SDT's organismic integration sub-theory (Deci & Ryan, 2002). For example, evidence has been advanced to support links between well-internalized (or self-determined) motives with greater physical self-worth in exercisers (Georgiadis, Biddle, & Chatzisarantis, 2001; Wilson & Rodgers, 2002), as well as, the role of more controlling (or non-self-determined) motives in relation to increased anxiety associated with physique evaluations in exercise settings (Thørgersen-Ntoumani & Ntoumanis, 2006).

While the aforementioned studies are informative and consistent with SDT, they only partially address Deci and Ryan's (2002) arguments concerning the relation between psychological need fulfillment and well-being considering the distinction between needs and motives outlined within SDT (Deci & Ryan, 2002; Vallerand, 2001). Previous studies of SDT's basic psychological needs sub-theory in exercise have focused more closely on the role of fulfilling competence, autonomy, and relatedness needs in relation to the motives regulating exercise behaviour (Hagger, Chatzisarantis & Harris, 2006; Markland, 1999; Wilson, Rodgers, & Fraser, 2002). Closer inspection of the available evidence testing links between psychological need satisfaction and affective markers of well-being in exercise indicate a restrictive focus on feelings of choice (Daley & Maynard, 2003; Parfitt & Gledhill, 2004) that represent merely a portion of the content domain defining perceived autonomy within SDT (Deci & Ryan, 2002; Reeve, Nix, & Hamm, 2003; Ryan & Deci, 2006). One notable exception is a recent study that supported the importance of perceived autonomy within exercise programs in terms of predicting satisfaction with life in adult patients referred to exercise schemes from their physician (Edmunds, Ntoumanis, & Duda, 2007). Consequently, there appears to be considerable scope for further investigation of the importance attributed to satisfying the needs for competence, autonomy, and relatedness within exercise settings to variations in well-being.

Ryan (1995) noted that domain-specific studies of psychological need satisfaction will determine the extent to which the general principles set forth within SDT's sub-theories generalize effectively across behavioural domains such as physical activity. Drawing on Ryan's (1995) contention, and the dearth of available empirical studies in exercise contexts examining links between psychological need fulfillment and well-being, the overall purpose of this investigation was to examine the relationship between perceived competence, autonomy, and relatedness experienced by women who exercise with physical self-worth. Physical self-worth was chosen as the marker of well-being for three reasons. First, physical self-worth has been associated with indices of life adjustment in both men and women irrespective of the effects attributable to global self-esteem and social desirability (Sonstroem & Potts, 1996). Second, Fox (2000) noted that perceptions of autonomy and relatedness may be important avenues for the development of physical self-perceptions, yet limited attempts have been made to test this contention directly in exercise settings (Georgiadis et al., 2001; Wilson & Rodgers, 2002). Finally, recent work by Thøgersen-Ntoumani, Fox, and Ntoumanis (2005) argued for the inclusion of physical self-worth as an integral marker of mental well-being on the basis of emotional adjustment properties inextricably linked with physique-relevant self-perceptions. Considering that previous studies have linked more global assessments of well-being with exercise-specific indices of psychological need satisfaction (Edmunds et al., 2007), the selection of a domain-specific marker of well-being that is relevant to women's health seems logical and worthwhile given the longstanding relationship between enhanced physical self-worth and prolonged investment in health enhancing behaviours (Crocker, Sabiston, Kowalski, McDonough, & Kowalski, 2006).

STUDY 1

The purpose of study 1 was to examine the relationship between overall perceptions of psychological need satisfaction drawn from exercise and feelings of physical self-worth. On the basis of SDT (Deci & Ryan, 2002; Ryan & Deci, 2006) and previous research (Georgiadis et al., 2001; Wilson & Rodgers, 2002), it was hypothesized that perceived psychological need satisfaction would be positively associated with a greater sense of physical self-worth.

Method

Participants

A total of 118 women drawn from eighteen different physical fitness and exercise classes offered at a Canadian university participated in Study 1. All classes were offered via the non-credit instructional program housed within the university's campus recreation department. Each exercise class was supervised by a qualified exercise instructor and met twice per week for twelve consecutive weeks. Each class focused on cardiovascular activities as the primary mode of exercise, lasted for approximately fifty-five minutes, and consisted of a warm-up and cool-down period separated by exercise sessions conducted at a self-paced intensity. Participants ranged in age between 18 and 71 years at the time of data collection (M_{age} = 25.98; SD = 11.17) and reported body mass index values (BMI) values approximating the healthy range for this age cohort (M_{BMI} = 22.71; SD = 2.89 kg/m^2, 84.2% ≤ 24.99 kg/m^2 and > 18.00 kg/m^2).

Measures

Demographics

Participants provided their age and self-report estimates of height and weight that were converted into Body Mass Index (BMI) scores.

Psychological Need Satisfaction (PNS)

Participants completed three items assessing perceptions of competence ("feeling competent and capable in the exercises I attempt"), autonomy ("feeling autonomous and choiceful in the exercises I do"), and relatedness ("feeling related and connected to the people I exercise with") that were modified from the work of Sheldon and Elliot (1999). Following the stem, "To what extent do you typically have these experiences in your exercise classes…", participants responded to each item on a scale anchored at the extremes by 1 (Very little) and 7 (Very much). Although the use of such indicators has been questioned (Crocker & Algina, 1986), there is evidence to suggest that normally distributed scores from single-item indicators that adequately represent the focal construct of interest can be as useful (or futile) as their multi-item counterparts (Gardner, Cummings, Dunham, & Pierce, 1998). Previous research using both the original and exercise-specific versions of these items provides evidence of the criterion validity associated with scores from these indices in terms of predicting well-being (Sheldon & Elliot, 1999) and exercise motivation (Wilson et al., 2002). Given that the items were developed for the purpose of testing theoretical propositions advanced within the framework of SDT, and demonstrated satisfactory distributional properties in the present sample (see Table 1), their inclusion in this study appears justified.

**Table 1. Descriptive statistics for manifest items and
latent constructs used in SEM analyses**

Latent Subscales and items	M	SD	Skew.	Kurt.	FL	SE
Psychological Need Satisfaction						
PNS-Perceived Competence	5.64	0.94	-0.43	-0.11	0.74	0.11
PNS-Perceived Autonomy	5.68	0.98	-0.49	-0.26	0.78	0.12
PNS-Perceived Relatedness	4.65	1.44	-0.60	0.05	0.31	0.24
PSDQ-Physical Self-Worth						
PSDQ-PSC Item Parcel 1	4.57	0.95	-1.13	1.79	0.93	0.02
PSDQ-PSC Item Parcel 2	4.50	0.95	-0.66	0.09	0.98	0.02
PSDQ-PSC Item Parcel 3	4.67	0.93	-0.81	0.25	0.94	0.02

Note. PNS = Psychological Need Satisfaction. PSDQ-PSC = Physical Self-Worth Subscale of the PSDQ (Marsh et al., 1994). *Skew.* = Univariate Skewness. *Kurt.* = Univariate Kurtosis. *FL* = Standardized factor loading from SEM of the structural model. *SE* = Standard Error associated with each *FL* in the SEM of the structural model. Descriptive statistics for the latent PSDQ-PSC variable were as follows: (a) $M_{PSDQ-PSC}$ = 4.58; (b) $SD_{PSDQ-PSC}$ = 0.91; (c) $Skew._{PSDQ-PSC}$ = -0.87; and (d) $Kurt._{PSDQ-PSC}$ = 0.43 in the present sample. All manifest items loaded significantly on their target latent factors (all p's $\leq$ .05).

Physical Self-Worth

Participants completed the global physical self-concept subscale of the Physical Self-Description Questionnaire (PSDQ-PSC; Marsh, Richards, Johnson, Roche, & Tremayne, 1994). This subscale provides a global evaluation of the positive feelings a person holds about his/her physical self (Marsh et al., 1994; Marsh, 1996). Considerable research supports the factorial integrity and structural validity of PSDQ-PSC scores with multitrait-multimethod procedures (Marsh et al., 1994; Marsh, 1996). Participants responded to six items (sample item: "I feel good about the way I look and what I can do physically") on a 6-point Likert scale anchored at the extremes by 1 (False) and 6 (True). Consistent with the recommendations of Marsh et al. (1994), item parcels were formed by averaging consecutive pairs of items to reduce the 6 individual items into 3 item parcels (2 items/parcel) which were then averaged to form a global PSDQ-PSC score per participant.

Data Collection Procedures and Analyses

Data were collected from intact groups (n > 15 in most instances) on two separate occasions separated by a period of 10 weeks. Participants were informed about the nature of the study, given the opportunity to ask questions pertaining to their involvement, and provided written informed consent prior to completing the questionnaires at the end of a regularly scheduled exercise class. Standard instructions were given to each group by the same investigator to reduce the potential for between-groups effects associated with test administration (Crocker & Algina, 1986). Participants completed demographic and PNS items during week 2 and PSDQ-PSC items during week 12 of their exercise classes.

Data analyses proceeded in three stages. First, the data were screened for outliers, non-response error, and evaluated for conformity with relevant statistical assumptions. Second, descriptive statistics, bivariate correlations, and internal consistency (Cronbach's Coefficient α; Cronbach, 1951) reliability statistics were computed. Third, structural equation modeling analyses (SEM) were used to determine the veracity of a conceptual model positing latent PSDQ-PSC scores as a function of latent PNS scores. Conventional standards were specified for all SEM models including loading items exclusively on relevant factors, correlating latent factors, not freeing error terms to correlate, and setting the loading of a manifest item to 1.0 to define each latent factor's scale (West, Finch, & Curran, 1995). An array of model fit indices recommended for small samples were used to evaluate the models tested via SEM (i.e., χ^2, *Comparative Fit Index* [*CFI*], *Incremental Fit Index* [*IFI*], *Root Mean Square Error of Approximation* [*RMSEA*]; West et al., 1995). While definitive criteria indicating acceptable model fit remains controversial in hypothesis-testing applications of SEM (Hu & Bentler, 1999; Marsh, Hau, & Wen, 2004), *CFI* and *IFI* values exceeding 0.90 and 0.95 typically indicate acceptable and excellent fit respectively (Hu & Bentler, 1999). *RMSEA* values exceeding 0.10 are undesirable and less than 0.05 suggest an excellent fit to the data (Browne & Cudeck, 1993). Maximum likelihood estimation procedures were used for all SEM analyses given that alternative estimation procedures for non-normal data require large sample sizes (Hu & Bentler, 1995).

Results

Preliminary Analyses

An inspection of participant responses indicated no missing data on any PNS or PSDQ-PSC item and no extreme scroes were evident in the sample data. Distributional characteristics of the data (see Table 1) along with a histogram of standardized residuals suggested no extreme univariate responses within the sample data (i.e., z-scores $\geq |4.0|$ SD's from the mean/item). Mardia's coefficient (10.92) suggested tolerable multivariate kurtosis although three cases were removed from subsequent analyses based on the observed Mahalanobis d^2 values (33.84, 18.93, and 18.08; all p's < 0.01). The internal consistency reliability estimate for PSDQ-PSC scores was 0.96 in the present sample. Inspection of the bivariate correlations (see Table 2) indicated a positive pattern of relationships between scores on each psychological need satisfaction indicator, as well as, positive correlations ranging from weak-to-moderate in magnitude between perceptions of psychological need satisfaction and PSDQ-PSC scores. Age was also positively correlated with perceived relatedness.

Main Analyses

A conceptual model drawn from SDT (Deci & Ryan, 2002; Ryan & Deci, 2006) was specified and tested using SEM procedures advocated for the evaluation of psychological models (MacCallum & Austin, 2000). For the purposes of this SEM analysis, PNS item scores were used as manifest indicators of a latent psychological need satisfaction construct which is an approach used in previous SDT research (Hagger et al., 2006). Confirmatory factor analysis of the full measurement model comprising one latent psychological need satisfaction factor and one latent PSDQ-PSC factor defined by 3 unique manifest items/factor was specified and tested in accordance with the recommendations of Anderson and Gerbing (1988). No grave concerns were noted in the fit of the measurement model to the sample data

(χ^2 = 16.03; df = 8; p = 0.04; *CFI* = 0.98; *IFI* = 0.98; *RMSEA* [90% *Confidence Interval*] = 0.09 [0.02-0.16]; ϕ PNS.PSDQ-PSC = 0.43, p < 0.01). Examination of the global model fit indices testing the structural model with SEM indicated marginal departure from the reference independence model (χ^2 = 16.03; df = 8; p = 0.04). Joint consideration of the pattern of global model fit indices (*CFI* = 0.98; *IFI* = 0.98; *RMSEA* [90% *Confidence Interval*] = 0.09 [0.02-0.16]) combined with the distribution of standardized residuals (93.33% z's ≤ |1.0|; 0% z's ≥ |2.0|), and pattern of standardized factor loadings (see Table 1) implied that the structural model provided a reasonable account for the sample data. Nevertheless, the confidence interval surrounding the *RMSEA* point estimate was larger than desired (Hu & Bentler, 1999) and the magnitude of the standardized factor loading exhibited by the perceived relatedness item on the target latent factor was less than the recommended threshold value of 0.40 (Ford, MacCallum, & Tate, 1986). An examination of the standardized path coefficient (γ = 0.43) embedded in the structural model indicated that global perceptions of psychological need satisfaction predicted greater endorsement of physical self-worth and accounted for a modest portion of the variance (R^2 = 0.18).

Table 2. Bivariate correlations between demographic variables, PNS, and PSDQ-PSC scores

Variables	1.	2.	3.	4.	5.	6.
Age	-					
BMI	.11	-				
PNS-Competence	-.15	-.06	-			
PNS-Autonomy	-.06	-.11	.56[*]	-		
PNS-Relatedness	.19[*]	.10	.24[*]	.28[*]	-	
PSDQ-PSC	.05	-.02	.34[*]	.40[*]	.21[*]	-

Note: PNS = Perceived Psychological Need Satisfaction. PSDQ-PSC = Physical Self-Worth subscale of the Physical Self-Description Questionnaire (Marsh et al., 1994). Correlations in the matrix are based on pairwise comparisons and sample size is equivalent across each element in the matrix.
* = p<.05(two-tailed significance)

Summary of Study 1

The purpose of study 1 was to test the relationship between perceived psychological need satisfaction experienced via exercise participation and feelings of physical self-worth in physically active women. The results of the bivariate analyses indicated that perceived competence, autonomy, and relatedness were positively associated with greater endorsement of physical self-worth in exercise class participants. The multivariate analysis revealed that feelings of psychological need satisfaction experienced during the initial stages of exercise class participation predicted subsequent perceptions of worth pertaining to the physical self. Consequently, feelings of physical worth may be, at least in part, a function of the extent to which women feel effective, volitional, and socially connected within the context of structured exercised classes.

STUDY 2

The purpose of study 2 was to examine the unique contributions to feelings of physical self-worth afforded to the satisfaction of competence, autonomy, and relatedness needs within exercise settings and determine the importance of gender on the psychological need fulfillment-physical self-worth relationship. In this regard study 2 sought to extend the results of study 1 by examining the unique effects attributable to satisfying each psychological need proposed within SDT (Deci & Ryan, 2002) on perceptions of physical self-worth in females. Further consideration of the degree to which the effect of psychological need fulfillment on physical self-worth is sensitive to the exerciser's gender was also investigated. Gender was selected as the moderator variable for two reasons. First, consistent gender differences in physical self-worth across the lifespan have been noted (Fox, 1997). This robust finding has lead Fox (2000) to recommend analysing self-perceptual processes separately for men and women to prevent the obfuscation of subtle differences stemming from collapsing samples across gender. Second, the link between psychological need satisfaction and well-being is considered universal within SDT and therefore "must apply across ages, genders, and cultures" (Deci & Ryan, 2002, p.23). Consistent with this tenet of SDT (Deci & Ryan, 2002; Ryan & Deci, 2006), it was hypothesized that (a) stronger physical self-worth would be associated with greater endorsement of psychological need fulfillment via exercise, and (b) gender would not moderate the perceived psychological need satisfaction-physical self-worth relationship.

Method

Participants

A total of 84 male (M_{age} = 21.16; SD_{age} = 1.47) and 163 female (M_{age} = 20.95; SD_{age} = 2.39) university students enrolled in undergraduate academic classes at a Canadian university provided data for study 2. Participants did not receive academic credit or remuneration for involvement in this study. Consistent with study 1, the BMI values approximated the healthy range for this age cohort (Males M_{BMI} = 25.28 kg/m^2; SD_{BMI} − 2.87, 44.0% ≤ 24.99 kg/m^2; Females M_{BMI} = 22.63 kg/m^2; SD_{BMI} = 3.35, 81.6% ≤ 24.99 kg/m^2), and considerable variability in physical activity behaviour was evident (Males M_{METS} = 62.17; SD_{METS} = 28.29; Females M_{METS} = 58.62; SD_{METS} = 27.73; 63.6% of the overall sample reported engaging in ≥ 3 strenuous exercise sessions/week for the past 7 days). All physical activity scores were derived from the summary index of the Godin Leisure Time Exercise Questionnaire (GLTEQ; Godin & Shepherd, 1986).

Measures

Demographics

Participants completed self-report questions pertaining to gender, age, height and weight that were converted to BMI scores.

Psychological Need Satisfaction in Exercise

Participants completed the 18-item Psychological Need Satisfaction in Exercise Scale (PNSE; Wilson, Rogers, Rodgers, & Wild, 2006) as an index of their perceived psychological need satisfaction drawn specifically from exercise contexts. A stem statement anchored each item in terms of how participants usually felt while exercising (i.e., "The following statements represent different feelings people have when they exercise. Please answer the following questions by considering how you typically feel while you are exercising."). Participants responded to each PNSE item on a scale anchored by 1 (False) and 6 (True). Sample items characterizing each PNSE construct included: (a) "I feel that I am able to complete exercises that are personally challenging" (PNSE-Perceived Competence; 6 items); (b) "I feel free to choose which exercises I participate in" (PNSE-Perceived Autonomy; 6 items); and (c) "I feel attached to my exercise companions because they accept me for who I am" (PNSE-Perceived Relatedness; 6 items). Wilson et al. (2006) have reported evidence supporting the structural validity and invariance of PNSE scores across gender, as well as, patterns of convergence with proxy markers of need satisfaction (Wilson et al., 2006) and motivation (Wilson, Mack, Muon, & LeBlanc, 2007) in samples of physically active undergraduate students that are consistent with SDT.

Physical Self-Worth

Participants completed the PSDQ-PSC subscale described in study 1, and the item parcel method advocated by Marsh et al. (1994) was applied to the sample data.

Data Collection Procedures and Analyses

Data were collected from intact groups ($n > 50$ in most instances). Participants were informed about the nature of the study, given the opportunity to ask questions pertaining to their involvement, and provided written informed consent prior to completing the questionnaires at the end of a regularly scheduled class. Standard instructions were given to each group by the same investigator to reduce the potential for between-groups effects associated with test administration (Crocker & Algina, 1986). Data analyses proceeded in three stages. First, the data were screened for outliers, patterns of non-response errors, and evaluated against relevant statistical assumptions. Second, descriptive statistics, bivariate correlations, and internal consistency (Cronbach's Coefficient α; Cronbach, 1951) reliability statistics were computed. Third, a series of simultaneous moderated regression models were calculated to examine the effects of gender on the relationship between perceived psychological need satisfaction and physical self-worth. Moderated regression examines the synergistic interactions between a set of predictor variables (i.e., perceived competence, autonomy, and relatedness) with a proposed moderator (i.e., gender) on a criterion variable (i.e., physical self-worth) to determine if the predictor's relationship with the criterion variable differs as a function of the moderator's influence (Aiken, West, & Pitts, 2003). The procedures advocated by Aiken et al. (2003) for the specification and interpretation of moderated effects in multiple regression applications were used. Each psychological need satisfaction score was centered by subtracting the raw score from the mean scores for the total sample. An arbitrary contrast code one unit apart was assigned designating the gender (men = 0.500; women = -0.500) of each participant. Interaction terms were created for each psychological need satisfaction score by forming the cross product term with the moderator (i.e., the contrast code for gender) such that a significant contribution from the interaction terms would indicate that the contribution of perceived psychological need satisfaction to feelings of physical self-worth differs as a function of the participant's gender (Aiken et al., 2003).

Table 3: Descriptive statistics, reliability estimates, and bivariate correlations between psychological need satisfaction and physical self-worth scores

Variables	M	SD	Skew	Kurt	1.	2.	3.	4.	5.	6.
Total Sample										
Age	21.02	2.14	5.22	42.89	-					
BMI	23.51	3.43	1.30	3.80	.26*	-				
PNSE-Competence	5.21	0.68	-0.84	0.41	-.05	-.08	0.90			
PNSE-Autonomy	5.56	0.53	-1.09	0.34	.02	-.09	.42*	0.90		
PNSE-Relatedness	4.50	0.92	-0.78	0.64	.06	-.06	.18*	-.01	0.87	
PSDQ-PSC	4.59	1.04	-0.79	0.17	.02	-.20*	.48*	.20*	.13*	0.96
Female Subsample										
Age	20.95	2.40	5.53	41.26	-					
BMI	22.60	3.34	2.07	8.20	.26*	-				
PNSE-Competence	5.06	0.69	-0.81	0.47	-.07	-.30*	0.90			
PNSE-Autonomy	5.50	0.56	-0.89	-0.07	.04	-.14	.43*	0.92		
PNSE-Relatedness	4.42	0.89	-0.72	0.77	.03	-.17*	.24*	.04	0.88	
PSDQ-PSC	4.41	1.03	-0.75	0.08	-.02	-.37*	.43*	.19*	.16*	0.95
Male Subsample										
Age	21.17	1.49	0.89	1.55	-					
BMI	25.29	2.89	0.73	0.79	.28*	-				
PNSE-Competence	5.48	0.59	-0.94	-0.12	-.09	.02	0.87			
PNSE-Autonomy	5.68	0.46	-1.56	1.82	-.11	-.22*	.29*	0.84		
PNSE-Relatedness	4.65	0.97	1.00	0.80	.14	.02	-.01	-.17	0.86	
PSDQ-PSC	4.92	0.98	1.03	0.79	.10	-.20	.46*	.11	.01	0.97

Note. PNSE = Psychological Need Satisfaction in Exercise Scale (Wilson et al., 2006). PSDQ-PSC = Physical Self-Description Questionnaire-Physical Self Worth subscale (Marsh et al., 1994). Reliability indices (Cronbach's Coefficient α; Cronbach, 1951) are placed along the principal diagonal. Skew = Univariate Skewness. Kurt = Univariate Kurtosis. Correlations in the matrix are based on pairwise comparisons and sample size is equivalent across each element in the matrix for the total sample and gender-based subsamples.

* = $p<.05$(two-tailed significance)

Results

Preliminary Analyses

No out of range responses were noted and no missing data were evident in the sample responses. Examination of the univariate distributional properties revealed two extreme respondents (one male and one female with z-scores ≥ 4.0 SD's away from the mean) on the PNSE-Perceived Autonomy subscale which were discarded from subsequent analyses. No other univariate distributional concerns were noted in the psychological data (see Table 3) although both age and BMI scores deviated from normality (see Table 3). One multivariate outlier was noted (Mahalonobis $d^2 = 81.06$, $p < 0.01$) and was removed. An inspection of the scatterplot of standardized residuals suggested that linearity and homoscedasticity were tenable assumptions in all multiple regression analyses. Internal consistency reliability estimates (see Table 3) ranged from 0.84 to 0.97 respectively across PNSE and PSDQ-PSC scores. An inspection of the bivariate correlation matrix (see Table 3) indicated that perceived psychological need satisfaction scores exhibited weak-to-moderate positive associations with PSDQ-PSC scores although perceived competence was clearly the dominant correlate of physical self-worth in this sample followed by perceived autonomy then perceived relatedness respectively.

Main Analyses

Simultaneous moderated multiple regression analyses were used to evaluate the relationship between perceived competence, autonomy, and relatedness experienced in exercise contexts with physical self-worth. Three separate regression analyses were conducted with gender as the moderator variable using the procedures advocated by Aiken et al. (2003). The variance inflation factor (VIF), tolerance value (TV), condition index (CI), and variance proportion (VP) values were inspected to determine the degree of collinearity in each regression model (Pedhazur, 1997). Both the VIF (range = 1.08-1.38) and TV (range = 0.72-0.98) suggested the presence of collinearity in the data. However, inspection of the CI's (range = 1.00-2.11) indicated minimal evidence of collinearity with only two VP values exceeding 0.50 for the regression models concerning perceived competence and autonomy. A closer inspection of the data indicated that both VP's exceeding 0.50 were associated with the centered predictor variables and their corresponding interaction term.

Summary of Study 2

The purpose of study 2 was to examine the contribution of satisfying each psychological need proposed within SDT to feelings of physical self-worth and to determine the degree to which gender moderated this relationship. Consistent with study 1, elevated perceptions of competence, autonomy, and relatedness were associated with the endorsement of more favourable evaluations of the physical self. The magnitude of the relationships varied with perceived competence exhibiting the strongest association with physical self-worth while perceived relatedness was clearly the weakest correlate in this sample. The results of study 2 extend the findings of study 1 by demonstrating that gender does not moderate the psychological need satisfaction-physical self-worth relationship in active exercisers.

Table 4: Simultaneous multiple regression analyses examining the moderating influence of gender on the perceived psychological need satisfaction-physical self-worth relationship

Predictor Variables	F	df	Adj. R^2	β	t	p-value
PNSE-Competence				0.47	7.24	<.01
Gender				0.11	1.76	.08
Interaction Term	26.80	3, 243	0.24	0.02	0.27	.79
PNSE-Autonomy				0.18	2.56	.01
Gender				0.21	3.44	< .01
Interaction Term	8.70	3, 243	0.09	-0.05	-0.71	.48
PNSE-Relatedness				0.13	1.96	.05
Gender				0.23	3.77	< .01
Interaction Term	7.95	3, 243	0.08	-0.10	-1.52	.13

Note. PNSE = Psychological Need Satisfaction in Exercise Scale (Wilson et al., 2006). Adj. R^2 = Adjusted R-Squared value. β = Standardized Beta-Coefficients. All F-values > |3.00| significant at $p < .01$ respectively. The degrees of freedom vary as a function of the removal of cases exhibiting large (≥|3.0|) standardized residual values per regression model.

CONCLUSION

The overall purpose of this investigation was to empirically test Deci and Ryan's (2002) contentions regarding the importance of psychological need fulfillment to well-being in an applied domain. This purpose was achieved through an examination of the relationship between perceived competence, autonomy, and relatedness drawn from exercise settings to physical self-worth in women. Results of two studies make it apparent that feeling capable and volitional within exercise settings, and to a lesser extent feeling connected with others in this context, appears to be associated with elevated well-being reflected by feeling adequate about the self physically. Perhaps of greater theoretical interest is the evidence provided in study 2 that supports the consistent effect attributable to perceptions of competence, autonomy, and relatedness in relation to physical self-worth across gender. This observation lends further credence to Deci and Ryan's (2002) contention that basic psychological need fulfillment as proposed within the SDT framework has a direct relationship with well-being that is universal in nature and not differentiated across gender.

Observations from both the SEM and moderated regression analyses supported our initial hypotheses and suggest that environments (such as exercise contexts) which encourage people to make meaningful connections with others, while engaging volitionally and effectively in challenging tasks, have direct links with greater feelings of adequacy and worth about the physical self. Extrapolating from these findings, it would appear that satisfying the basic psychological needs as proposed within the framework of SDT (Deci & Ryan, 2002) represents plausible routes for shaping physical self-worth which is encouraging given that these emotions represent an integral albeit small portion of well-being (Fox, 1997; Thøgersen-Ntoumani et al., 2005). This observation is largely in line with Fox's (2000) contentions regarding the importance of feeling autonomous in the activities undertaken in physical activity settings accompanied by a sense of connection with others to a healthy self-perceptual system. Perhaps of greater interest within this investigation were the results of the moderator analysis conducted in study 2 that supported Deci and Ryan's (2002) contention that a fundamental feature distinguishing psychological needs concerns their direct link with well-being which is theorized to be unaffected by gender. Such support is encouraging considering that few SDT-based studies have examined the degree of consistency inherent in motivational processes across gender (Standage, Duda, & Ntoumanis, 2005) despite the centrality of such assertions within SDT's basic psychological needs sub-theory (Deci & Ryan, 2002).

Despite the consistency of this study's findings with SDT and Fox's (2000) commentary, a noticeable pattern of variation was evident in the magnitude of the relationships observed between competence, autonomy, and relatedness perceptions and physical self-worth. Close inspection of the data from the moderated regression analyses implies that feeling physically competent was the most salient need warranting satisfaction in exercise contexts for women to hold more positive evaluations of their physical selves followed sequentially by perceived autonomy and then more closely by feelings of relatedness. This observation is in line with a larger body of physical self-perception literature that suggests feelings of physical adequacy (or competencies) that emanate from effective interactions with one's surroundings foster and maintain feelings of self-worth germane to the physical self (Crocker et al, 2006; Fox, 2000). On the basis of this study, it seems reasonable to suggest that health professional interested in enhancing women's well-being by improving their feelings regarding the physical self through exercise would do well to structure the environment in such a way to maximize effective functioning in the pursuit of mastering challenging exercise tasks. To limit the focus of intervention programs towards satisfying the need of competence via exercise, however, seems restrictive and is not advocated on the basis of the present study. The small effect sizes attributable to perceived autonomy and relatedness in relation to physical self-worth evident in Table 4 are noteworthy. Practitioners interested in promoting or maintaining well-being may wish to consider engaging women in a manner that fosters a sense of self-direction or volitional endorsement in an inclusive environment. This recommendation is predicated on the assumption that small effects hold credence when they illustrate the importance of theoretically relevant processes, such as psychological need fulfillment via exercise participation for example, to a complex criterion like well-being (Abelson, 1985; Rosenthal & Rubin, 1983).

While the results of the present study imply that substantial benefits in terms of domain-specific well-being can likely be garnered from environments that allow women to feel effective and volitional in their exercise pursuits, the observations concerning the role of perceived relatedness appear less clear. Evidence at both the bivariate and multivariate levels of analyses in studies 1 and 2 did not provide convincing support for convergent validity of the assessment methods used to capture perceived relatedness. These observations are not wholly consistent with SDT where Deci and Ryan (2002) have argued that psychological needs operate in a complimentary rather than mutually exclusive manner and therefore might be expected to co-vary more uniformly. Nevertheless, comparable observations are hardly novel in applications of SDT's basic psychological needs sub-theory to physical activity contexts. Previous research examining basic psychological need satisfaction with Canadian (Kowal & Fortier, 2000) and British (Reinboth & Duda, 2006) athletes report inconsistent relationships between need satisfaction indices whereas investigations of French (Sarrazin, Vallerand, Guillet, Pelletier, & Curry, 2002) and American (Gagné, Ryan, & Bargman, 2003) youth sport athletes report weak-to-strong patterns of inter-relationships between need satisfaction indices.

The mixed-pattern of relationships evident between perceived relatedness and feelings of competence and autonomy within exercise contexts implies that additional instrument development and evaluation research is needed given that this construct has proven challenging to assess (Wilson et al., 2003). Nevertheless, the consistently small associations evident in studies 1 and 2 between feeling related to other exercisers and physical self-worth were initially unexpected and raise interesting questions regarding the role of relatedness to others within exercise contexts. It seems plausible, for example, that the importance of relatedness to others within exercise settings is at least in part a function of the degree of internalization accompanying women's regulation of this important health behaviour. Ryan and Deci (2003) have argued that relatedness serves as the catalyst for assimilating cultural norms and valued identities with the self. Extrapolating from this argument, it seems reasonable to suggest that the importance affixed to feeling connected may be more salient in exercise initiates whose sense of physical self-worth may be tied to the social evaluations received from salient referents within the exercise environment. Alternatively, it may be that proximal supports for relatedness within exercise contexts play a less functional role if individuals satisfy their need for relatedness distally within other life contexts (Ryan & Deci, 2000; Vallerand, 1997). The interplay between context-specific and distal supports for relatedness, as well as competence and autonomy-based psychological needs, remains a fruitful avenue for further inquiry to disentangle the relative synergies (or conflicts) evident in the processes that impact women's well-being. Considering these interpretations within the context of this investigation, the relatively weak relationships exhibited by perceived relatedness with physical self-worth compared with the satisfaction of competence and autonomy needs does not appear wholly inconsistent with SDT (Deci & Ryan, 2002) and extols the importance of examining the unique role afforded each psychological need proposed by Deci and Ryan (2002).

One additional point of interest stemming from the present investigation concerns the manner in which perceived psychological need satisfaction was measured and subsequently analyzed. In the multiple regression analyses conducted in study 2, perceptions of competence, autonomy, and relatedness were examined individually rather than amalgamating the scores into a global need satisfaction index as used in study 1 and previous research (Hagger et al., 2006). As a result of this approach, it is evident that fulfilling competence needs in exercise settings appears to exert the strongest influences on feelings of physical self-worth while satisfaction of autonomy and relatedness needs respectively exert weaker albeit meaningful effects. Previous arguments from Koestner and Losier (2002) have questioned the practice of aggregating data derived from instruments designed to measure motivational processes specific to SDT (Deci & Ryan, 1985; 2002) and it seems plausible that their sentiments apply to the measurement of psychological need satisfaction in exercise contexts. Future studies could explore this issue more carefully by examining the unique and combined contributions of satisfying SDT-based psychological needs at various points in the adoption of habitual exercise behaviours to determine the relative strength of satisfying each psychological need at different points in time on physical self-worth formation and change.

LIMITATIONS AND FUTURE DIRECTIONS

Although the results of this investigation are theoretically interesting and hold practical appeal, a number of limitations should be recognised and future directions advanced to further our understanding of the role afforded basic psychological needs in the promotion of women's well-being via exercise. First, this study employed non-probability based sampling techniques in cross-sectional non-experimental designs that afford minimal confidence in the external or internal validity of the data (Pedhazur & Pedhazur Schmelkin, 1991). Future studies would do well to examine issues pertinent to the satisfaction of basic psychological needs in large population-based samples, as well as, samples that demonstrate distinct criteria of interest for testing the claim of universality attributable to basic psychological needs within SDT (e.g., age, ethnicity, culture). Such approaches may wish to consider the advantages of multi-wave designs that could provide greater insight into the dynamic influence of each SDT-based psychological need on well-being. This line of inquiry would offer more detailed insight into the causal implications of Deci and Ryan's (2002) arguments concerning the role of psychological need fulfillment in relation to well-being. Second, this study relied exclusively on self-report instruments and a single domain-specific marker of well-being. The measurement of well-being is contentious at best yet emerging arguments suggest that the assessment of well-being should include global context-free indicators alongside more domain-specific markers (Thøgersen-Ntoumani et al., 2005). Future studies in exercise contexts may wish to embrace this perspective by including biological (Ryff, Singer, & Love, 2004) and neural activation (Urry et al., 2004) markers of well-being to accompany domain-specific markers like physical self-worth to circumvent issues of common methods variance that can unduly inflate relationships amongst self-report variables (Pedhazur & Pedhazur Schmelkin, 1991). Finally, more careful attention to the type of well-being being assessed is also advocated in future studies. Ryan and Deci (2001) have distinguished between eudaimonic and hedonic well-being with the latter focusing merely on the pursuit of happiness whereas the former centres on the notion of complete and authentic functioning within life. Within the SDT framework, fulfillment of basic psychological needs is implicated in the endorsement of eudaimonic well-being more so than hedonic well-being and it would appear that systematic efforts to address this contention would seem like a logical next step for research in this area.

In summary, the purpose of this study was to examine the contribution of perceived competence, autonomy, and relatedness as key psychological needs proposed by Deci and Ryan (1985; 2002) within SDT to physical self-worth in exercisers. The results of study 1 supported the omnibus influence of exercise settings supporting the satisfaction of SDT's psychological needs on global physical self-worth. Study 2 indicated that the relationship between satisfying competence, autonomy, and relatedness needs via exercise and feelings of physical self-worth was not moderated by gender. Overall, the results of this investigation are novel insofar as previous studies examining the physical self have focused largely on perceptions of physical competency or adequacy as opposed to processes more inextricably tied to the needs for autonomy and relatedness (Crocker et al., 2006; Fox, 2000) which appear worthy of consideration. Collectively, the results of this investigation provide support for Deci and Ryan's (2002) premise that social contexts providing an opportunity for individuals to satisfy competence, autonomy, and relatedness needs are associated with a greater sense of well-being which in this case was evident in terms of associations with a person's sense of physical self-worth. These findings also corroborate Fox's (2000) contention regarding the plausibility of alternative routes to physical self-worth other than mere competencies, and suggest Deci and Ryan's (2002) argument concerning the universal effects of need satisfying experiences on indices of well-being holds promise in exercise contexts. The unique contribution of this investigation is that both studies represent initial attempts to unravel the mechanisms associated with physical self-worth in physically active women using SDT as a guiding theoretical framework. Collectively, the results of the present investigation lend preliminary support to the importance of satisfying SDT's psychological needs within exercise contexts for the promotion of well-being and future research extending this line of inquiry appears justified.

REFERENCES

Abelson, R. P. (1985). A variance explanation paradox: When a little is a lot. *Psychological Bulletin, 97*, 128-132.

Aiken, L. S., West, S. G., & Pitts, S. G. (2003). Multiple linear regression. In J.A. Schinka & W.F. Velicer (Eds), *Handbook of Psychology Volume 2-Research Methods in Psychology* (pp. 483-501). Hoboken, NJ: Wiley.

Anderson, J. C., & Gerbing, D. W. (1988). Structural equation modeling in practice: A review and recommended two-step approach. *Psychological Bulletin, 103*, 411-423.

Baumeister, R. F., & Leary, M. R. (1995). The need to belong: Desire for interpersonal attachments as a fundamental human motivation. *Psychological Bulletin, 117*, 497-529.

Browne, M. W., & Cudeck, R. (1993). Alternative ways of assessing model fit. In K. A. Bollen & J. S. Long (Eds.), *Testing Structural Equation Models* (pp. 136-162). Newburg Park, CA: Sage.

Crocker, L., & Algina, J. (1986). *Introduction to classical and modern test theory.* Belmont, CA: Wadsworth.

Crocker, P. R. E., Sabiston, C. M., Kowalski, K. C., McDonough, M. H., & Kowalski, N. (2006). Longitudinal assessment of the relationship between physical self-concept and health related behaviour and emotion in adolescent girls. *Journal of Applied Sport Psychology, 18,* 185-200.

Cronbach, L. J. (1951). Coefficient alpha and the internal structure of tests. *Psychometrika, 16,* 297-234.

Daley, A. J., & Maynard, I. W. (2003). Preferred exercise mode and affective responses in physically active adults. *Psychology of Sport & Exercise, 4*, 347-356.

DeCharms, R. (1968). *Personal causation: The internal affective determinants of behavior.* New York, NY: Academic Press.

Deci, E. L., & Ryan, R. M. (1985). *Intrinsic motivation and self-determination in human behavior.* New York: Plenum Press.

Deci, E. L., & Ryan, R. M. (2002). *Handbook of self-determination research.* Rochester, NY: University of Rochester Press.

Edmunds, J., Ntoumanis, N., & Duda, J. L. (2007). Adherence and well-being in overweight and obese pateients referred to an exercise on prescription scheme: A self-determination theory perspective. *Psychology of Sport & Exercise, 8,* 722-740.

Ford, J., MacCallum, R., & Tait, M. (1986). The application of factor analysis in psychology: A critical review and analysis. *Personnel Psychology, 39,* 291-314.

Fox, K. R. (1997). *The physical self: From motivation to well-being.* Champaign, IL: Human Kinetics.

Fox, K. R. (2000). The effects of exercise on self-perceptions and self-esteem. In S. J. H. Biddle, K. R. Fox, & S. H. Boutcher (Eds), *Physical activity and psychological well-being* (pp. 88-117). London, UK: Routledge.

Gagné, M., Ryan, R. M., & Bargman, K. (2003). Autonomy support and need satisfaction in the motivation and well-being of gymnasts. *Journal of Applied Sport Psychology, 15,* 372-390.

Gardner, D. G., Cummings, L. L., Dunham, R. B., & Pierce, J. L. (1998). Single-item versus multiple-item measurement scales: An empirical example. *Educational & Psychological Measurement, 58,* 898–906.

Georgiadis, M. M., Biddle, S. J. H., & Chatzisarantis, N. (2001). The mediating role of self-determination in the relationship between goal orientations and physical self-worth in Greek exercisers. *European Journal of Sport Sciences, 1,* 1-9.

Godin, G. & Shepherd, R. J. (1985). A simple method to assess exercise behaviour in the community. *Canadian Journal of Applied Sport Sciences, 10,* 141-146.

Hagger, M. S., Chatzisarantis, N. L. D., & Harris, J. (2006). From psychological need satisfaction to intentional behaviour: Testing a motivational sequence in two behavioural contexts. *Personality & Social Psychology Bulletin, 32,* 131-148.

Hu, L., & Bentler, P. M. (1999). Cutoff criteria for fit indexes in covariance structure analysis: Conventional criteria versus new alternatives. *Structural Equation Modeling: A Multidisciplinary Journal, 6,* 1-55.

Iyengar, S. S., & DeVoe, S. E. (2003). Rethinking the value of choice: Considering cultural mediators of intrinsic motivation. In V. Murphy-Berman & J. Berman (Eds.), *Cross-cultural differences in perspectives on the self* (pp. 129-174). London: University of Nebraska Press.

Koestner R., & Losier, G. F. (2002). Distinguishing three ways of being highly motivated: A closer look at introjection, identification, and intrinsic motivation. In E. Deci & R. M. Ryan, (Eds) *Handbook of self determination research* (pp. 101-123). Rochester, NY: University of Rochester Press.

Lindwall, M., Rennemark, M., Halling, A., Berglund, J., & Hassmén, P. (2007). Depression and exercise in elderly men and women: Findings from the Swedish National Study on Aging and Care (SNAC). *Journal of Aging & Physical Activity, 15,* 41-55.

MacCallum, R. C., & Austin, J. T. (2000). Applications of structural equation modeling in psychological research. *Annual Review of Psychology, 51,* 201–226.

Markland, D. (1999). Self-determination moderates the effects of perceived competence on intrinsic motivation in an exercise setting. *Journal of Sport & Exercise Psychology, 21,* 350-360.

Marsh, H. W. (1996). Physical self-description questionnaire: Stability and discriminant validity. *Research Quarterly for Exercise & Sport, 67,* 249-262.

Marsh, H. W., Hau, K. T., & Wen, Z. (2004). In search of golden rules: Comment on hypothesis testing approaches to setting cutoff values for fit indexes and dangers in overgeneralizing Hu and Bentler's (1999) findings. *Structural Equation Modeling: A Multidisciplinary Journal, 11*, 320-341.

Marsh, H. W., Richards, G. E., Johnson, S., Roche, L., & Tremayne, P. (1994). Physical self-description questionnaire: Psychometric properties and multitrait-multimethod analysis of relations to existing instruments. *Journal of Sport & Exercise Psychology, 16*, 270-305.

Parfitt, G., & Gledhill, C. (2004). The effect of choice of exercise mode on psychological responses. *Psychology of Sport & Exercise, 5*, 111-117.

Pedhazur, E. J. (1997). *Multiple regression in behavioral research: Explanation and prediction*. Orlando, Florida: Harcourt Brace.

Pedhazur, E. J., & Pedhazur Schmlekin, L. (1991). *Measurement, design, and analysis: An integrated approach*. Hillsdale, NJ: Lawrence Erlbaum.

Pelletier, L. G., Fortier, M. S., Vallerand, R. J., & Brière, N. M. (2001). Associations among perceived autonomy support, forms of self-regulation, and persistence: A prospective study. *Motivation & Emotion, 25,* 279-306.

Reeve, J., Nix, G., & Hamm, D. (2003). Testing models of the experience of self-determination in intrinsic motivation and the conundrum of choice. *Journal of Educational Psychology, 95*, 375-392.

Reinboth, M., & Duda J. L. (2006). Perceived motivational climate, need satisfaction and indices of well-being in team sports: A longitudinal perspective. *Psychology of Sport and Exercise, 7*, 269–286.

Reinboth, M., Duda, J. L., & Ntoumanis, N. (2004). Dimensions of coaching behavior, need satisfaction, and the psychological and physical welfare of young athletes. *Motivation and Emotion, 28*, 297-313.

Rosenthal, R. & Rubin, D. (1983). A note on percent of variance explained as a measure of the importance of effects. *Journal of Applied Social Psychology, 9*, 395-396.

Ryan, R. M. (1995). Psychological needs and the facilitation of integrative processes. *Journal of Personality, 63*, 397-428.

Ryan, R. M., & Deci, E. L. (2006). Self-regulation and the problem of human autonomy: Does psychology need choice, self-determination, and will? *Journal of Personality, 74,* 1557-1586.

Ryan, R. M., & Deci, E. L. (2001). On happiness and human potentials: A review of research on hedonic and eudaimonic well-being. In S. Fiske (Ed.), *Annual Review of Psychology* (Vol. 52; pp. 141-166). Palo Alto, CA: Annual Reviews.

Ryan, R. M., & Deci, E. L. (2000). Self-determination theory and the facilitation of intrinsic motivation, social development, and well-being. *American Psychologist, 55*, 68-78.

Ryff , C.D., Singer, B.H., & Love, G.D. (2004). Positive health: Connecting well-being with biology. *Philosophical transactions of the royal society of london B, 359*, 1383-1394.

Sarrazin, P., Vallerand, R. J., Guillet, E., Pelletier, L. G., & Cury, F. (2002). Motivation and dropout in female handballers: A 21-month prospective study. *European Journal of Social Psychology, 32,* 395-418.

Schwarz, B. (2000). Self-Determination: The tyranny of freedom. *American Psychologist, 55*, 79-88.

Sheldon, K. M., & Elliot, A. J. (1999). Goal striving, need satisfaction, and psychological well-being: The self-concordance model. *Journal of Personality & Social Psychology, 76,* 482–497.

Sheldon, K. M., Williams, G., & Joiner, T. (2003). *Self-determination theory in the clinic.* New Haven, CT: Yale University Press.

Sheldon, K. M., Elliot, A. J., Kim, Y., & Kasser, T. (2001). What is satisfying about satisfying events? Comparing ten candidate psychological needs. *Journal of Personality & Social Psychology, 80,* 325-339.

Sonstroem R. J., & Potts, S. A. (1996). Life adjustment correlates of physical self-concepts. *Medicine & Science in Sports & Exercise, 28,* 619-625.

Standage, M., Duda, J. L., & Ntouamnis, N. (2005). A test of self-determination theory in school physical education. *British Journal of Educational Psychology, 75,* 411-433.

Thøgersen-Ntoumani, C., & Ntoumanis, N. (2006). The role of self-determined motivation in the understanding of exercise-related behaviours, cognitions and physical self-evaluations. *Journal of Sports Sciences, 24,* 393-404.

Thøgersen-Ntoumani, C., Fox, K. R., & Ntoumanis, N. (2005). Relationships between exercise and three components of mental well-being in corporate employees, *Psychology of Sport & Exercise, 6,* 609-627.

Urry, H. L., Nitschke, J. B., Dolski, I., Jackson, D. C., Dalton, K. M., Mueller, C. J., Rosenkranz, M. A., Ryff, C. D., Singer, B. H., & Davidson, R.J. (2004). Making a life worth living: Neural correlates of well-being. *Psychological Science, 15,* 367-372.

Vallerand, R. J. (2001). A hierarchical model of intrinsic and extrinsic motivation in sport and exercise. In G.C. Roberts (Ed.), *Advances in motivation in sport and exercise* (pp. 263-319). Champaign, IL: Human Kinetics.

West, S. G., Finch, J. F., & Curran, P. J. (1995). Structural equation models with nonnormal variables: Problems and remedies. In R. H. Hoyle (Ed.), *Structural equation modeling: Concepts, issues, and applications* (pp. 56-75). Thousand Oaks, CA: Sage.

White, R. W. (1959). Motivation reconsidered: The concept of competence. *Psychological Review, 66,* 297-333.

Wilson, P. M., & Rodgers, W. M. (2002). The relationship between exercise motives and physical self-esteem in female exercise participants: An application of Self-Determination Theory. *Journal of Applied Biobehavioral Research, 7,* 30-43.

Wilson, P. M., & Rodgers, W. M. (2007). Self-determination theory, exercise, and well-being. In M. S. Hagger & N. L. D. Chatzisarantis (Eds.), *Intrinsic motivation and self-determination in exercise and sport* (pp. 101-112). Champaign, IL: Human Kinetics.

Wilson, P. M., Rodgers, W. M., & Fraser, S. N. (2002). Examining the psychometric properties of the behavioral regulation in exercise questionnaire. *Measurement in Physical Education & Exercise Science, 6,* 1-21.

Wilson, P. M., Mack, D. E., Muon, S., & LeBlanc, M. E. (2007). What role does psychological need satisfaction play in motivating exercise participation? In L. A. Chiang (Ed.), *Motivation of exercise and physical activity* (pp. 35-52). Hauppauge, NY: Nova Science Publishers.

Wilson, P. M., Rodgers, W. M., Blanchard, C. M., & Gessell, J. G. (2003). The relationships between psychological needs, self-determined motivation, exercise attitudes, and physical fitness. *Journal of Applied Social Psychology, 33,* 2373-2392.

Wilson, P. M., Rogers, W. T., Rodgers, W. M., & Wild, T. C. (2006). The Psychological Need Satisfaction in Exercise Scale. *Journal of Sport & Exercise Psychology, 28,* 231-251.

AUTHOR'S NOTE

The first and second authors were supported by grants from the Social Sciences and Humanities Research Council of Canada (SSHRC Grants #410-2005-1485, #820-2006-0017, #410-2007-1832) during manuscript preparation. The collection of data reported in study 2 was funded by an internal SSHRC seed grant awarded to the first author from Brock University.

In: Progress in Exercise and Women's Health Research   ISBN 1-60456-014-5
Editor: Janet P. Coulter, pp. 159-175   © 2008 Nova Science Publishers, Inc.

Chapter 5

RESPONSIBILITY AND ACTIVITY

THE PERSONAL-SOCIAL RESPONSIBILITY MODEL: EXPLORING A NOVEL APPROACH TO PROMOTING GENDER EQUITY AND INCREASING RELEVANCE FOR ADOLESCENT FEMALES IN PHYSICAL EDUCATION

Paul M. Wright[1], Michelle B. Stockton and Normand L. Hays
Department of Health and Sport Sciences
University of Memphis, Memphis, TN, (901) 678-3480

ABSTRACT

Due to the twin epidemic of obesity and physical inactivity, promoting physical activity has been identified as a major public health priority in the United States. Unfortunately, there is a precipitous decline in physical activity levels among adolescents and this decline is more pronounced for females than males. Improving the effectiveness of school-based physical education is one strategy to promote physical activity for this segment of the population, yet it has been demonstrated that females tend to be less engaged than males in physical education. Advocates for gender equity in physical education have recommended using the Personal-Social Responsibility Model (PSRM) to create a gender-sensitive learning environment. The PSRM is a student-centered instructional model that promotes positive social interactions by emphasizing respect, effort, self-direction, and caring. Moreover, the PSRM promotes the transfer of these responsibilities, or life skills, to other settings. The purpose of this study was to extend previous research by investigating possible gender differences related to the life goals and perceived obstacles of participants in a PSRM physical activity program. Specific research questions included: 1) What are the long- and short-term life goals of participants?; 2) What obstacles do participants perceive in pursuing these goals?; and 3)

---

[1] Corresponding author: pwright2@memphis.edu

Are there gender differences in participants' life goals and perceived obstacles? Qualitative analysis revealed several broadly relevant categories related to goals and obstacles, however, the salience of certain categories did seem to vary with gender. Implications for practice and research are discussed.

INTRODUCTION

A recent national survey in the United States (US) estimated that 60.5% of adults were overweight, 23.9% were obese, and 3.0% were extremely obese with a steady increase in prevalence rates occurring over the past two decades (CDC, 2006; Racette, Deusinger, & Deusinger, 2003). Unfortunately, the prevalence of overweight and obesity is also increasing in children and adolescents. Over the past 30 years obesity rates have quadrupled among children 6-11 years (4-19%), and have tripled among children 2-5 years (5-14%) and adolescents 12-19 years (5-17%) (Hedley et al., 2004; Ogden et al., 2006). Overweight and obesity are major risk factors for a multitude of physical, social, and psychological consequences in youth (Williams et al., 2005). Serious health consequences, such as type 2 diabetes, high blood pressure, and cardiovascular disease are being seen in overweight and obese children (Williams et al., 2005; WHO, 2006). These health risks are exacerbated by the social and psychological risks associated with obesity (i.e. poor self-esteem, body image dissatisfaction in adolescents, etc.) (Strauss, 2000; Strauss & Pollack, 2003). If obesity trends continue, obesity is projected to affect over 20% of children in 2010, become the leading cause of preventable morbidity and mortality, and eventually reverse the increase in life expectancy in the US (Olshansky et al., 2005; van Baal et al., 2006).

Recognizing the potentially devastating health consequences of childhood obesity, it is important to focus on the determinants known to be inciting the obesity epidemic. In its most basic form, obesity results from an imbalance between energy intake and expenditure leading to an accumulation of adipose tissue. Thus, physical inactivity has been consistently cited as one of the leading predictors for the increasing trend of overweight and obesity (Hill & Melanson, 1999). In fact, trends for physical inactivity mimic those of obesity. There is a precipitous decline in physical activity levels among adolescents. Several studies have reported physical activity levels declining by as much as 50% during adolescence (Aaron, Storti, Robertson, Kriska, & LaPorte, 2002; Kimm et al., 2000). Low levels of physical activity were also reported from the National Longitudinal Study of Adolescent Health which indicated that the majority of adolescents do not participate in moderate physical activity five or more times per week (Gordon-Larsen et al., 2004).

It has been established that physical activity behaviors (Kelder et al, 1994; Kohl et al., 1998; Pate et al., 1996) and obesity status (CDC, 2005; Fox, 2003) tend to track into adulthood. This combined with the overwhelming evidence that shows the health benefits associated with physically active lifestyles (i.e. reductions in risk factors for several chronic diseases, reductions in anxiety, improvements in body image, mood, self-confidence, and self-esteem) highlights the need for the adoption of positive health behaviors at young ages to ensure optimal health throughout the lifespan (AHA, 2005; UNH, 2002; USHHS 1996,1998). Therefore, it is no surprise the promotion of physical activity has been identified as a major public health priority by the Surgeon General, the Centers for Disease Control and

Prevention, and the U.S. Department of Health and Human Services (CDC, 1997; USDHHS, 1996, 2000, 2001).

Because adolescents spend the majority of their days in a school setting, improving the effectiveness of school-based physical education is a key strategy to promote physical activity for children and adolescents (NASPE, 2004). Unfortunately, it has been demonstrated that females tend to be less engaged than males in traditional physical education programs. For instance, McKenzie et al. (2004) have reported that girls tend to be less active than boys whether participating in coeducational or separate physical education programs. According to Vertinsky (1992), traditional physical education is often biased toward males and lacks gender-sensitivity. While some researchers report that gender-stereotyping in physical education has decreased (Hopwood & Carrington, 1994), others suggest gender stereotypes are still frequently reproduced by male and female physical educators (Brown & Evans, 2004; McCaughtry, 2004). Stereotypical thinking on the part of physical education teachers is likely to influence curricular decisions and thereby have an impact on students' understanding of gender roles (Harrison & Worthy, 2001). Whether due to inherent differences or socialization factors, research supports that boys and girls do tend to have distinct physical activity preferences (Greenwood, Stillwell, & Byars, 2001). These activity preferences often align with traditional notions of gender. For example, one qualitative study of middle school physical education revealed, "Both boys and girls felt that contact sports like football and wrestling were better suited for boys and that low intensity sports such as gymnastics and volleyball were better suited for girls" (Osborne, Bauer, & Sutliff, 2002: 88). Other findings from this study suggested that a more competitive learning environment frequently leaves girls feeling alienated in physical education.

Beveridge and Scruggs (2000) propose that gender equity in physical education can be promoted through changes in the teaching style, curriculum, and learning environment. They contend, "Girls are often more cooperative, social, creative, and mature than their male counterparts" (p. 25). This observation is supported by research showing adolescent girls tend to choose social and game-like activities when presented with an option (Prusak & Darst, 2002). Having choices appears to be a key factor and an effective tool in motivating adolescent girls in physical education (Prusak, Treasure, Darst, & Pangrazi, 2004). Further, Beveridge and Scruggs (2000) recommend introducing student-centered activities such as cooperative learning and peer-teaching to engage and motivate girls. They also suggest using the Personal-Social Responsibility Model (PSRM) to create a gender sensitive learning environment because it incorporates many of these practices.

The PSRM is an instructional model that was developed to promote life skills among underserved youth through physical activity (Hellison, 2003). Students are expected to respect the rights and feelings of others by controlling their tempers, including everyone in the activity, and resolving conflicts peacefully. They are encouraged to focus on effort and improvement rather than competition and comparison. Also, students are encouraged to direct their own progress through decision-making, goal setting, and independent work. As much as possible, students are given opportunities to take on leadership roles and exhibit caring behavior toward each other. Students are given opportunities to practice these roles and responsibilities during the physical activity lesson. Discussions before and after the activity promote further awareness of and reflection on these responsibilities. The ultimate aim of the PSRM is to transfer the learned responsibilities and life skills to other settings (Hellison, 2003).

The PSRM's practical effectiveness has been established in numerous program evaluations and research studies (for reviews, see Hellison & Martinek, 2006; Hellison & Walsh, 2002). Most of these have focused on implementation and immediate impact in the program setting. This literature indicates the model is effective in creating a positive learning environment and getting participants to take on increasingly active and responsible roles in the program. Some studies have demonstrated the transfer of PSRM life skills such as effort and self-control to the classroom setting (Martinek, Schilling, & Johnson, 2001). While no experimental studies have been conducted to date, descriptive statistical analysis in a recent study demonstrated positive trends on a number of academic outcomes for PSRM program participants versus a strong comparison group (Wright, Li, Ding & Pickering, 2007).

Although no studies have directly examined the impact the PSRM might have on physical activity levels, the potential of its positive influence does seem to exist. For instance, several qualitative studies and evaluations have noted high levels of enjoyment, effort, and motivation among participants in PSRM programs (see Hellison & Walsh, 2002 and Hellison & Martinek, 2006). One recent study demonstrated with a series of valid and reliable measures that participants in a PSRM program had generally high levels of intrinsic motivation, perceived a task-oriented motivational climate, and felt the program was both enjoyable and useful (Wright et al., 2007). Another study demonstrated significant positive correlations between scores on an intrinsic motivation scale and scales that assess personal and social responsibility among students in an urban physical education program (Li, Wright, Rukavina, & Pickering, 2007). All of the variables noted here are associated with higher levels of participation in physical activity as well as exercise adherence (Li & Lee, 2004). The link to exercise adherence is also supported by a series of recent studies demonstrating many participants in community-based PSRM programs feel high levels of connection and commitment that lead to sustained voluntary participation spanning several years in some cases (Hellison & Wright, 2003; Schilling, 2001; Schilling, Martinek, & Carson, 2007).

Most of the PSRM studies reviewed above focused on co-educational programs and included male and female participants in their sampling. However, only one PSRM study has specifically explored the issue of gender. Wright and Ding (2005) reviewed quantitative and qualitative program evaluation data from 35 (14 boys and 21 girls) African American students from an inner-city high school who participated in a PSRM program. Participants gave positive ratings overall on effort and enjoyment scales (Duda & Nicholls, 1992); the girls' means on both scales were actually more positive than the boys'. Qualitative findings indicated both boys and girls found the curriculum to be relevant; the instructors demonstrated a commitment to gender equity; and that girls were especially positive about student-centered activities such as peer assessment. In sum, the findings supported the notion that the PSRM is effective in promoting gender equity.

Wright and Ding's (2005) findings were focused on perceptions of the in-program experience. However, a key aim of the PSRM is the transfer of life skills to other settings. Transfer is often promoted through goal-setting exercises and discussions about real life situations (Hellison, 2003; Hellison et al., 2000; Martinek, Schilling, & Johnson, 2001). This emphasis on transfer and life skills represents a unique element not present in many physical activity programs. Given the apparent success of these strategies in making PSRM programs relevant and meaningful, there is value in better understanding the life goals and perceived obstacles of program participants. In order to effectively reach all participants, it is important for PSRM practitioners and researchers to consider potential gender differences. Therefore, the purpose of this study was to investigate possible gender differences related to the life goals and perceived obstacles of participants in a PSRM physical activity program. Specific research questions included: 1) What are the long- and short-term life goals of participants?; 2) What obstacles do participants perceive in pursuing these goals?; and 3) Are there gender differences in participants' life goals and perceived obstacles?

Context

The context for this study was the Tai Chi Tiger program that had been offered for several consecutive years as a form of engaged scholarship. Using the framework of service-bonded inquiry (Martinek & Hellison, 1997; Martinek, Hellison, & Walsh, 2004), the first author delivered this PSRM-based Tai Chi program to students in an inner-city high school. Tai Chi is a traditional Chinese exercise originally developed as a martial art. It is a graceful, non-competitive, wellness oriented physical activity that has been recommended for use in secondary physical education (Chen & Sherman, 2002). A more detailed description of the Tai Chi Tiger curriculum and its implementation can be found elsewhere (Wright & Burton, in press; Wright, Li, Ding, & Pickering, 2007). The same curriculum was delivered to three in tact classes over a two-year period by the first author, a certified Tai Chi instructor with ten years of experience implementing and evaluating PSRM programs. PSRM strategies implemented in this curriculum included: promoting awareness and reflection of responsibility through discussion; providing opportunities to take on responsible roles such as leadership during the activity; and allowing participants to be more active in making decisions and evaluating themselves. Participants learned several slow, graceful movements from traditional Tai Chi as well as the corresponding martial arts applications. Participants had opportunities to lead the class in warm up exercises and Tai Chi movements. Peer-teaching as well as self- and peer-assessment strategies were also incorporated. Participants were led through reflections and goal-setting exercises to promote the transfer of PSRM responsibilities and life skills into other settings. These activities are described in greater detail below.

METHOD

Participants and Setting

Participants were a convenience sample of 79 (38 girls and 41 boys) adolescents with a mean age of 15.2 years. All participants were African American and attended an inner-city high school in the southern region of the US. Each participant was enrolled in one of three different co-educational physical education classes in which the Tai Chi Tiger program was delivered. Twenty-three participants (29.1%) were enrolled in a class that received the program during the 2003-2004 academic year and the remaining 56 participants (70.9%) were enrolled in one of two classes that received the program in the 2004-2005 academic year. While a larger number of students was involved in the program, the current sample consisted of those who secured active parental consent and completed the data source analyzed in this study. Data presented here come from a larger, on-going evaluation study that was approved by the university's Institutional Review Board and the school's principal.

Data Collection and Procedures

The 20-lesson Tai Chi Tiger curriculum was integrated into a required physical education course that met for 50 minutes every day throughout the academic year. Most classes were taught in the school's gymnasium but a classroom was available for occasional lectures, discussions, and data collection. Approximately half way through the 20-lesson program, participants had been introduced to the core PSRM responsibilities of respect, effort, self-direction, and leadership. They had also experienced more active roles such as peer-teaching. At this point in the program, a greater emphasis was placed on the notion of transfer. In a classroom-based discussion, participants were introduced to the concept of goal-setting. The first author/instructor explained the goal-setting process and discussed its value. Participants were introduced to the concept of long- and short-term goals. They were instructed to think of long-term goals as something they would like to do, have, or become as adults, i.e. after high school. They were told to think of short-term goals as stepping-stones that would take them closer to reaching their long-term goal. There was also discussion about obstacles participants might face in pursuit of their goals. Obstacles were defined as anything that might stop them or interfere with them working toward and achieving their goals. Throughout the presentation, the first author/instructor provided examples and asked participants to share their own. In addition to checks for understanding, he encouraged participants to ask questions if they needed clarification. When satisfied that all participants understood the concepts, he and a research assistant administered a goal-setting worksheet. Participants were asked to write in a long-term goal, a related short-term goal, and at least one obstacle that might prevent them from reaching these goals. Most participants provided brief responses and completed the worksheet in less than ten minutes. The first author/instructor provided individualized, written feedback to participants' responses the following week and used participant examples to highlight the relevance of the PSRM in subsequent group discussions. The original goal-setting worksheets were retained as artifacts and subsequently analyzed in this study.

Data Analysis

Qualitative data analysis was conducted by the first and third authors. At the time of this study, the first author had several years of experience using qualitative research methods and teaching doctoral level classes on the topic. The third author was a doctoral candidate who had taken an introductory course and received additional training in qualitative research methods. The first author was directly involved in the delivery of the Tai Chi Tiger program as the lead instructor. The third author had no direct role or connection to the program. Capitalizing on these different perspectives, researcher triangulation was used to enhance the trustworthiness of the study (Lincoln & Guba, 1985; Patton, 2002).

Participants' original responses were re-written verbatim in a computer program to facilitate data management and analysis. Responses related to the three different topics (long-term goals, short-term goals, and obstacles) were first analyzed using constant comparison and inductive analysis to identify patterns and develop categories (LeCompte & Priesle, 1993). This first phase of analysis was conducted without regard to gender. Categories were identified based on their prevalence in the overall data set. Independently, the first and third author read all responses to a given topic several times until patterns began to emerge. Each developed a set of discrete categories that characterized the data. After both researchers developed a preliminary set of categories, the two sets were compared and refined through discussion until consensus was reached. The categories representing each topic were finalized after precise definitions were written that could be consistently applied to the raw data with complete agreement between the two researchers.

For all three topics, many participants provided responses that conveyed more than one idea. Therefore, the number of discrete responses that were coded for each category exceeds the number of actual participants in the sample. For example, one boy gave the following response for his long-term goal, "I would like to go to a 4 year university and go and play professional basketball". This particular response was ultimately coded as contributing to two long-term goal categories, *academics* and *athletics*.

Ryan and Bernard (2000) note the value of quantifying raw qualitative data that have been systematically coded or categorized. This approach was useful in the current study due to the sample size, the nature of our raw data and our desire to disaggregate findings by gender. Organized around final categories in each topic area, the data were disaggregated by gender. Frequencies and percentages were calculated to assess response patterns by gender.

RESULTS

Long Term Goals

Table 1 summarizes the findings related to long-term goals. The vast majority of 113 discrete long-term goals identified by boys and girls fell into one of four categories: *athletics/celebrity* (23.0%); *academics* (25.7%); *professions requiring a degree* (24.8%); and *professions not requiring a degree* (16.8%). Only 11 (9.7%) of the long-term goals did not fit conceptually into one of these four categories.

Table 1. Number and Percentage of 113 Long-Term Goals by Gender and Category

Category	Male (subtotal = 59)		Female (subtotal = 54)		Combined (total = 113)	
	Number	Percentage	Number	Percentage	Number	Percentage
Athletics/ Celebrity	21	35.6%	5	9.3%	26	23.0%
Academics	15	25.4%	14	25.9%	29	25.7%
Profession requiring degree	5	8.5%	23	42.6%	28	24.8%
Profession not requiring degree	13	22%	6	11.1%	19	16.8%
Other	5	8.5%	6	11.1%	11	9.7%

The definitions for each of these categories as well as narrative examples from boys and girls are presented in Table 2.

Table 2. Definitions and Narrative Examples for Long-Term Goal Categories

Category	Definition	Narrative Example	
		Male	Female
Athletics/ Celebrity	Related to professional athletics or celebrity status connected to the entertainment industry.	I want to be a professional basketball player.	I want to make it in the WNBA.
Academics	Connected to higher education.	Getting a Ph.D.	Finishing school and go to college.
Profession requiring degree	Required the equivalent of a bachelor's degree or higher.	I want to be a lawyer.	My long term goal is to become a physician or a pediatrician because those are the two things that I would like to look up to be in life.
Profession not requiring degree	Recognized career that requires specialized training.	To be a police officer.	My goal is to be a beautician after high school.
Other	Aspirations that were difficult to link with others because they were very broad, vague, or unique.	I hope I get better at math.	I want to have a good career and family.

The proportion of boys and girls who shared long-term goals related to *academics* were quite similar, 25.4% and 25.9%, respectively. Also, there was little difference in the proportion of long-term goals that did not fit cleanly into one of the major categories. The largest difference by gender was in the category of *profession requiring a degree*. Girls (42.6%) were much more likely than boys (8.5%) to share goals of this type. Consistent with the previous finding, boys were twice as likely as girls (22.0% vs. 11.1%) to identify *professions not requiring a degree*. Boys were much more likely to have goals related to *athletics/celebrity* than girls, 35.6% and 9.3%, respectively.

Short Term Goals

Table 3 summarizes the findings related to short-term goals. The 102 discrete short-term goals generated by participants were placed into four different categories: *athletics* (47.1%); *academics* (12.7%); *career preparation* (17.6%); and *persistence* (22.5%).

Table 3. Number and Percentage of 102 Short-Term Goals by Gender and Category

Category	Male (subtotal = 52)		Female (subtotal = 50)		Combined (total = 102)	
	Number	Percentage	Number	Percentage	Number	Percentage
Athletics/ Celebrity	27	51.9%	21	42.0%	48	47.1%
Academics	9	17.3%	4	8.0%	13	12.7%
Career Preparation	5	9.6%	13	26.0%	18	17.6%
Persistence	11	21.2%	12	24.0%	23	22.5%

Definitions and narrative examples for each of these categories can be found in Table 4.

Table 4: Definitions and Narrative Examples for Short-Term Goal Categories

Category	Definition	Narrative Example	
		Male	Female
Athletics	Connected in some way to sports participation.	Practice everyday in the school gym for I can get better in basketball.	During high school I would have to play sports and learn about how things work in the sports life.
Academic Outcomes	Includes some mention of academic outcomes such as graduating or getting into college.	I want to graduate from high school and college.	I need to stay in school and go to college and take some class.
Career Preparation	Refers to activities specifically related to a career identified in the same participant's long-term goal.	Reading books about computers, find out different colleges I can go to and be a computer technician.	I want to work in a beauty shop. [long-term goal was to be a beautician]
Persistence	Short-term goals revolving around behaviors and attitudes needed to persevere and achieve goals.	My goal is to work harder in school, to get good grades.	What I need to do to reach my goal is to stay in class do my work and don't hang around the crowd.

Boys were more likely than girls to identify short-term goals related to *athletics* (51.9% vs. 42.0%) and *academics* (17.3% vs. 8.0%). However, girls were more likely than boys to identify short-term goals that connected directly to *career preparation* (26.0% vs. 9.6%). Girls were slightly more likely to identify goals connected to *persistence* (24.0% vs. 21.2%).

Obstacles

Participants were asked to identify obstacles that might prevent them from reaching their goals. Table 5 summarizes the findings related to these obstacles. In total, 118 discrete obstacles were identified. These were placed into seven different categories: *negative peer influence* (21.2%); *getting into trouble* (6.8%); *lack of persistence* (24.6%); *substance abuse* (11.9%); *circumstance* (18.6%); *self-control issues* (7.6%); and *no obstacles* (9.3%).

Table 5. Number and Percentage of 118 Obstacles by Gender and Category

Category	Male (subtotal = 61)		Female (subtotal = 57)		Combined (total = 118)	
	Number	Percentage	Number	Percentage	Number	Percentage
Negative Peer Influence	14	23.0%	11	19.3%	25	21.2%
Getting into Trouble	3	4.9%	5	8.8%	8	6.8%
Lack of Persistence	12	19.7%	17	29.8%	29	24.6%
Substance Abuse	12	19.7%	2	3.5%	14	11.9%
Circumstance	11	18.0%	11	19.3%	22	18.6%
Self-Control Issues	3	4.9%	6	10.5%	9	7.6%
Obstacles	6	9.8%	5	8.8%	11	9.3%

Table 6 contains definitions and narrative examples for each of these categories.

Table 6: Definitions and Narrative Examples for Obstacle Categories

Category	Definition	Narrative Example	
		Male	Female
Negative Peer Influence	Identifies the negative influence of other individuals.	Gangs, bad friends, and not studying.	Peer pressure.
Getting into Trouble	Mentions actions that break laws or rules and/or refers to negative consequences.	Like going to jail and having a record.	Like getting in trouble.
Lack of Persistence	Recognizes that goals may not be reached do to lack of focus, effort, or determination.	Laziness-main problem.	I might get lazy and not study, read, or ask questions.
Substance Abuse	Involves some mention of alcohol, tobacco, or illicit drugs.	Things that would stop me would probably be drugs, low self esteem, and people who might try to put me down.	Drugs, people such as bad influences on you.
Circumstance	References situations or life circumstances that may or may not be under the individual's control.	If the Lord take my life.	Teen pregnancy.
Self-Control Issues	Conveys problems with controlling words and actions, i.e. losing temper.	Fighting.	My temper and my attitude.
No Obstacles	Responses that expressed strong determination and a belief that no obstacles could hold the individual back.	Nothing!	No one can stop me.

Differences were quite small (less than two percentage points) in two of the categories, *circumstance* and *no obstacles*. Boys were more likely to identify obstacles related to *negative peer influence* (23.0% vs. 19.3%) and *substance abuse* (19.7% vs. 3.5%). Girls were more likely than boys to mention *getting into trouble* (8.8% vs. 4.9%), *lack of persistence* (29.8% vs. 19.7%), and *self-control issues* (10.5% vs. 4.9%).

CONCLUSION

The purpose of this study was to investigate possible gender differences related to the life goals and perceived obstacles of participants in a PSRM physical activity program. In the broader field of physical education pedagogy, there is an increasing interest in understanding girls' experiences (Flintoff & Scraton, 2006). This mirrors a growing appreciation among social scientists in the complexity of affective development in adolescent girls (Garbarino, 2007; Pipher, 1994; Simmons, 2002). While there is a strong body of evidence supporting the PSRM as an instructional model, gender issues require further exploration. Wright and Ding (2005) provided momentum for this line of inquiry by demonstrating PSRM's potential to promote gender equity. Findings from that study and others suggest a key to the model's effectiveness rests in the ability to establish relevance for participants beyond the program setting (Wright & Burton, in press; Wright & Ding, 2005; Wright et al., 2007). Making physical education relevant to students is a characteristic of successful programs, especially in urban environments (Ennis, 1999). By understanding participants' life goals and perceived obstacles, practitioners may be able to increase their program's relevance. Regarding goals and obstacles of participants in this study, all categories applied to boys and girls. This indicates the categories were broadly relevant and not gender specific. With that said, the salience of some categories did seem to vary with gender.

Relative to goals, boys were more likely to have aspirations related to athletics. This was seen in both the long- and short-term goals. Girls, on the other hand, were more focused on professions. They were much more likely than boys to set goals related to professions requiring academic degrees. However, the two groups were equally likely to report academic goals related to higher education. Boys were less likely overall to set goals involving professions, and when they did, they were more likely than girls to name professions that did not require degrees. The girls' focus on career goals was also highlighted by the fact that they were more likely to set short-term goals that were directly linked to a profession cited in their long-term goal.

Obstacle categories also applied broadly to both genders. Because the setting for this study was an impoverished inner-city neighborhood, it is not surprising that issues such as gangs, drug abuse, criminal activity, academic failure, and fighting emerged as concerns. Although the rate of teen pregnancy in this neighborhood and school community was very high, only two girls identified this issue as an obstacle to achieving their goals. In terms of gender differences in the obstacle categories, boys were much more likely to refer to substance abuse and girls were more likely to report lack of persistence as obstacles. It is interesting to note that girls were slightly more likely than boys to identify obstacles related to getting into trouble and self-control issues such as fighting. This finding is noteworthy in light of recent social trends related to the prevalence of defiant and physically aggressive behaviors among adolescent girls (Garbarino, 2007; Simmons, 2002).

Implications for Practice

The results of this study are directly relevant to practitioners working in physical education settings, but may be transferable to other contexts such as after-school programs and summer camps. Indeed, many PSRM programs are offered in community-based programs (Hellison et al., 2000). We encourage practitioners to engage participants in a similar process rather than simply generalizing these findings. With that said, these findings may provide a useful starting point for discussions of transfer. These findings support the reliance of PSRM practitioners on goal-setting exercises and discussions of transfer (Hellison, 2003). Based on this sample, it appears adolescents are fully capable of engaging in such discussions in the context of a PSRM program with a reasonable degree of sophistication and honesty. A key challenge, of course, is to connect these discussions to the physical activity program. The PSRM literature is replete with strategies to accomplish this (in particular, see Hellison, 2003 and Hellison et al., 2000). It is worth noting that the core responsibilities of the PSRM can be linked to many of the categories that emerged in this study. For example, the issue of persistence emerged in short-term goals and obstacles. In the Tai Chi Tiger program, the first author/instructor capitalized on this by highlighting the relevance of effort, a core PSRM responsibility. Effort was framed as a life skill that could be practiced in the program and applied in other situations such as schoolwork. In a similar way, obstacles related to self-control and getting into trouble were linked to the PSRM responsibility of respect. Good decision-making regarding substance abuse and negative peer influence was connected to the PSRM responsibility of self-direction.

Based on the current findings, we encourage practitioners to highlight the importance of careers and higher education as they promote the idea of transfer in PSRM programs. These topics were relevant to many participants this study and often linked in concrete ways to their own life goals. Walsh has provided a good example of this approach in his career club curriculum that combines the PSRM with a focus on possible futures (Martinek, Hellison, & Walsh, 2004). One strong element of his approach is the emphasis on procedural knowledge such as learning the steps required to enter a given career. Findings in the current study indicate that female participants may be more likely to think about their futures in this way. With this said, we caution practitioners against assuming what obstacles or concerns are relevant to participants based on gender stereotypes or the results of a single study. As noted by Wright and Ding (2005), gender equity is not achieved by neglecting the boys in order to balance an historical injustice. Rather, it means providing content, initiating discussions, and creating a learning environment that does not systematically exclude or marginalize anyone. The current study indicates it is possible to accomplish this in PSRM programs. However, the teacher or program leader must have an awareness of gender differences and a commitment to assuring equity.

Implications for Research

Findings from the current study may be of interest to researchers designing interventions to address physical inactivity and obesity, especially those involving African American adolescent females. This segment of the population is potentially at the highest risk for the ill effects of inactivity and sedentary living, including obesity, cardiovascular disease, diabetes, and some forms of cancer (Kimm et al., 2002; Taylor et al., 2002; Tershakovec, Kuppler, Zemel, & Stallings, 2002). Gender and race/ethnicity have been shown to be predictors of obesity prevalence in that females have higher obesity rates compared to males, and obesity rates are higher in African American girls compared to Caucasian girls (CDC, 2005; Swallen, Reither, Haas, & Meier, 2005). In fact, over the last three decades, the most dramatic increases in the prevalence of overweight in the US have been reported in African-American girls (Troiano et al., 1995). Regarding physical activity, studies have found that girls are less active than boys, and African American girls are less active than Caucasian girls (CDC, 2005). In a recent study of 1,668 adolescent girls, African American girls spent less time engaged in moderate to vigorous physical activity and more time in sedentary activities than their Caucasian counterparts (Felton, et al., 2002). The PSRM represents a field-tested set of instructional strategies that appears to effectively engage and motivate male and female African American adolescents in physical activity programs (see Hellison & Walsh, 2002 and Hellison & Martinek, 2006). Moreover, research indicates PSRM programs can foster commitment and sustained participation among participants (Hellison & Wright, 2003; Schilling, 2001; Schilling, Martinek, & Carson, 2007). Therefore, while the ultimate aims of the PSRM relate to social-emotional development, we propose that further study of the PSRM's effectiveness in promoting physical activity and combating obesity in school-based physical education as well as community-based programming is warranted.

REFERENCES

Aaron, D. J., Storti, K. L., Robertson, R. J., Kriska, A. M., & LaPorte, R. E. (2002). Longitudinal study of the number and choice of leisure time physical activities from mid to late adolescence. *Arch Pediatr Adolesc Med, 156*, 1075-1080.

American Heart Association. (AHA). (2005). Overweight in children and adolescents. *Circulation*. 2005, 111, 1999-2012. Retrieved on September 16, 2006, from *http://circ.ahajournals.org/cgi/content/full/111/15/1999*.

Beveridge, S., & Scruggs, P. (2000). TLC for better PE: Girls and elementary physical education. *Journal of Physical Education, Recreation and Dance, 71*, 22-27.

Brown, D., & Evans, J. (2004). Reproducing Gender? Intergenerational links and the male PE teacher as a culture conduit in teaching physical education. *Journal of Teaching in Physical Education, 23*, 48-70.

Center for Disease Control and Prevention (CDC). (1997). Guidelines for school and community programs to promote lifelong physical activity among young people. *Morbidity and Mortality Weekly Report, 1997; 46, (No. RR-6)*

Center for Disease Control and Prevention (CDC). (1999). Physical Activity and Health: A Report to the Surgeon General. Retrieved March 24, 2007, from *http://www.cdc.gov/nccdphp/sgr/adults.htm*.

Center for Disease Control and Prevention (CDC). (2000). Promoting Better Health for Young People Through Physical Activity and Sports: A Report to the President. Retrieved July 7, 2007, from *http://www.cdc.gov/HealthyYouth/physicalactivity/promoting_health/references*

Center for Disease Control and Prevention (CDC). (2005). Prevalence of overweight among children and adolescents: United States, 1999-2002. Retrieved September 16, 2006, from National Center for Health Statistics website: *http://www.cdc.gov/nchs/products/pubs/pubd/hestats/overwght99.htm*.

Centers for Disease Control and Prevention (CDC). (2006). Overweight and obesity: contributing factors. Retrieved January 17, 2006, from http://www.cdc.gov/nccdphp/dnpa/obesity/contributing_factors.htm.

Chen, D., & Sherman, C. (2002). Teaching balance with Tai Chi: Strategies for college and secondary school instruction. *Journal of Physical Education, Recreation & Dance, 73*, 31-37.

Duda, J. L., & Nicholls, J. (1992). Dimensions of achievement motivation in schoolwork and sport. *Journal of Educational Psychology, 84*, 1-10.

Ennis, C. D. (1999). Communicating the value of active, healthy lifestyles to urban students. *Quest, 51*, 164-169.

Felton, G. M., Dowda, M., & Ward, D. S. (2002). Differences in physical activity between black and white girls living in rural and urban area. *Journal of School Health, 72*, 250-255.

Flintoff, A., & Scraton, S. (2006). Girls and physical education. In D. Kirk, D. MacDonald, and M. O'Sullivan (Ed.s), *The Handbook of Physical Educaton* (pp. 767-783. Thousand Oaks, CA: Sage.

Fox, K. (2003). Childhood obesity and the role of physical activity. *JRSH* 2003; 124:34-39.

Gabarino, J. (2006). *See Jane hit: Why girls are growing up more violent and what we can do about it*. New York: Penguin Press.

Gordon-Larsen, P., Nelson, M. C., & Popkin, B. M. (2004). Longitudinal physical activity and sedentary behavior trends: adolescence to adulthood. *Am J Prev Med, 27*(4), 277-283.

Greenwood, M., Stillwell, J., & Byars, A. (2001). Activity preferences of middle school physical education students. *Physical Educator, 58*, 26-29.

Harrison, L., & Worthy, T. (2001). "Just like all the rest" Developing awareness of stereotypical thinking in physical education. *Journal of Physical Education, Recreation and Dance, 72*, 21-24.

Hedley, A. A., Ogden, C. L., Johnson, C. L., Carroll, M. D., Curtin, L. R., et al. (2004). Prevalence of overweight and obesity among US children, adolescents, and adults, 1999-2002. *JAMA, 291*(23), 2847-2850.

Hellison, D. (2003). *Teaching responsibility through physical activity* (2nd ed.). Champaign, IL: Human Kinetics.

Hellison, D., Cutforth, N., Martinek, T., Kallusky, J., Parker, M., & Steihl, J. (2000). *Youth development and physical activity: Linking universities and communities*. Champaign, IL: Human Kinetics.

Hellison, D., & Walsh, D. (2002). Responsibility-based youth programs evaluation: Investigating the investigations. *Quest, 54*, 292-307.

Hellison, D., & Wright, P. M. (2003) Retention in an urban extended day program: A process-based assessment. *Journal of Teaching in Physical Education, 22*, 369-381.

Hill, J. O., & Melanson, E. L. (1999). Overview of the determinants of overweight and obesity: current evidence and research issues. *Med Sci Sports Exerc, 31*(11), S515-521.

Hopwood, T., & Carrington, B. (1994). Physical education and femininity. *Educational Research, 36*, 237-246.

Kelder S. H., Perry C. L., & Klepp, K. I. (1993). Community-wide youth exercise promotion: long-term outcomes of the Minnesota Heart Health Program and the Class of 1989 Study. *Journal of School Health, 63*(5), 218-223.

Kimm, S. Y., & Obarzanek, E. (2002). Childhood obesity: a new pandemic of the new millennium. *Pediatrics, 110*(5), 1003-1007.

Kohl, H., & Hobbs, K. (1998). Development of physical activity behaviors among children and adolescents. *Pediatrics, 101*, 549-554.

LeCompte, M. D., & Preissle, J. (1993). *Ethnography and qualitative design in educational research*. San Diego, CA: Academic Press.

Li, W., & Lee, A. M. (2004). A review of conceptions of ability and related motivational constructs in achievement motivation. *Quest, 56*, 439-461.

Li, W., Wright, P. M., Rukavina, P., & Pickering, M. (2007). Measuring Students' Perceptions of Personal and Social Responsibility and its Relationship to Enjoyment in Urban Physical Education. Paper presented at the 2007 American Educational Research Association National Conference, Chicago, IL.

Lincoln, Y. S., & Guba, E. G. (1985). *Naturalistic inquiry*. Beverly Hills, CA: Sage.

Martinek, T., & Hellison, D. (1997). Service-bonded inquiry: The road less traveled. *Journal of Teaching in Physical Education, 17*, 107-121.

Martinek, T., Hellison, D., & Walsh, D. (2004). Service-bonded inquiry revisited: A research model for the community-engaged professor. *Quest, 56*, 397-412.

Martinek, T., Schilling, T., & Johnson, D. (2001). Evaluation of a sport and mentoring program designed to foster personal and social responsibility in underserved youth. *The Urban Review , 33*, 29-45.

McCaughtry, N. (2004). Learning to read gender relations in schooling: Implications of personal history and teaching context on identifying disempowerment for girls. *Research Quarterly for Exercise and Sport, 75*, 400-412.

McKenzie, T. L., Prochaska, J. J., Sallis, J.F., & LaMaster, K. J. (2004). Coeducational and single-sex physical education in middle schools: Impact on physical activity. *Research Quarterly for Exercise and Sport, 75*, 446-449.

National Association for Sport and Physical Education. (2004). *Moving into the future. National standards for physical education (2nd ed)*. Reston, VA: NASPE Publications.

Ogden, C. L., Carroll, M. D., Curtin, L. R., McDowell, M. A., Tabak, C. J., et al. (2006). Prevalence of overweight and obesity in the United States, 1999-2004. *JAMA, 295*(13), 1549-1555.

Olshansky, S. J., Passaro, D. J., Hershow, R. C., Layden, J., Carnes, B. A., et al. (2005). A potential decline in life expectancy in the United States in the 21st century. *N Engl J Med, 352*(11), 1138-1145.

Osborne, K., Bauer, A., & Sutliff, M. (2002). Middle school students' perceptions of coed versus non-coed physical education. *Physical Educator, 59*, 83-89.

Pate R. R., Heath, G. W., Dowda, M., & Trost, S. G. (1996). Associations between physical activity and other health behaviors in a representative sample of US adolescents. *American Journal of Public Health, 86*(11), 1577-1581.

Patton, Q. M. (2002). *Qualitative research and evaluation methods (3rd ed.)*. Thousand Oaks, CA: Sage.

Pipher, M. (1994). *Reviving Ophelia: Saving the selves of adolescent girls*. New York: Riverhead Trade.

Prusak, K. A., & Darst, P. W. (2002). Effects of types of walking activities on actual choices by adolescent female physical education students. *Journal of Teaching in Physical Education, 21*, 230-241.

Prusak, K. A., Treasure, D. C., Darst, P. W., & Pangrazi, R. P. (2004). The effects of choice on the motivation of adolescent girls in physical education. *Journal of Teaching in Physical Education, 23*, 19-29.

Racette, S. B., Deusinger, S. S., & Deusinger, R. H. (2003). Obesity: overview of prevalence, etiology, and treatment. *Physical Therapy, 83*, Retrieved September 16, 2006, from http://www.ptjournal.org/cgi/content/full/83/3/276.

Ryan, G. W., & Bernard, H. R. (2000). Data management and analysis methods. In N.K. Denzin & Y.S. Lincoln (Ed.s), *Handbook of Qualitative Research,* (2nd ed., pp. 769-802). Thousand Oaks, CA: Sage.

Schilling, T. (2001). An investigation of the commitment among participants in an extended day physical activity program. *Research Quarterly for Exercise and Sport, 72*, 355-365.

Schilling, T., Martinek, T., & Carson, S. (2007). Youth leaders' perceptions of commitment to a responsibility-based physical activity program. *Research Quarterly for Exercise and Sport, 78*, 48-60.

Simmons, R. (2002). *Odd girl out: The hidden culture of aggression in girls*. New York: Harcourt.

Strauss, R. S. (2000). Childhood obesity and self-esteem. *Pediatric, 105*(1), 1-5.

Strauss, R. S., & Pollack, H. A. (2003). Social marginalization of overweight children. *Arch Pediatr Adolesc Med, 157*, 733-738.

Swallen, K., Reither, E., Haas, S., & Meier A. (2005). Overweight, obesity, and health-related quality of life among adolescents: The National Longitudinal Study of Adolescent Health [Abstract]. *Pediatrics, 115*, 340-347.

Taylor, W., Chan, W., Cummings, S., Simons-Morton, B., Day, R., Sangi-Haghpeykar, H., et al. (2002). Healthy growth: Project description and baseline finding. *Ethnic Diseases, 12*, 567-577.

Tershakovec, A., Kuppler, K., Zemel, B., & Stallings, V. (2002). Age, sex, ethnicity, and body composition, and resting energy expenditure of obese African American and white children and adolescents. *American Journal of Clinical Nutrition, 75*, 867-871.

Troiano, R., Flegal, K., Kuczmarski, R., Campbell, S., & Johnson, C. (1995). Overweight prevalence and trends for children and adolescents. The National Health and Nutrition Examination Surveys, 1963-1991. *Archives of Pediatric & Adolescent Medicine, 149*, 1085-1091.

U.S. Department of Health and Human Services. (USDHHS). (1996). Physical activity and health: A report of the Surgeon General. Atlanta, GA: U.S. Dept. of Health and Human Services, Centers for Disease Control and Prevention.

U.S. Department of Health and Human Services. (USDHHS). (2000). Healthy People 2010: conference edition. Washington, D.C.: U.S. Department of Health and Human Services.

U.S. Department of Health and Human Services, Office of the Surgeon General. (2001). *The Surgeon General's Call to Action to Prevent and Decrease Overweight and Obesity*. Rockville, Md: US Department of Health and Human Services.

University of New Hampshire Cooperative Extension (UNH). (2002). Promoting physical exercise and activity in children. Retrieved on January 18, 2007, from www.ceinfo.unh.edu.

van Baal, P. H., Hoogenveen, R. T., de Wit, G. A., & Boshuizen, H. C. (2006). Estimating health-adjusted life expectancy conditional on risk factors: results for smoking and obesity. *Popul Health Metr, 4*, 14.

Vertinsky, P.A. (1992) Reclaiming space, revisioning the body: The quest for gender-sensitive physical education. *Quest, 42*, 373-396.

Williams, J., Wake, M., Hesketh, K., Maher, E., & Waters, E. (2005). Health-related quality of life of overweight and obese children. *JAMA, 293*(1), 70-76.

World Health Organization (WHO). (2006). Obesity and overweight. Retrieved September 16, 2006, from http://www.who.int/dietphysicalactivity/publications/facts/obesity/en.

Wright, P. M., & Burton, S. (in press). Examining the implementation and immediate outcomes of a personal-social responsibility model program for urban high school students. *Journal of Teaching in Physical Education.*

Wright, P. M., & Ding, S. (2005). Promoting gender equity in urban physical education through curricular innovation. Paper included in *Proceedings of the 3rd Annual National Conference on Girls and Women in Physical Activity.* Shreveport, LA.

Wright, P. M., Li, W., Ding, S.,& Pickering, M. (2007). Impact of the Personal and Social Responsibility Model on Urban High School Students' Academic Outcomes. Paper presented at the 2007 American Educational Research Association National Conference, Chicago, IL.

In: Progress in Exercise and Women's Health Research
Editor: Janet P. Coulter, pp. 177-192
ISBN 1-60456-014-5
© 2008 Nova Science Publishers, Inc.

Chapter 6

PHYSICAL ACTIVITY INTERVENTIONS IN AFRICAN AMERICAN WOMEN

Ashutosh Atri[1] and Manoj Sharma[2]

[1]University of Texas, 1800 El Paseo Street, # 1214Houston, TX 77054
[2]Health Promotion & Education, University of Cincinnati, PO Box 210068, Cincinnati, OH 45221-0068

ABSTRACT

The health status of African American women continues to lag behind their white counterparts. Despite the beneficial effects of physical activity on health African American women remain the least physically active subgroups within the United States. The purpose of this article was to review physical activity promotion and weight loss interventions targeted towards African American women who were 18 years or older. In order to collect the materials for the study, a search of Academic Search Premier, CINAHL, ERIC, and MEDLINE databases was carried out for the time period 2000 June 2007. A total of 11 interventions met the search criteria. Only four out of the 11 interventions were rooted in behavioral theories. The theories used were social action theory, social cognitive theory, behavior choice treatment and the social ecological model. Future interventions need to reify behavioral theories. Seven out of the 11 studies made accommodations for cultural sensitivity while four interventions made no mention of the concept. However, out of the seven studies only one study distinguished cultural sensitivity into its superficial and deep dimensions and addressed both those realms. Future interventions need to be culturally sensitive. With regard to process evaluation only one intervention included a formative and a process evaluation component. Future interventions need to utilize process evaluations. In terms of the duration, three of the interventions were brief (up to 12 weeks), four were middle range (five to six months) and four were 12 months long. Interventions that did not employ theoretical frameworks

---

[1] Corresponding author: (Phone) (740) 406-0284, (E-mail) ashutosh_atri@hotmail.com

[2] Corresponding author: (Phone) (513) 556-3878, (Fax) (513) 556-3898 and (E-mail) manoj.sharma@uc.edu.

were longer in duration than the ones which did. If more interventions are theory based they can be more efficient and shorter in duration. Most of the interventions focused on short term changes right after the intervention and it is essential to have measures at least at six months after the intervention to see for the retention of behavior change. On the whole, interventions have resulted in modest changes in behaviors and have shown mixed results with indicators of physical inactivity thereby necessitating more effective use of theoretical approaches.

INTRODUCTION

Despite accounting for a mere 12 % of the US population African Americans have the poorest health status indicators in the country (United States Department of Health and Human Services [USDHHS], 1995). The health status of African American women continues to lag behind their white counterparts regardless of the major improvements in mortality rates, heart disease, stroke, and obesity, (USDHHS, 1995). African Americans continue to be two times more likely than whites to have hypertension, obesity, and high fat intake. Poor nutrition, smoking, alcohol, and drug abuse are reported to occur commonly in African American women thereby increasing the risk for several chronic conditions. Coronary heart disease, hypertension and diabetes are found much more commonly in African American women in comparison to other ethnic groups.

The African American female health concerns are further compounded by the obesity epidemic. It deserves concern due mainly to two reasons- first the widening reaches of the obesity epidemic as the American baby boomers age and secondly, the fact that the epidemic is disproportionately concentrated in the black population. Although body weight increases with age for most people, African American women display a marked excess of obesity compared with women of other ethnicities and with men (Mokdad, Serdula, Dietz, Bowman, Marks, & Koplan, 1999). Consequently, rates are elevated in this group for a number of obesity-related health outcomes, including certain cancers. As 20% of cancer incidence in women is attributable to obesity and obesity increases cancer mortality, black women represent a high-risk group for such obesity-related cancers as colon cancer, breast cancer, multiple myeloma, and endometrial cancer.

Modifiable risk factors that promote obesity include high-risk dietary and physical activity patterns. Despite the fact that physical activity has been known to reduce the morbidity and mortality from these and other conditions, research demonstrates that African American women remain the least physically active subgroups within the United States (Young & Stewart, 2006). Crespo and colleagues (2000) found that African Americans are more likely to have a sedentary lifestyle than whites. Further African American women are considerably more likely than white women to be overweight. Alarming is the revelation that, these differences appear to be independent of socioeconomic status (Troiano & Flegal, 1998; Crespo, Smit, Andersen, Carter-Pokras, & Ainsworth, 2000).

The purpose of this article was to review physical activity promotion and weight loss interventions targeted towards healthy African American women who were 18 years or older. Recent interventions in this area have been reviewed and recommendations for the field of health education have been provided. The review has been limited to interventions focusing exclusively on the African American female population resident within the United States.

METHODS

In order to collect the materials for the study, a search of Academic Search Premier, CINAHL, ERIC, and MEDLINE databases was carried out for the time period 2000 - June 2007. The criteria for inclusion of the studies were:

- Publication in English language;
- Publication between 2000 and June 2007 (however, also included were any previous studies that were published in the specified time period);
- Location of the study in the United States;
- Focus on African American women with women older than 18 years of age.

Exclusion criteria were publications in languages other than English, publications prior to 2000, studies conducted outside of the United States and studies that focused on three or more ethnic groups, studies in which the target population was drawn from hospital populations and/or populations diagnosed with more than one chronic conditions, was composed of more than one ethnic group and if the interventions focused predominantly on elderly populations or African American children. Studies comparing findings from African American women with not more than one ethnic group were included.

RESULTS

We were able to locate 11 such interventions. These have been summarized in Table 1 below.

Table 1. Summary of physical activity promotion and weight loss interventions targeted towards African American women

Study/age/year	Participants (n)	Theory	Intervention	Duration	Major Findings
SisterTalk (Gans et. al, 2003) 30-60 years 1999	373 African American women	Social Action Theory	A cable television delivered weight control program	12 months	
Breast health/weight loss (Fitzgibbon et al., 2005) 35-65 years 2001	64 black women	Social Cognitive Theory	Reduce weight Reduce dietary fat Increase physical activity Increase breast self examination competence	20 week	Frequency of regular physical activity, duration of physical activity and intensity higher for intervention group than control group
Church based intervention by Young & Stewart (2006) 25-70 years 2004	196 women	None	Church based aerobic exercise intervention designed to increase physical activity	6 months	No significant change in the increases in physical activity levels in a church based aerobic & a stretch & health intervention

Table 1. Continued

Study/age/year	Participants (n)	Theory	Intervention	Duration	Major Findings
Randomized pilot trial (Newton & Perry , 2004) 30-69 years 2002	60 women	None	Culturally sensitive exercise counseling Standard behavior exercise counseling Physician advice	6 months	Home-based exercise counseling programs are effective for improving fitness. Addition of culturally tailored components may not be sufficient to produce better outcomes than standard behavioralcounseling .
Behavioral Choice Treatment (Sbrocco et al., 2005) 18-55 yrs 2003	20 African American women	Behavior choice treatment	How to stop dieting and utilize health behaviors for health outcomes Computerized Self monitoring Two week meal plans and recipe booklets	12 week	1) African American church group experienced significant weight change 2) Higher adherence to the intervention by church based group in comparison to the university group
Fight Cancer with Fitness (Yancey et al., 2006) 21-77 years	366 African American women	Social ecological model	Weekly two hour sessions including exercise instruction and skills training in balanced exercise regimens Nutrition education about a low fat complex carbohydrate diet	8 week	1) Weight stability in the intervention group at 2 months 2) Intervention & control group fitness improved 3) Long term fitness (waist circumference stability) not found in intervention group
Steps to soulful living (Karanja et al. 2002) 35-53 years 2000	66 African American women	None	1) Weekly group counseling meetings 2) Exercise classes at a community center 3) Nutrition & behavior modification topics	6 months	1) Duration of exercise of participants increased 2) Significant changes in reported intake of total energy and dietary fat 3) Mean weight loss of 3.7 ±5.1 kg

Table 1. Continued

Study/age/year	Participants (n)	Theory	Intervention	Duration	Major Findings
Changes in steps per day by (Banks-Wallace & Conn, 2005) 25-68 years 2003	21 sedentary African American women	None	1) Monthly group meetings focusing on health promotion topics and group exercises 2) Home based walking component encouraging increase in walking & selecting partners	12 months	Positive impact on walking in sedentary hypertension prone African American women
Healthy Body/Healthy Spirit (Resnicow et al, 2002, 2005) 18-85 years 2005	906 individuals mostly women	None	1) Standard nutrition and Physical activity (PA) materials 2) Culturally targeted self-help nutrition & PA materials, 3) Telephone counseling calls	12 months	a) Self-help interventions more likely to induce change in fruit and vegetable intake and physical activity than educational materials b) Motivational interviewing further increased fruits & vegetable consumption but not physical activity in the self-help culturally targeted materials.
Project Joy (Yanek et al., 2001) 40 and older 2001	529 women	None	1) Weekly nutrition & physical activity sessions 2) Group prayers & health messages with scriptures 3) Church sponsored events	12 months	1) Significant change for 11 cardiovascular risk factors in intervention group. 2) Higher number of sessions attended, older age, higher baseline BMI & inclusion in the active intervention groups were significant predictors of weight loss.
Rush Medical Center study (Staffileno et al., 2007) 18-45 years 2002-2004	24 women	None	1) Lifestyle physical activity (walking, stair climbing etc.) 2) Private educational sessions reviewing lifestyle physical activity	8 week	1) Exercise group had significant reduction in systolic blood pressure 2) No significant change in ambulatory blood pressure

The first intervention was designed and evaluated by Gans and colleagues (2003) and named "Sister Talk." This was a culturally sensitive intervention for black women that built on the previous successes of group weight loss programs, but used cable TV to provide a home-based alternative to the traditional, center-based intervention approach. Community networking and both qualitative and quantitative interview techniques from the fields of social marketing and cultural anthropology were used to involve black women from Boston in the design and implementation of a program that would be practical, appealing, and culturally sensitive. The core "Sister Talk" intervention consisted of 12 one hour weekly programs broadcast live on cable TV. The "SisterTalk" behavioral change approach was based on Social Action Theory (SAT), an approach that integrates cognitive and social processes known to influence the acquisition and long-term maintenance of lifestyle behaviors. The researchers attempted to address the superficial and deep structures of cultural competence and conducted 28 focus groups with a total of 193 black women at nine different community sites over an eight and a half month period from August 1997 to May 1998. The quantitative data from this survey were analyzed by exploring frequency distributions, e.g., prevalence of various attitudes or behaviors. The open-ended survey responses helped the researchers to obtain depth of understanding of the range and nature of possible barriers and facilitators to weight control. Overall, the marketing survey data confirmed and in some cases added to our understanding of the issues and helped them to determine the proper emphasis for certain content in "Sister Talk."

Some of the insights gathered from the evaluation of this program were that at least 12–18 months of intensive formative research is usually required for maximum cultural tailoring and effectiveness when the topic and/or population have been understudied. The intervention also brings out the value of having both white and black moderators at each focus group. Having a black focus group moderator was important for gaining the trust of the community, while having a white moderator was helpful in probing further on issues and examples that the black moderator may have glossed over as "common knowledge." The "Sister Talk" program could easily be adapted for black women in other parts of the United States. Given the comprehensiveness of the behavioral principles used in "Sister Talk," this program could provide a useful starting point for development of weight control programs for other ethnic and racial groups.

The second intervention by Fitzgibbon and colleagues (2005) involved a pilot intervention to test the feasibility and efficacy of conducting a combined (breast health/weight loss) intervention in the African American women. Citing the disproportionate mortality rates among black women as compared to white women as their motivation, these researchers conducted a randomized pilot intervention trial to assess the feasibility and efficacy of a combined breast health/weight loss intervention. Sixty four overweight or obese Black women, ages 35–65 participated in the intervention. The primary objectives were to determine whether a 20-week (twice weekly) intervention could decrease weight and dietary fat intake and increase both physical activity and breast self-exam (BSE) proficiency. High retention rates (96% and 89%) marked both the cohorts in which this project was implemented. Both cohorts showed increased proficiency in BSE in the intervention versus the control group (2.4 vs. −0.4, $p < 0.05$; 3.3 vs. −0.2, $p < 0.001$, respectively), but only cohort two showed decreased percent body weight (4.0% decrease vs. 0.9% increase, $p < 0.01$), increased physical activity frequency (2.4 vs. 0.1 times/week, $p < 0.05$), and a trend for decreased dietary fat (−2.6% kcal vs. 0.0% kcal, $p = 0.07$) in the intervention compared to the control group.

The study is one of its kinds in that it focuses on combined intervention strategies and makes a cause for the same. It documents the feasibility of recruiting, randomizing, and retaining women in a combined intervention and demonstrated weight loss and associated lifestyle changes. Of note is the fact, that studies exploring the linkage between weight and breast cancer have produced contradictory results. The study proves that the challenge of how to effecting change in diverse behaviors (breast health, physical activity, and dietary intake consistent with weight loss) that are complementary in the sense that they are related to reducing breast cancer risk but require different methods to effect change, is well possible and feasible.

The third intervention was done by Young & Stewart (2006) which sought to evaluate a six-month, church-based aerobic exercise intervention to increase physical activity among African American women against a health lecture and stretching condition. Participants were 196 women from 11 churches. Churches were randomized to an Aerobic Exercise or Health N Stretch intervention. Similar to the approach taken by Fitzgibbon and colleagues (2005) these researchers incorporated formative research to develop culturally appropriate intervention for use in the trial. Based on multiple focus groups some of the themes incorporated into the final interventions were:

- Health concerns, weight control, and the influence of others were motivators to start exercise.
- Feeling good and having energy were motivators to continue exercising.
- Social support and enjoyment were motivating forces for starting a physical activity program.

Some of the more important findings from the qualitative aspect of the study were that group based activities were preferred and aerobic dance type of activities were desired. These researchers found that physical activity was not different in Aerobic Exercise and Stretch N Health. Low attendance plagued both the interventions. Both groups reduced physical inactivity prevalence from baseline (26% and 18% decline, respectively). They also discovered that higher baseline social support predicted change in physical activity, regardless of treatment assignment. Young & Stewart (2006) also recommend future research to identify factors that would enhance physical activity level participation in order to reduce health disparities for this population subgroup at high risk of sedentary behavior-related diseases. The researchers explore the two primary dimensions of cultural sensitivity and advocate incorporating both the surface and the deep structures into any study focusing on this group.

The fourth intervention (Newton & Perri, 2004) compares the effects of three home-based exercise promotion programs for African Americans. Sixty, sedentary African-American adults were randomly assigned to either a standard behavioral counseling group (n=22), a culturally sensitive counseling group (n=20), or a physician advice comparison group (n=10). The key study outcomes measured at baseline and after six months included cardio-respiratory fitness and physical activity. Acculturation was examined as a moderating variable. Participants in all three groups reported significant increases in walking, but significant improvements in fitness were observed only in the two intervention groups. Participants in the culturally sensitive intervention reported significantly higher levels of exercise social support compared to members of the other two groups. These findings show that home-based exercise counseling programs are effective for improving fitness, yet the addition of culturally tailored components may not be sufficient to produce better outcomes than standard behavioral counseling.

The fifth intervention (Sbrocco, et al. 2005) compared adherence to Behavioral Choice Treatment (BCT), a 12-week obesity treatment program that promoted weight loss and exercise, among 22 Caucasian-American and 10 African-American overweight women in a university setting to 10 African-American overweight women in a church setting. Behavioral Choice Treatment (BCT) promotes moderate behavior change that can be comfortably and therefore permanently maintained. Participants obtained feedback from computerized eating diaries and kept exercise logs. Percentage of dietary fat consumed during treatment differed by group (F $_{(3, 35)}$59.27, p<0.01). Univariate analysis of variance indicated that the Caucasian-American group consumed less dietary fat than either the African-American university group (t $_{(38)}$ =4.29, p<0.01) or the African-American church group (t $_{(38)}$ =2.64, p<0.05). A trend was also seen for the African-American university group to consume less dietary fat than the African-American church group (t$_{(38)}$=1.81, p<0.07).Results indicated that both university groups exhibited comparable eating pathology at pre and post-treatment and comparable weight loss, despite the African-American sample attending fewer sessions. The African-American church group exhibited less disordered eating attitudes, less interpersonal distrust (e.g., reluctance to form close relationships or sense of alienation) at pre-treatment and experienced significantly greater weight loss than either university group. All groups lost weight and maintained these losses at 12-month follow-up. Preliminary results suggest treatment setting may play an important role in treatment adherence and sample characteristics.

The sixth intervention (Yancey et al., 2006) tested the efficacy of an eight week culturally targeted nutrition and physical activity intervention called African American Women Fight Cancer with Fitness (FCF) in producing cancer protective anthropometric, physiological, psychological and behavioral changes in African American women. A randomized, attention-controlled, two-group trial was conducted in a black owned commercial gym with a sample of 366 predominantly healthy, obese African American women. A free one year membership to the study site gym was provided to participants in both groups. Data were collected at baseline, two, six, and 12 months. Sample retention at one year was 71%. While weight loss was not a focus of the intervention, the intervention included skills training in a balanced regular exercise regimen and nutrition education promoting a low far, complex carbohydrate rich diet, emphasizing the cancer preventive benefits of increased fruit and vegetable intake. The authors' found that this intervention produced modest short-term improvements in body composition, but the economic incentive of a free one-year gym membership provided to all participants was a more potent intervention than the education and social support intervention tested. They also found that the results of their study imitated results from similar studies on Caucasian female populations where significant changes immediately post intervention are followed by decay with time. However, longer-term fitness enhancement remains elusive and demands research and policy attention. The results suggest that there may be policy implications in that employer-/insurer-subsidized gym memberships may require interventions targeting other levels of change (e.g., physical or social/environmental) to foster sustainable fitness improvements.

The seventh intervention (Karanja et al, 2002) was titled "Steps to Soulful Living" (Steps) and purported to adapt a contemporary weight loss intervention to be culturally and structurally appropriate for African American women. Through a formative qualitative research approach the intervention was tailored specifically for this ethnic group. The actual intervention was conducted with 69 participants, 39 of whom participative in the formative focus groups. The interventions were composed of 26 weekly group meetings with 15-25 participants. The meetings were divided into two halves. The first half dealt with weighing and self report exercise activity for the previous week and the second half comprised of sharing meals and discussing how the participants attempted to reduce the fat content in each shared dish. Nutrition and behavior modification were also discussed. The focus groups helped pinpoint multiple key elements that were vital to the intervention delivery. Some of these were increasing identification between counselors and participants, increasing social support of participants, using demonstrative formats for information delivery, family and community involvement and increasing program ownership by the participants. Compared to baseline the average number of hours participants exercised increased significantly throughout the intervention. The proportion of participants meeting the study goal of maintaining at least one day of food records each week increased steadily and peaked during weeks 13-18 but declined in the last 8 weeks of the study. In the 42 participants who completed the baseline questionnaires percent energy intake from fat fell six points. The participants lost a mean of 3.3% of their body weight during the intervention. Further analyses dictated that the most important predictor of weight loss was baseline body weight. The study produced multiple insights regarding the feasibility of programs targeting physical activity and/or weight loss in African American women. The weight losses though modest are significant enough to positively impact high-normal blood pressures in this ethnic group. The attendance and 6 month follow up rates are comparable to other large clinical trials. The researchers attribute the successes of their intervention to the multiple cultural adjustments made to the interventions to tailor it better to the African American group.

The eighth intervention (Banks-Wallace, & Conn 2005) attempted to explain the changes in steps per day as a result of a pilot study promoting walking. A pre post single group design was used to assess this 12 month intervention followed with a six month follow up with 21 sedentary African American women 25-68 years of age. The intervention itself included a 3 hour monthly group meeting and a home based walking component. The monthly sessions were divided into multiple constituents. In the first 20-30 minutes the participants and researchers shared life context information, thereafter a professional story teller shared a story reflecting the topic of the day (the topics focused on heart healthy nutrition, importance of physical activity and so on) and this was followed by a 40 minute interactive learning module. Further, time was also allotted for group physical activity during each session. Group walks through the surrounding neighborhoods served as the primary form of physical activity. Personal incentives were raffled during the monthly meetings to increase participation. The home based component included providing the participants a copy of the Stanford walking kit which was designed to encourage a gradual increase in walking over a six weeks period. Women were also encouraged to find a partner with whom they could share their walking goals, barriers to walking, successes and new problem solving insights. Baseline data regarding steps each day was assessed through the use of pedometers and outcome data was collected every three months between group sessions and for 6 months post intervention. The major focus of this intervention was on walking as a means of increasing physical activity. A total of 21 women were formally entered into the study (age range 25-68 years). A greater percentage of women participated in the data collection visits in comparison to those attending monthly intervention sessions. A total of 13 women participated in the 12 month post intervention period and 15 took part in the 18 month post intervention follow up. Variables among individual participants across data collection periods made it more feasible to discuss the changes in steps in terms of trends than in terms of statistical significance. At the end of the six month follow up assessment point mean steps increased by 1,425 (37%) from baseline for the total group and by 2,379 (51%) for the subgroup of 10 participants who participated in all three data collections (done at six,12 and 18 months). While the study found that the intervention positively impacted walking among sedentary African American women the increase in steps was smaller in comparison to other contemporary interventions. The researchers speculate on the possibilities that the increase in steps may have been affected at least partly as a result of the racial identity of the participants. It is also recommended that multi phased interventions may be more effective in increasing the physical activity of African American women.

The ninth intervention titled Healthy body/Healthy spirit was a multi component faith based intervention (Resnicow et al., 2002, 2005) that attempted to explore the effectiveness of culturally tailored self help diet and physical activity interventions versus standard health education materials not tailored for the African American population. Further, the intervention attempted to explore whether multiple telephone counseling calls (motivational interviewing) could increase fruit and vegetable intake and physical activity in an African American population. The intervention was composed of a three group cluster randomized design grouping by churches and included two data collection points: baseline and after one year of follow up.

The study was conducted in a set of socio economically diverse churches in the Atlanta metropolitan area. Sixteen churches were randomly assigned to three intervention conditions.

Group one (five churches) received standard nutrition and physical activity intervention materials, Group two (six churches) received culturally targeted self-help nutrition and physical activity intervention materials, and Group three (five churches) received the same intervention as Group two plus four telephone counseling calls.

In designing the culturally targeted materials for this project a qualitative approach was employed which included a series of focus groups (four addressing fruits & vegetables and four addressing physical activity) with members of local Black churches not participating in this project. This "diagnostic" research yielded numerous elements for surface and deep structure tailoring, including food preferences, cooking practices, and exercise patterns relevant to this population. Deep structure issues that emerged include unique attitudes regarding body image, concerns among many women regarding the effort to redo their hair after exercising, safety concerns in some neighborhoods, and lack of time for exercise due to extensive church and family commitments.

At baseline, 1,056 individuals were recruited across the 16 churches. The number of participants per church averaged 66 (range = 44–88). Of the initial sample, 906 (86%) were assessed at 1-year follow-up. Follow-up rates in the three intervention groups were 89%, 90%, and 82% respectively. The cohort was predominantly female with a mean age of 46 years.

The telephone calls for Group three participants were completed for 85%, 79%, 74%, and 73% for Calls one through four, respectively. Overall, in Group three, 5.5% received 0 calls, 2.3% received one call, 9.4% received two calls, 9.7% received three calls, and 73.1% received all four calls. For Call one, 62% of participants chose to work on fruits & vegetables, and at Call 3, 57% chose to work on fruits & vegetables. Results on fruits & vegetables intake indicated that the change in fruits & vegetables intake was largest in Group three and intermediate in Group two. Individuals in Groups two and three who reported using the cookbook and watching most or all of the fruits & vegetables video showed a significantly greater increase in fruits & vegetables intake than did those not using these materials. Likewise, individuals who reported using the activity guide showed a significantly greater increase in physical activity than did those not using the guide. Although those who reported watching most or all of the activity video showed a greater increase in activity than did those not watching the activity video, these differences were not statistically significant. Regular use of the pedometer was associated with a greater increase in activity, and this difference was statistically significant for moderate/vigorous activities and the index of exercise items. Approximately 45% of the participants reported making a moderate or large change in one health behavior but no change in the other. Specifically, this included 21% who reported a large fruits & vegetables change but no change in physical activity, 9% who reported a moderate fruits & vegetables change but no physical activity change, 10% who reported a large physical activity change and no fruits & vegetables change, and 5% who reported moderate physical activity change but no fruits & vegetables change. The remaining 17% of participants reported making multiple changes. Across all three experimental groups, the most common pattern of multiple changes was a large change for both fruits & vegetables and physical activity. The other three possible change patterns, large change in fruits & vegetables and moderate change in physical activity, large change in physical activity and moderate change in fruits & vegetables, and moderate change in both fruits & vegetables and physical activity were infrequent, in the range of 1%–3%. For fruits & vegetables, there was a clear additive effect for the motivational interviewing component, whereas for physical activity, motivational interviewing did not appreciably enhance the impact of the self-help culturally targeted materials.

The tenth intervention (Yanek, Becker, Moy, Gittelsohn, & Koffman, 2001) tested the impact on cardiovascular risk profiles of African American women 40 years and older after one year of participation in one of three church based nutrition and physical activity strategies. The program also attempted to assess the extent to which a strong spiritual component can impact a standard behavioral group intervention in a church. The researchers designed three strategies a behavioral model based on standard group methods with weekly sessions (SI), the same model supplemented with a spiritual and church cultural component (SP) and a control group of non spiritual, self-help interventions (SH). Interventions were designed at the individual level and implemented at the group level in a church setting. Themes and feedback gathered through focus groups and interviews were incorporated both into the interventions and the questionnaires to assess nutrition, physical activity, smoking cessation, and operational and feasibility of the program. Thereafter, churches were recruited if they met the eligibility criteria some of which were a primarily African American congregation, location in the urban core of Baltimore and high interest in local activities. Sequential enrollment of the churches continued until a sample of 490 women was obtained. The assignment of the church to one of the three groups was done by random selection.

Standard intervention churches held weekly sessions on nutrition and physical activity. Based on the social learning theory these sessions attempted to enhance individual self efficacy.

Each session included 30 minutes of moderate intensity aerobic activity. Spiritual intervention churches received the standard interventions in addition to a spiritual component and church contextual component. Weekly sessions included group prayers and health messages enriched with scriptures. The self help group included materials from the American heart association on healthy eating and physical activity. Baseline screening was offered to all eligible participants in all interventions and attempted to assess the demographics and medical history, anthropometrics and blood pressure and heart rate, blood lipid and glucose levels, dietary nutrient intake, smoking and carbon monoxide levels and physical activity. One year follow up screening was done and to increase follow up pastors' support and multiple incentives were employed.

A total of 529 women were enrolled in the program and from this cohort 50.5% (n=267) were in the spiritual group, 35.5% (n= 188) were in the standard group, and 14.0% (n=74) were in the self help group. Most participants had completed high school, three out of four were employed, slightly more than half had hypertension, and more than 40% had arthritis. The standard intervention (SI) and the spiritual models had no real differences and were combined and the results compared with the self help group. Within the active intervention groups there was a statistically significant change for 11 of the 13 cardiovascular risk factors and a modest change in the amount of energy expenditure. Higher number of sessions attended, older age, higher baseline BMI and inclusion in the active intervention groups were significant predictors of weight loss. This program revealed several insights. The researchers contend that it was impractical to devise a church based intervention which is not spiritual. Further, unlike previous studies where weight loss is attenuated within as little as one year this study demonstrated a persistence of weight loss and also multiple favorable biological benefits. Community interventions at the church level have a definitive chance of influencing the participants' health with continual support and reinforcement.

The eleventh intervention was a single blind clinical trial conducted at Rush University Medical Center, Chicago that comprised of an eight week individualized home based physical activity program consisting of lifestyle physical activity (Staffileno, Minnick, Coke, & Hollenberg, 2007). The intervention was preceded by a pre randomization three weeks screening and thereafter randomization into exercise or no exercise group. The target population was drawn from US born African American women, aged 18-45 years with high normal or stage 1 hypertension.

The pre randomization screening established baseline blood pressure, a physical examination and a complete blood count following which participants were randomly assigned to the exercise and the no exercise groups. Participants in the exercise group wee instructed to engage in lifestyle physical activity with an aim accumulating 150 minutes of physical activity per week. A 60 minutes private education session was imparted to participants prior to their starting the physical activity. The session reviewed health benefits of physical activity, safety issues, goal setting and self monitoring, identification of physical activity barriers and ways of incorporating activity into everyday life and finally ways of individualizing physical activity. Further, at biweekly clinic visits key topics from the education sessions were reinforced. The purpose of the intervention as per the researchers was to find simple ways to integrate physical activity into everyday living by "making physical activity habits as routine as brushing teeth and combing hair". Weight, body mass index, self report physical activity and adherence to the physical activity regimen were regularly recorded.

There were no differences in the exercise and no exercise groups in terms of the baseline age, body mass index or blood pressure. Post intervention the exercise group demonstrated a significant reduction in the systolic blood pressure and a reduction in the blood pressure status from stage 1 hypertension to pre-hypertension. The non exercise group had a non significant decrease in the systolic blood pressure. The study found statistically and clinically significant reduction in the blood pressures and a high degree of adherence to the intervention (72% self reported frequency and 87% self reported duration) in the form of fidelity to the prescribed frequency and duration but not always to the intensity of physical activity. The research demonstrates that lifestyle based approaches can be applied to hypertension prone populations especially the African American female population and can produce significant outcomes.

CONCLUSION

The purpose of this article was to review physical activity promotion and weight loss interventions targeted towards healthy African American women over the ages of 18 years within the United States of America conducted during 2000 and June 2007. Needless to say, the numbers of interventional studies available are far fewer in numbers than expected based on the sheer magnitude of the physical inactivity and obesity epidemic within the African American population, especially the women population. There is a compelling need for more interventions in this field.

Only four out of the 11 interventions reviewed by us were rooted in behavioral theories and/or models. The social action theory, social cognitive theory, behavior choice treatment and the social ecological model were employed by one intervention each. Health promotion interventions need to be embedded in theories and models for multiple reasons. They can be benchmarked against existent programs based on the same theories and conclusions can be drawn. If a theory based intervention works fine, it can often be generalizable to a much broader audience and population and setting than an intervention not designed around a theory. In theory based interventions if intervening constructs are measured it is easy to identify which components work and that can lead to improvement in efforts as well as the theory.

Cultural sensitivity is a concept that has come to the forefront of public health in general and health education and promotion in particular. Health educators are increasingly realizing the fact that health programs involving non dominant ethnic groups and minority cultures need to be tailored to the norms and rules prevalent in that group especially so if the program is being adapted from an earlier intervention that produced results for an ethnically different group. The concept of cultural sensitivity pervades all aspects of a program right from the program design and content up to the program delivery and intervention execution stage. Resnicow and colleagues (2005) have defined cultural sensitivity as "the extent to which ethnic/cultural characteristics, experiences, norms, values, behavioral patterns and beliefs of a target population as well as relevant historical, environmental and social forces are incorporated in the design, delivery, and evaluation of targeted health promotion interventions". Cultural tailoring has been defined as the process of creating culturally sensitive interventions. Interventions with a good natured cultural component may still not be entirely culturally sensitive because they lack in either the superficial or the deep dimension of cultural sensitivity. We found that seven out of the 11 studies made accommodations for cultural sensitivity while four interventions made no mention of the concept. However, out of the seven studies only one study distinguished cultural sensitivity into its superficial and deep dimensions and went about addressing both those realms (Resnicow, 2005). Most of the interventions that did incorporate the concept of cultural sensitivity into the design incorporated it through focus groups with African American women during the formative phase of the study and tailored the intervention and the materials as per the feedback received.

We also found during our review that a formal process evaluation was not in built into most of the interventions. Only one study included a formative and a process evaluation component. Even though some studies speak about program adherence a formal evaluative component is lacking in most of them.

In terms of the duration, three of the interventions were brief: two eight week interventions and one intervention running for 12 weeks. Four were middle range with three interventions of six month's duration and one intervention of around five months duration. The remaining four interventions were each 12 months long. Interventions that did not employ theoretical frameworks were longer in duration than the ones which did. For example, three out of the 4 brief interventions were theory based. If more interventions are theory based they can be more efficient and shorter in duration.

All of our interventions have focused on individual level behavior change approaches and none has tried to address broader policy and environmental level changes. Most of the interventions have focused on short term changes right after the intervention and it is essential

to have measures at least at six months after the intervention to see for the retention of behavior change. Only two of the eleven studies have longitudinally explored the behavior change for long term decay and persistence. On the whole, interventions have resulted in modest changes in behaviors and mixed results with indicators of physical inactivity thereby necessitating more effective use of theoretical approaches.

RECOMMENDATIONS FOR FUTURE INTERVENTIONS

As previously mentioned most interventions did address the concept of cultural sensitivity in a very cursory manner. We believe that a more detailed and meticulous approach is required for better outcomes and long term behavior changes. Future interventions would do well to address the superficial and deep dimensions of cultural sensitivity both.

Moreover, for interventions to be effective they should be built around pre existing and often rigorously tested theoretical framework. This helps in two ways- first it ensures the credibility of the study and second it helps in applying the same design in different settings with minor modifications. It can also be benchmarked against other interventions based on the same theory. More interventions need to measure constructs from behavioral theories so that it can be discerned which components work and to what extent.

We also found that retention remains a problem for most of the studies and recommend exploratory studies that would research ways to maximize retention. Retention could be addressed during the formative stages of the program itself and incorporated as one of the many themes in a focus group that intends to gather insight that would help in the program design.

Finally, long term measurements of impact variables need to be taken. It is essential to have measures at least at six months after the intervention to see for the retention of behavior change.

REFERENCES

Banks-wallace, J., & Conn, V. (2005). Changes in steps per day over the course of a pilot walking intervention. *The ABNF Journal: Official Journal of the Association of the Black Nursing Faculty in Higher Education, Inc, 16*(2), 28-32.

Crespo, C. J., Smit, E., Andersen, R. E., Carter-Pokras, O., & Ainsworth, B. E. (2000). Race/ethnicity, social class and their relation to physical inactivity during leisure time: Results from the third national health and nutrition examination survey, 1988–1994. *American Journal of Preventive Medicine, 18*, 46–53.

Drayton-brooks, S., & White, N. (2004). Health promoting behaviors among african american women with faith-based support. *The ABNF Journal: Official Journal of the Association of the Black Nursing Faculty in Higher Education, Inc*, 15(5), 84-90.

Fitzgibbon, M. L., Stolley, M. R., Schiffer, L. S., Sanchez-Johnsen, l. A. P., Wells, A. M., & Dyer, A. D. (2005). A combined breast health/weight loss intervention for black women. *Preventive Medicine, 40*(4), 373-383.

Gans, K. M., Kumanyika, S. K., Lovell, H. J., Risica, P. M., Goldman, R., Odoms-Young, A. et al. (2003). The development of sister talk: A cable tv-delivered weight control program for black women. *Preventive Medicine, 37*(6), 654-667.

Karanja, N., Stevens, V., Hollis, J., & Kumanyika, S. (2002). Steps to soulful living (steps): A weight loss program for African-American women. *Ethnicity & Disease, 12*(3), 363-371.

Mokdad, A. H., Serdula, M. K., Dietz, W. H., Bowman, B. A., Marks, J. S. & Koplan, J. P. (1999). The spread of the obesity epidemic in the United States, 1991-1998. *Journal of American Medical Association, 282*(16), 1519-1522.

Newton, R. L. & Perri, M. (2004). A randomized pilot trial of exercise promotion in sedentary african-american adults. *Ethnicity & Disease, 14*(4), 548-557.

Resnicow, K., Jackson, A., Braithwaite, R., Di Iorio, C., Blisset, D., Rahotep, S. et al. (2002). Healthy body/healthy spirit: A church-based nutrition and physical activity intervention. *Health Education Research, 17*(5), 562-573.

Resnicow, K., Jackson, A., Blissett, D., Wang, T., Mccarty, F., Rahotep, S. et al. (2005). Results of the healthy body healthy spirit trial. *Health Psychology, 24*(4), 339-48

Sbrocco, T., Carter, M. M., Lewis, E. L., Vaughn, N. A., Kalupa, K. L., King, S. et al. (2005). Church-based obesity treatment for African-American women improves adherence. *Ethnicity & Disease, 15*(2), 246-255.

Staffileno, B., Minnick, A., Coke, L., & Hollenberg, S. (2007). Blood pressure responses to lifestyle physical activity among young, hypertension-prone African-American women. *The Journal Of Cardiovascular Nursing, 22*(2), 107-17.

Troiano, P., & Flegal, K. (1998). Overweight children and adolescents: Description, epidemiology, and demographics. *Pediatrics, 101*, 497 504.

United States Department of Health and Human Services. (1995). *Healthy people 2000 review 1994.* Washington, DC: Government Printing Office.

Yancey, A. K., Mccarthy, W. J., Harrison, G. G., Wong, W. K., Siegel, J. M., & Leslie, J. (2006). Challenges in improving fitness: results of a community-based, randomized, controlled lifestyle change intervention. *Journal Of Women's Health, 15*(4), 412-429.

Yanek, L., Becker, D., Moy, T., Gittelsohn, J., & Koffman, D. (2001). Project joy: Faith based cardiovascular health promotion for African American women. *Public Health Reports, 116* (suppl. 1), 68-81.

Young, D. R., & Stewart, K. J. (2006). A church-based physical activity intervention for African American women. *Family & Community Health, 29*(2), 103-117.

In: Progress in Exercise and Women's Health Research ISBN 1-60456-014-5
Editor: Janet P. Coulter, pp. 193-211 © 2008 Nova Science Publishers, Inc.

Chapter 7

THEORETICAL FRAMEWORKS IN EXERCISE AND WOMEN'S HEALTH RESEARCH

Birte Dohnke[1] *and Sonia Lippke*[2]

[1]Center for Gender in Medicine (GiM); Charité - Universitätsmedizin Berlin; Germany
[2]Health Psychology; Freie Universität, Berlin; Germany

ABSTRACT

Physical exercise contributes to primary and secondary prevention of heart diseases, hypertension, stroke, diabetes, and cancer. In women physical inactivity is additionally associated with specific risks for mortality and morbidity. However, many women do not engage in sufficient physical exercise. Although women know quite well that this unhealthy habit increases the risk of myocardial infarction, they frequently underestimate their personal risk to die from vascular diseases. But basic knowledge rarely meets with corresponding habits. In addition, women-typical motives (i.e., perceived pros and cons) and high barriers (i.e., low self-efficacy beliefs) play the central role in motivation to engage in regular physical activity which can best be explained by gender roles and corresponding norms, expectations, and experiences. This chapter describes how gender roles and corresponding norms, expectations, and experiences influence women's physical activity and its changes as well as how interventions may be better tailored to women needs. The introduction gives a review about health risks of physical inactivity and health benefits of physical activity; and prevalences, knowledge, motives, and barriers in women are described. This evidence, however, is not sufficient to better design women-specific interventions due to the complex nature of the process of health behaviour change. Consequently, we introduce the Health Action Process Approach (HAPA) as theoretical framework to integrate this evidence and identify women-typical characteristics. Implications for theory-based research on women's adoption and maintenance of health enhancing physical exercise is outlined. The chapter concludes with strategies how to design exercise promotion interventions theory-based tailored to particularly women needs.

---

[1] Corresponding author: Phone: +49 30 – 450 539 079, Fax : +49 30 – 450 539 989 and Email: birte.dohnke@charite.de

Key Words: women; physical activity; Health Action Process Approach; sex differences; gender roles

INTRODUCTION

Lifestyle accounts for an enormous extent in morbidity and mortality. Particularly physical inactivity is in this regard of focal importance (Willett, 2002). That is, a lack of physical activity contributes to incidence and progression of many chronic degenerative diseases such as cardiovascular diseases, hypertension, stroke, diabetes, and cancer (Willett, 2002).

In women, there moreover arise specific risks: Physical inactivity, thus, is associated with a considerable higher risk for diabetes (Meisinger *et al.*, 2005) than in men. Conversely, physical activity rather lowers the risk for myocardial infarction more than in men (Yusuf *et al.*, 2004). Physical activity, in addition, seems to be associated with a lessened incidence of osteoporosis in women and contributes to an essential risk reduction of cardiovascular diseases as well as cancer (Gregg *et al.*, 2003).

Based on this evidence, prevention guidelines have been invented especially for women which recommend among others physical activity independently on women's individual risk status. The renewed guidelines for prevention of CVD in women, for example, advises women to accumulate a minimum of 30 minutes of moderate-intensity physical activity (e.g., brisk walking) on most, and preferably all, days of the week (Mosca *et al.*, 2007). Women, moreover, who want to lose weight or sustain weight loss, should accumulate a minimum of 60 to 90 minutes of moderate-intensity physical activity on most, and preferably all, days of the week.

Prevalence of Inactivity in Women

Numerous surveys point out that more women than men do not follow at all or only insufficiently the recommended lifestyle (King *et al.*, 2000; S. B. Martin *et al.*, 2000; Trost *et al.*, 2002). In Canada, for example, about every second woman (49%) and 44% of men was physically inactive (Statistics Canada, 2007). As can be seen in Figure 1, less than every forth female citizen was physically active (24%) whereas almost every third male citizen was physically active (29%).

In several countries, the same picture is drawn by epidemiological data: For example in the United States of America (US), prevalence rates indicate that 12% of women (8% of men) were never active in 2005 (Centers for Disease Control and Prevention, 2007). Approximately 28% women (31% men) engaged in regular leisure-time physical activity, but according to overall physical activity only 16% of women (17% of men) engaged in high impact activity. In Germany, the prevalence of physical inactivity demonstrates that 38% of women (37% of men) were inactive in 2003 (Lampert *et al.*, 2005). In contrast, two-thirds of both women and men engaged in sport, 28% of women (21% of men) at least two hours per week. These are according to international guidelines (Mosca et al., 2007) merely 16-28% of women and thereby fewer women than men who are sufficiently active.

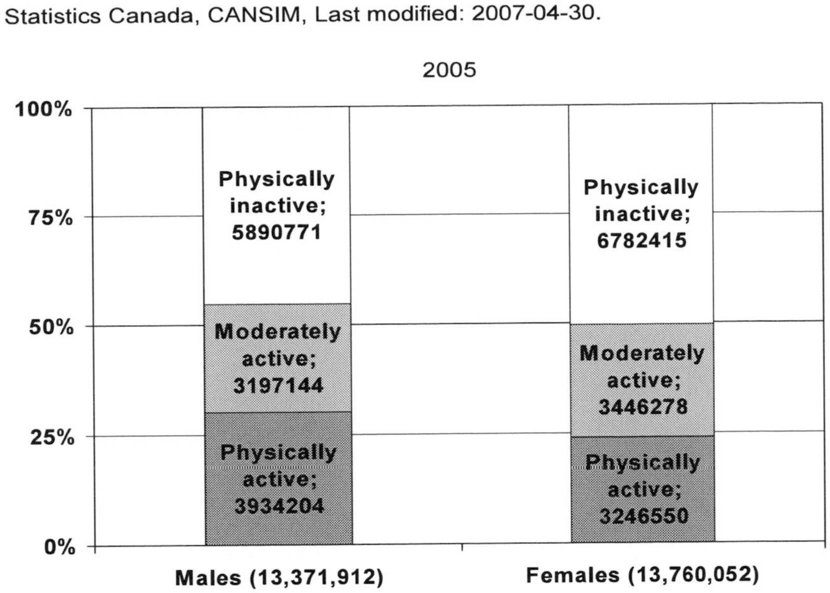

Figure 1. Intensity of participation in leisure time physical activity among men and women in Canada.

Prevalence rates of physical activity in women, however, strongly depend on women's definitions and interpretations of physical activity and consequently on the assessments (Abel *et al.*, 2001; Bull *et al.*, 2001; Tudor-Locke *et al.*, 2003). A multi-method study on African-American and American Indian women, for example, revealed that 'physical activity' is typically considered to be structured 'exercise' and not incidental activities of daily life (Tudor-Locke et al., 2003). 'Leisure', in comparison, was interpreted from a cultural perspective as being lazy. Consequently, if physical activity and exercise are differentiated, more women (82%) describe themselves as currently engaging in regular physical activity than in regular exercise (55%) as a telephone survey on 2,912 US women demonstrated (Bull et al., 2001).

Similarly, more women (77%) report engaging in lifestyle activity combining exercises, sports, physically active hobbies, vigorous household chores, and occupational physical activity than in exercises including participation in exercises, sports, or physically active hobbies (25%) or in regular exercise (11%) as the US Women's Determinants Study on 2,912 US middle- and older-aged minority women revealed (A. A. Eyler *et al.*, 1999). Public health studies, accordingly, suggest considering habitual physical activity such as daily walking and biking due to their high significance in women's activity spectrum. Indicators of habitual physical activity, thus, demonstrate typically higher rates of daily walking and biking among women, whereas indicators of sport and exercise demonstrate lower physical activity among women (Abel et al., 2001; K. Meyer *et al.*, 2004). This reveals in sum that women are not generally less physically active than men but that their patterns of physical activity are qualitatively different. They are rather as active as men, if besides sport activity likewise habitual physical activity such as walking or bicycling (Abel et al., 2001; K. Meyer et al., 2004) or physical activity of low or medium intensity (King et al., 1992) are considered.

Women in comparison to men, however, seem to try more often to increase their health-enhancing physical activity, but also failed more often (Assaf *et al.*, 2003). In a study with 1,152 individuals living with Type 2 Diabetes, Plotnikoff and colleagues found that sex was significantly related to an increase of physical activity: Women were less successful than men to change their behaviour (Plotnikoff *et al.*, 2007). Correspondingly, intervention studies aiming at increasing physical activity and health indicators typically find that girls and women benefit less than boys and men, respectively (Bolognesi *et al.*, 2006; Prochaska & Sallis, 2004).

Knowledge of Women

How can it be explained that many women's lifestyle differs so much from the lifestyle recommendations and partly more than men's lifestyle? One explanation might be that health education failed to inform women sufficiently about the significance of a healthy, i.e., physically active lifestyle. A nationally representative sample in the European Union, in this regard, revealed that significantly fewer women (16%) than men (20%) believed physical activity to be an important influence on health (Margetts *et al.*, 1999). The American Heart Association National Study, more specific, demonstrated that in fact all interviewed 1,024 US women perceived exercise to be a heart disease prevention strategy (Mosca *et al.*, 2004). However, only 46% of the women knew heart disease to be the leading cause of death for women and again only 13% perceived heart disease to be their greatest health problem. In addition, a population-based survey with 28,090 participants showed that fewer women (17%) than men (23%) correctly named physical inactivity as stroke risk factor (Müller-Nordhorn *et al.*, 2006). This underestimation of women's general as well as their personal health risks is alerting, since persons who are aware of their personal risk factors such as lack of physical activity more frequently alter just this risk behaviour (R. Martin *et al.*, 2005).

Motives and Barriers of Women

A further explanation may be looked for among the motives and barriers which underlie particularly the behaviour of women. At the same time, it is to be noted firstly that sex differences in physical activity are not so much associated with the biological sex as in fact with the gender role (Gill, 2007; Helgeson, 2005; Waldron, 1997). That is, norms and expectations which go along with being female versus male, for example, to be caring, emotionally expressive, polite, and helpful. These expectations are indeed linked to the biological sex, but eminently dependent on the particular socio-cultural context and vary, therefore, with age, education, income, and ethnicity. As a consequence, one needs to differentiate sex and gender by considering further aspects as mediator or moderator of possible sex differences such as gender role self-concept, age, education, income, and ethnicity (see below).

In the past, sport was associated with masculine attributes such as brawn, fortitude, fighting spirit, and aggressiveness. It was, hence, deemed as a male domain and done only by few women because such stereotypical beliefs affect expectancies and behaviour toward girls and women (Darlison, 2000). In a study with approximately 1,500 mothers and their 11- to

12-year-old children, for example, mothers' gender stereotypic beliefs influenced their perceptions of the child's abilities in the sport domain moderated by the sex of their child (Jacobs & Eccles, 1992). That is, mothers with more gender stereotypic beliefs in sports believed their daughters to have lower sport abilities but their sons to have higher sport abilities. In addition, mothers' perceptions mediated the influence of past sport performance on children's self-perceptions of sport ability. Similarly, Fredricks and Eccles (2005) showed in a longitudinal study that both mothers and fathers held gender-stereotyped beliefs about athletics and were gender-typed in their behaviours and that their perceptions of their children had the strongest unique relationship with children's beliefs and participation both concurrently and over time. The results confirmed that girls had lower perceived competence, value, and participation, despite the absence of gender differences in motor proficiency, and suggested that the full set of parent socialization factors influenced children's outcomes (Fredricks & Eccles, 2005).

Those experiences may shape girls' and women's motives and barriers in relation to sport and physical actitivy. In this manner, many girls and women still follow rather feminine *motives* referring to weight, appearance, and health, and less frequent fun- or performance-related motives (Klomsten *et al.*, 2005; Zunft *et al.*, 1999). Women rather make a habit of physical activity, if they expect a lot of benefits hereby (Cox *et al.*, 2003), and if they have a strong motive of "joy" (Titze *et al.*, 2005). Women with only few motives and with poor health seem to disengage from regular sport such as running (Titze et al., 2005). Poor health is generally a barrier to engage in physical activity among women (A. A. Eyler, 2003; A. E. Eyler *et al.*, 2002; King et al., 2000; Sternfeld *et al.*, 2000).

At the same time, women perceive many *barriers* which, from their viewpoint, hinder them from engaging in physical activity. Thus, every fourth female participant in an US survey stated lack of time and every fifth family duties, tiredness, energy scarcity, and shyness due to appearance (King *et al.*, 2000). Comparably more often women than men reported the barriers „not the sportive type" or „no energy" (A. E. Eyler et al., 2002; King et al., 2000; Zunft et al., 1999). Moreover, they stated more frequently "care for children/elderly" as obstacle. These barriers are not absolutely women-typical but may affect women differently due to gender role expectancies: They often do believe not or barely not to have leisure time beyond their domestic and familial duties (Frankish et al., 1998; Tudor-Locke et al., 2003).

It is, hence, no wonder that sport-related *self-efficacy* beliefs (i.e., beliefs to be able to be physically active even in face of barriers) are relevant correlates of physical activity particularly in girls and women (A. E. Eyler et al., 2002; Motl *et al.*, 2002, 2005; Sternfeld *et al.*, 1999; Trost et al., 2002). For example, in a random sample of 2,636 ethnically diverse women, aged 20 to 65, those with high self-efficacy were 4 times more likely to engage in high levels of sports and exercise than those with low self-efficacy (Sternfeld et al., 1999). Perceived self-efficacy predicted also increase or maintenance of regular physical activity among girls and women (Cox et al., 2003; Motl et al., 2005).

Moreover, sport-related *social support* was found to be an important predictor of physical activity in girls and women (De Bourdeaudhuij & Sallis, 2002; A. A. Eyler et al., 1999; A. E. Eyler et al., 2002; O'Brien Cousins, 1995; Sternfeld et al., 1999; Titze et al., 2005; Trost et al., 2002). In a random sample of 2,636 ethnically diverse women in the age of 20 to 65, for example, women with high social support were 2.34 times more likely to engage in high levels of sports and exercise than women with low social support (Sternfeld et al., 1999).

Survey data from 327 community-dwelling women aged 70 to 98 demonstrated, correspondingly, insufficient social support for exercise to be a key barrier to participation also in late life (O'Brien Cousins, 1995). Similarly, women with high levels of social support were less likely to be sedentary than those with low support, even after adjusting for race/ethnicity as demonstrated by the US Women's Determinants Study, i.e., a sample of 2,912 middle- and older-aged women (A. A. Eyler et al., 1999). In addition, longitudinal findings of lifestyle interventions studies found social support to be an important mediator for successful behaviour change. These lifestyle interventions aim at increasing social support as an important facilitator of behaviour change. Such programmes are, for example, the PrimeTime or Mediterranean Lifestyle Program targeting postmenopausal women with CHD or diabetes, respectively (Toobert et al., 1998; Toobert et al., 2005). Evaluations of these programmes typically find that women benefit from peer support beside social–cognitive strategies in relation to modification of multiple lifestyle behaviours including physical activity.

Together, insufficient knowledge, suboptimal motives, high barriers, low self-efficacy beliefs, and lack of social support might be explanations for greater differences between actual lifestyle and lifestyle recommendations in women than in men. But how can interventions better be tailored to women's needs so that they more easily engage in regular physical activity? The presented evidence so far is not sufficient to answer this question due to the complex nature of the process of health behaviour change. That is, many studies consider different single aspects or use different theoretical backdrops to examine possible predictors of physical activity in women. They provide, thereby, only singular findings which do not demonstrate which factor is actually how important in concert with others. The process of health behaviour change, however, is more complex in nature: That is, some factors might be important in deciding to engage in physical activity whereas others might be important only in maintaining or disengaging from regular physical activity. Consequently, we introduce a theoretical framework which integrates different aspects and theories. On basis of this theory and its evidence women-typical characteristics will be discussed in the following.

THEORETICAL FRAMEWORK ON HEALTH BEHAVIOUR CHANGE

The Health Action Process Approach (HAPA) (Schwarzer, 1992, 2001) is a model that explains the process of health behaviour change by explicitly integrating continuous and stage assumptions, and being thereby a hybrid model. At the same time, the HAPA integrates variables from motivational theories, which aim to predict goals, and behaviour-enabling models, which include post-decisional facets such as plans (i.e., implementation intentions). The model was tested in different health behaviour domains as physical activity and exercise behaviour (Schwarzer, in press; Schwarzer et al., 2007). In the following, the model will be described in more detail.

The HAPA makes a distinction between a motivational phase and a volitional/post-decision phase of health behaviour change. The basic idea is that individuals experience a shift of mindset when moving from the first (motivational) phase to the second (volitional) phase. The moment when people commit themselves to a goal, for example, to engage in regular exercise they enter the volitional phase. In this phase, a division into two sub-phases appears to be meaningful where people can be labelled as either intenders or actors. Firstly, they intend to act but still remain inactive. Secondly, they have already adopted the intended behaviour. Thus, three phases or stages can be distinguished as shown in Figure 2. In the

(1)   ***Non-Intentional Stage***, a behavioural goal needs to be developed. Afterwards, individuals enter

(2)   ***Intentional Stage***, when they have already set a goal but still remain inactive (or at least not active at the recommended level), while the exercise behaviour is being planned and prepared. If these plans are translated into action, individuals reside in

(3)   ***Action Stage***. They are then physically active at the recommended goal behaviour level.

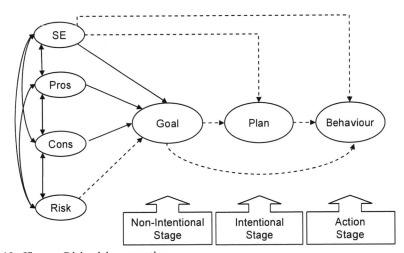

Note: SE, self-efficacy; Risk, risk perception.

Figure 2. The Health Action Process Approach (Schwarzer, 1992).

In the *non-intentional stage*, a goal has not been set so far and needs to be developed. In this motivational phase, first, risk perception is a distal antecedent. That is, risk perception is sufficient to enable the undecided person to set a behaviour goal. Furthermore, it is a prerequisite for a contemplation process and further elaboration of thoughts about behavioural consequences and personal capacities. Because risk perception operates at a stage-specific level and has an effect only in the motivational phase, its effect on goal setting is represented by a dashed line in Figure 2 (Lippke *et al.*, 2005). Second, outcome expectancies ('pros' as positive outcomes and 'cons' as negative consequences from the goal behaviour) are assumed as being most important in the non-intentional phase, in specific, when balancing the pros and cons of a new behaviour. Third, the belief in one's capabilities to perform a desired action (i.e., self-efficacy) is necessary for pursuit of goal behaviour. That is, perceived self-efficacy plays a role in the motivational phase by promoting goal setting but maintains important also in the later stages for behaviour implementation (Lippke et al., 2005), indicated by the solid arrow in Figure 2.

After a goal has been set, the *intentional stage* is entered. The person has strong goals but is not performing the behaviour yet. The goal has to be transformed into detailed plans on how to perform the behaviour. Instructions on the goal pursuit may contain assisting goals and precise action plans (also called implementation intentions; Gollwitzer, 1999). These plans state when, where and how the goal behaviour will be initiated, thereby cognitive links between concrete opportunities and the intended behaviour will be built. After goal setting, the regarded variables change their dominance and interplay. Risk perception has no further influence while outcome-expectancies remain important. Self-efficacy is also important in the planning and initiation process, especially if barriers occur or no enabling situation arises. Self-efficacy keeps the goal strong and the plans flexible to compensate for setbacks and stay on track to initiation (Schwarzer, 2001).

If the goal behaviour has been initiated, the individual enters the *action stage*. In this, the behaviour has to be controlled by cognitions in order to be maintained. Self-regulatory skills are substantial for the maintenance process. Effort has to be invested, useful situations for implementation of the new behaviour have to be detected, and distractions have to be resisted. The behaviour will mainly be directed by self-efficacy (Schwarzer, 2001) because these beliefs regulate how effort is invested and persistence is managed if barriers and setbacks occur. The performed behaviour has to be maintained, and relapses have to be managed by action control strategies. Due to individuals having to first set a goal which then may be translated into plans and behaviour, this process is stage-specific; only individuals in intentional and action stages are more likely to make plans and subsequently perform the goal behaviour as indicated by dashed lines in Figure 2 (Lippke et al., 2004b). Also the influence of self-efficacy on post-decisional processes, such as planning and behaviour performance, depends on whether one has decided to change (here it is crucial to believe in one's own competences) or not (here only goal setting can be supported by self-efficacy).

Moreover, the HAPA also includes situational barriers and resources such as social support which are proposed to play a role in the volitional phase (Schwarzer, 1992, 2001). However, not much work has been done on these aspects to date.

Model predictions were confirmed for both women and men in a study with 560 orthopaedic rehabilitation patients using gender separating analysis (Lippke *et al.*, 2004a). In addition, it was found that both women and men are equally successful in making plans and benefiting from them in terms of engaging in regular physical activity (Lippke et al., 2004a). However, particular dissimilarity was found in studies on special aspects of the HAPA. These will be described in the next paragraph and followed by a theoretical conclusion for gender sensitive studies on physical activity.

Integration of Empirical Evidence on Women's Exercise Behaviour

Women-typical motives and barriers indicate at present in correlation with the HAPA several reasons why women do frequently not engage in sufficient physical activity although they know about a healthy lifestyle.

Underestimated Health Risk

At first, most women seem to underestimate their personal risk for myocardial infarction and stroke (Mosca et al., 2004; Müller-Nordhorn et al., 2006). Consequently, health education seems to have not sufficiently succeeded to sensitize also women for the subject of vascular diseases. In addition, one might assume that women do not feel to be personal addressed or motivated by information about or knowledge of health risks due to physical inactivity. In order to change this, those messages via mass media or educational brochures shall be increasingly effective which present also the frequency and severity of health consequences of an unhealthy (i.e., inactive) lifestyle especially in women. It might be beneficial thereby that women are typically more concerned about their health than men (Helgeson, 2005) and accordingly more interested in health issues. As a consequence, women might theoretically easily be motivated to change their lifestyle to a healthy and physically active one if risks are explained in a more women-specific and thereby higher self-relevant manner. However, effects of different kinds of risk communication among women were not tested empirically so far. Consequently, more research is needed using the general and furthermore gender-sensitive strategy to measure risk perception (see below).

Negative Outcome Expectancies and Doubts on Self-Efficacy

The main reason of health education's or risk information's failure so far can apparently be attributed to the fact that most women have unfavourable expectancies regarding consequences of regular physical activity and their own self-efficacy. Women hold indeed positive outcome expectancies regarding physical activity. There is evidence, however, that many women rather expect unspecific or only few benefits of physical activity (O'Brien Cousins, 2000; Titze et al., 2005). One might assume in theory though that motivation accompanied by specific and as many as possible positive outcome expectancies is more sustainable (Cox et al., 2003). That is, a woman is more likely to maintain her physical activity if she perceives specific benefits (such as an increase in her endurance capacity of 10 minutes) which are easier appraised as personal success than unspecific benefits (such as increased attractiveness or better health).

Evidence, conversely, emphasises that women often hold many and in part very specific negative outcome expectancies. Regarding physical activity, for example, 143 older women reported in a study 19 negative consequences such as pain and breathlessness in comparison to only 6 positive consequences (O'Brien Cousins, 2000). Another study demonstrated that 447 women expected as many negative as positive consequences from exercise (O'Hea *et al.*, 2003). Following this, an offensive und active discussion of such negative expectancies is recommended which may qualify their relevance resulting in a positive decision balance.

Low self-efficacy, finally, is an important motivational problem because women typically doubt their behavioural competence more than men, e.g., to maintain regular physical activity in face of barriers. They also perceive in part more barriers than men. Because high self-efficacy is crucial for motivation and behaviour change, women-specific interventions should intensively target self-efficacy. They should address stage-specific barriers which for example hinder adoption or maintenance of physical activity, and encourage women thereby to be able to cope successfully with anticipated barriers.

Insufficient Action Plans and Coping Plans

But even women who intent to engage in regular physical activity often fail to implement their goals due to lacking knowledge how to attain their goals in detail. Action plans may help: Individuals can be supported to anticipate conditions and possibilities to engage in regular physical activity and to concretely plan the how, when and where. A girl or woman who prefers moderate activities without pressure to perform could choose „gym class Thursdays at the YMCA " or „jogging through the woods Mondays after work" which fits to her daily routine (cf., Mota & Esculcas, 2002). In contrast, a woman who is interested in competitive sport could join a tennis or volleyball association.

If women adopt the intended physical activity they have to maintain it as long as possible: They have to invest effort and perseverance. That is, maintenance of physical activity requires an active self-regulation process which can be supported by attainable sub-goals and incentives. Because even in this sub-process of a lifestyle change distractions and risk situations may occur, it is additionally important to possess about different coping options. Here, conscious coping plans may help (Ziegelmann et al., 2006). A woman who already (unsuccessfully) changed her lifestyle can try to use her experiences. Because she supposedly know already in which situation it is particularly difficult for her to be physically active and when or in which way regular physical activity is only difficult to arrange with her everyday life. These are, even in case of failures, consequences that may promote the current lifestyle change. One example for an intervention combining action planning and coping planning to enhance a commercial weight reduction program especially for women was presented by Luszczynska and colleagues (Luszczynska et al., 2007). In this study, targeting physical activity and nutrition, women who made actions plan and coping plans lost twice as much weight than women who participated only in the commercial programme (i.e., control group). Plans, as hypothesised, mediated the effects of the intervention on weight and body mass index change.

Lack of Social Support

Another reason of women's failure to be sufficiently physically active might be too little social support or their lower benefit from social support. In the domain of smoking, for example, many studies indicate that women are less likely to benefit from social support than men (Carlson et al., 2002; Murray et al., 1995). Moreover, social norms have to be mentioned in the context of social influences. That is, subjective norms (i.e., social pressure prescribing approved behaviour) and descriptive norms (i.e., partner's behaviour informing about behaviour of others) play a role in health behaviour change (Rivis & Sheeran, 2003). Social norms, however, may be mutually contradictory (Cialdini & Trost, 1998). Women, for example, are more concerned with health, but are also socialised to take care of others due to existing gender role expectancies (Helgeson, 2005). Whereas the first mentioned aspect of the female gender role might foster social pressure to engage in regular physical activity (i.e., subjective activity norm), the second aspect undermines it. In addition, girls and women may feel under social pressure to engage in physical activity (strong subjective activity norm), but are less likely to have a physically active mother and female friends, respectively, (weak descriptive activity norm) due to still lower physical activity prevalences in girls and women than in boys and men. Based on this, more systematic research is needed aiming at investigating the role of different social influences on physical activity in women within a theoretical framework of health behaviour change.

Finally, it should be again noted that sex differences in physical activity are less associated with the biological sex but with the gender role and corresponding norms and expectations (Gill, 2007; Helgeson, 2005; Waldron, 1997). More complex social models demonstrate that further aspects contribute to mediation or moderation of these differences such as gender role self-concept (i.e., identification with the own gender role), age, education, income, and ethnicity. That is, differences in physical activity and underlying motivation are linked to the biological sex, but eminently vary with those aspects.

IMPLICATIONS FOR THEORY-BASED RESEARCH

Our review so far strongly indicates that theory-based research on physical activity in women should carefully consider possible gender biases when measuring social-cognitive and physical activity behaviour.

Measures of Physical Activity

Physical activity is primarily a social behaviour and in its meaning and expressive form fundamentally linked to gender. We provided evidence that traditional measures of physical activity often and solely focusing on sports and exercise may lead to underestimation of physical activity in women when ignoring kinds of physical activity that comprise more habitual activities such as riding the bike to work, going for walks, or performing physically exhausting household chores (D. Meyer et al., 2003; K. Meyer et al., 2004; Sternfeld et al., 1999). More specific, assessing the type and amount of sport activities (e.g., walking, cycling), physical activities during everyday work days and leisure time (i.e., housework, gardening, climbing stairs, etc.) covers gender-specific sports and physical activity behaviour in a more sophisticated but realistic way than the only questions about vigorous activities where the heart beats rapidly and one is sweating. The scale by Godin and Shepart (1985b) or modified version (Plotnikoff et al., 2007) provides such a measurement: It is asked about

A) Strenuous physical activity: heart beats rapidly, sweating (e.g., running, jogging, hockey, soccer, squash, cross country skiing, judo, roller skating, vigorous swimming, vigorous long distance bicycling, vigorous aerobic dance classes, heavy weight training);

B) Moderate physical activity: not exhausting, light perspiration (e.g., fast walking, baseball, tennis, easy bicycling, volleyball, badminton, easy swimming, alpine skiing, popular and folk dancing); and

C) Mild physical activity: minimal effort, no perspiration (e.g., easy walking, yoga, archery, fishing, bowling, lawn bowling, shuffleboard, horseshoes, golf, snowmobiling).

Such a gender sensitive assessment allows conducting a more appropriate measure of 'general physical activity' and classifies considerably more women as practising a health promoting lifestyle. This, consequently, prevents measurement bias in prevalence estimations and misclassifications, i.e., assignment to non-intentional, intentional and action stage (cf., Bull et al., 2001).

Measurement of Risk Perception

Health knowledge and risk perception is highly vulnerable to bias and in its amount fundamentally linked to the assessment. We provided evidence that women are typically more concerned about their personal health as their family's health, but often underestimate their personal health risk particularly for vascular diseases. That is, measures of risk perception that ask women to estimate their absolute risk for several diseases or health problems may lead to greater underestimations in women (e.g., "How likely is it you will have a stroke sometime in your life?", with the verbal anchors "very unlikely" to "very likely"). Assessing personal risk perception rather in comparison to persons of their own sex and age (cf., Schwarzer, in press; Weinstein, 1980) should reduce the amount of underestimation and provides thereby more valid evidence of women's risk perception (e.g., "Compared to an average person of your sex and age, how are your chances of getting a stroke?", with the verbal anchors "much below average" to "much above average").

Measurement of Outcome Expectancies

Results indicate that traditional measures of outcome expectancies that focus only positive consequences of physical activity may lead to biased model predictions in women when leaving out negative consequences of physical activity. More specific, assessing the expectations of positive (e.g., weight loss, prevention of heart attack) and negative (e.g., great effort, time) consequences of physical activities covers gender-specific motives in a more realistic way and allows conducting a more appropriate measure of 'decision balance'. However, women and men might value some outcome expectancies differently. Weight loss, for example, may be a positive outcome in women but negative in men, because men often wish conversely to build muscles (McCabe & Ricciardelli, 2003). Women, however, seem to be more likely to use diet than exercise as a method of weight loss, while men seem to be equally likely to select exercise or dieting (McElhone *et al.*, 1999). These differences should be kept in mind when constructing and selecting measurements.

Measurement of Barriers and Self-Efficacy

Evidence demonstrated that women often perceive many and in part women-typical barriers which prevent them from regular physical activity. Taking into account that women often doubt their behaviour competencies, i.e., perceive weak self-efficacy (Godin & Shephard, 1985a), measures of self-efficacy should carefully consider women-typical barriers.

Measurement and Manipulation of Self-Regulatory Strategies such as Plans

Non-experimental research mainly focus on level of action plans (i.e., its concreteness) and the degree of appropriate self-regulatory strategies regarding given barriers (Schwarzer, in press). Assessing action plans and coping plans has thereby to consider women-typical barriers particularly social barriers such as family duties. Intervention research, moreover, might scrutinize also plan contents and matching of action plans and coping plans in more detail.

Measurement of Social Influences

We outlined that social influences play an important role in physical activity among women. That is, domain-specific social support should be integrated as important resource in theory-based research. Measures, thereby, might include different sources and different kinds of social support. Thus, women may be asked to report support provided by husband and/or family and friends (cf., Toobert et al., 2005) such as accompany, propose, remind, and encourage (cf., De Bourdeaudhuij & Sallis, 2002). Moreover, social norms should be considered (cf., De Bourdeaudhuij & Sallis, 2002).

Data Analysing Strategies

When analyzing models predicting physical activity and the interplay of social-cognitive variables, sex might be included as moderator: Testing possible sex differences in prediction models might shed more light into differences between women and/or men particularities in women. However, the previous theory-based studies so far could detect no or not many sex differences (e.g., Lippke et al., 2004a).

Acting on the great discussion in sport psychology on whether sex differences actually exist or rather other factors explain theses differences, we again have to note that sex differences in physical activity are not so much associated with the biological sex as in fact with the gender role (Gill, 2007; Helgeson, 2005; Waldron, 1997). These norms and expectations which go along with being female versus male are indeed linked to the biological sex, but eminently vary with age, education, income, and ethnicity. As demonstrated throughout the review, gender role expectations shape girls' and women's activity behaviour as their perceived motive, perceived barriers and self-regulation strategies. Model testing, as a consequence, should carefully consider further possible mediators or moderators such as gender role identification, age, education. This strategy of data analysis may help to close sex differences or to identify subgroups of women (and men) which are at high risk for inactivity, respectively.

In sum, combining gender-sensitive approaches with theoretical frameworks such as the HAPA is a promising way to gain more appropriate evidence to develop theory- and evidence-based interventions that are better adjusted to women-typical needs. How this can be done in particular will be explicated in the following.

INTERVENTION DEVELOPMENT AND APPLICATION

The HAPA can be applied as described to explain why many women despite existing knowledge often do not engage in a healthy lifestyle. It opens ways to develop promising effective interventions by targeting them on motivation or motivational problems of women. Prior to every motivational counselling it has to be diagnosed in which psychological stage a person is, that is, whether a lifestyle change is intended or which experience already exists (e.g., see Bolognesi et al., 2006; Britt *et al.*, 2004; Marcus & Forsyth, 2003; Resnicow *et al.*, 2002).

A person who is unmotivated and intends no lifestyle change (i.e., non-intentional stage) should primary informed about risks of the current life style. Thereby counselling of women should particularly take into account that information has a high self-relevance. Neutrally communicated pros and cons of a changed lifestyle can create an awareness of problem. For this several brochures or individual cost-benefits analyses exist which can be worked out by a person self-administered (Bolognesi et al., 2006; Marcus & Forsyth, 2003).

A person who is motivated and intends a lifestyle change (i.e., intentional stage) the counselling should focus on personal and health-related benefits of a change. In addition, reasons which a person prevents from acting should be clarified. If a person is ready for a change individual plans of how to translate the goal into behaviour and possible coping strategies helps. This can also be carried out as a written planning intervention (Lippke et al., 2004b; Sniehotta *et al.*, 2006; Ziegelmann et al., 2006).

A person who already acts and changes his/her lifestyle but has still difficulties to maintain this change (i.e., action stage) the counselling should promote self-reflection of pros and behavioural competences. Women-specific programmes to enhance self-efficacy might help women better than generic interventions where women may feel not targeted personally. If necessary action plans and coping plans are adapted if it turns out in everyday life that the activity is not realisable as planned or unexpected barriers hinder or compromise maintenance (Bolognesi et al., 2006; Marcus & Forsyth, 2003; Schwarzer, in press).

Basically, counselling should avoid to arguing or to persuading (Marcus & Forsyth, 2003). In contrast, previous positive experiences and resources of a person have to be identified and to be increased. Encouragement means generally to strengthen a person's self-efficacy beliefs (Schwarzer, in press).

CONCLUSION

Differences exist between men's and women's physical activity. These differences are originated by gender roles and corresponding norms, expectations, and experiences. Interventions considering women's needs and obstacles may be better tailored to women and, thereby, made more effective. However, designing women-specific interventions is challenging due to the complex nature of the process of health behaviour change. The Health Action Process Approach (HAPA) was introduced as theoretical framework to integrate finding and to better identify women-typical characteristics. Research on women's adoption and maintenance of health enhancing physical exercise should be sensitive to gender differences. Designing exercise promotion interventions theory-based especially tailored to women needs more evidence-based practice. Some first recommendations for gender sensitive programmes direct towards an increase of suitable physical activities and their antecedents.

REFERENCES

Abel, T., Graf, N., & Niemann, S. (2001). Gender bias in the assessment of physical activity in population studies. *Soz Praventivmed, 46*(4), 268-272.

Assaf, A. R., Parker, D., Lapane, K. L., Coccio, E., Evangelou, E., & Carleton, R. A. (2003). Does the Y chromosome make a difference? Gender differences in attempts to change cardiovascular disease risk factors. *J Womens Health (Larchmt), 12*(4), 321-330.

Bolognesi, M., Nigg, C. R., Massarini, M., & Lippke, S. (2006). Reducing obesity indicators through brief physical activity counseling (PACE) in Italian primary care settings. *Ann Behav Med, 31*(2), 179-185.

Britt, E., Hudson, S. M., & Blampied, N. M. (2004). Motivational interviewing in health settings: A review. *Patient Educ Couns, 53*(2), 147-155.

Bull, F. C., Eyler, A. A., King, A. C., & Brownson, R. C. (2001). Stage of readiness to exercise in ethnically diverse women: A U.S. Survey. *Med Sci Sports Exerc, 33*(7), 1147-1156.

Carlson, L. E., Goodey, E., Bennett, M. H., Taenzer, P., & Koopmans, J. (2002). The addition of social support to a community-based large-group behavioral smoking cessation intervention: Improved cessation rates and gender differences. *Addict Behav, 27*(4), 547-559.

Centers for Disease Control and Prevention. (2007). Physical activity among adults: United states, 2000 and 2005. from http://www.cdc.gov/nchs/products/pubs/pubd/hestats/physicalactivity/physicalactivity.htm

Cialdini, R. B., & Trost, M. R. (1998). Social influence: Social norms, conformity and compliance. In D. T. Gilbert, S. T. Fiske & G. Lindzey (Eds.), *The handbook of social psychology* (4th ed., Vol. 2, pp. 151-192). New York: McGraw-Hill.

Cox, K. L., Gorely, T. J., Puddey, I. B., Burke, V., & Beilin, L. J. (2003). Exercise behaviour change in 40 to 65-year-old women: The SWEAT study (sedentary women exercise adherence trial). *Br J Health Psychol, 8*(Pt 4), 477-495.

Darlison, E. (2000). Geschlechterrolle und Sport [Sex role and sports]. *Orthopade, 29*(11), 957-968.

De Bourdeaudhuij, I., & Sallis, J. (2002). Relative contribution of psychosocial variables to the explanation of physical activity in three population-based adult samples. *Prev Med, 34*(2), 279-288.

Eyler, A. A. (2003). Personal, social, and environmental correlates of physical activity in rural midwestern white women. *Am J Prev Med, 25*(3 Suppl 1), 86-92.

Eyler, A. A., Brownson, R. C., Donatelle, R. J., King, A. C., Brown, D., & Sallis, J. F. (1999). Physical activity social support and middle- and older-aged minority women: Results from a US survey. *Soc Sci Med, 49*(6), 781-789.

Eyler, A. E., Wilcox, S., Matson-Koffman, D., Evenson, K. R., Sanderson, B., Thompson, J., Wilbur, J., & Rohm-Young, D. (2002). Correlates of physical activity among women from diverse racial/ethnic groups. *J Womens Health Gend Based Med, 11*(3), 239-253.

Frankish, C. J., Milligan, C. D., & Reid, C. (1998). A review of relationships between active living and determinants of health. *Soc Sci Med, 47*(3), 287-301.

Fredricks, J. A., & Eccles, J. S. (2005). Family socialization, gender, and sport motivation and involvement. *Journal of Sport & Exercise Psychology, 27*(1), 3-31.

Gill, D. (2007). Gender and cultural diversity. In G. Tenenbaum & R. C. Eklund (Eds.), *Handbook of sport psychology* (3 ed.). New York: Wiley.

Godin, G., & Shephard, R. J. (1985a). Gender differences in perceived physical self-efficacy among older individuals. *Percept Mot Skills, 60*(2), 599-602.

Godin, G., & Shephard, R. J. (1985b). A simple method to assess exercise behavior in the community. *Can J Appl Sport Sci, 10*(3), 141-146.

Gollwitzer, P. M. (1999). Implementation intentions: Strong effects of simple plans. *Am Psychol, 54*, 493-503.

Gregg, E. W., Cauley, J. A., Stone, K., Thompson, T. J., Bauer, D. C., Cummings, S. R., & Ensrud, K. E. (2003). Relationship of changes in physical activity and mortality among older women. *JAMA, 289*(18), 2379-2386.

Helgeson, V. S. (2005). *The psychology of gender* (2nd ed.). Upper Saddle River, NJ: Prentice Hall.

Jacobs, J. E., & Eccles, J. S. (1992). The impact of mothers' gender-role stereotypic beliefs on mothers' and children's ability perceptions. *J Pers Soc Psychol, 63*(6), 932-944.

King, A. C., Blair, S. N., Bild, D. E., Dishman, R. K., Dubbert, P. M., Marcus, B. H., Oldridge, N. B., Paffenbarger, R. S., Jr., Powell, K. E., & Yeager, K. K. (1992). Determinants of physical activity and interventions in adults. *Med Sci Sports Exerc, 24*(6 Suppl), S221-236.

King, A. C., Castro, C., Wilcox, S., Eyler, A. A., Sallis, J. F., & Brownson, R. C. (2000). Personal and environmental factors associated with physical inactivity among different racial-ethnic groups of U.S. Middle-aged and older-aged women. *Health Psychol, 19*(4), 354-364.

Klomsten, A. T., Marsh, H. W., & Skaalvik, E. M. (2005). Adolescents' perceptions of masculine and feminine values in sport and physical education: A study of gender differences. *Sex Roles, 52*(9-10), 625-636.

Lampert, T., Mensink, G. B., & Ziese, T. (2005). Sport und Gesundheit bei Erwachsenen in Deutschland [Sport and health among adults in Germany]. *Bundesgesundheitsblatt Gesundheitsforschung Gesundheitsschutz, 48*(12), 1357-1364.

Lippke, S., Ziegelmann, J. P., & Schwarzer, R. (2004a). Behavioral intentions and action plans promote physical exercise: A longitudinal study with orthopedic rehabilitation patients. *Journal of Sport & Exercise Psychology, 26*, 470-483.

Lippke, S., Ziegelmann, J. P., & Schwarzer, R. (2004b). Initiation and maintenance of physical exercise: Stage-specific effects of a planning intervention. *Research in Sports Medicine, 12*, 221–240.

Lippke, S., Ziegelmann, J. P., & Schwarzer, R. (2005). Stage-specific adoption and maintenance of physical activity: Testing a three stage model. *Psychology of Sport and Exercise, 6*, 585-603.

Luszczynska, A., Sobczyk, A., & Abraham, C. (2007). Planning to lose weight: Randomized controlled trial of an implementation intention prompt to enhance weight reduction among overweight and obese women. *Health Psychol, 26*(4), 507-512.

Marcus, B., & Forsyth, L. A. (2003). *Motivating people to be physically active*. Champaign, IL: Human Kinetics Publishers.

Margetts, B. M., Rogers, E., Widhal, K., Remaut de Winter, A. M., & Zunft, H. J. (1999). Relationship between attitudes to health, body weight and physical activity and level of physical activity in a nationally representative sample in the European Union. *Public Health Nutr, 2*(1A), 97-103.

Martin, R., Johnsen, E. L., Bunde, J., Bellman, S. B., Rothrock, N. E., Weinrib, A., & Lemos, K. (2005). Gender differences in patients' attributions for myocardial infarction: Implications for adaptive health behaviors. *Int J Behav Med, 12*(1), 39-45.

Martin, S. B., Morrow, J. R., Jr., Jackson, A. W., & Dunn, A. L. (2000). Variables related to meeting the CDC/ACSM physical activity guidelines. *Med Sci Sports Exerc, 32*(12), 2087-2092.

McCabe, M. P., & Ricciardelli, L. A. (2003). Body image and strategies to lose weight and increase muscle among boys and girls. *Health Psychol, 22*(1), 39-46.

McElhone, S., Kearney, J. M., Giachetti, I., Zunft, H. J., & Martinez, J. A. (1999). Body image perception in relation to recent weight changes and strategies for weight loss in a nationally representative sample in the European Union. *Public Health Nutr, 2*(1A), 143-151.

Meisinger, C., Lowel, H., Thorand, B., & Doring, A. (2005). Leisure time physical activity and the risk of type 2 diabetes in men and women from the general population. The MONICA/KORA Augsburg cohort study. *Diabetologia, 48*(1), 27-34.

Meyer, D., Leventhal, H., & Gutmann, M. (2003). Common-sense models of illness: The example of hypertension. In P. Salovey & A. J. Rothman (Eds.), *Social psychology of health*. (pp. 9-20). New York: Psychology Press.

Meyer, K., Niemann, S., & Abel, T. (2004). Gender differences in physical activity and fitness - association with self-reported health and health-relevant attitudes in a middle-aged swiss urban population. *J Public Health, 12*, 283-290.

Mosca, L., Banka, C. L., Benjamin, E. J., Berra, K., Bushnell, C., Dolor, R. J., Ganiats, T. G., Gomes, A. S., Gornik, H. L., Gracia, C., Gulati, M., Haan, C. K., Judelson, D. R., Keenan, N., Kelepouris, E., Michos, E. D., Newby, L. K., Oparil, S., Ouyang, P., Oz, M. C., Petitti, D., Pinn, V. W., Redberg, R. F., Scott, R., Sherif, K., Smith, S. C., Jr., Sopko, G., Steinhorn, R. H., Stone, N. J., Taubert, K. A., Todd, B. A., Urbina, E., & Wenger, N. K. (2007). Evidence-based guidelines for cardiovascular disease prevention in women: 2007 update. *Circulation, 115*(11), 1481-1501.

Mosca, L., Ferris, A., Fabunmi, R., & Robertson, R. M. (2004). Tracking women's awareness of heart disease: An american heart association national study. *Circulation, 109*(5), 573-579.

Mota, J., & Esculcas, C. (2002). Leisure-time physical activity behavior: Structured and unstructured choices according to sex, age, and level of physical activity. *Int J Behav Med, 9*(2), 111-121.

Motl, R. W., Dishman, R. K., Ward, D. S., Saunders, R. P., Dowda, M., Felton, G., & Pate, R. R. (2002). Examining social-cognitive determinants of intention and physical activity among black and white adolescent girls using structural equation modeling. *Health Psychol, 21*(5), 459-467.

Motl, R. W., Dishman, R. K., Ward, D. S., Saunders, R. P., Dowda, M., Felton, G., & Pate, R. R. (2005). Comparison of barriers self-efficacy and perceived behavioral control for explaining physical activity across 1 year among adolescent girls. *Health Psychol, 24*(1), 106-111.

Müller-Nordhorn, J., Nolte, C. H., Rossnagel, K., Jungehülsing, G. J., Reich, A., Roll, S., Villringer, A., & Willich, S. N. (2006). Knowledge about risk factors for stroke. A population-based survey with 28 090 participants. *Stroke, 37*(4), 946-950.

Murray, R. P., Johnston, J. J., Dolce, J. J., Lee, W. W., & O'Hara, P. (1995). Social support for smoking cessation and abstinence: The lung health study. Lung health study research group. *Addict Behav, 20*(2), 159-170.

O'Brien Cousins, S. (1995). Social support for exercise among elderly women in Canada. *Health Prom Int, 10*(4), 273.

O'Brien Cousins, S. (2000). "my heart couldn't take it": Older women's beliefs about exercise benefits and risks. *J Gerontol B Psychol Sci Soc Sci, 55*(5), P283-294.

O'Hea, E. L., Wood, K. B., & Brantley, P. J. (2003). The transtheoretical model: Gender differences across 3 health behaviors. *Am J Health Behav, 27*(6), 645-656.

Plotnikoff, R. C., Lippke, S., Karunamuni, N., Eves, N., Courneya, K. S., Sigal, R., & Birkett, N. (2007). Co-morbidity, functionality and time since diagnosis as predictors of physical activity in individuals with type 1 or type 2 diabetes. *Diabetes Res Clin Prac, 78*, 115-122.

Prochaska, J. J., & Sallis, J. F. (2004). A randomized controlled trial of single versus multiple health behavior change: Promoting physical activity and nutrition among adolescents. *Health Psychol, 23*(3), 314-318.

Resnicow, K., DiIorio, C., Soet, J. E., Ernst, D., Borrelli, B., & Hecht, J. (2002). Motivational interviewing in health promotion: It sounds like something is changing. *Health Psychol, 21*(5), 444-451.

Rivis, A., & Sheeran, P. (2003). Descriptive norms as an additional predictor in the theory of planned behaviour: A meta-analysis. *Curr Psychol, 22*(3), 218-233.

Schwarzer, R. (1992). Self-efficacy in the adoption and maintenance of health behaviors: Theoretical approaches and a new model. In R. Schwarzer (Ed.), *Self-efficacy: Thought control of action* (pp. 217-243). Washington, DC, USA: Hemisphere Publishing Corp.

Schwarzer, R. (2001). Social-cognitive factors in changing health-related behaviors. *Current Directions in Psychological Science, 10*(2), 47-51.

Schwarzer, R. (in press). Modeling health behavior change: How to predict and modify the adoption and maintenance of health behaviors. *Applied Psychology: An International Review*.

Schwarzer, R., Schüz, B., Ziegelmann, J. P., Lippke, S., Luszczynska, A., & Scholz, U. (2007). Adoption and maintenance of four health behaviors: Theory-guided longitudinal studies on dental flossing, seat belt use, dietary behavior, and physical activity. *Ann Behav Med, 33*(2), 156-166.

Sniehotta, F. F., Scholz, U., & Schwarzer, R. (2006). Action plans and coping plans for physical exercise: A longitudinal intervention study in cardiac rehabilitation. *Br J Health Psychol, 11*(1), 23-37.

Statistics Canada. (2007, Last modified: 2007-04-30). Physical activity, by age group and sex. Table 105-0433 and catalogue no. 82-221-x. from http://www40.statcan.ca/l01/cst01 /health46.htm

Sternfeld, B., Ainsworth, B. E., & Quesenberry, C. P. (1999). Physical activity patterns in a diverse population of women. *Prev Med, 28*(3), 313-323.

Sternfeld, B., Cauley, J., Harlow, S., Liu, G., & Lee, M. (2000). Assessment of physical activity with a single global question in a large, multiethnic sample of midlife women. *Am J Epidemiol, 152*(7), 678-687.

Titze, S., Stronegger, W., & Owen, N. (2005). Prospective study of individual, social, and environmental predictors of physical activity: Women's leisure running. *Psychology of Sport and Exercise, 6*(3), 363-376.

Toobert, D. J., Glasgow, R. E., Nettekoven, L. A., & Brown, J. E. (1998). Behavioral and psychosocial effects of intensive lifestyle management for women with coronary heart disease. *Patient Educ Couns, 35*(3), 177-188.

Toobert, D. J., Strycker, L. A., Glasgow, R. E., Barrera Jr, M., & Angell, K. (2005). Effects of the mediterranean lifestyle program on multiple risk behaviors and psychosocial outcomes among women at risk for heart disease. *Ann Behav Med, 29*(2), 128-137.

Trost, S. G., Owen, N., Bauman, A. E., Sallis, J. F., & Brown, W. (2002). Correlates of adults' participation in physical activity: Review and update. *Med Sci Sports Exerc, 34*(12), 1996-2001.

Tudor-Locke, C., Henderson, K. A., Wilcox, S., Cooper, R. S., Durstine, J. L., & Ainsworth, B. E. (2003). In their own voices: Definitions and interpretations of physical activity. *Womens Health Issues, 13*(5), 194-199.

Waldron, I. (1997). Changing gender roles and gender differences in health behavior. In D. S. Gochman (Ed.), *Handbook of health behavior research* (Vol. I, pp. 303-328). New York: Plenum Press.

Weinstein, N. D. (1980). Unrealistic optimism about future life events. *J Pers Soc Psychol, 39*, 806-820.

Willett, W. C. (2002). Balancing life-style and genomics research for disease prevention. *Science, 296*(5568), 695-698.

Yusuf, S., Hawken, S., Ounpuu, S., Dans, T., Avezum, A., Lanas, F., McQueen, M., Budaj, A., Pais, P., Varigos, J., & Lisheng, L. (2004). Effect of potentially modifiable risk factors associated with myocardial infarction in 52 countries (the interheart study): Case-control study. *Lancet, 364*(9438), 937-952.

Ziegelmann, J. P., Lippke, S., & Schwarzer, R. (2006). Adoption and maintenance of physical activity: Planning interventions in young, middle-aged, and older adults. *Psychology and Health, 21*, 145-163.

Zunft, H. J., Friebe, D., Seppelt, B., Widhalm, K., Remaut de Winter, A. M., Vaz de Almeida, M. D., Kearney, J. M., & Gibney, M. (1999). Perceived benefits and barriers to physical activity in a nationally representative sample in the european union. *Public Health Nutr, 2*(1A), 153-160.

In: Progress in Exercise and Women's Health Research   ISBN 1-60456-014-5
Editor: Janet P. Coulter, pp. 213-227   © 2008 Nova Science Publishers, Inc.

Chapter 8

EFFECTS OF WEIGHT-BEARING AND NON-WEIGHT BEARING EXERCISE ON BONE MINERAL DENSITY DURING SHORT-TERM WEIGHT LOSS IN OVERWEIGHT PREMENOPAUSAL WOMEN

Joanne Loethen and Pamela S. Hinton
Department of Nutritional Sciences
University of Missouri-Columbia, USA

ABSTRACT

Background

Weight reduction in overweight and obese individuals reduces morbidity and mortality from chronic diseases associated with excess adiposity. Weight loss, however, negatively affects bone health by decreasing bone mass and bone mineral density.

Objective

The purpose of the present study was to examine the effects of short-term weight loss with and without non-weight bearing aerobic exercise on bone mineral content (BMC) and density (BMD) in overweight premenopausal females.

Methods

Twenty overweight to class I obese, sedentary, non-smoking women aged 18 to 35 years, participated in this 6-week weight loss intervention study designed to produce a 5% reduction in body weight. Participants were randomly assigned to either the diet only (D) or the diet plus non-weight bearing exercise (D+E) group. The D group achieved weight loss via moderate energy restriction; the D+E group reduced energy intake and increased energy expenditure by 250-400 kcal/day through non-weight bearing aerobic exercise. Exercise training consisted primarily of cycling on a stationary bike 5 days/week at approximately 60% of measured maximum oxygen consumption (75% maximal heart rate) for 45 minutes/day. Anthropometrics, maximal oxygen consumption (VO$_2$max), BMD and BMC of the total body, hip and lumbar spine were measured at baseline and post-weight loss. Dietary intake was monitored using written food diaries; pre- and post-weight loss diets were analyzed using Food Processor 8.0. Repeated measures two-way ANOVA was used to test for significant time and group effects, as well as for group by time interactions. Post hoc t-tests and Tukey's test were used for significant main effects and interactions, respectively. Data were analyzed using SigmaStat (Version 2.03, SPSS Inc.).

Results

D and D+E groups were not significantly different at baseline in age, body weight, BMI, percent body fat, or VO$_2$max. Body weight and BMI decreased significantly in both groups from baseline to post-weight loss ($p<0.05$) and there was no group by time interaction; however, the D+E group exhibited a significant reduction in percent body fat (~5%), while the D group did not. As expected, there was a significant group by time interaction for VO$_2$max; aerobic capacity increased significantly in the D+E group ($p<0.05$), confirming compliance with the exercise training. Average energy intake decreased by 971 ± 158 and 468 ± 98 kcal/d in the D and D+E groups, respectively. There were no significant group differences in BMD or BMC at any site before or after weight loss. Neither group showed any significant changes in BMD or BMC. However, hip BMD showed a tendency to decline with weight loss (time main effect, $p=0.079$).

Conclusion

The present study suggests that a 6-wk moderate weight reduction with or without non-weight bearing aerobic training does not cause any significant changes in BMD or BMC in premenopausal overweight women. Long-term weight loss, however, may result in measurable reductions in BMD, as suggested by the observed decrease in hip BMD ($p=0.079$). Aerobic exercise, regardless of whether it is weight bearing or non-weight bearing, is known to promote health benefits beyond that of bone density, and, therefore, should be an important component of any weight loss program.

INTRODUCTION

Overweight and obesity are prevalent health hazards within the U.S. population. Currently 65% and 31% of American adults are overweight and obese, respectively [1]. Hypertension, coronary heart disease, type 2 diabetes, and numerous other chronic diseases are associated with excess body fat, thus raising the cost of health care and reducing the life expectancy of the current population and future generations [2]. Weight reduction in overweight and obese individuals, especially modest long-term weight loss, is a well-established method of reducing the risk for chronic disease and early mortality in this population. Although the loss of excess body weight is important to achieve optimal health benefits, weight reduction negatively affects bone health by decreasing bone mass and bone mineral density [3-13]. Over time, excessive bone loss can compromise bone strength, increase fracture risk and place an individual at a greater risk of developing osteopenia, osteoporosis, and other bone-related diseases.

Bone health is a crucial, but often overlooked, factor when considering an individual's overall health and quality of life. Any compromise in bone strength can have detrimental and debilitating effects on one's functional capacity, mobility, and thus quality of life. In 2004, approximately 34 million American men and women were believed to have low bone mass while another 10 million were diagnosed with having osteoporosis (National Osteoporosis Foundation, 2004). This compromise in bone health is accompanied by a greater risk for fracture, possible immobilization, and increased health care costs for all those affected.

Maintaining bone health throughout life is essential to delaying and/or preventing the onset of osteoporosis, osteopenia, and other bone-related diseases that may result from excessive bone loss. Although bone loss is primarily associated with aging and tends to be most prevalent in females, low bone mass can appear at any age and among all populations [10] . Weight loss, decreased activity level, and poor nutritional status are just a few of the factors can that influence bone throughout the life cycle [10]. Obtaining optimal bone health in the early and middle stages of life will aid in reducing fracture risk, sustaining normal daily activities, and maintaining the quality of life throughout the aging process.

The relationship between body weight and bone mass has been well established. Individuals with a high body weight tend to have a higher bone mass and less bone turnover than their lighter counterparts [14]. Excess body weight, as indicated by a body mass index (BMI) ≥ 25 kg/m^2, also is associated with increased bone mineral density (BMD) and decreased bone resorption, while individuals with a lower BMI often have reduced BMD, increased resorption, and, subsequently, a greater risk for fracture [14-19]. Total body fat is another parameter that is one of the most consistent predictors of BMD, and correlates positively with BMD [15, 20]. The relationship between body weight, fat content, and bone mass seems to be more pronounced in females; however, men show similar associations between body weight, body fat, and bone status [14, 21]. Thus, it appears that maintaining a higher body weight may be helpful in achieving greater bone mass.

Current weight status and/or energy availability is another predictor of bone health. Positive and negative energy balance have differential effects on the rate of bone turnover and elicit varying responses on the skeletal structure [4, 7, 11-13, 22, 23]. Weight reduction induced by a very low calorie diet (405 kcal/day) has been shown to result in rapid bone loss, whereas subsequent weight regain re-establishes initial BMD [7]. More moderate energy restriction results in a similar, yet less pronounced relationship between weight flux and bone mass [4, 8]. While weight loss stimulates the entire remodeling process (both formation and resorption), bone resorption is favored and likely is to blame for the reduction in BMD. Furthermore, the extent of bone loss induced by weight reduction appears to be dependent on the rate, amount, and duration of the weight loss regimen [4, 22].

Whether weight loss-induced bone loss during early adulthood translates to an increased risk for osteoporosis later in life is not yet clear. Age-related bone loss is inevitable [24]; however, some suggest that obtaining a higher peak bone mass early in life will reduce an individual's chances for or delay the onset of osteoporosis and other bone-related diseases [25]. The same is true for adults who are able to maintain balance between bone formation and resorption further into aging. For example, should an individual avoid a significant imbalance of bone resorption and formation until the age of 50, he or she will have a lower risk of developing osteoporosis than if that same imbalance had developed ten years earlier. Therefore, it is important to maintain balance between bone resorption and formation throughout the life cycle, which appears to be difficult in those aiming to lose weight.

The importance of physical activity to bone health has been well established through studies comparing physically active individuals to sedentary controls [26, 27]. Furthermore, the type of physical activity (i.e. aerobic vs. resistance training) and the degree of impact (high impact vs. low impact) during exercise have been suggested to reflect the extent to which bone is affected. High-impact and weight-bearing exercises have a greater positive effect on bone mass (via enhanced bone formation) than low-impact and non-weight bearing activity in female athletes [28, 29] and postmenopausal [30] women, respectively. The mechanism by which physical activity promotes bone density is the mechanical load placed on bone which produces a signal to activate bone cells, stimulate bone turnover, and promote a remodeling process that favors bone formation [31]. The bone structure thus adapts to the mechanical stress placed on it by increasing bone mass and density. In contrast, the absence of or decrease in mechanical loading on the skeletal system results in a significant decline in bone mass [27, 32]. Although normal daily activities can produce mechanical loads that are sufficient to promote bone remodeling in most individuals, these activities may not be enough for an individual who already is in a state of low bone mass or negative bone balance, such as during weight loss.

Weight loss intervention studies involving caloric restriction plus exercise have indicated the importance of including physical activity during weight reduction to prevent or decrease the amount of bone loss. Villareal, et al [22] observed no changes in BMD after 12 months of exercise-induced weight loss in adult men and women, while weight loss without exercise showed significant decreases in BMD of the lumbar spine, hip, and intertrochanter. Similar results have been documented by Ryan et al [23] following 6 months of diet-induced weight loss with or without exercise in postmenopausal women. Although exercise did not prevent a decline in BMD of the total body, regional BMDs of the femoral neck and greater trochanter regions were maintained throughout the 6-month intervention. In yet another study, women who increased their physical activity the most during an 18-month lifestyle intervention displayed lesser bone loss when compared to less active women [6]. Thus, it is evident that even though weight loss significantly reduces BMD, physical activity may help to reduce and possibly even prevent the bone loss that accompanies weight reduction.

While much evidence supports the notion that exercise may benefit bone health, particularly in individuals undergoing weight loss, little research has been performed to investigate the effects of non-weight bearing aerobic activity during weight reduction. The studies involving weight loss and exercise primarily have involved resistance training and/or weight-bearing aerobic activity (i.e. walking, jogging, stair climbing). To our knowledge, no research studies have investigated a weight loss intervention involving non-weight bearing aerobic activity (i.e. cycling, swimming) exclusively. Due to the reduced mechanical loading stimuli encountered during non-weight bearing activity, it is expected that this type of training will not have as great a benefit on bone mass as weight-bearing exercise training; however, any exercise stimulus regardless of the type, may provide some benefit over a weight loss regimen that contains no exercise training whatsoever. Leg strength has been shown to be a significant predictor of hip BMD in Caucasian young women [33], and a significant association between femoral neck BMD and lower limb muscle mass was observed in postmenopausal women [34]. Assuming that exercise, including non-weight bearing exercise training, promotes an increase and/or maintenance of muscle mass, the preservation of muscle mass may be one way that non-weight bearing exercise could benefit bone mass. Also, the strain of exercise-induced muscle contraction on bone is another manner in which BMD is influenced by non-weight bearing activity.

Thus, the purpose of the present study was to compare changes in BMD and BMC during short-term weight loss achieved via caloric-restriction and non-weight bearing aerobic exercise with caloric restriction alone in overweight premenopausal females.

METHODS

Subjects. Originally, thirty-four women, aged 18 to 35 years, volunteered for this study. Participants primarily were recruited by posters, fliers, and mass email to the University of Missouri-Columbia faculty, staff, and students and by word of mouth. To be eligible, women had to be weight stable, not currently dieting, and not participating in a regular exercise program at the time of recruitment or for three months prior. Subjects were screened by an initial interview and health history questionnaire. Subjects were overweight to class I obese (BMI 25-35 kg/m^2), non-smokers, generally healthy, and were not on any medications that would alter calcium or bone metabolism. Upon providing written informed consent and completing baseline testing, subjects were randomly assigned to either the diet only (D) or the diet plus non-weight bearing exercise (D+E) weight loss program designed to produce a 5% reduction in body weight over a 6-week period.

Dietary analysis and dietary intervention. Prior to beginning the study, all subjects submitted a 3-day written diet log for two week days and one weekend day which then was used to evaluate baseline diet composition. Throughout the study, dietary intake was monitored using written food diaries and the last three days of the diary were used to evaluate post-weight loss diet composition. Pre- and post-weight loss diets were analyzed using the Food Processor 8.0 computer program. Subjects in the D group were instructed to reduce their caloric intake by 500-750 kcal/day. Strategies to achieve this reduction in energy intake included: eliminating "empty calories" (e.g. soda, added fat); substituting high-fat foods with low-fat options; and reducing portion size. Subjects in the D+E group were advised to reduce their energy intake by 300-500 kcal/day, while also expending 250-400 kcal/day through non-weight bearing aerobic exercise 5 days per week. Each participant met with a nutritionist 1-2 times/week in order to weigh-in and receive diet counseling based on her progress. Both interventions aimed to produce a gradual weight loss of 1-2 pounds/week over a 6-week period.

Exercise intervention. Exercise training of subjects in the D+E group consisted primarily of cycling on a stationary bike 5 days/week at approximately 60% of measured maximum oxygen consumption (75% maximal heart rate) for 45 minutes/day. Subjects also were given the option of participating in other non-weight bearing aerobic activities, such as swimming; however, subjects primarily opted to cycle. Each week, D+E subjects were required to complete at least 3 of their 5 exercise sessions under the supervision of a laboratory staff member at the "fitness center" located in McKee Gymnasium. Subjects were given the option of completing 2 of the 5 sessions on their own with instruction to perform only non-weight bearing aerobic activities. During their second week of exercise, subjects in the D+E group performed a 30-minute submaximal VO_2 test to estimate energy expenditure during each exercise session. Caloric expenditure was then calculated by taking the total number of calories expended during the 30-minute test and adding half of this value to the total to get an estimate of kcals expended during a 45-minute session. Participants in the D group were instructed to continue their sedentary lifestyle and not to begin any formal exercise program during their participation in the study.

Body composition. Initial body weight was recorded at each subject's first diet counseling session with the study nutritionist. Throughout the study, body weight was obtained 1-2 times per week either during the appointments with the nutritionist or prior to a scheduled exercise session. Height and weight were determined at baseline and post-weight loss and were used to calculate body mass index (BMI) by dividing the subjects' weight in kg by height (m) squared. Body composition was assessed using two methods: DXA analysis and skinfold measurement. DXA body fat measurements were obtained during a total body scan.

VO_2 testing. Maximal aerobic capacity was assessed in all subjects before and after weight loss to confirm adherence to the exercise program (D+E) or sedentary lifestyle (D). Testing was performed using a ParVo Medics TrueOne® 2400 metabolic measurement system (ParVo Medics, Inc.) on a stationary bike (Ergomedic 828E Monark, G1H Sweden) using the following protocol. Following a five-minute warm-up with no resistance, testing began and the workload was increased to 0.5 kp, after which the workload was increased an additional 0.5 kp every two minutes until the subject was unable to continue. The subject was asked to maintain a constant, self-determined cadence throughout the duration of the test. Subjects wore a headpiece connected to a bi-directional valve and attached to a rubber mouthpiece (Hans Rudolph 2726 Series). This valve was then connected to the metabolic cart by a plastic tube so that a breath-by-breath analysis could be obtained. A true VO_2max was believed to be attained when two of the following criteria were met: a plateau in oxygen uptake with an increased workload; a respiratory exchange ratio >1.10; and a maximal heart rate within 10bts/min of the age-predicted maximal value. Testing also was terminated if the subject began experiencing discomfort or if she was unable to maintain the established cadence. Heart rate monitors (Polar B1, Polar Electro Oy, Finland) were used to monitor and record heart rate values during exercise testing as well as during supervised sessions of the D+E group. Measured VO_2max was used to assess the fitness status of subjects at baseline and follow-up, and also was used to prescribe a target heart rate for subjects in the D+E group during their exercise sessions.

BMD and BMC. Bone mineral density (BMD) and bone mineral content (BMC) of the total body, left hip, and lumbar spine were measured at baseline and post-weight loss using dual-energy x-ray absorptiometry (DXA, Hologic Delphi A). Standardized procedures for patient positioning and use of DXA software were followed. Scans were analyzed with Hologic software. Fasting blood samples were also taken between 06:00 and 10:00 at baseline and follow-up for further analysis of bone turnover at a later date.

Statistical analysis. Repeated measures two-way ANOVA was used to test for significant main effects of group and time, as well as group by time interactions. Data were analyzed by SigmaStat statistical software (SigmaStat Version 2.03, SPSS Inc.). Tukey's test was used for post-hoc comparisons when the group-by-time interaction was significant. Student's t-tests were used to test for differences between groups in age, as well as duration of weight loss.

RESULTS

A total of twenty women completed the study (D, n=10 and D+E, n=10). Fourteen of the 34 who initially volunteered dropped out due to inability to meet the weight loss requirement within the given period, inability to comply with the exercise component of the D+E protocol, or for personal reasons. One woman in the D+E group became pregnant, was unable to complete the post-weight loss DXA scan, and, therefore, was excluded from the final BMD and BMC analyses. Data also were missing for the hip scan of one woman in the D group.

Average duration of weight loss to achieve a 5% reduction in body weight was 5.0 weeks in the D group and 6.3 weeks in the D+E group. Compliance rate of exercise sessions in the D+E group was high; all subjects completed an average of five sessions per week with ~75% of these sessions completed in our supervised facility.

Participants in the D and D+E groups were not significantly different at baseline in age, body weight, BMI, percent body fat, or VO$_2$max (Table 1). Body weight and BMI decreased significantly in both groups from baseline to post-weight loss ($p<0.05$) and there was no group by time interaction. No significant changes were seen in percent body fat of the D group from baseline to follow-up, but a significantly greater decrease (~5% reduction) occurred in the D+E group after the intervention ($p=0.003$) as opposed to the D group.

Table 1. Subject characteristics of subjects before and after a diet-induced or diet + non-weight bearing exercise-induced weight loss intervention

	DIET ONLY (D)			DIET+EXERCISE (D+E)		
	Baseline	Post-Wt Loss	% change	Baseline	Post-Wt Loss	% change
Age (yr)	26.0±2.0			25.0±1.0		
Height (cm)	166.1±1.9			164.0±2.0		
Duration of weight loss (wks)	5.0±0.3			6.3±0.3†		
Body weight (kg)	77.3±0.2	73.2±0.2*	-5.3	75.2±0.2	71.2±0.2*	-5.3
BMI (kg/m²)	28.0±0.1	26.6±0.1*	-5.0	27.9±0.1	26.4±0.1*	-5.4
Body fat (%)	37.0±0.3	36.8±0.3	-0.5	37.5±0.4	35.6±0.4*	-5.1†
VO2max (L/min)	1.9±0.1	1.8±0.1	-5.3	1.7±0.1	1.9±0.1*	11.8†
VO2max (mls/kg/min)	24.9±0.7	24.8±0.7	-0.4	23.9±0.7	27.8±0.7	16.3*

Values are means ± SE. N=10 for diet only group. N=9 for diet+exercise group.
Body fat reflects measurements obtained from DXA analysis
* Significantly different from baseline, $p<0.05$
† Significantly different from D group, $p<0.05$

There was a significant group by time interaction for maximal oxygen consumption. VO_2max did not change from baseline in the D group, but increased significantly in the D+E group ($p<0.05$). This result confirms compliance of the D+E group with the exercise training. There was no significant difference in aerobic capacity between groups following weight loss. As expected, weight reduction reflected a significant improvement of relative VO_2max in the D+E group. A small, but insignificant decrease of relative VO_2max occurred in the D group after weight loss.

Daily caloric intake decreased significantly in both the D and D+E groups from baseline to follow-up ($p<0.005$), and the D group had a significantly greater reduction compared to the D+E group ($p<0.05$) (Table 2). Average caloric intake decreased 971 ± 158 and 468 ± 98 kcal/d in the D and D+E groups, respectively. Calcium intake was not significantly different between groups and declined similarly regardless of intervention type. Average reduction in calcium intake of all subjects was 312 ± 76 mg/d. Vitamin D intake showed no significant difference after weight loss and did not differ between groups. No significant differences existed between the groups in regards to percent calories from fat, carbohydrate, or protein. Percent of energy from fat decreased similarly in all subjects (combined average of 7% kcal reduction) at post-testing compared to baseline. In contrast, percentages of energy from carbohydrate and protein increased in all subjects (combined averages of 5% and 4.7%, respectively). Submaximal VO_2 testing indicated an average caloric expenditure of 242 ± 14 kcals per 45-minute exercise session for subjects in the D+E group.

Table 2. Daily intakes of subjects before and after a diet-induced or diet + non-weight bearing exercise-induced weight loss intervention

	DIET ONLY (D)			DIET+EXERCISE (D+E)		
	Baseline	Post-Wt Loss	Change	Baseline	Post-Wt Loss	Change
Energy (kcal/d)	2227±93	1256±93*	-971±158	1772±98	1304±98*	-468±98†
Fat (%kcal)	35±2	29±2	-6	33±2	23±2	-10
CHO (%kcal)	48±2	53±2	+5	54±2	59±2	+5
PRO (%kcal)	16±1	19±1	+3	14±1	20±1	+6
Calcium (mg/d)	885±76	584±76*	-301±98	749±80	424±80*	-325±123
Vitamin D (µg/d)	2.15±0.38	1.19±0.38	-44.84	1.42±0.40	1.26±0.40	-11.67

Values are means ± SE. N=10 for diet only group. N=9 for diet+exercise group.

* Significantly different from baseline, $p<0.05$

† Significantly different from D group, $p<0.05$

BMD and BMC. No significant differences existed between the groups for BMD or BMC measurements of total body, lumbar spine, left hip, femoral neck, or Ward's triangle either before or after weight loss (Table 3). Due to missing data from one subject in the D+E group, post-weight loss values reflect combined data of 10 subjects from the D group plus 8 subjects from the D+E group (N=18). Several subjects were unable to remove external artifacts or piercings that were within the lumbar spine scan area. Because high density objects can interfere with the scan, these participants were not include in the SBMC analysis, and thus only a limited number of subjects were included in that particular data set. This may help to explain the considerably large, yet insignificant change in SBMC after weight loss (Table 3). For these subjects, SBMD was calculated by excluding the lumbar vertebra affected the external artifact or piercing. Neither group showed any significant changes in BMD or BMC at any of the specific sites. However, hip BMD showed a tendency to decline with weight loss (time main effect, $p=0.079$).

Mean T-scores (±SD) for BMD of the D and D+E groups prior to intervention were, respectively, 0.3±0.9 and -0.2±0.6 for the total body, 0.8±0.8 and 0.0±0.7 for the lumbar spine, and 0.7±0.8 and 0.3±1.4 for the hip. T-scores are based on mean BMD values for a reference population of young adult females. The mean T-scores of the subjects indicate that the participants were generally within the normal range for BMD. In the D+E group, one subject had a total body T-score between -1.0 and -2.5, while another subject had a hip T-score in this same range, which suggests low bone mass and possible osteopenia in these two women.

DISCUSSION

The present study suggests that a 6-wk moderate weight reduction with or without non-
weight bearing aerobic training does not cause any significant changes in BMD or BMC in 18-35 year old overweight women as indicated by DXA analysis. Furthermore, the inclusion of non-weight bearing exercise during moderate weight reduction did not invoke any differences in BMD or BMC values compared with a weight reduction program that did not involve regular aerobic exercise. Despite the lack of change in BMD and BMC measurements after 6-wks of weight reduction, the results from this study must not be disregarded without further consideration.

BMD, BMC, and weight reduction. BMD and BMC are two of the most common measurements used to diagnose osteoporosis and low bone mass, and BMD is believed to be the strongest predictor of future osteoporotic fracture [35]. Research has identified decreases in BMD and BMC values after weight reduction [4, 7, 8, 36]; however, weight loss interventions that include an exercise training component appear to attenuate bone loss compared to exercise-free interventions [6, 22, 23]. Although BMD and BMC decrease as a result of weight loss, it is well understood that the entire bone remodeling process can take up to 6 months to complete [37]; therefore, the 6-wk duration of the present study may not have been sufficient to reflect any statistically significant changes in bone mass or bone mineral content. It is worth noting, however, that hip BMD showed a tendency to decline with weight loss (time main effect, $p=0.079$). The majority of weight loss studies that have documented changes in BMD and BMC have lasted anywhere from three months to two years in duration, which may explain why significant changes in bone density were observed in previous studies as opposed to the results seen here.

Influence of exercise. High-impact loading and weight-bearing activity are known to have a positive effect on the skeletal system. This concept has been evidenced through studies involving female athletes with various loading characteristics [28, 29], as well as in sedentary postmenopausal women who adopt a regular weight-bearing exercise routine [30]. In contrast, a reduction in this weight-bearing stimulus through bed rest [27] or reduced activity level [32] can negatively effect bone density to the extent that future risk for fracture becomes a significant concern. Weight loss also causes a reduction in the weight-bearing stimulus due to a decrease in the amount of body weight that the skeleton is required to support. In a sense, the skeletal system adapts to the demand, or lack of demand, placed on it based on the load that it is required to bear. Women in the current study were subjected to a reduction in mechanical load over a 6-wk period due to a 5% reduction in body weight, yet failed to display any change in BMD or BMC from baseline to post-weight loss measurements. This suggests that the weight reduction may have been too modest and too short in duration in order to reflect any significant changes in BMD or BMC. In addition, all of the women were previously sedentary and none increased their amount of weight-bearing activity throughout the study, regardless of intervention type; thus, only the weight-bearing action of the participants would have been that of their normal daily activities. The inclusion of non-weight bearing exercise training by women in the D+E group would increase their overall activity level, but would not intentionally increase their amount of weight-bearing activity over that of the D group; therefore, the two treatment groups in the present study can be assumed to have maintained their levels of weight-bearing activity in a similar fashion. The inclusion of non-weight bearing activity in the D+E group did not appear to influence BMD or BMC any differently from that of the D group. Despite no changes in BMD or BMC of either group in the current study, we believe that if the weight loss were to continue beyond 6 weeks, noticeable changes in BMD and BMC may have occurred. A tendency of hip BMD to decrease after 6 weeks of weight reduction indicates that a longer duration and/or a larger sample size may have resulted in a significant change.

To our knowledge, no other studies have been conducted to investigate the effects of non-weight bearing activity during a weight loss intervention. However, researchers have observed a lower BMD in competitive athletes who are primarily involved in non-weight bearing activities (i.e. cyclists, swimmers) [28, 29, 38, 39]. This evidence taken together with the results of our study, suggest that only weight-bearing activities play a significant role in promoting bone density in the short term. The inclusion of non-weight bearing activity during short-term weight reduction does not reflect any differences in BMD or BMC compared to weight reduction without any exercise component.

Table 3. Bone mineral content and bone mineral density of subjects before and after diet-induced or diet+ non weight bearing exercise weight loss

	DIET ONLY			DIET+EXERCISE		
	Baseline	Post-Wt Loss	% change	Baseline	Post-Wt Loss	% change
TBBMC	2346.8±10.0	2364.3±10.0	0.7	2242.1±10.5	2252.7±11.8	0.5
TBBMD	1.142±0.005	1.151±0.005	0.8	1.101±0.005	1.103±0.006	0.2
SBMC	63.20±3.33	57.45±3.53	-9.1[#]	61.06±3.16	57.75±3.78	-5.4[#]
SBMD	1.131±0.004	1.122±0.004	-0.8[#]	1.073±0.004	1.068±0.005	-0.5[#]
HBMC	31.55±0.67	32.43±0.67	2.8	31.37±0.71	30.49±0.79	-2.8
HBMD	1.032±0.005	1.018±0.005	-1.4	0.976±0.006	0.968±0.006	-0.8
FNBMC	4.48±0.03	4.48±0.03	0.0	4.18±0.03	4.23±0.04	1.2
FNBMD	0.921±0.006	0.926±0.007	0.5	0.866±0.007	0.857±0.008	-1.0
WARD BMC	0.94±0.02	0.94±0.02	0.0	0.99±0.02	0.97±0.03	-2.0
WARDBMD	0.823±0.008	0.822±0.009	-0.1	0.814±0.008	0.816±0.009	0.2

Values are means ± SE. N=10 for diet only group. N=8 for D+E group.

One participant from D+E was excluded due to missing post-weight loss data.

No significant differences existed between groups for any variables

[#]Data excludes 3 participants due to the presence of external artifacts within the scan area

Calcium and Vitamin D. The existing results of our study are similar to the findings of Shapses, et al [40] and Riedt, et al [41] who each conducted a program of 6-month weight reduction in premenopausal overweight women. Neither group noticed a significant change in bone mass after weight loss, as indicated by DXA analysis; however, both studies also involved the investigation of varying levels of calcium intake during weight loss and may not be directly comparable to our findings. Calcium intakes for all of our participants decreased similarly over the 6-week period and intakes at both time points (baseline and post-weight loss) were well below the recommended daily intake of 1,300 mg/day. It has been suggested that bone loss during moderate weight reduction in premenopausal women is not largely influenced by low calcium intakes [40], whereas in postmenopausal women calcium supplementation is crucial to bone health during periods of weight loss [13]. All of the subjects in the present study had similar calcium intakes as well as similar decreases in calcium intake over the 6-wk period; thus calcium did not likely play a large role in the existing findings. Analysis of serum bone turnover markers may give further insight into the influence of calcium intake and the status of bone mineralization.

Vitamin D intakes were not significantly different between groups nor did they noticeably change over the 6-wk period. Roughly half of the subjects in this study participated between July and September, while the other half completed the study somewhere between the months of September and January. Because seasonal variation has been known to influence bone health, determination of serum 25(OH)D levels would be more suitable to accurately assess the Vitamin D status of each participant, depending on her season of participation.

Other factors influencing bone health. Age, menopausal status, and body fat mass are other factors that may play a role in bone status. Aging and menopause (in women) are both associated with a loss of bone mass [26, 42] and their effects on bone likely result from reduced physical activity, lower circulating levels of sex steroid hormones, and/or decreased muscle mass. These factors did not likely contribute to our findings, since all women in our study were similar in age (18-35 yrs) and were well below the age of menopausal onset.

Fat mass may also contribute to bone status [15, 20], although whether or not this occurs and the mechanism by which fat mass promotes bone health are still highly debated. Participants in the D+E group reduced body fat percent to a greater extent than those in the D group, but again, no significant differences were observed in BMD or BMC of either group, so alterations in fat mass may not have played a significant role in the results of this study.

Study limitations. Other possible variables and confounding factors that may have contributed to the lack of change in bone density of our subjects include small sample size, varying levels of occupational weight-bearing activity, and varying durations of weight loss (several subjects required ~5 wks to achieve the weight loss, while others took a full 6-7 wks to obtain their goal weight). Better control of these variables may have reflected more significant changes in BMD and BMC over the intervention period and should be considered in future investigations.

CONCLUSION

In conclusion, our results suggest that moderate, short-term weight loss does not significantly affect bone density in overweight, adult women. Furthermore, the influence of short-term weight loss on BMD does not differ when non-weight bearing aerobic exercise training is included in the weight loss program. Despite a lack of change in BMD as indicated by DXA analysis, future analysis of serum bone turnover markers will help obtain a better evaluation of the status of bone mineralization of the participants in this study. Also, the inclusion of aerobic activity, regardless of whether it is weight bearing or non-weight bearing, is known to promote health benefits beyond that of bone density, and therefore must be emphasized as an important component of any weight loss program.

REFERENCES

[1]   Flegal KM, Carroll MD, Ogden CL, Johnson CL. Prevalence and trends in obesity among US adults, 1999-2000. *JAMA,* 2002;288,1723-7.

[2]   Pi-Sunyer FX. The obesity epidemic: pathophysiology and consequences of obesity. *Obes Res,* 2002;10 Suppl 2,97S-104S.

[3]   Ramsdale SJ, Bassey EJ. Changes in bone mineral density associated with dietary-induced loss of body mass in young women. *Clin Sci (Lond),* 1994;87,343-8.

[4]   Fogelholm GM, Sievanen HT, Kukkonen-Harjula TK, Pasanen ME. Bone mineral density during reduction, maintenance and regain of body weight in premenopausal, obese women. *Osteoporos Int,* 2001;12,199-206.

[5]   Shapses SA, Riedt CS. Bone, body weight, and weight reduction: what are the concerns? *J Nutr,* 2006;136,1453-6.

[6] Salamone LM, Cauley JA, Black DM, Simkin-Silverman L, Lang W, Gregg E, Palermo L, Epstein RS, Kuller LH, Wing R. Effect of a lifestyle intervention on bone mineral density in premenopausal women: a randomized trial. *Am J Clin Nutr,* 1999;70,97-103.

[7] Compston JE, Laskey MA, Croucher PI, Coxon A, Kreitzman S. Effect of diet-induced weight loss on total body bone mass. *Clin Sci (Lond),* 1992;82,429-32.

[8] Van Loan MD, Johnson HL, Barbieri TF. Effect of weight loss on bone mineral content and bone mineral density in obese women. *Am J Clin Nutr,* 1998;67,734-8.

[9] Pritchard JE, Nowson CA, Wark JD. Bone loss accompanying diet-induced or exercise-induced weight loss: a randomised controlled study. *Int J Obes Relat Metab Disord,* 1996;20,513-20.

[10] Services USDoHaH. Bone Health and Osteoporosis: a report of the Surgeon General. 2004.

[11] Ricci TA, Heymsfield SB, Pierson RN, Jr., Stahl T, Chowdhury HA, Shapses SA. Moderate energy restriction increases bone resorption in obese postmenopausal women. *Am J Clin Nutr,* 2001;73,347-52.

[12] Jensen LB, Kollerup G, Quaade F, Sorensen OH. Bone minerals changes in obese women during a moderate weight loss with and without calcium supplementation. *J Bone Miner Res,* 2001;16,141-7.

[13] Ricci TA, Chowdhury HA, Heymsfield SB, Stahl T, Pierson RN, Jr., Shapses SA. Calcium supplementation suppresses bone turnover during weight reduction in postmenopausal women. *J Bone Miner Res,* 1998;13,1045-50.

[14] Reid IR. Relationships among body mass, its components, and bone. *Bone,* 2002;31,547-55.

[15] Reid IR, Ames R, Evans MC, Sharpe S, Gamble G, France JT, Lim TM, Cundy TF. Determinants of total body and regional bone mineral density in normal postmenopausal women--a key role for fat mass. *J Clin Endocrinol Metab,* 1992;75,45-51.

[16] Papakitsou EF, Margioris AN, Dretakis KE, Trovas G, Zoras U, Lyritis G, Dretakis EK, Stergiopoulos K. Body mass index (BMI) and parameters of bone formation and resorption in postmenopausal women. *Maturitas,* 2004;47,185-93.

[17] Cifuentes M, Johnson MA, Lewis RD, Heymsfield SB, Chowdhury HA, Modlesky CM, Shapses SA. Bone turnover and body weight relationships differ in normal-weight compared with heavier postmenopausal women. *Osteoporos Int,* 2003;14,116-22.

[18] Ravn P, Cizza G, Bjarnason NH, Thompson D, Daley M, Wasnich RD, McClung M, Hosking D, Yates AJ, Christiansen C. Low body mass index is an important risk factor for low bone mass and increased bone loss in early postmenopausal women. Early Postmenopausal Intervention Cohort (EPIC) study group. *J Bone Miner Res,* 1999;14,1622-7.

[19] Tremollieres FA, Pouilles JM, Ribot C. Vertebral postmenopausal bone loss is reduced in overweight women: a longitudinal study in 155 early postmenopausal women. *J Clin Endocrinol Metab,* 1993;77,683-6.

[20] Aloia JF, Vaswani A, Ma R, Flaster E. To what extent is bone mass determined by fat-free or fat mass? *Am J Clin Nutr,* 1995;61,1110-4.

[21] Hannan MT, Felson DT, Dawson-Hughes B, Tucker KL, Cupples LA, Wilson PW, Kiel DP. Risk factors for longitudinal bone loss in elderly men and women: the Framingham Osteoporosis Study. *J Bone Miner Res,* 2000;15,710-20.

[22] Villareal DT, Fontana L, Weiss EP, Racette SB, Steger-May K, Schechtman KB, Klein S, Holloszy JO. Bone mineral density response to caloric restriction-induced weight loss or exercise-induced weight loss: a randomized controlled trial. *Arch Intern Med,* 2006;166,2502-10.

[23] Ryan AS, Nicklas BJ, Dennis KE. Aerobic exercise maintains regional bone mineral density during weight loss in postmenopausal women. *J Appl Physiol,* 1998;84,1305-10.

[24] Espallargues M, Sampietro-Colom L, Estrada MD, Sola M, del Rio L, Setoain J, Granados A. Identifying bone-mass-related risk factors for fracture to guide bone densitometry measurements: a systematic review of the literature. *Osteoporos Int,* 2001;12,811-22.

[25] Theintz G, Buchs B, Rizzoli R, Slosman D, Clavien H, Sizonenko PC, Bonjour JP. Longitudinal monitoring of bone mass accumulation in healthy adolescents: evidence for a marked reduction after 16 years of age at the levels of lumbar spine and femoral neck in female subjects. *J Clin Endocrinol Metab,* 1992;75,1060-5.

[26] Uusi-Rasi K, Sievanen H, Vuori I, Pasanen M, Heinonen A, Oja P. Associations of physical activity and calcium intake with bone mass and size in healthy women at different ages. *J Bone Miner Res,* 1998;13,133-42.

[27] Krolner B, Toft B. Vertebral bone loss: an unheeded side effect of therapeutic bed rest. *Clin Sci (Lond),* 1983;64,537-40.

[28] Taaffe DR, Robinson TL, Snow CM, Marcus R. High-impact exercise promotes bone gain in well-trained female athletes. *J Bone Miner Res,* 1997;12,255-60.

[29] Heinonen A, Oja P, Kannus P, Sievanen H, Haapasalo H, Manttari A, Vuori I. Bone mineral density in female athletes representing sports with different loading characteristics of the skeleton. *Bone,* 1995;17,197-203.

[30] Dalsky GP, Stocke KS, Ehsani AA, Slatopolsky E, Lee WC, Birge SJ, Jr. Weight-bearing exercise training and lumbar bone mineral content in postmenopausal women. *Ann Intern Med,* 1988;108,824-8.

[31] Takahashi H, Nihon Seikei Geka Gakkai. Meeting. Mechanical loading of bones and joints. Tokyo ; New York: Springer; 1999.

[32] Bikle DD, Halloran BP. The response of bone to unloading. *J Bone Miner Metab,* 1999;17,233-44.

[33] Liang MT, Bassin S, Dutto D, Braun W, Wong N, Pontello AM, Cooper DM, Arnaud SB. Bone mineral density and leg muscle strength in young caucasian, Hispanic, and asian women. *J Clin Densitom,* 2007;10,157-64.

[34] Gentil P, Lima RM, Jaco de Oliveira R, Pereira RW, Reis VM. Association between femoral neck bone mineral density and lower limb fat-free mass in postmenopausal women. *J Clin Densitom,* 2007;10,174-8.

[35] Cummings SR, Bates D, Black DM. Clinical use of bone densitometry: scientific review. *JAMA,* 2002;288,1889-97.

[36] Riedt CS, Cifuentes M, Stahl T, Chowdhury HA, Schlussel Y, Shapses SA. Overweight postmenopausal women lose bone with moderate weight reduction and 1 g/day calcium intake. *J Bone Miner Res,* 2005;20,455-63.

[37] Favus MJ, American Society for Bone and Mineral Research. Primer on the metabolic bone diseases and disorders of mineral metabolism. 6th ed. Washington, DC: American Society for Bone and Mineral Research; 2006.

[38] Nichols JF, Palmer JE, Levy SS. Low bone mineral density in highly trained male master cyclists. *Osteoporos Int,* 2003;14,644-9.

[39] Beshgetoor D, Nichols JF, Rego I. Effect of training mode and calcium intake on bone mineral density in female master cyclist, runners, and non-athletes. *Int J Sport Nutr Exerc Metab,* 2000;10,290-301.

[40] Shapses SA, Von Thun NL, Heymsfield SB, Ricci TA, Ospina M, Pierson RN, Jr., Stahl T. Bone turnover and density in obese premenopausal women during moderate weight loss and calcium supplementation. *J Bone Miner Res,* 2001;16,1329-36.

[41] Riedt CS, Schlussel Y, von Thun N, Ambia-Sobhan H, Stahl T, Field MP, Sherrell RM, Shapses SA. Premenopausal overweight women do not lose bone during moderate weight loss with adequate or higher calcium intake. *Am J Clin Nutr,* 2007;85,972-80.

[42] Nguyen TV, Sambrook PN, Eisman JA. Bone loss, physical activity, and weight change in elderly women: the Dubbo Osteoporosis Epidemiology Study. *J Bone Miner Res,* 1998;13,1458-67.

In: Progress in Exercise and Women's Health Research
Editor: Janet P. Coulter, pp. 229-240

ISBN 1-60456-014-5
© 2008 Nova Science Publishers, Inc.

Chapter 9

TIMING OF POST-EXERCISE PROTEIN DOES NOT AFFECT GAINS IN LEAN MASS BUT MAY INFLUENCE LOSS OF FAT MASS IN WOMEN

Melissa J. Benton [1], *Pamela D. Swan* [2] *and Carol S. Johnston* [2]

[1] Valdosta State University
[2] Arizona State University

ABSTRACT

Background

Women are at heightened risk for loss of strength and functional ability due to sarcopenia as they age. Resistance training (RT) is an effective intervention against muscle loss, while ingestion of a post-exercise protein supplement may have an additive effect on muscle growth.

Purpose

The purpose of this study was to determine if timing of protein intake following RT would influence gains in lean mass in women.

[1] Correspondence to : College of Nursing, Valdosta State University
1300 N. Patterson St., Valdosta, GA 31698
Phone: 229-245-3775, email:mjbenton@valdosta.edu

Methods

Fifteen women (age 38 ± 10 years, BMI 27.8 ± 5.1 kg/m^2) completed 12 weeks of RT three times a week (36 sessions). Immediately (T0) or two hours (T2) after each training bout they received a high protein supplement (150 kcal, 25g protein, 5g carbohydrate, 3.5g fat). Maximal strength (1RM chest and leg press) and body composition (air displacement plethysmography) were measured at baseline and after completion of week 12.

Results

There were no significant differences between groups for gains in strength and lean mass. Both groups experienced similar increases in strength ($P < 0.01$) and gained an average of 0.43 ± 0.3 kg lean mass ($P = 0.11$). A significant difference between groups was observed for fat mass. Group T2 lost a significant amount of fat mass (-0.8 ± 0.6 kg) ($P = 0.03$) compared to Group T0 (-0.1 ± 0.7 kg).

Conclusion

In women engaged in a 12-week RT program, gains in lean mass are not affected by the timing of protein intake post exercise. However, a two-hour delay in intake following RT sessions results in significant decreases in fat mass.

Key Words: body composition, resistance training, strength

INTRODUCTION

Sarcopenia, the involuntary loss of muscle with age, is associated with loss of strength and functional ability. [1] Women in particular are vulnerable to sarcopenia due to lower peak muscle mass in early adulthood as well as a greater rate of loss with age compared to men. [2] Loss of this metabolically active skeletal muscle can lead to decreased resting energy expenditure [3, 4] placing women at additional risk for gains in fat mass leading to sarcopenic obesity. Independently of muscle, fat mass is positively associated with loss of function and disability in women. [5, 6] Hence, it is important to identify effective interventions that can maintain as well as promote gains in lean mass.

Resistance training (RT) can prevent or reverse many of the effects of aging, including sarcopenia. It stimulates muscle protein synthesis resulting in an increase in muscle mass in normal as well as overweight individuals. [7, 8] A regular RT program can not only result in muscle hypertrophy, [9, 10, 11] but can also promote fat loss by increasing the relative contribution of fat to overall energy expenditure. [12, 13] RT is a feasible intervention for promoting accretion of lean mass as well as possibly reducing fat mass in women as they age.

Dietary protein combined with RT may offer additional benefits for gains in lean mass.Conventional wisdom is that the ingestion of protein immediately after resistance exercise will augment muscle growth over and above what would be seen with RT alone. Circulation to working muscles is increased during and after exercise, allowing for enhanced delivery of amino acids for use in muscle protein synthesis. [14, 15] After an acute bout of resistance exercise, administration of essential amino acids combined with carbohydrate results in increased muscle protein synthesis for up to three hours after exercise. [16]

Only two studies to date have examined this effect in combination with a regular RT program. One study involved elderly men (74 $\pm$1 years) [17] and the other middle-aged men (34 $\pm$ 3 years). [18] However, women, since they are more vulnerable to muscle loss over the lifespan than men, need to be studied. This study was designed to evaluate the effect of timing of a high-protein supplement in relation to a high intensity RT program on body composition in women. It was hypothesized that the effect on women would be similar to that of elderly and middle-aged males and, after 12 weeks, protein supplementation given immediately post exercise would result in greater gains in lean mass than delayed supplementation given two hours after training.

METHODOLOGY

Following completion of informed consent and collection of baseline measurements participants were pair matched by age. Age was chosen as the matching variable due to the wide range of ages of the participants. Pair members were then randomized into one of two groups: (1) RT followed immediately by protein supplementation or (2) RT followed two hours later by protein supplementation.

Participants

Women (n=21) between the ages of 24 – 54 were recruited from a university campus and surrounding community. All reported generally good health and had no past history of cardiac disease or diabetes.

Measurement

Body composition was measured at baseline (week 0) and after completion (week 12) of the RT program. All measurements were taken in the morning between 6:30 – 9:30 am in a fasting state (no food for 12 hours). Participants were instructed to abstain from exercise, caffeine or alcohol for 24 hours before testing. Final measurements were completed 48 hours after the last RT session.

Body composition including absolute lean mass, absolute fat mass and % body fat was estimated using air displacement plethysmography (Bod Pod, LMI, Inc., Concord, CA). Participants were asked to wear a tight-fitting Lycra® bathing suit or an exercise bra and shorts in order to avoid air pockets, as well as a close fitting bathing cap with all hair tucked inside. All jewelry was removed prior to measurement. During the test participants were asked to sit in the closed measurement chamber without moving and breathe regularly. Lung volume was predicted using Bod Pod software version 1.80, Beta version. Air displacement plethysmography has been found to be a valid and reliable measure of body composition that in adults obtains comparable agreement (within 1%) with hydrostatic weighing (HW) and dual-energy X-ray absorptiometry (DEXA). [19]

Maximal strength was measured using the 1 repetition maximum (1RM) procedure described by Kraemer and Fry. [20] Participants were asked to rate each lift using a rating of perceived exertion (RPE) as suggested by McGuigan and Foster. [21] A maximal attempt was defined as actual failure or an RPE of 9-10 on a 10-point scale, [22] with a statement by the participant that another attempt could not be achieved. For initial testing a series of three 1RM tests were scheduled at least 24 hours apart. For each exercise (chest press, latissimus pulldown, leg press, shoulder press, seated row, leg extension, biceps curl, triceps pushdown) the highest weight lifted or pressed during the three trials was identified as the 1RM. A final 1RM test was conducted after completion of the RT program.

Resistance Training

The 12-week RT program (36 sessions) consisted of 3 sets of 8-12 repetitions of eight exercises (chest press, latissimus pulldown, incline leg press, shoulder press, seated row, leg extension, biceps curl, triceps pushdown) three times a week on non-consecutive days. Exercises were counterbalanced to avoid excessive fatigue of small muscle groups. To enhance muscular response, free weights and cables were used for all exercises except the incline leg press, which was plate loaded. [23] For efficiency and to limit the amount of rest between sets, exercises were paired into supersets (chest press-latissimus pulldown, leg press-shoulder press, seated row-leg extension, biceps curl-triceps pushdown). Initially, intensity was set at 10 repetitions at 50% 1RM for the first set of each exercise and 8-12 repetitions at 80% 1RM for the second and third set of each exercise. Resistance was increased 5-10% when participants were able to consistently complete 10-12 repetitions with good form for the second and third set of each exercise. As a surrogate measure of intensity, Figure 1 demonstrates the mean change in training volume (the maximum weight lifted 10 times) for chest press and leg press between week 1 and week 12 for all participants.

Diet

Participants were instructed not to change their diet during the course of the study. Three-day diet records were collected at the beginning (week 1) and end (week 12) of the RT period. Participants were instructed to report intake for *typical* days, but were otherwise allowed to choose which days they reported. Both verbal and written instructions for accurate completion of the records were provided, including description of food type and preparation method, and measurement of quantity consumed. Diets were analyzed using Food Processor version 7.6.

Participants were also instructed not to exercise on an empty stomach. If they had not eaten a regular meal within two hours they were to eat a light snack of approximately 150 kcal 30-60 minutes before exercising.

Protein Supplement

After each training session participants were given a ready-to-drink whey and casein-based high-protein supplement (Myoplex ® Carb Sense, EAS, Inc., Golden, CO, USA) containing 150 kcal, 25g protein, 5g carbohydrate and 3.5g fat (66% protein, 13% carbohydrate, 21% fat). One group (T0) drank the protein supplement within five minutes after completion of exercise and did not consume any other food or beverage except water for two hours. The second group (T2) waited for two hours following exercise without eating or drinking anything except water and then drank the protein supplement at exactly two hours post exercise.

Statistical Analysis

Data were analyzed using SPSS version 13.0 and reported as mean and standard error (SE). Significance was set at $P<0.05$. A two-factor repeated measures ANOVA was used to evaluate changes in body composition. The two factors were timing of supplementation (immediate vs. two hours post exercise) and change over time (weeks 1 and 12). A one-tailed t-test was used to evaluate combined changes in lean mass. Unpaired t-tests were used to evaluate changes in strength, perceived exertion and three-day dietary intake.

Table 1. Participant Demographic and Body Composition Characteristics

Characteristics	T0 (n=7)		T2 (n=7)	
	Week 1	Week 12	Week 1	Week 12
Age (yrs)	39 ± 3	39 ± 3	38 ± 4	38 ± 4
Mass (kg)	72.2 ± 4.3	72.4 ± 4.4	75.8 ± 7.6	75.7 ± 6.6
BMI (kg/m^2)	26.8 ± 1.6	26.9 ± 1.5	28.7 ± 2.3	28.7 ± 2.0
Lean Mass (kg)	45.7 ± 2.3	46.0 ± 2.4	44.4 ± 2.3	45.0 ± 2.4
% Lean Mass	63.7 ± 2.6	63.5 ± 2.7	59.9 ± 2.6	60.4 ± 2.7
Fat Mass (kg)	26.5 ± 4.2	26.4 ± 3.5	31.4 ± 4.2	30.6 ± 3.5*
% Body Fat	36.2 ± 2.6	36.1 ± 2.2	40.0 ± 2.6	39.5 ± 2.2**

Data presented as Mean ± SE $P<0.05$
*$P=0.03$ (time x group effect)
**$P=0.055$ (time x group effect)

Results

Five participants withdrew from the study – one due to pregnancy, two due to health problems not related to the study protocol, and two due to time constraints. A sixth participant was excluded due to failure to adhere to the study protocol. A seventh participant was dropped due to an error in body composition measurement such that she lost 3.9 kg of lean mass, which was greater than 3 standard deviations from the overall mean. Thus, 14 participants were included in the final analysis. Group characteristics are shown in Table 1. There was no difference between or within groups at baseline and 12 weeks for age, body mass or body mass index (BMI). Based on the self-reported three-day diet records there were no significant differences in mean 24-hour intake between groups for total calories, protein or fat (see Table 2).

Table 2. Dietary analysis of self-reported three-day diet records collected during weeks 1 and 12 of the resistance training program

	T0 (n=7)		T2 (n=7)	
	Week 1	Week 12	Week 1	Week 12
Kcal/day	1480 ± 152	1764 ± 198	1986 ± 190	2118 ± 166
Protein(gm)/day	73 ± 7	84 ± 6	72 ± 3	101 ± 6
Carbohydrates(gm)/day	184 ± 23	209 ± 25	269 ± 55	236 ± 28
Fat(gm)/day	50 ± 7	64 ± 11	68 ± 5	86 ± 5

Data presented as Mean ± SE

There were no significant differences between groups.

Overall adherence with the 12-week training protocol was 97% (T0 = 99%, T2 = 96%). Mean training time was 37 minutes per session. Group T0 averaged 37.6 ± 5.8 minutes per session while group T2 averaged 36.9 ± 5.3 minutes.

Table 3. 1RM Test Results for Chest Press and Leg Press

	T0 (n=7)		T2 (n=7)	
Characteristics	Week 1	Week 12	Week 1	Week 12
1RM Chest Press (lbs)	73 ± 17	109 ± 17**	43 ± 11	86 ± 11***
1RM Leg Press (lbs)	285 ± 47	540 ± 83***	186± 43	384 ± 46***
RPE for 1RM chest press at week 1 and same weight lifted at week 12	7.5 ± 1	4 ± 1 ***	9 ± 0.5	4 ± 1**
RPE for 1RM leg press at week 1 and same weight lifted at week 12	7.5 ± 1	3 ± 1***	8.5 ± 0.5	3 ± 1***

Data presented as Mean ± SE   **P=0.02   ***P < 0.01

The absolute amount of weight lifted one time (1RM) increased significantly in both groups while the rating of perceived exertion (RPE) for the same weight decreased significantly.

Strength

Upper (chest press) and lower (leg press) body strength was not significantly different between groups at baseline or after the 12-week RT program. Not surprisingly both groups had significant improvements in 1RM strength for chest and leg press as a result of the training program. Maximal strength for the chest press increased 49% (P=0.02) for group T0 and 98% (P<0.01) for group T2, while for the leg press, group T0 increased 89% (P<0.01) and group T2 increased 110% (P<0.01) (see Table 3). There were also no between-group differences in RPE values for 1RM chest and leg press tests. Both groups demonstrated significant decreases in perceived exertion after 12 weeks of training. Prior to the RT program RPE values for the 1RM chest press were 7.5 ± 1 and 9 ± 0.5 for groups T0 and T2 respectively, while after 12 weeks RPE values for the same weight decreased to 4 ± 1

(P<0.01) for group T0 and 4 ± 1 (P=0.02) for group T2. Similar changes occurred for the 1RM leg press, with initial RPE values reported as 7.5 ± 1 and 8.5 ± 0.5 for groups T0 and T2 respectively. Again, after the 12-week RT program RPE values for the same weight decreased to 3 ± 1 (P<0.01) for both groups (see Table 3).

Body Composition

At baseline and week 12 there were no significant differences in lean mass between groups (see Table 1). The mean gain in lean mass during the 12-week RT program was 0.43 ± 0.3 kg (P=0.11). For fat mass and percent body fat, group T0 lost an average of 0.1 ± 0.7 kg and 0.1% ± 0.4% respectively, while group T2 lost an average of 0.8 ± 0.7 kg (P=0.03) and 0.5% ± 0.4% (P=0.055). Only group T2 demonstrated a significant change in body composition during the 12-week period (see Table 1).

DISCUSSION

This is the first study to evaluate the effect of timing of a high-protein post-exercise supplement on changes in body composition in women involved in a high intensity RT program. Although this was a small study (n=14), data are suggestive that a two-hour delay in protein supplementation after RT will result in significant decreases in fat mass, without impeding gains in lean mass.

Two previous studies have evaluated the timing of a protein supplement after resistance training on elderly [17] or middle aged men. [18] Both studies support the enhanced effect on muscle growth of a protein supplement taken immediately post RT. Our current findings, however, suggest that in women whatever anabolic effect is exerted by protein supplementation during the two-hour post-exercise period occurs without regard to its timing. This apparent gender difference may be hormonally based. In studies involving males the anabolic effect of testosterone must always be considered. Testosterone levels in men can be significantly elevated in response to either an acute bout of RT [24] or a regular RT program lasting 6-8 weeks. [25] These increases in testosterone do not occur in women. [26] During the post-exercise period immediate ingestion of protein may enhance testosterone production in males resulting in greater gains in lean mass, whereas in women ingestion of protein at any time during the two-hour period when blood flow to working muscles is greatest results in similar gains in lean mass.

Intensity of training should also be considered when evaluating the differences found between the current study and the results of Esmarck et al. [17] and Doi et al. [18] Perhaps the effect of timing of protein supplementation is elicited or enhanced when training intensity is below a critical threshold (i.e. less anabolic). The current study utilized a high intensity RT program in untrained women. Neither of the earlier studies of the effect of timing of protein supplementation on men used a similarly intense training protocol. Esmarck et al. [17] used a beginning intensity of 10-12 repetitions at 100% 20RM for only three exercises (leg press, latissimus pulldown, leg extension) that did not reach an intensity of 8 repetitions at 100% 8RM until the sixth week of training (half way through the training program). The current study used an initial intensity of 80% 1RM with progressive increases throughout all 12 weeks of training that resulted in increases in training volume of 94% and 54% respectively for the chest and leg press (see Figure 1). Doi et al. [18] used 13 exercises at an intensity that allowed for 10-15 repetitions with 3 kg dumbbells initially and progressed to 4-5 kg dumbbells at the end of 12 weeks of training. Without the strong anabolic effect of high intensity training in the two prior studies, [17, 18] the timing of nutrition may have had a more profound effect on accretion of lean mass than was found in the current study. This is consistent with the findings of Welle and Thornton [27] who found that muscle protein synthesis after resistance exercise in older adults was influenced by the intensity of training rather than dietary protein.

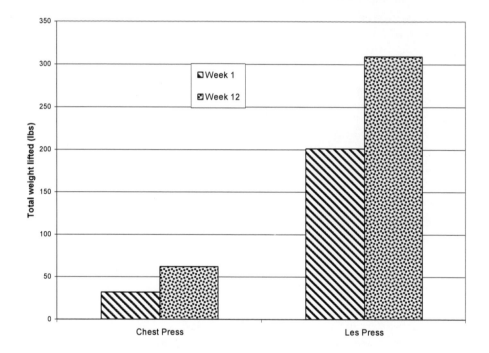

Figure 1. Mean change in training volume over 12 weeks for all participants. The maximum amount of weight lifted in 10 repetitions increased 94% for chest press and 54% for leg press.

Studies of the effect of varying training intensities on muscle growth have been inconsistent in their results. In elderly men and women, a 12-week high intensity training program has been found to stimulate greater gains in strength and hypertrophy than moderate intensity. [28] However, a one-year RT program comparing high and low intensities elicited similar gains in strength and muscle mass in a group of elderly women. [29] Our data indicate that in women the intensity of training alone may play a greater role in accretion of muscle than timing of protein supplementation in relation to resistance exercise. Clearly, more research on RT intensity in women is needed.

To date, there have been no studies of the effect of a regular RT program on body fat in women without the addition of either dietary restriction or endurance exercise. Binzen, Swan and Manore [12] studied the metabolic effect of an acute bout of resistance exercise on energy expenditure (VO_2) and fat utilization (respiratory exchange ratio) in ten young, trained women. During the two-hour post-exercise period both overall energy expenditure and fat utilization were significantly increased in a fasting state. In the current study, group T2 duplicated the conditions studied by Binzen, Swan and Manore [12] in that they remained fasting for the two-hour period after exercise until ingesting the high-protein supplement. Over a 12-week period the enhanced post-exercise fat utilization predicted by Binzen, Swan and Manore [12] could have resulted in a significant decrease in body fat in these individuals.

Although no studies have been conducted regarding the effect of immediate post-exercise protein on energy expenditure and fat burning, two studies [30, 31] have examined the effect of delayed nutrition. Bielinski, Schutz and Jequier [30] administered a mixed nutrient meal (18% protein, 55% carbohydrate, 27% fat) to ten young, trained males 30 minutes after a three-hour treadmill run at 50% VO_{2max} or after a similar period of rest. They found that fat utilization after exercise was enhanced compared to after rest and that it was not blunted by meal ingestion. However, nutrient ingestion did not occur for a full 30 minutes after exercise. This was the period during which Binzen, Swan and Manore [12] found the most profound change in fat burning, which peaked within 30 minutes after exercise. Possibly, when even a 30-minute delay occurs in provision of nutrition, the fat burning stimulus provided by exercise is not blunted. This would be consistent with the findings of the present study.

Bosher et al. [31] examined the effect of either a high fat (18% protein, 37% carbohydrate, 45% fat) or high carbohydrate (20% protein, 79% carbohydrate, 1% fat) meal ingested 45 minutes after an acute bout of resistance exercise on fat burning in nine young, trained males. Compared to a fasting (water only) state, there was no significant difference in fat utilization during the two-hour post-exercise period. However, as previously discussed, nutrient administration did not occur for 45 minutes after completion of the resistance exercise bout, during which time the acute shift towards increased fat utilization would have occurred. Ingestion of a meal at this time may not have been sufficient to reverse the enhanced fat burning process once stimulated by exercise. It may be only during the critical first minutes after completion of exercise that increases in fat utilization can be blunted.

It should be noted that one weakness of the present study was the inability to control for diet. Although instructed not to change their diet during the 12-week training program, all participants reported an increase in overall calories as well as protein and fat. However, any differences between groups were not statistically significant and neither group gained or lost a significant amount of weight during the 12 weeks. The only significant difference observed between groups was in body composition, with group T2 demonstrating a decrease in fat mass. However, since dietary intake was not significantly different between groups this loss of body fat in group T2 was unlikely the result of diet per se. In fact, group T2 reported a greater overall intake of calories, protein and fat per day than group T0, such that they were more likely to have gained rather than lost fat mass based solely on dietary intake.

CONCLUSION

Twelve weeks of high intensity RT are well tolerated and can significantly increase upper and lower body strength in untrained women. In addition, such a training program results in modest (mean 0.43 ± 0.3 kg) gains in lean mass that do not reach statistical significance (P =

0.11) but may reflect physiological significance, especially in women who are at high risk for loss of lean mass over time.

Protein supplementation immediately following exercise over 12 weeks of RT does not significantly affect accretion of lean mass in women. However, a two-hour delay in protein intake following RT sessions may result in enhanced fat utilization leading to significant decreases in fat mass. This has potential significance for women whose training goal includes fat loss as well as muscle gain, especially in light of research indicating that women obtain less benefit from RT programs than men [32-34] that may discourage their participation in resistance exercise.

REFERENCES

[1] Frontera WR, Hughes VA, Lutz KJ, Evans WJ. A cross-sectional study of muscle strength and mass in 45- to 78-yr-old men and women. *J Appl Physiol.* 1991 Aug;71(2):644-50.

[2] Kyle UG, Genton L, Hans D, Karsegard L, Slosman DO, Pichard C. Age-related differences in fat-free mass, skeletal muscle, body cell mass and fat mass between 18 and 94 years. *Eur J Clin Nutr.* 2001 Aug;55(8):663-72.

[3] Menozzi R, Bondi M, Baldini A, Venneri MG, Velardo A, Del Rio G. Resting metabolic rate, fat-free mass and catecholamine excretion during weight loss in female obese patients. *Br J Nutr.* 2000 Oct;84(4):515-20.

[4] Webb P. Direct calorimetry and the energetics of exercise and weight loss. *Med Sci Sports Exerc.* 1986 Feb;18(1):3-5.

[5] Ramsay SE, Whincup PH, Shaper AG, Wannamethee SG. The relations of body composition and adiposity measures to ill health and physical disability in elderly men. *Am J Epidemiol.* 2006 Sep 1;164(5):459-69.

[6] Lebrun CE, van der Schouw YT, de Jong FH, Grobbee DE, Lamberts SW. Fat mass rather than muscle strength is the major determinant of physical function and disability in postmenopausal women younger than 75 years of age. *Menopause.* 2006 May-Jun;13(3):474-81.

[7] Hasten DL, Pak-Loduca J, Obert KA, Yarasheski KE. Resistance exercise acutely increases MHC and mixed muscle protein synthesis rates in 78-84 and 23-32 yr olds. *Am J Physiol Endocrinol Metab.* 2000 Apr;278(4):E620-6.

[8] Yarasheski KE, Pak-Loduca J, Hasten DL, Obert KA, Brown MB, Sinacore DR. Resistance exercise training increases mixed muscle protein synthesis rate in frail women and men >/=76 yr old. *Am J Physiol.* 1999 Jul;277(1 Pt 1):E118-25.

[9] Donnelly JE, Sharp T, Houmard J, Carlson MG, Hill JO, Whatley JE, et al. Muscle hypertrophy with large-scale weight loss and resistance training. *Am J Clin Nutr.* 1993 Oct;58(4):561-5.

[10] Marks BL, Ward A, Morris DH, Castellani J, Rippe JM. Fat-free mass is maintained in women following a moderate diet and exercise program. *Med Sci Sports Exerc.* 1995 Sep;27(9):1243-51.

[11] Ross R, Pedwell H, Rissanen J. Response of total and regional lean tissue and skeletal muscle to a program of energy restriction and resistance exercise. *Int J Obes Relat Metab Disord.* 1995 Nov;19(11):781-7.

[12] Binzen CA, Swan PD, Manore MM. Postexercise oxygen consumption and substrate use after resistance exercise in women. *Med Sci Sports Exerc.* 2001 Jun;33(6):932-8.

[13] Osterberg KL, Melby CL. Effect of acute resistance exercise on postexercise oxygen consumption and resting metabolic rate in young women. *Int J Sport Nutr Exerc Metab.* 2000 Mar;10(1):71-81.

[14] Biolo G, Tipton KD, Klein S, Wolfe RR. An abundant supply of amino acids enhances the metabolic effect of exercise on muscle protein. *Am J Physiol.* 1997 Jul;273(1 Pt 1):E122-9.

[15] Tipton KD, Rasmussen BB, Miller SL, Wolf SE, Owens-Stovall SK, Petrini BE, et al. Timing of amino acid-carbohydrate ingestion alters anabolic response of muscle to resistance exercise. *Am J Physiol Endocrinol Metab.* 2001 Aug;281(2):E197-206.

[16] Rasmussen BB, Tipton KD, Miller SL, Wolf SE, Wolfe RR. An oral essential amino acid-carbohydrate supplement enhances muscle protein anabolism after resistance exercise. *J Appl Physiol.* 2000 Feb;88(2):386-92.

[17] Esmarck B, Andersen JL, Olsen S, Richter EA, Mizuno M, Kjaer M. Timing of postexercise protein intake is important for muscle hypertrophy with resistance training in elderly humans. *J Physiol.* 2001 Aug 15;535(Pt 1):301-11.

[18] Doi T, Matsuo T, Sugawara M, Matsumoto K, Minehira K, Hamada K, et al. New approach for weight reduction by a combination of diet, light resistance exercise and the timing of ingesting a protein supplement. *Asia Pac J Clin Nutr.* 2001;10(3):226-32.

[19] Fields DA, Goran MI, McCrory MA. Body-composition assessment via air-displacement plethysmography in adults and children: a review. *Am J Clin Nutr.* 2002 Mar;75(3):453-67.

[20] Kraemer WJ, Fry AC. Strength testing: development and evaluation of methodology. In: Foster PJMC, editor. *Physiological Assessment of Human Fitness.* Champaign, IL: Human Kinetics; 1995. p. 115-38.

[21] McGuigan MR, Foster C. A new approach to monitoring resistance training. *Strength and Conditioning Journal.* 2004;26(6):42-7.

[22] Borg GA. Psychophysical bases of perceived exertion. *Med Sci Sports Exerc.* 1982;14(5):377-81.

[23] Stone M, Plisk S, Collins D. Training principles: evaluation of modes and methods of resistance training--a coaching perspective. *Sports Biomech.* 2002 Jan;1(1):79-103.

[24] Kraemer WJ, Marchitelli L, Gordon SE, Harman E, Dziados JE, Mello R, et al. Hormonal and growth factor responses to heavy resistance exercise protocols. *J Appl Physiol.* 1990 Oct;69(4):1442-50.

[25] Kraemer WJ, Staron RS, Hagerman FC, Hikida RS, Fry AC, Gordon SE, et al. The effects of short-term resistance training on endocrine function in men and women. *Eur J Appl Physiol Occup Physiol.* 1998 Jun;78(1):69-76.

[26] Kraemer WJ, Fleck SJ, Dziados JE, Harman EA, Marchitelli LJ, Gordon SE, et al. Changes in hormonal concentrations after different heavy-resistance exercise protocols in women. *J Appl Physiol.* 1993 Aug;75(2):594-604.

[27] Welle S, Thornton CA. High-protein meals do not enhance myofibrillar synthesis after resistance exercise in 62- to 75-yr-old men and women. *Am J Physiol.* 1998 Apr;274(4 Pt 1):E677-83.

[28] Kalapotharakos VI, Michalopoulou M, Godolias G, Tokmakidis SP, Malliou PV, Gourgoulis V. The effects of high- and moderate-resistance training on muscle function in the elderly. *J Aging Phys Act.* 2004 Apr;12(2):131-43.

[29] Taaffe DR, Pruitt L, Pyka G, Guido D, Marcus R. Comparative effects of high- and low-intensity resistance training on thigh muscle strength, fiber area, and tissue composition in elderly women. *Clin Physiol.* 1996 Jul;16(4):381-92.

[30] Bielinski R, Schutz Y, Jequier E. Energy metabolism during the postexercise recovery in man. *Am J Clin Nutr.* 1985 Jul;42(1):69-82.

[31] Bosher KJ, Potteiger JA, Gennings C, Luebbers PE, Shannon KA, Shannon RM. Effects of different macronutrient consumption following a resistance-training session on fat and carbohydrate metabolism. *J Strength Cond Res.* 2004 May;18(2):212-9.

[32] Bamman MM, Hill VJ, Adams GR, Haddad F, Wetzstein CJ, Gower BA, et al. Gender differences in resistance-training-induced myofiber hypertrophy among older adults. *J Gerontol A Biol Sci Med Sci.* 2003 Feb;58(2):108-16.

[33] Hakkinen K, Pakarinen A, Kraemer WJ, Newton RU, Alen M. Basal concentrations and acute responses of serum hormones and strength development during heavy resistance training in middle-aged and elderly men and women. *J Gerontol A Biol Sci Med Sci.* 2000 Feb;55(2):B95-105.

[34] Hakkinen K, Kraemer WJ, Newton RU, Alen M. Changes in electromyographic activity, muscle fibre and force production characteristics during heavy resistance/power strength training in middle-aged and older men and women. *Acta Physiol Scand.* 2001a Jan;171(1):51-62.

In: Progress in Exercise and Women's Health Research
Editor: Janet P. Coulter, pp.241-253
ISBN 1-60456-014-5
© 2008 Nova Science Publishers, Inc.

Chapter 10

CENTRAL ITALY: PHYSICAL ACTIVITY OF FEMALE RESIDENTS FROM PISA PROVINCE

E Matteucci and O Giampietro

Department of Internal Medicine, University of Pisa, Italy.

ABSTRACT

Regular moderate-intensity exercise has been shown to decrease all-cause mortality and age-related morbidity. Improved cardiovascular, metabolic, endocrine, and psychologic health has been documented. The 'effective' dose of exercise needed to elicit effects likely to be of clinical importance as well as and the concept of accumulation of activity has been extensively debated. Despite this, the major part of adult population does not currently exercise at the recommended levels. Italian public health surveillance systems do not usually include assessments of this type of physical activity. We examined physical activity behaviours of participants in a lifestyle, nutritional, cardiovascular, and immunologic screening survey conducted in Pisa, central Italy. Demographic, socio-economic and lifestyle information was obtained by Lifestyle European Prospective Investigation of Cancer and Nutrition (EPIC) questionnaire (including questions on education, socioeconomic status, occupation, history of previous illness and disorders of surgical operations, lifetime history of consumption of tobacco and alcoholic beverages, and physical activity). Smoking habits, educational level, occupational status, daily number of hours engaged in housework, weekly number of hours engaged in physical activities during leisure (walking, cycling, gardening, exercise) and during job (sitting most of the time; light activity, walking around; handiwork with some effort; heavy work) were assessed.

Among 116 women (age 44±13 years, range 17 to 73 years) 66% worked, mainly in sedentary and light jobs. Their educational level was the following: 46% secondary, 34% high, 20% graduate. They spent 2.7±1.3 hours/day in housework activities, 2.0±1.7 hours/week in exercise, 1.3±0.5 hours/day in physical activities (including walking, cycling, gardening, and exercise). Increasing physical activity was associated with reduced body mass index. On the contrary, housework activities were not significantly associated with body weight. Time spent in housework decreased with increasing educational level, whereas leisure time physical activities correspondingly increased. Increasing age was associated with reduced physical activity and increased housework. Women' behaviours were compared with those of 93 men of similar age.

These preliminary data are discussed to analyse which could be the most effective methods in lifestyle epidemiology among those presently available. Indeed, although it should be advisable a European survey of lifestyle with particular attention to exercise and physical activity, the lack of standardisation of the assessment methods remains the main methodological drawback for carrying out such studies in practice.

INTRODUCTION

Regular physical activity, such as walking, running, or swimming, produces cardiovascular adaptations that increase exercise capacity, endurance, and skeletal muscle strength. Moderate-intensity exercise has been shown to decrease all-cause mortality and age-related morbidity. Improved cardiovascular, metabolic, endocrine, and psychologic health has been documented [1]. The 'effective' dose of exercise needed to elicit effects likely to be of clinical importance as well as and the concept of accumulation of activity has been extensively debated. Despite this, the major part of adult population does not currently exercise at the recommended levels [2]. Italian public health surveillance systems do not usually include detailed assessments of this type of physical activity.

DEFINITION OF TERMS

Physical activity is defined as any bodily movement produced by the contraction of skeletal muscle that results in energy expenditure beyond resting expenditure. Leisure-time physical activity refers to those activities one participates in during free time. Occupational physical activity is that associated with the performance of a work. *Exercise* (or exercise training) is a subcategory of leisure-time physical activity and consists in planned, structured, and repetitive bodily movements that are performed to improve or maintain one or more components of *physical fitness*, defined as a physiologic state of well-being that allows one to meet the demands of daily living sport performance. The term of healthy-related physical fitness refers to the body's ability to produce energy without the use of oxygen. The total *dose* of physical activity depends on the characteristics of the intensity, frequency (number of sessions per day or week), duration of each session, and mode/type. The absolute *intensity* reflects the actual rate of energy expenditure and can be expressed as oxygen uptake, kcal or kJ per minute, or *metabolic equivalents*, METs (1 MET = 3.5 $\cdot$ ml $O_2 \cdot kg^{-1} \cdot min^{-1}$). The relative intensity refers to the percent of aerobic power utilised during exercise and is expressed as percent of maximal heart rate or percent of VO_2 max. Borg's Rating of Perceived Exertion (RPE) scale classifies the intensity relative to the individual perception of effort.

Levels of heart rate and blood pressure increase in response to acute exercise. Changes of heart rate and blood pressure relative to baseline levels in response to an extended period of endurance training are indices of cardiovascular adaptability. There is evidence for considerable heterogeneity in the individual responsiveness of physiological indicators of risk factors to regular physical activity, whose major apparent determinant are age, sex, and ethnic origin. Genetic and environmental factors seem to determine the familial aggregation of human heterogeneity in response to regular physical activity [4].

HEALTH BENEFITS OF PHYSICAL ACTIVITY

Regular physical activity and high fitness level are associated with a reduced all-cause and cardiovascular-related mortality [1, 5]. Moreover, routine physical activity is effective in the primary and secondary prevention of chronic diseases such as cardiovascular disease, diabetes mellitus, obesity, hypertension, cancer, osteoporosis, and depression [1]. Chronic adaptations brought about by regular physical activity include: improved body composition, improved lipoprotein profiles, improved glucose homeostasis, reduced blood pressure, reduced systemic inflammation, decreased blood coagulation, changes in endothelial function, improved psychological status.

Both men and women who reported increased levels of physical activity showed reductions in relative risk of death from any cause and from specific diseases. There appears to be a graded linear dose-response relation. Currently recommended minimum volume of exercise for health benefits is 1000 kcal per week that is equivalent to 1 hour of moderate walking 5 days a week. The American Heart Association developed evidence-based guidelines specifically designed for cardiovascular disease prevention in women [6]. Lifestyle interventions included physical activity: women should be encouraged to accumulate a minimum of 30 minutes of moderate-intensity physical activity on most, and preferably all, days of the week. A systematic review of the literature regarding primary prevention of cardiovascular-related death in women confirmed the graded inverse relationship between physical activity and cardiovascular disease risk. The protective effects were seen with as little as 1 hour of walking per week [7].

Exercise interventions are associated with a decreased incidence of type 2 diabetes, particularly among people at high risk of diabetes [8]. Regular physical activity is also effective in the management of diabetes [9]. Routine moderate physical activity has been also associated with reduced incidences of breast and colon cancer [10]. Exercise training programs prevent bone loss in pre- and post-menopausal women as well as the risk and number of falls [11-12].

The minimal and optimal amounts of physical activity needed to produce specific beneficial outcomes must be better defined. For example, the key features of cardio-protective exercise seem to include its intensity relative to individual capacity [13]. Frequency of exercise is also important with respect to the time-courses over which the acute effects of exercise (decreased blood pressure, improved insulin sensitivity, attenuation of the post-prandial rise in plasma triglycerides) disappear. Scientific evidence that several short sessions of moderate physical activity during the day (accumulation of activity) are as effective in eliciting chronic training effect as one longer session of the same total duration is still limited. Moreover, further research is required to clarify the differential effects on health outcomes of low intensity exercise in comparison with high intensity exercise, when the energy expended is equivalent.

ENERGY METABOLISM DURING AND AFTER EXERCISE

The rate of carbohydrate utilisation during prolonged exercise is tightly regulated to match the energy needs of the working muscles [14]. At the onset of exercise, blood flow and glucose delivery to the working muscles increase; plasma insulin concentration falls, while glucagon and catecholamine production increases. Blood glucose concentration is maintained constant by liver glycogenolysis and gluconeogenesis (from lactate, alanine, and glycerol).

The rate of fat oxidation during exercise depends on the rate of carbohydrate utilisation, availability of carbohydrate and fatty acids, relative exercise intensity, and training status. Maximal rates of fatty acid oxidation are usually attained at low exercise intensities (~40% of VO_2 max). The absolute work rate determines the total quantity of fuel required during exercise, the relative exercise intensity determines the fuel mixture. The relative exercise intensity, in turn, varies as a function of aerobic training level, age, sex, and health status. The contribution of fat oxidation decreases with increasing exercise intensity, whereas it compensates for the progressive depletion of muscle glycogen and triglyceride stores during prolonged exercise (beyond 30 minutes). Diet and adaptation to endurance exercise training can modify the crossover point for the relative exercise intensity at which the predominant fuel shifts from fat to carbohydrate. Exercise has three separate effects on muscle glucose transport: 1) an acute, insulin-independent stimulation of glucose transport, 2) a successive increase in the sensitivity of the glucose transport process to insulin, 3) an adaptive increase in GLUT4 protein.

Regularly performed endurance training induces metabolic and morphological adaptations in skeletal muscle. Chronic adaptations include an increase in the activities of key enzymes of the mitochondrial electron transport chain and in mitochondrial protein concentration, increased capillary supply [15]. Resistance exercise training should also be effective in enhancing the skeletal muscle cellular antioxidant capacity [16] that is a key variable in determining cellular redox status and survival.

Furthermore, exercise is a potent regulator of postprandial lipid metabolism [17]. However, the hypotriglyceridemic effect of exercise is rapidly reversed in the absence of recent exercise. Thus, it is due to acute metabolic changes following individual exercise sessions, rather than long-term adaptations to training. Both increased lipoprotein lipase-mediated triglyceride clearance and reduced VLDL secretion are the probably contributing mechanisms.

METHODS OF EVALUATING PHYSICAL ACTIVITY AND FITNESS

Physical fitness seems to be similar to physical activity in its relation to morbidity and mortality, but is more strongly predictive of health outcomes [1]. Practically, the assessment of physical fitness is not feasible in large population-based studies. Protocols designed to evaluate the individuals components of health-related physical fitness assess body composition (body mass index, waist circumference, skinfold thickness), aerobic fitness, anaerobic fitness, and musculoskeletal fitness (muscular strength, endurance, and flexibility) [18]. Direct assessment of the maximum aerobic power (VO_2 max) is complex and expensive. Thus, aerobic fitness is usually measured indirectly by submaximal tests or incremental to maximal tests (the Bruce protocol). Before starting an exercise program, individual maximum heart rate should be determined during an incremental to maximal test. Heart rate can be used to estimate VO_2 max: the lower heart rate for a given workload, the higher level of aerobic fitness. Alternatively, exercise time or METs are used.

Anaerobic capacity is defined as the maximal amount of adenosine triphosphate resynthesised via anaerobic metabolism by the whole organism during a specific mode of short-duration maximal exercise (usually short-term cycling power tests or running tests) [19]. There is no perfect test to evaluate it. Maximal blood lactate as an estimate of anaerobic capacity has been discussed due to its high variability partially related to the confounding influence of acute changes in blood volume. Physical activity is a complex set of behaviours not easily measurable, with four main dimensions: frequency (occasions per week), intensity, time (duration of the bout), and type. Various approaches have been used to assess physical activity: self-reported surveys (diaries, logs, recall questionnaires, retrospective quantitative history, and global self-reports), job classification, behavioural observation, motion sensors, physiologic markers (heart rate, doubly labelled water), indirect and direct calorimetry. The pros and cons of each of the various methods to assess physical activity or change in activity have been extensively evaluated [20].

Physical activity surveys have been developed to quantify the frequency of participation in moderate- or vigorous-intensity activities performed during leisure time, or for household chores, transportation and occupational activities. Self-reported surveys have been used most frequently. Fortunately, population-based investigations have demonstrated an inverse gradient of health risk across self-reported activity groups [1]. A critical element of the self-management approach is the availability of an easily administered questionnaire that assesses physical activity levels among adults and older adults.

A recent literature review identified 53 self-reported questionnaires (available in English) that have been used in the past 25 years to assess physical activity with adults [21]. All but 12 of the 53 questionnaires did meet at least four of the review criteria: 1) dimensions, 2) complexity, 3) recall time frame, 4) use as an outcome measure, 5) reliability/validity/responsiveness, 6) cultural adaptability, 7) purpose of development. However, none of them was judged completely acceptable because too complex or not adequately validated.

THE PREVALENCE OF PHYSICAL INACTIVITY

Physical inactivity is a modifiable risk factor for a variety of chronic diseases and its prevalence is higher than that of all other modifiable risk factors. Centers for Disease Control and Prevention (CDC) analysed data from the Behavioral Risk Factor Surveillance System (BRFSS) surveys for 2001 (214,500 respondents) and 2003 (264,684 respondents) [22]. The BRFSS is a population-based, random-digit-dialed telephone survey administered to U.S. civilian, nonistitutionalised adults aged ≥18 years in the 50 states and the District of Columbia. Since 2001, the questionnaire includes items about moderate and vigorous physical activity in three domains (household work, transportation, and discretionary/leisure time) to quantify its frequency, duration, and intensity in a usual week. Respondents are classified as active at the minimum recommended level if they report moderate-intensity activity at least 30 minutes per day, 5 or more days per week, or vigorous-intensity activity at least 20 minutes per day, 3 or more days per week. Respondents are classified as inactive if they report no activity of 10 minutes or more per week of moderate or vigorous intensity. In 2003, 54.1% of U.S. adults did not engage in physical activity at the minimum recommended level. From 2001 to 2003, the prevalence of adults physically active remained unchanged (45.3% and 45.9%, respectively). Previously, the prevalence of U.S. adults achieving the recommended levels of physical activity was *apparently* increased from 2000 (26.2%) to 2001 (45.3%) due to the addition of nonsports-related examples, such as heavy yard work and housework.

Until recently, internationally comparable data on levels of physical activity across the European Region have not been collected; moreover, public health surveillance systems have not included assessments of moderate-intensity physical activity, focusing on exercise of vigorous intensity. Because of the uneven availability of data on levels of physical activity in countries as well as the lack of harmonised measures and indicators to be used, it is difficult to estimate trends across the Region. The scarcity of data from repeated surveys across the European Region highlights an important issue for policy-makers: monitoring physical activity at a population level using consistent measures over time. According to the World Health Organisation [23], a survey of EU countries in 2002 showed that the prevalence of adults (aged ≥15 years) classified as sufficiently active was only 31%, ranging from about 44% in The Netherlands to 26% in Italy and 23% in Sweden. Thus, two thirds of the adult population did not reach recommended levels of physical activity. Data from the Istituto Nazionale di Statistica (ISTAT) show that in Italy, in 2003, 41.6% of people aged ≥3 years was physically inactive, 37.6% reported some physical activity, and only 20.8% reported regular participation in sports-related activities (www.istat.it). From 1999 to 2003 the millions of inactive individuals increased from 19.5 to 23.0 (available from: coni.it/fileadmin/ user_upload/_temp_/mondo_sportivo/osservatori/documenti/Evol_03_15-3-05.pdf).

OUR EXPERIENCE WITH LIFESTYLE EPIC QUESTIONNAIRE

We examined physical activity behaviours of participants in a lifestyle, nutritional, cardiovascular, and immunologic screening survey conducted in Pisa, central Italy [24-26]. Demographic, socio-economic and lifestyle information was obtained by Lifestyle European Prospective Investigation of Cancer and Nutrition (EPIC) questionnaire. The EPIC study is a multi-centre prospective study involving 23 administrative study centres in 10 countries since 1992. The study populations were not representative of the general population because the choice was influenced by practical possibilities of obtaining adequate participation and ensuring long-term follow-up. EPIC study used self-administered, scanner-readable food-frequency and lifestyle questionnaires whose development, reproducibility, and relative validity were described in detail previously [27-29]. The standardised lifestyle questionnaire includes questions on education, socioeconomic status, occupation, history of previous illness and disorders of surgical operations, lifetime history of consumption of tobacco and alcoholic beverages, professional and non-professional physical activity. Smoking habits, school level (primary, secondary, high, graduate), occupational status (full time, part time, no work), daily number of hours engaged in housework, weekly number of hours engaged in physical activities during leisure (walking, cycling, gardening, exercise) and during job (sitting most of the time; light activity, walking around; handiwork with some effort; heavy work) were assessed.

METHOD

A total of 204 subjects were recruited from the local community and completed the life style questionnaire: 116 women (age 44±13 years, range 17 to 73 years) and 93 men (age 46±14 years, range 16 to 77 years). The sample included 38 patients with type 1 diabetes mellitus, 76 first-degree relatives of type 1 patients (44 parents and 32 siblings), and 95 healthy subjects. All subjects gave informed consent and the ethical committee of the hospital approved the study proposal. The medical examination included standardised personal and family health history, physical examination, blood chemistry analysis, and graded exercise test [24-26].

The BMI was calculated as body weight/height^2 (in kg/m^2). Arterial blood pressure was measured twice after at least 10 minutes of rest while the patient was in the sitting position. Sitting systolic and diastolic blood pressure (Korotkoff V) were measured twice and averaged after 10 minutes rest. Mean blood pressure (MBP) was calculated as diastolic BP + 1/3 (systolic BP – diastolic BP). Current smokers were defined as subjects smoking one or more cigarette, cigar or pipe per day. Ex smokers were subjects who had smoked in the past. Educational level was defined as the higher level (primary, secondary, high, graduate). Occupational status was evaluated as work full time, work part time, no work. Subjects reported the daily number of hours they engaged in housework as well as the weekly number of hours they engaged in physical activities during leisure (walking, cycling, gardening, exercise) and during work (sitting most of the time; light activity, walking around; handiwork with some effort; heavy work). Average number of rooms per household member was recorded.

The results are expressed as mean±SD. Data not normally distributed were logarithmically transformed before t-tests and ANOVA. The cut-off level for statistical significance was set at P <0.05. The unpaired Student's t-test (two-tailed) in combination with Bonferroni corrections for multiple hypotheses testing and Mann-Whitney U-test were used to determine significant differences between independent groups. Statistical analyses comparing more than two groups were performed using ANOVA and Kruskal-Wallis rank test. Comparison of categories was by chi-square test. We estimated the associations by Spearman rank correlation analysis, stepwise regression analysis and multiple linear regression (Statview Package, Abacus Concepts, Berkeley, California).

RESULT

Table1 presents the health characteristics and demographics estimated from the lifestyle EPIC questionnaire by gender. The distribution of age and education was similar for female and male respondents. Women had lower body mass and mean blood pressure than man and the highest percentage of non-smokers (60% vs 44%, p<0.05). Overall, 29% of respondents were not currently employed; the proportion of non-workers was higher in women (34%) than in man (23%). The frequency distribution of professional activity evidenced that a sedentary or standing professional activity was most common (30% and 25% of respondents, respectively). Higher proportions of respondents with a manual or heavy manual professional activity were observed in men (26%) than in women (9%). Almost no man performed household activities, whereas the mean duration of household activities was 2.7 hours per day in women (Figure 1). Time dedicated to physical activity (walking, cycling, gardening, repairing, and exercise) was higher in men than in women (Figure 1) because of a high participation in exercise (or sporting activities that included gymnastics, running, playing tennis, swimming, etc.) and cycling (Table 1).

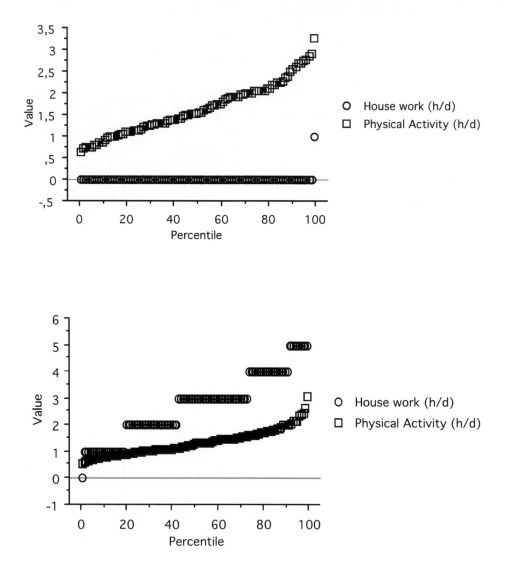

Figure 1. Percentile plots of time dedicated to house work and recreational activities for men (black circles and red rectangles, respectively, in the higher panel) and women (lower panel).

Unexpectedly, increasing physical activity was associated with reduced body mass index in women (r = -0.21, p<0.05; Figure 2) but not in men. On the contrary, housework activities were not significantly associated with body weight. Among women, time spent in housework decreased with increasing educational level, whereas leisure time physical activities correspondingly increased (Figure 3). Employment status, on the contrary, did not change the distribution of physical activity (data not shown). Increasing age was associated with reduced physical activity (r = -0.2, p<0.05) and increased housework (r = 0.6, p<0.001).

Table 1. Clinical characteristics, demographic and lifestyle information of the study participants estimated from the lifestyle EPIC questionnaire by gender.

Characteristic	Women	Men	p<
n	116	93	
Age (years)	44±13	46±14	
BMI (kg/m^2)	25±4	26±3a	0.05
MBP (mmHg)	90±12	95±10	0.01
Smoker/non/ex	30/70/16	27/41/25	0.05
School (prim/second/high/graduate)	1/53/39/23	0/43/29/21	
Work (full-time/part-/out)	53/24/39	62/9/22	0.01
Type (sedentary)/standing/handi/heavy)	34/33/7/3	28/19/13/11	0.05
Physical activity			
(hours/day)	1.3±0.5	1.6±0.6	0.001
Exercise (hours/week)	2.0±1.7	2.7±2.0	0.05
House work (hours/day)	2.7±1.3	0.01±0.1	0.001
Rooms/household member	1.5±0.6	1.5±0.6	

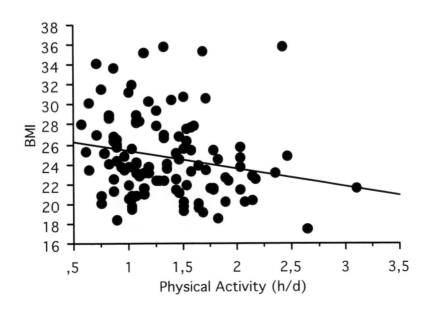

Figure 2. Relationship between time dedicated to recreational activities and body mass index in women.

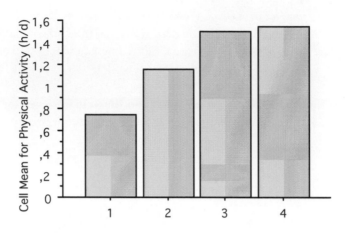

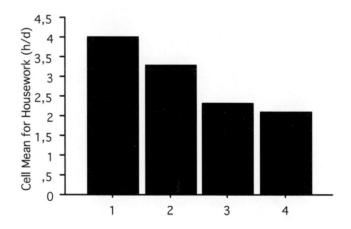

Figure 3. Time spent in recreational physical activity (upper panel) and house work (lower panel) as a function of educational level (1 primary; 2 secondary, 3 high, 4 graduate) among women.

CONCLUSION

The results of present study confirm previous observations on Italian lifestyle obtained by the lifestyle EPIC questionnaire [29] yet highlight some differences. The baseline data of Haftenberger et al [29] were collected between 1992 and 2000, whereas ours between January and July 2001. In Pisa, frequency distribution of type of professional activity differed from that previously observed in the near Florence: the proportion of non-workers was lower among women. Professional activities were mainly sedentary or standing. In general, participation in walking and gardening was lower, participation in sports and cycling was higher in Pisa compared with Florence. We cannot compare our data on the unequal distribution of time dedicated to household activity among men and women because only women were investigated in Florence. However, data from other EPIC centres confirmed that, in women, time spent on household activities was the highest in the centres of the Mediterranean countries with a mean duration even higher than that we observed in Pisa. Moreover, our findings evidenced that educational level, not employment status, strongly influenced the distribution of physical activity.

A complex range of factors influences the likelihood that an individual, group, or community will be physically active [23]. Factors in the macro environment include socioeconomic, cultural, and environmental conditions. Factors in the micro environment include the conduciveness of living and working environments to physical activity, and social support toward sedentary activities. Individual factors also influence people's choices.

Although it should be advisable a European survey of lifestyle with particular attention to exercise and physical activity, the lack of standardisation of the assessment methods remains the main methodological drawback for carrying out such studies in practice. These preliminary data prompted us to evaluate which could be the most effective methods in lifestyle epidemiology among those presently available. In general, questionnaire-based surveys present the best option for assessments covering large number of people, although all information is self-reported and subject to potential misclassification bias. The most reliable surveys use validated questionnaires that allow the findings to be generalised and, if repeat surveys use the same methods, trends can be analysed. However, recall surveys have some drawbacks [20]. They require effort by the respondent if the time frame is long enough. Remembering details of prior participation in physical activity may be difficult especially for older individuals. Obtaining the data also generates expenses of administering the survey, training the interviewers, ensuring quality control, and processing data.

ABBREVIATIONS

BMI	Body Mass Index
BRFSS	Behavioral Risk Factor Surveillance System
CDC	Centers for Disease Control and Prevention
EPIC	European Prospective Investigation of Cancer and Nutrition
MBP	Mean Blood Pressure
MET	Metabolic Equivalent
RPE	Rating of Perceived Exertion
WHO	World Health Organisation
ISTAT	Istituto Nazionale di Statistica

REFERENCES

[1]   Warburton, DER; Nicol, CW; Bredin, SSD. Health benefits of physical activity: the evidence. *CMAJ*, 2006, 174, 801-809.

[2]   Ford, ES; Giles, DW; Dietz, WH. Prevalence of the metabolic syndrome among US adults: findings from the third national health and nutrition examination survey. *JAMA*, 2002, 287, 356-359.

[3]   Howley, ET. Type of activity: resistance, aerobic and leisure versus occupational physical activity. *Med Sci Sports Exerc,* 2001, 33, S364-S369.

[4]   Bouchard, C; Rankinen, T. Individual difference in response to regular physical activity. *Med Sci Sports Exerc*, 2001, 33, S446-S451.

[5]   Thompson, PD; Buchner, D; Pina, IL; Balady, GJ; Williams, MA; Marcus, BH; Berra, K; Blair, SN; Costa, F; Franklin, B; Fletcher, GF; Gordon, NF; Pate, RR; Rodriguez, BL; Yancey, AK; Wenger, NK; American Heart Association Council on Clinical Cardiology Subcommittee on Exercise, Rehabilitation, and Prevention; American Heart Association Council on Nutrition, Physical Activity, and Metabolism Subcommittee on Physical Activity. Exercise and physical activity in the prevention and treatment of atherosclerotic cardiovascular disease: a statement from the Council on Clinical Cardiology (Subcommittee on Exercise, Rehabilitation, and Prevention) and the Council on Nutrition, Physical Activity, and Metabolism (Subcommittee on Physical Activity). *Circulation*, 2003, 107, 3109-3116.

[6]   Mosca, L; Appel, LJ; Benjamin, EJ; Berra, K; Chandra-Strobos, N; Fabunmi, RP; Grady, D; Haan, CK; Hayes, SN; Judelson, DR; Keenan, NL; McBride, P; Oparil, S; Ouyang, P; Oz, MC; Mendelsohn, ME; Pasternak, RC; Pinn, VW; Robertson, RM; Schenck-Gustafsson, K; Sila, CA; Smith, SC Jr; Sopko, G; Taylor, AL; Walsh, BW; Wenger, NK; Williams, CL; AHA. Evidence-based guidelines for cardiovascular disease prevention in women. American Heart Association scientific statement. *Arterioscler Thromb Vasc Biol*, 2004, 24, 29-50.

[7]   Oguma, Y; Shinoda-Tagawa, T. Physical activity decreases cardiovascular disease risk in women: review and meta-analysis. *Am J Prev Med,* 2004, 26, 407-418.

[8]   Tuomilehto, J; Lindstrom, J; Eriksson, JG; Valle, TT; Hamalainen, H; Ilanne-Parikka, P; Keinanen-Kiukaanniemi, S; Laakso, M; Louheranta, A; Rastas, M; Salminen, V; Uusitupa, M; Finnish Diabetes Prevention Study Group. Prevention of type 2 diabetes mellitus by changes in lifestyle among subjects with impaired glucose tolerance. *N Engl J Med,* 2001, 344, 1343-1350.

[9]   Boule, NG; Haddad, E; Kenny, JP; Wells, GA; Sigal, RJ. Effects of exercise on glycemic control and body mass in type 2 diabetes mellitus: a meta-analysis of controlled clinical trials. *JAMA*, 2001, 286, 1218-1227.

[10] Lee, IM. Physical activity and cancer prevention – data from epidemiologic studies. *Med Sci Sports Exerc*, 2003, 35, 1823-1827.

[11] Wolff, I; Croonenborg, JJ; Kemper, HC; Kostense, PJ; Twisk, JW. The effect of exercise training programs on bone mass: a meta-analysis of published controlled trials in pre- and postmenopausal women. *Osteoporos Int*, 1999, 9, 1-12.

[12] Gregg, EW; Pereira, MA; Caspersen, CJ. Physical activity, falls, and fractures among older adults: review of the epidemiologic evidence. *J Am Geriatr Soc*, 2000, 48, 883-893.

[13] Hardman, AE. Physical activity and health: current issues and research needs. *Int J Epidemiol*, 2001, 30, 1193-1197.

[14] Holloszy, JO; Kohrt, WM; Hansen, PA. The regulation of carbohydrate and fat metabolism during and after exercise. *Front Biosci*, 1998, 3, 1011-1027.

[15] Hawley, JA. Adaptations of skeletal muscle to prolonged, intense endurance training. *Clin Exp Pharmacol Physiol*, 2002, 29, 218-222.

[16] Parise, G; Phillips, SM; Kaczor, JJ; Tarnopolsjy, MA. Antioxidant enzyme activity is up-regulated after unilateral resistance exercise training in older adults. *Free Radic Biol Me,* 2005, 39, 289-295.

[17] Gill, JMR; Hardman, AE. Exercise and postprandial lipid metabolism: an update on potential mechanisms and interactions with high-carbohydrate diets. *J Nutr Biochem*, 2003, 14, 122-132.

[18] Warburton, DER; Nicol, CW; Bredin, SSD. Prescribing exercise as preventive therapy. *CMAJ*, 2006, 174, 961-974.

[19] Green, S; Dawson, B. Measurement of of anaerobic capacities in humans. Definitions, limitations and unsolved problems. *Sports Med* 1993, 15, 312-327.

[20] Haskell, WL; Kiernan, M. Methodologic issues in measuring physical activity and physical fitness when evaluating the role of dietary supplements for physically active people. *Am J Clin Nutr*, 2007, 72, 541S-550S.

[21] Topolski, TD; LoGerfo, J; Patrick, DL; Williams, B; Walwick, J; Patrick, MB. The rapid assessment of physical activity (RAPA) among older adults. *Prev Chronic Dis*, 2006, 3 (*available from: http://www.cdc.gov/pcd/issues/2006/oct/06_0001*).

[22] Centers for Disease Control and Prevention (CDC). Adult participation in recommended levels of physical activity - United States, 2001 and 2003. *MMWR Morb Mortal Wkly Rep*, 2005, 54, 1208-1212.

[23] World Health Organization, Regional Office for Europe. *Physical activity and health in Europe: evidence for action.* Eds: Cavill, N; Kahlmeier, S; Racioppi, F. Publisher: Copenhagen, 2006.

[24] Matteucci, E; Passerai, S; Mariotti, M; Fagnani, F; Evangelista, I; Rossi, L; Giampietro, O. Dietary habits and nutritional biomarkers in Italian type 1 diabetes families: evidence of unhealthy diet and combined-vitamin-deficient intakes. *Eur J Clin Nutr*, 2005, 59, 114-122.

[25] Matteucci, E; Malvaldi, G; Fagnani, F; Evangelista, I; Giampietro, O. Redox status and immune function in type 1 diabetes families. *Clin Exp Immunol*, 2004, 136, 549-554.

[26] Matteucci, E; Rosada, J; Pinelli, M; Giusti, C; Giampietro, O. Systolic blood pressure response to exercise in type 1 diabetes families compared with healthy control individuals. *J Hypertens*, 2006, 24,1745-1751.

[27] Pisani, P; Faggiano, F; Krogh, V; Palli, D; Vineis, P; Berrino, F. Relative validity and reproducibility of a food frequency dietary questionnaire for use in the Italian EPIC centres. *Int J Epidemiol*, 1997, 26, S152-160.

[28] Pasanisi, P; Berrino, F; Bellati, C; Sieri, S; Krogh, V. Validity of the Italian EPIC questionnaire to assess past diet. *IARC Sci Publ*, 2002, 156, 41-44.

[29] Salvini, S; Saieva, C; Sieri, S; Vineis, P; Panico, S; Tumino, R; Palli, D. Physical activity in the EPIC cohort in Italy. *IARC Sci Publ*, 2002, 156, 267-269.

In: Progress in Exercise and Women's Health Research
Editor: Janet P. Coulter, pp. 255-269

ISBN 1-60456-014-5
© 2008 Nova Science Publishers, Inc.

Chapter 11

EARLY ADOLESCENT GIRLS' PSYCHOSOCIAL HEALTH IN THE LIGHT OF THEIR SPORTS ACTIVITY BEHAVIOR

Noémi Keresztes and Bettina F. Piko
University of Szeged, Hungary

ABSTRACT

The lack of sports activity and its impact on public health is a serious concern in modern society, while its benefical effects are indicated by many empirical researches. Besides many somatic health benefits, physical activity is closely related to higher level of psychosocial health, psychological well-being, positive mood and mental health. Sports activity behavior is established during late childhood and early adolescence, similar to other health behaviors. While regular sports activity is a natural part of children's lifestyle, it starts to decrease during adolescence, particularly among girls, and therefore, they are an important target group to get involved in health promotion programs. The main goal of our present study is to analyze early adolescent girls' psychosocial health in the light of their sports activity behavior. Our data collection was going on among elementary school girls (N=247) living in Szeged, Hungary, by using a self-administered questionnaire. Data suggest that in this age period most of them regularly take part in sports activity. In their choice of sports type, primarily they prefer individual sports. In terms of individual sports, they prefer dancing and running. The most popular team sports are the following among them: handball and basketball. Among psychosomatic symptoms, headache, low-back pain and chronic fatigue are the most frequent. We have pointed out that in their psychosocial health, sports activity plays an important role. Girls who take part in regular sports activity and are engaged in sports activity at a higher level or in an organized sports club indicate their own health and fitness higher, have lower levels of psychosomatic symptoms. More active girls also tended to avoid regular smoking and drinking and watched for their diet more often. In addition, subjective factors of sports activity (e.g., liking sports and evaluating sports as important) may also contribute to develop motivations towards regular sports activity.

Our findings suggest that the role of sports activity behavior in psychosocial health is an important focus of research. These research results may be useful in health promotion programs targeted adolescent girls.

Keywords: early adolescents, girls, psychosocial health, sports activity behavior

INTRODUCTION

The lack of sports activity and its impact on public health is a serious concern in modern society since physically inactive lifestyle is associated with poor health outcomes. Therefore, promoting sports activity and searching for health protective effects of sports are promoted and receive priority in public health policy (Garreth, Brasure, Schmitz, Schultz, & Huber, 2004; Mutrie, & Blamey, 2004).

Previous researches have suggested that regular participation in sports activity has long-term health benefits. Many studies provide empirical rationale for somatic, psychological and psychosocial benefits of regular sports activity, even among children and adolescents (Marcoux, Sallis, McKenzie, Marshall, Armstrong, & Goggin, 1999; Sallis, McKenzie, Alcaraz, Kolody, Faucette, & Hovell, 1997). For example, sports activity is closely related to lower health risk and lower rate of morbidity and mortality of numerous chronic diseases, such as obesity, high blood pressure, musculoskeletal and cardiovascular diseases (Macintyre, 2004). Psychosocial health benefits are particularly important in adolescence. Adolescents who are engaged in regular sports activity are less likely to smoke, watch television, and more likely to eat a healthy diet (Pate, Heath, Dowda, & Trost, 1996, Steptoe, Wardle, Fuller, Holte, Justo, Sanderman, & Wichstrom, 1997). Young people who exercise regularly also report better psychological well-being, self-perceived health and self-perceived fitness (Piko, 2000, Piko, & Keresztes, 2006). In addition, active involvement in sports activity has substantial benefical effects in terms of maintaining positive mood and promoting mental health (Thøgersen-Ntoumani, Fox, & Ntoumanis, 2005).

Habits of leisure time sports activity, similar to other health behaviors, such as smoking, alcohol and diet control, are established during late childhood and early adolescence (Perkins, Jacobs, Barber, & Eccles, 2004). The regular leisure time sports activity is a natural part of children's lifestyle (Kulig, Brenner, & McManus, 2003). In childhood and during adolescence, team sports and organized sports (such as handball, football, basketball) are more frequent than in any other age groups, particularly among boys (Vilhjalmsson, & Kristjansdottir, 2003). On the other hand, girls may prefer individual and nonregular sports, such as dancing or running. Whereas sports activity is popular among children, it starts to decrease during adolescence, particularly among girls (Telama, & Yang, 2000). According to a recent study, among girls, the transition between early and middle adolescence is accompanied by a significant increase in leisure-time sedentary behavior, e.g, watching TV, videos, playing video games (Hardy, Bass, & Booth, 2007). Longitudinal studies have found that this decreasing tendency is particularly strong in terms of regular and organized sports activity (Kimm, Glynn, Kriska, Fitzgerald, Aaron, Similo, McMahon, & Barton, 2000). There is a strong decline during early adolescence, between childhood and puberty, and another one in postadolescence, between puberty and adulthood. Not surprisingly, the occurrence of obesity also tends to increase during these transitory life periods (Gordon-Larsen, Adair, Nelson, & Popkin, 2004).

As mentioned previously, the situation of girls is more disadvantageous. Gender differences are especially great in the engagement of regular and heavy sports activity. Studies on gender roles reveal a positive relationship between masculine identity and sports (Lantz, & Schroeder, 1999). As a consequence, boys seem to value competition and achievement in sports more than girls. A study appears to indicate different socially constructed gender role orientations between males and females in sports activity (Koca, Asci, & Kiraczi, 2005). In connection with this, studies reveal that girls and boys have very different motivational structure. Boys are primarily motivated by showing competitive drive, demonstrating their physical power and achieving goals, whereas girls are more motivated by reaching a nice figure or a healthy body (Koivula, 1999). Gender differences in sports activity may be explained by three hypotheses: the enrollment hypothesis, the withdrawal hypothesis and the activity differential hypothesis (Lenskyj, 1990). This first hypothesis is particularly relevant during adolescence, that is, girls are less engaged in sports clubs and other organized sports activities. Some studies show that girls have more negative experiences in connection with physical education and lower interest and involvement in leisure time sports activity than boys (Coakley, & White, 1992; Ennis, 1996). Negative experiences of physical education may contribute to a feeling of helplessness and reduced effort in adolescent girls (Vilhjalmsson, & Kristjansdottir, 2003). All in all, adolescent girls are an important target group to get involved in health promotion programs (Sallis, Zakarian, Hovell, & Hofstetter, 1996).

The role of sports activity in disease prevention is inevitable. However, it is more difficult to justify the beneficial effects of sports in children's and adolescents' health. This may be explained by health processes during this age period which needs a special approach to health status evaluation. The measurements of health status may take several dimensions, namely, physical, psychological, and social (Piko, 1999). In modern society, the psychosocial dimension tends to play an important role in determining health and illness (Link, & Phelan, 1995). This is particularly true among children and adolescents since most young people are free of serious physical illness, yet they experience and report considerable psychosomatic and psychological distress symptomatology (Egger, Costello, Erkanli, & Angold, 1999; Piko, Barabas, & Boda, 1997). Due to the lack of serious physical illness, children and especially adolescents tend to use psychosocial health variables (such as psychosomatic health complaints) and health behaviors (such as smoking or sports activity) as a frame of reference to health perceptions (Krause, & Jay, 1994; Piko, Barabas, & Boda, 1997). As a consequence, we may conclude that the interconnections between self-perceived health, health behaviors (such as sports activity) and psychosomatic health complaints may be an issue to understand health processes during adolescence.

Self-perceived health is a widely used global health indicator (Piko, & Keresztes, 2007; Tremblay, Dahinten, & Kohen, 2003). There is a close connection between sports activity and youth's evaluation of their own health (Piko, 2000). That is, those who are engaged in more sports activity, evaluate their own health and fitness significantly higher. Sports activity has both a direct and indirect (e.g., by decreasing smoking or depression) beneficial effect on self-perceived health (Pastor, Balaguer, Pons, & Garcia-Merita, 2003).

In addition to self-perceived health and self-perceived fitness, the prevalence of psychosomatic symptoms is a predictive factor of the psychosocial dimension of health. As a psychosocial health variable, psychosomatic symptoms, such as sleep disorders, low-back pain, tension headache and chronic fatigue are quite common in adult as well as in adolescent populations (Eriksen, Svendsrød, Ursin, & Ursin, 1998; Haugland, Wold, Stevenson, Aaroe, & Woynarowska, 2001). Adolescent girls particularly tend to report high levels of psychosomatic symptoms (Piko, Keresztes, & Pluhár, 2006). These symptoms have been found to be a good indicator of adolescents' increased introspectiveness, symptom reporting orientations and subjective health perceptions (Erginoz, Alikasifoglu, Ercan, Uysal, Ercan, Albayrak Kaymak, & Ilter, 2004). In addition, there is a close connection between self-perceived health, sports activity and the occurrence of psychosomatic symptoms (Piko, 2000). Sports activity may also lower adolescents' depressive symptomatology and increase their psychological well-being (Piko, & Keresztes, 2006), and improve children's overall quality of life (Jirojanakul, Skevington, & Hudson, 2003).

In the present study of Hungarian adolescent girls, we examined the prevalence and indicators of their sports activity behavior with special attention to their psychosocial health. Namely, we examined levels of psychosomatic symptoms, health behavior, self-perceived health and fitness in the light of their sports activity behavior.

METHODS

Participants and Procedure

Data were collected from middle school students using randomly selected classes (10% of this type in this urban area) from four schools in distinct school districts in Szeged, Hungary. Thus, this sample well represents middle school children living in Szeged town. The total number of students sampled was 600. Of the questionnaires, 548 were returned and analyzed, yielding a response rate of 92 percent. 54.7 percent (N = 301) of the sample was male and 44.9 percent (N = 247) female. The subsample of girls (N = 247) was used as a unit of this study to investigate psychosocial health influences of early adolescent girls. The age range of the respondents was 10 to 15 years of age (Mean = 12.2 years, S.D. = 1.2 years).

Data were collected during the autumn semester of 2003, using a self-administered questionnaire. Parents were informed of the study with their consent obtained prior to data collection. A standardized procedure of administration was followed. Trained graduate students distributed the questionnaires to students in each class after briefly explaining the study objectives and giving the necessary instructions. Students completed the questionnaires during the class period. The quesionnaires were anonymous and voluntary.

MEASURES

The self-administered questionnaire included items on sociodemographics, prevalence of sports activity, self-perceived health, self-perceived fitness, psychosomatic symptoms, other health behaviors and other sports-related items.

Sports Activity

Regarding sports activity, the following question was asked: "How many times in the last school year have you participated in sports activity (for at least a half hour) besides school physical education?" Response categories were: "not besides school", "occasionally besides school", "regularly (on a weekly basis) besides school" (Keresztes, Piko, Pluhar, & Page, in press; Luszczynska, Gibbons, Piko, & Teközel, 2004). Those who received exemption from school P.E. were exluded from the study.

Other Sport-Related Variables

The following items were measured: level (e.g., hobby, competition) and organization (school, sports club, with friends, alone) of sports activity, type of sports (individual, team sports), and some subjective factors (e.g., liking sports and evaluating school P.E.) (Keresztes, Pluhar, & Piko, 2003).

Self-Perceived Health and Fitness

Self-perceived health was measured by a question concerning how respondents prefer to report their health compared with peers of their age. The response could be ranked by 4 items and were coded as poor = 1, fair = 2, good = 3 and excellent = 4. Self-perceived fitness was measured using a similar 4-point scale (Lamb, 1992; Piko, 2000).

Psychosomatic Symptoms

The following self-reported psychosomatic symptoms were investigated: low-back pain, tension headache, sleeping problems, chronic fatigue, stomach pyrosis, tension diarrhea and palpitations. The aim of this measure was to obtain information on the frequency of these symptoms during the past 12 months, that is, an overall picture of psychosomatic health status (Piko, Barabas, & Boda, 1997). Adolescents were asked: "During the past 12 months, how often have you had a low-back pain?"...etc. Responses were coded as: often = 3, sometimes = 2, seldom = 1, and never = 0. The final scale had a range of 0 to 21 and was reliable with a Cronbach's alpha of 0.70.

Other Health Behaviors

Smoking and alcohol use, as the most common and legal forms of substance were measured. The following questions were asked: "How many times in the last three months have you smoked cigarettes/drunk alcohol?" Response categories in terms of smoking were the following: "not at all", "occasionally", "regularly (on a daily basis)". Response categories in terms of drinking were the following: "not at all", "occasionally", "regularly (on a weekly basis)". In addition, diet control as a preventive health behavior was measured. The following question was asked: "How many times in the last three months have you paid attention to what you have eaten (that is, tried to eat a healthy diet)?" Response categories were the following: "not at all/a little", "about half of the time", "most of the time" (Luszczynska, Gibbons, Piko, & Teközel, 2004).

Statistical Analyses

SPSS for MS Windows Release 11.0 programme was used in the calculations with maximum significance level set to .05. The analysis began with an examination of the descriptive statistics (mean, S.D.; frequencies). Significant differences between variables were determined by Chi-square tests and ANOVA.

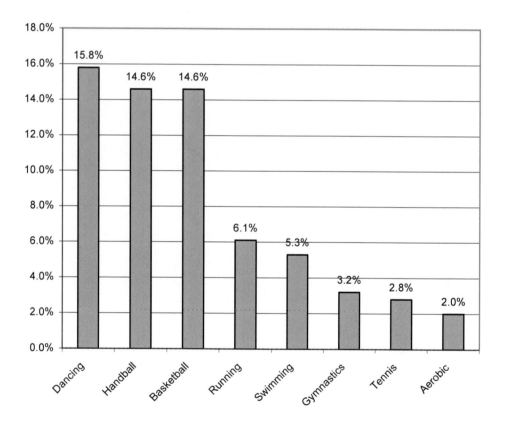

Figure 1 shows the most popular sports activities among adolescents girls. Among them: dancing, handball, basketball, running, swimming, gymnastics, tennis and aerobic were the most popular sports.

RESULTS

Gender Differences in Early Adolescents' Sports Activity

Table 1 presents gender differences in sport-related variables. There were no gender differences in the frequencies of sports activity ($p > .05$), however, boys were more engaged in team sports (65.8% of the boys and 42.7% of the girls; $p < .001$). In addition, boys were more engaged in organized sports and the level of their sports activity was also higher ($p < .01$). More boys evaluated school Physical Education as important as a school subject and expressed a higher level of liking sports ($p < .01$).

Table 1. Gender differences in sport-related variables

	Girls (%) (N = 247)	Boys (%) (N = 301)
Frequency of sports activity		
Not besides school	12.8	11.3
Occasionally besides school	20.2	19.1
Regularly besides school	67.1	69.6
Type of sports***		
Team sports	42.7	65.8
Individual sports	57.3	34.2
Level of sports activity**		
Hobby level	46.9	37.5
Planning to compete	16.2	13.1
Competition	36.9	49.5
Organization of sports activity**		
In school	27.4	18.6
Sports club	35.9	49.8
With friends	11.8	13.7
Alone	24.9	17.9
Evaluation of Physical Education**		
More important than other subjects	17.4	28.0
Equivalent to other subjects	51.7	41.3
Less important than other subjects	22.5	18.9
Impossible to compare	8.5	11.9
Liking sports**		
1- not at all	5.8	3.7
2	3.3	3.7
3	16.5	12.5
4	41.6	30.1
5- very much	32.9	50.0

Note. Chi-square tests. *$p < 0.05$; **$p < .01$; ***$p < .001$

Descriptive Statistics for Psychosocial Health among Adolescent Girls

Descriptive statistics for psychosocial health have pointed out that tension headache, low-back pain and chronic fatigue were the most frequent psychosomatic symptoms among these girls. More than 10% of them reported they often had these symptoms in the last 12 months. Among girls, 60.1% evaluated their own health as good and 57.9% of them evaluated their fitness to be good. The occurrence of smoking was 12.7% in this sample of adolescent girls (3.7% of them reported smoking on a daily basis). The rate of alcohol use was 24.8%, the rate of weekly use was 4.7%. More than one-third of them (38.3%) most of the time paid attention to their diet, whereas 32.5% did it half of the time and 29.2% not at all or a little.

Table 2. Frequencies of psychosocial health variables among adolescent girls (N = 247)

	%
Self-perceived health	
Poor	0.4
Fair	5.8
Good	57.9
Excellent	36.0
Self perceived fitness	
Poor	1.2
Fair	13.2
Good	60.1
Excellent	25.5
Psychosomatic symptoms (often)	
Tension headache	10.3
Low-back pain	11.5
Sleeping problems	4.9
Chronic fatigue	11.2
Stomach pyrosis	1.2
Tension diarrhea	5.8
Palpitations	4.1
Smoking	
Not at all	87.3
Occasionally	9.0
Regularly (daily)	3.7
Alcohol use	
Not at all	75.2
Occasionally	20.1
Regularly (weekly)	4.7
Diet control	
Not at all/a little	29.2
Half of the time	32.5
Most of the time	38.3

Relation between Sports Activity Behavior and Self-Perceived Health and Fitness

As Chi-square tests revealed, girls who were engaged in regular sports activity besides school evaluated their own health and fitness higher than their less active peers. Among regularly active girls, 32.7% reported excellent fitness and 38.5% excellent health, whereas students who did not take part in sports activity besides school reported significantly poorer values (Only 6.9% of them reported excellent self-perceived fitness and 26.7% excellent self-perceived health). In addition, we found that in connection with self-perceived health and fitness the level of sports activity was also important since respondents at a higher level reported better self-perceived health and fitness. 47.7% of the girls who were engaged in competitions evaluated their own fitness to be excellent and 46.1% of them evaluated their own health at the same level. In contrast, among less active students, only 15.1% reported excellent fitness and 34.2% excellent health. According to the organization of sports activity, we pointed out that girls belonging to organized sports clubs evaluated their own fitness and health higher than the others. Among girls from sports clubs 35.7% reported excellent fitness and 45.2 % excellent health.

Table 3. Self-perceived fitness and health in the light of the frequency of sports activity among adolescent girls

Self-perceived fitness***	**Frequency of sports activity (%)**			
	Not besides school	*Occasionally besides school*	*Regularly school*	*besides*
Poor	6.9	-	0.6	
Fair	27.6	25.0	6.8	
Good	58.6	62.5	59.9	
Excellent	6.9	12.5	32.7	
Self-perceived health*	**Frequency of sports activity (%)**			
	Not besides school	*Occasionally besides school*	*Regularly school*	*besides*
Poor	-	-	0.6	
Fair	13.3	8.5	3.1	
Good	60	59.6	57.8	
Excellent	26.7	31.9	38.5	

Note. Chi-square tests. *p<0.05; ***p<.001

Relation between Sports Activity Behavior and Psychosomatic Symptoms

Analyses of variance revealed that the frequency and level of sports activity played an important role in the occurrence of psychosomatic symptoms among adolescents girls (p<.05). For example, girls who were engaged in regular sports activity reported the lowest level of psychosomatic symptoms (mean score: 12.2). Likewise, girls who were engaged in sports competitions (mean score: 11.8) or just were to plan it (mean score: 11.6) reported significantly lower levels of psychosomatic symptoms as compared to those who took part in sports activities only at a hobby level (mean score: 13.1). Whether sports activity was organized or nonorganized did not play a role, although those who took part in sports clubs reported the lowest level of symptoms (mean score: 11.9).

Table 4. Self-perceived fitness and health in the light of the level of sports activity among adolescent girls

Level of sports activity (%)			
Self-perceived fitness***	Hobby level	Planning tocompete	Competition
Poor	1.4	-	-
Fair	17.8	7.7	5.7
Good	65.8	76.9	46.6
Excellent	15.1	15.4	47.7
Level of sports activity (%)			
Self-perceived health*	Hobby level	Planning tocompete	Competition
Poor	1.4	-	-
Fair	5.5	-	4.5
Good	58.9	71.1	49.4
Excellent	34.2	28.9	46.1

Note. Chi-square tests. *p<0.05; ***p<.001

Table 5. Self-perceived fitness and health in the light of the organization of sports activity among adolescent girls

Organization of sports activity (%)				
Self-perceived fitness***	In school	Sports club	With friends	Alone
Poor	1.5	4.8	14.8	3.4
Fair	10.8	59.5	63	22.4
Good	61.5	35.7	22.2	58.6
Excellent	26.2			15.5
Organization of sports activity (%)				
Self-perceived health*	In school	Sports club	With friends	Alone
Poor	-	1.2	-	-
Fair	7.7	4.8	-	7.1
Good	61.5	48.8	64.3	64.3
Excellent	30.8	45.2	35.7	28.6

Note. Chi-square tests *p<0.05; ***p<.001

Table 6. Psychosomatic symptoms in the light of sports activity behavior among adolescents girls

Psychosomatic symptoms scale			
Variables	Mean	S.D.	ANOVA Significance level
Frequency of sport activity			
Not besides school	12.4	3.3	
Occasionally besides school	13.0	2.9	p<0.05
Regularly besides school	12.2	3.8	
Level of sports activity			
Hobby	13.1	3.8	
Planning to compete	11.6	2.9	p<0.05
Competition	11.8	3.3	
Organization of sports activity			
In school	12.9	3.7	
Sports club	11.9	3.1	p>0.05
With friends	12.7	3.4	
Alone	12.7	3.9	

Note. Analysis of variance (ANOVA)

Relation between sports activity behavior and other health behaviors

Among the variables of sports activity behavior, organization of sports did not play a role. The frequency of sports activity was associated with diet control; those who were engaged in regular sports reported a more frequent diet control ($p < .05$; Chi-square test). Furthermore, level of sports activity was associated with smoking and drinking; those who reported sports activity at a competition level did not smoke ($p < .01$) or drink ($p < .05$) regularly. On the other hand, those who reported sports activity at a hobby level tend to smoke or drink more often.

Table 7. Health behaviors in the light of sports activity behavior among adolescent girls

Health behaviors	Frequency of sports activity (%)			Level of sports activity (%)			Organization of sports activity (%)			
	Not besides school	Occasionally besides school	Regularly besides school	Competition	Planning to compete	Hobby	In school	Sports club	With friends	Alone
Smoking										
Not at all	87.1	89.8	86.4	85.2	100.0	84.8	87.5	90.6	89.3	81.0
Occasionally	3.2	6.1	11.1	14.8	-	8.0	12.5	7.1	7.1	10.3
Regularly	9.7	4.1	2.5	-	-	7.1	-	2.4	3.6	3.4
	p>0.05			p<0.01			p>0.05			
Drinking										
Not at all	71.0	79.2	73.0	73.6	84.6	71.7	75.0	72.6	64.3	78.0
Occasionally	25.8	18.8	23.9	26.4	15.4	23.0	23.4	25.0	35.7	15.3
Regularly	3.2	2.1	3.1	-	-	5.3	1.6	2.4	-	6.8
	p>0.05			p<0.05			p>0.05			
Diet control										
Not at all/a little	30.0	25.5	29.4	31.8	21.6	29.5	34.9	28.6	32.1	24.1
Half of the time	43.3	46.8	27.0	29.5	32.4	33.0	31.7	26.2	32.1	37.9
Most of the time	26.7	27.7	43.6	38.6	45.9	37.5	33.3	45.2	35.7	37.9
	p<0.05			p>0.05			p>0.05			

Note. Chi-square tests

DISCUSSION

In the present study, we examined the prevalence and indicators of early adolescent girls' sports activity behavior and their psychosocial health. We also examined levels of psychosomatic symptoms, self-perceived health and fitness in the light of their sports activity behavior. The lack of physical activity is a serious public health concern (Garreth, Brasure, Schmitz, Schultz, & Huber, 2004; Mutrie, & Blamey, 2004) not only among adults but also among youth, particularly among girls (Telama, & Yang, 2000). Therefore, there is a need of further research to focus on girls' sports activity behavior in their teenage years. Previous studies also provide empirical rationale for somatic, psychological and psychosocial benefits of physically active lifestyle (Marcoux, Sallis, McKenzie, Marshall, Armstrong, & Goggin, 1999; Sallis, McKenzie, Alcaraz, Kolody, Faucette, & Hovell, 1997). Thus, girls should be encouraged to engage in more sports activity to benefit from its favorable effects (Sallis, Zakarian, Hovell, & Hofstetter, 1996).

In comparison to boys, there were no gender differences in the frequencies of sports activities, that is, adolescent girls in this sample were engaged in sports activity quite regularly. This finding was similar to a previous research, although the regularity was found to be different: most of the girls were engaged in sports activity once or twice a week, whereas boys of the same age preferred taking part sports activity three or more times a week (Keresztes, Pluhar, & Piko, 2003). In addition, boys were more engaged in team sports and organized sports and the level of their sport activity was also higher. These findings were similar to previous results (Kimm et al., 2000; Telama, & Yang, 2000). All in all, boys also evaluated the importance of sport and liked school Physical Education higher than girls.

Among girls, the most popular sports were the following: dancing, basketball, handball and running. As literature suggests, girls prefer individual sports (Aaron, Storti, Robertson, Kriska, & LaPorte, 2002) in contrast to boys. Most of them took sports activity at a hobby level, but the rate of those who compete regularly was also high. According to the organization of sports, we found that most of them attended sports clubs, although at a lower amount than boys did. Besides, they took sports in school and alone. Joint (nonorganized) sports activity with friends at a hobby level was rare in this age-group. Comparing these results to boys, other studies also reported girls' lower enrollment in sports clubs (Vilhjalmsson, & Kristjansdottir, 2003).

Subjective evaluations and opinions may also be important for adolescents in terms of their motivation towards sports activity. Our results indicated that most of the respondents liked Physical Education as a school subject and they thought that this subject was equivalent to the others or even more important. Liking sports may help develop a motivation towards regular sports activity to become a substantial factor of lifestyle and leisure time (Sallis, Prochaska, & Taylor, 2000).

Analyzing girls' psychosocial health we found that in this age period most of them evaluated their own health and fitness to be good, whereas previous studies had pointed out that boys significantly tended to report better self-perceived health and fitness (Due, Holstein, & Marklund, 1991). Similarly to other studies, tension headache, low-back pain and chronic fatigue were the most commonly mentioned psychosomatic symptoms (Eriksen, Svendsrød, Ursin, & Ursin, 1998; Haugland, Wold, Stevenson, Aaroe, & Woynarowska, 2001). The occurrence of psychosomatic symptoms is an important psychosocial health indicator since adolescent girls tend to report common psychosomatic symptoms more often as compared to boys (Piko, Keresztes, & Pluhár, 2006).

Examining the role of sports activity behavior in psychosocial health we found that certain aspects of sports activity had significant influences on psychosocial health among early adolescent girls. Similar to other studies, girls who were engaged in regular sports activity evaluated their own health and fitness higher than their less active peers (Piko, & Keresztes, 2006). Besides frequency of sports activity, the level and organization of sports were also determinant. For example, girls belonging to organized sports club evaluated their own fitness and health higher than the others and reported lower frequencies of psychosomatic symptoms. Likewise, girls who were engaged in sports activity at a competition level or just were to plan it, reported better self-perceived health and fitness and lower levels of psychosomatic symptoms. In addition, there was an association between certain aspects of sports activity and health behaviors among adolescents girls. Previous studies revealed a positive association between adolescents physical activity and their favorable health behavior (Pate et al., 1996; Steptoe et al., 1997). Among the variables of sports activity behavior in this sample of adolescent girls, the frequency of sports activity was associated with diet control, whereas the level of sports activity was associated with smoking and drinking. All in all, those who were more physically active avoided smoking and drinking and watched for their diet more often.

As a summary, we may conclude that sports activity behavior had a strong influence on psychosocial health and health behavior among early adolescent girls. Regular sports activity is an asset in preventing psychosocial health problems among female adolescents, therefore, girls may be an important target group in school health promotion programs.

REFERENCES

Aaron, D.J., Storti, K.L., Robertson, R.J., Kriska, A. & LaPorte, R. (2002). Longitudinal study of the number and choice of leisure time physical activities from mid to late adolescence. *Archives of Pediatrics & Adolescent Medicine,* 156, 1075-1080.

Coakley, J., & White, A. (1992). Making decision: Gender and sport participation among British adolescents. *Sociology of Sport Journal,* 9, 20-35.

Due, P., Holstein, B. E. & Marklund, U. (1991). Self-reported health status among students in Scandinavia. *Nordic Medicine,* 106, 71-74.

Egger, H.L., Costello, E.J., Erkanli, A, & Angold, A. (1999). Somatic complaints and psychopathology in children and adolescents: stomach aches, musculoskeletal pains, and headaches. *Journal of the American Academy of Child and Adolescent Psychiatry,* 38, 852-860.

Ennis, C.D. (1996). Students' experiences in sport-based physical education: More than apologies are necessary. *Quest,* 48, 453-456.

Erginoz, E., Alikasifoglu, M., Ercan, O., Uysal, O., Ercan, G., Albayrak Kaymak, D., & Ilter, O. (2004). Perceived health status in a Turkish adolescent sample: Risk and protective factors. *European Journal of Pediatrics,* 163, 485-494.

Eriksen, H.R., Svendsrød, R., Ursin, G., & Ursin, H. (1998). Prevalence of subjective health complaints in the Nordic European countries in 1993. *European Journal of Public Health,* 8, 294-298.

Garreth, N.A., Brasure M, Schmitz, K.H., Schultz, M.M., & Huber, M.R. (2004). Direct cost to a health plan. *American Journal of Preventive Medicine,* 27, 304-309.

Gordon-Larsen, P., Adair, L.S., Nelson, M.C., & Popkin, B.M. (2004). Five-year obesity incidence in the transition period between adolescence and adulthood: The National Longitudinal Study of Adolescent Health. *American. Journal of Clinical Nutrition,* 80, 569-575.

Hardy, L.L., Bass, S.L., & Booth, M.L. (2007). Changes in sedentary behavior among adolescent girls: A 2.5-year prospective cohort study. *Journal of Adolescent Health,* 40, 158-165.

Haugland, S., Wold, B., Stevenson, J., Aaroe, L.E. & Woynarowska, B. (2001). Subjective health complaints in adolescence: A cross-national comparison of prevalence and dimensionality. *European Journal of Public Health,* 11, 4-10.

Jirojanakul, P., Skevington, S.M., & Hudson, J. (2003). Predicting young children's quality of life. *Social Science & Medicine,* 57, 1277-1288.

Keresztes, N., Pluhár, Zs., & Piko, B. (2003). Frequency of physical activity and sporting types among middle school children. *Hungarian Review of Sports Science,* 4, 43-47. (in Hungarian)

Keresztes, N., Piko, B., Pluhar, Zs. & Page, R.M. (in press). Social influences in leisure time sport activity among early adolescents. *The Journal of Royal Society for the Promotion of Health.*

Kimm, S.Y.S., Glynn, N.W., Kriska, A.M., Fitzgerald, S.L., Aaron, D.J., Similo, S.L., McMahon, R.P., & Barton, B.A. (2000). Longitudinal changes in physical activity in a biracial cohort during adolescence. *Medicine and Science in Sports and Exercise,* 32, 1445-1454.

Koca, C., Asci, F.H., & Kiraczi, S. (2005). Gender role orientation of athletes and nonathletes in a patriarchal society: A study in Turkey. *Sex Roles: A Journal of Research,* 3-4, 217-225.

Koivula, N. (1999). Sport participation: Differences in motivation and actual participation due to gender typing. *Journal of Sporting Behavior,* 22, 360–380.

Krause, N.M., & Jay, G.M. (1994). What do global self-rated health items measure? *Medical Care,* 32, 930-942.

Kulig, K., Brenner, N.D., & McManus, T. (2003). Sexual activity and substance use among adolescents by category of physical activity plus team sports participation. *Archives of Pediatrics & Adolescent Medicine,* 157, 905-912.

Lamb, K.L. (1992). Correlates of self-perceived fitness. *Perceptual & Motor Skills,* 74, 907-914.

Lantz, C.D, & Schroeder, P.J. (1999). Endorsement of masculine and feminine gender roles: Differences between participation and identification with the athletic role. *Journal of Sporting Behavior,* 22, 545–557.

Lenskyj, H. (1990). Power and play: Gender and sexuality issues in sport and physical activity. *International Review of the Sociology of Sport,* 25, 235-245.

Link, B.G., & Phelan, J. (1995). Social conditions as fundamental causes of disease. *Journal Health and Social Behavior,* extra issue, 80-94.

Luszczynska, A., Gibbons, F.X., Pikó, B.F., & Teközel, M. (2004). Self-regulatory cognitions, social comparison, and perceived peers' behaviours as predictors of nutrition and physical activity: A comparison among adolescents in Hungary, Poland, Turkey, and USA. *Psychology and Health,* 19, 577-93.

Macintyre, S. (2004). Socio-economic differences in cardiovascular disease and physical activity: Stereotypes and reality. *The Journal of the Royal Society for the Promotion of Health,* 124, 66-69.

Marcoux, M.F., Sallis, J.F., McKenzie, T.L., Marshall, S., Armstrong, C.A., & Goggin, K.J. (1999). Process evaluation of a physical activity self-management program for children: SPARK. *Psychology & Health,* 14, 659-677.

Mutrie, N., & Blamey, A. (2004). Getting the inactive implications for public health policy. *The Journal of the Royal Society for the Promotion of Health,* 124, 16-17.

Pastor, Y., Balaguer, I., Pons, D., & Garcia-Merita, M. (2003). Testing direct and indirect effects of sports participation on perceived health in Spanish adolescents between 15 and 18 years of age. *Journal of Adolescence,* 26, 717-730.

Pate, R.R., Heath, G.W., Dowda, M., & Trost, S.G. (1996). Association between physical activity and other health behaviors in a representative sample of US adolescents. *American Journal of Public Health,* 86, 1577-1781.

Perkins, D.F., Jacobs, J.E., Barber, B.L., & Eccles, J.S. (2004). Childhood and adolescent sport participation as predictors of participation in sports and fitness activities during young adulthood. *Youth & Society,* 35, 495-520.

Piko, B. (1999). Teaching the mental and social aspects of medicine in Eastern Europe: Role of the WHO definition of health. *Administration and Policy in Mental Health,* 26, 435-438.

Piko, B., Barabas, K., & Boda, K. (1997). Frequency of common psychosomatic symptoms and its influence on self-perceived health in a Hungarian student population. *European Journal of Public Health,* 7, 243-247.

Piko, B. (2000). Health-related predictors of self-perceived health in a student population: The importance of physical activity. *Journal of Community Health,* 25, 125-137.

Piko, B., & Keresztes, N. (2006). Physical activity, psychosocial health and life goals among youth. *Journal of Community Health,* 31, 136-145.

Piko, B., Keresztes, N., & Pluhár, Zs. (2006). Aggressive behavior and psychosocial health among children. *Personality and Individual Differences,* 40, 885-895.

Piko, B., & Keresztes, N. (2007). Self – perceived health among early adolescents: The role of psychosocial health. *Pediatrics International,* 49, 577-583.

Sallis, J.F., Zakarian, J.M., Hovell, M.F., & Hofstetter, C.R. (1996). Ethnic, socioeconomic and sex differences in physical activity among adolescents. *Journal of Clinical Epidemiology,* 49, 125-134.

Sallis, J.F., McKenzie, T.L., Alcaraz, J.E., Kolody, B., Faucette, N., & Hovell, M.F. (1997). The effects of a 2-year physical education program (SPARK) on physical activity and fitness in elementary school students. *American Journal of Public Health,* 87, 1328-1334.

Sallis, J.F., Prochaska, J.J., & Taylor, W.C. (2000). A review of correlates of physical activity of children and adolescents. *Medicine and Science in Sports and Exercise,* 32, 963-975.

Steptoe, A., Wardle, J., Fuller, R., Holte, A., Justo, J., Sanderman, R., & Wichstrom, L. (1997). Leisure time physical exercise: prevalence, attitudinal correlate and behavioral correlates among young Europeans from 21 countries. *Preventive Medicine,* 26, 845-854.

Telama, R., & Yang, X. (2000). Decline of physical activity from youth to young adulthood in Finland. *Medicine and Science in Sports and Exercise,* 32, 1617–1622.

Thøgersen-Ntoumani, C., Fox, K.R., & Ntoumanis, N. (2005). Relationships between exercise and three components of mental well-being in corporate employees. *Psychology of Sport and Exercise,* 6, 609-627.

Tremblay, S., Dahinten, S., & Kohen, D. (2003). Factors related to adolescents' self-perceived health. *Health Report,* 14 Supplement, 7-16.

Vilhjalmsson, R., & Kristjansdottir, G. (2003). Gender differences in physical activity in older children and adolescents: the central role of organized sport. *Social Science & Medicine,* 56, 363-74.

INDEX

B

C

F

G

H

N

O

Q

R

S

T

U

V

W

X

Y